# THEORIES OF CIVIL
# VIOLENCE

Other Works By James Rule

*Measuring Political Upheaval*, 1965, by Charles Tilly and James Rule.
*Private Lives and Public Surveillance*, 1973.
*Insight and Social Betterment*, 1978.
*The Politics of Privacy*, 1980, by James Rule, Doug McAdam, Linda
    Stearns, and David Uglow.

# THEORIES OF CIVIL VIOLENCE

JAMES B. RULE

UNIVERSITY OF CALIFORNIA PRESS
BERKELEY   LOS ANGELES   LONDON

University of California Press
Berkeley and Los Angeles, California

University of California Press, Ltd.
London, England

©1988 by
The Regents of the University of California

Library of Congress Cataloging-in-Publication Data

Rule, James B., 1943–
   Theories of civil violence/James B. Rule.
   p.   cm.
   Bibliography: p.
   Includes index.
   ISBN 0-520-06278-7 (alk. paper)
   1. Violence.   2. Riots.   3. Revolutions.   I. Title.
HM281.R84 1988                              87-34235
303.6'2—dc19                                CIP

Printed in the United States of America

1   2   3   4   5   6   7   8   9

*to Lewis A. Coser*
*Master Sociologist of Conflict and Violence*
*Political Activist and Scholar of Politics*
*Sociologue Engagé and Detached Critic*
*Publicist, Teacher, Teacher of Teachers*
*Wise Colleague, Sage Advisor, Generous Advocate*
*Mentor and Friend*

*In the Year of his Accession to the status*
*of Distinguished Professor Emeritus*

# Contents

# Foreword

In writing this book, I have sought to weigh my words. I have grown convinced that clarity of thinking in social science absolutely requires clarity and economy of expression. Especially in discussion of theoretical issues, important ideas are readily lost in thickets of verbiage. Worse, obscurantism offers to many an irresistable temptation to conceal trivial or confused ideas in pompous, mystifying, overweening language. For all the concern among social scientists for mathematical formulation as a guarantee of intellectual exactitude, we fail to exploit opportunities for exact expression in ordinary English.

This book is an analytical history of major theories of the origins and characteristics of collective violence within polities—riot, rebellion, civil war, and the like. Sometimes called the "problem of order," sometimes the "Hobbesian problem," this issue is often alleged to be the most fundamental on the agenda of social science. Whether it really is *the* most fundamental I cannot say. But it is certainly a very long-standing issue, and one closely enmeshed with other key theoretical strands.

My goal is to use the history of theorizing on this important theme as a forum for considering the nature and possibilities of social science theories *in general*. Above all, I want to examine this cross-section of the history of social and political thought to assess the prospects for cumulation and progress in social science.

In pursuing these ends, I have much to say about the virtues and flaws of theories under consideration. I am sure that every reader will find at least one point of disagreement, and many will find a great deal more. In keeping with my efforts at clarity, I have taken pains to make the sense of my positions unmistakable, thus presenting the clearest possible target for rejoinder. The greatest favor any reader could do would be to read with the same care and thoroughness that I have attempted in the writing.

xi

If that much can be done, any response should help raise the quality of debate on these subjects.

Nearly every major school and tendency in the history of social and political thought has offered some theoretical account of civil violence. In the past twenty-five years, moreover, we have seen an explosion of writing on the subject, including both theorizing and research. Such an embarrassment of riches presents both opportunities and hazards. To attempt to consider every contribution to these debates would be deadly; worse, it would subvert the real purpose. A dramatist, seeking to convey boredom, must not succeed in boring the audience. Similarly, my goal is to assess in depth the major alternative theoretical responses to the Hobbesian problem, not to rehearse the entire literature.

Thus the need for some principle of selection. I have tried to identify the major, distinctive theoretical accounts of civil violence and, for each of these broad positions, to lay out and consider the strongest arguments for and against. Where the literature includes empirical research bearing on the theory, I have sought to assess such research with the same thoroughness.

In making these assessments, I have tried to keep a high ratio of works consulted to those actually discussed. The latter include what I consider the most influential or the most weighty expositions—the most distinctive theoretical statements, the most telling research studies. But often what has been influential has not, on scrutiny, appeared intellectually weighty, and vice-versa. So I have tried to attend both to works that have mattered to other thinkers on these subjects and to works that *should* matter.

Still, in the interest of economy, I have had to forgo discussion of many estimable works. Every reader familiar with the literature probably will find at least a few favorite studies absent from my discussion, perhaps even ones of his or her own authorship. Such omissions do not necessarily reflect a low evaluation of the works involved. My effort has been to focus on *theories* in their intellectual distinctiveness, avoiding redundancy as much as possible. I have tried to keep asking how the various theoretical positions differ in their approach to empirical material, what each has to say that is peculiar to it, and how particular research studies help us to assess the strengths and weaknesses of the positions involved. The inevitable result has been that many important works do not come in for discussion, where the theoretical ideas involved are adequately developed elsewhere.

Another kind of tough judgment call has had to do with the extent of attention given to various classic expositions of theoretical positions. Many important early writers have provided *bases* for modern theories of civil violence, while mostly leaving it to intellectual posterity to specify the precise empirical implications of their theories for this subject. Thus the question: How much extrapolation of a great thinker's ideas is justified, before one begins putting words unwarrantedly in another's mouth? Conveying in the abstract the principles on which I have decided such questions is very difficult. The best I can do is to note that it seemed essential to discuss writings of Marx and Engels in some detail, whereas de Tocqueville is mentioned only in passing. Rich as de Tocqueville's work is, its implications for when and where to expect violent collective strife within polities seem less clear-cut than those of Marx. To be sure, de Tocqueville offers insights into the causes of specific upheavals, most obviously the French Revolution of 1789. But I find any attempt to bring these arguments together in a single theory of civil violence more speculative than in the case of Marx.

Naturally I hope that this book makes a contribution in its own right to social theory. But the kind of contribution that I feel is most urgently needed may not be what all readers expect. The conviction is widespread that "scientific progress" in the study of social life can only come via one of two royal intellectual roads. One of these is the collection and analysis of new and more elaborate data; the other is the relentless creation of new theoretical wrinkles of one kind or another, presented under such labels as breakthrough, new departure, and reorientation.

Obviously new ideas and new forms of evidence are always welcome. And here and there I have yielded to the virtuous temptation to entertain new theoretical formulations or to identify evidence that, if assembled, would hold special interest. But such observations are not my main purpose here. More important is my effort to show that many promising theoretical ideas long available in the literature remain unexploited. For reasons on which I speculate in Chapter Nine, the intellectual community tends to shift its attention to new theoretical views and new forms of evidence before fully digesting the possibilities at hand. If the goal is to build enduring theoretical insights, we need deeper, more thorough judgments on the theoretical positions already before us.

But perhaps that is not really the goal. Perhaps we propound theories of social and political life simply to dramatize our feelings about it; or to counter the dramatizations of other, antagonistic theories; or to inspire or justify social action of the sort to which we are inclined anyway, or for any number of other relatively transient reasons. If so, then expectations that theoretical accomplishments should endure are misplaced. Instead, we should expect the concerns and intellectual criteria reflected in social theory to shift constantly with the changing intellectual appetites of each age. This book provides certain support for this view of social theory, as noted in Chapter Nine.

Nevertheless, I have approached my task here as though cumulation and progress were reasonable expectations of social theory, as though it were proper to expect questions asked and answered at earlier stages of inquiry on civil violence to make an enduring difference to the conduct of inquiry later on. I have sought to trace continuities in theoretical themes over time and to weigh the forces that conduce to cumulation and continuity against those that seem to block these things.

Whether we should expect theories to be enduring and cumulative or transient and suited to passing intellectual needs, then, should hardly be prejudged at this point. It is bootless to speculate a priori on whether the study of social life is essentially scientific or essentially something else without attending to the actual patterns and processes by which theoretical ideas come and go. We need a broad conspectus of intellectual developments over an extended period. For these purposes, the history of theories of civil violence offers an apposite case in point.

---

This book is the first of a two-volume sequence. The sequel will deal with cumulation and progress in social thought more generally.

Both works grow out of long-standing interests in civil violence and social theory. These interests date back to my undergraduate days as a student of Lewis Coser, now my colleague at Stony Brook. His influence on my thinking on these subjects cannot adequately be recorded here. In gratitude for his extraordinary intellectual and moral support for the scholarly efforts of myself and countless others, I dedicate this book to him.

The idea of writing a book of this kind dates back at least fifteen years; actual creation of the book has been going on since 1981. During this period I have relied enormously on criticisms and other guidance from many friends and colleagues. These include Ronald Aminzade, Said Arjomand, Bernard Barber, Lewis Coser, Steven Finkel (coauthor of Chapter Seven), Mark Granovetter, Ted Gurr, George Homans, David Lee, Theodore Lowi, Gary Marx, Doug McAdam, Maurice Pinard, Art Stinchcombe, John Sumser, Charles Tilly, Axel Van Den Berg, Ekkart Zimmermann, and a number of others. My gratitude to all of these good colleagues is deep and sincere. Some of them have taken special trouble to provide me with particularly long and detailed comments, in efforts to disabuse me of what they consider unfortunate ideas. I have not always been willing or able to accept all this painstaking advice. But I offer these critics instead a satisfaction nearly as good: I hereby formally admit that they have made me squirm.

In addition to this fine substantive advice, indispensable practical and editorial attention has been provided by a number of thoughtful and dedicated people, including Michael Aronson, Carla Gonzalez, Berenice Hoffman, Robin Miller, Ellen Parnell, and Carole Roland.

It is a pleasure to acknowledge institutional support for this study from a variety of sources, including the Research Foundation of the State University of New York, Columbia University, the John Simon Guggenheim Foundation, and the Center for Advanced Study in the Behavioral Sciences (Stanford).

And finally, I must also acknowledge several institutions that, on reflection, determined that their support would be better extended elsewhere, including the Hoover Institution (on war, revolution and peace), the Harry Frank Guggenheim Foundation (devoted to studies of the causes and consequences of dominance, aggression, and violence), and the Institute for Advanced Study (Princeton).

Let credit be given where credit is due. As always, responsibility for the shortcomings of the work rests strictly with the author.

James B. Rule
Port Jefferson, New York
December 1986

# Introduction

This book has two purposes. First, it is a history of theories of civil violence, and of theoretically oriented research on this subject. Second, it is a study of social theory itself. I intend these two pursuits to facilitate each other. By analyzing the history of theories on one central issue in social science, I hope to illuminate the nature and possibilities of social science theories in general.

---

Conflict of interest inheres in social life. True, social relations may provide many of our deepest personal gratifications, our most profound sense of meaning, or indispensable opportunities for self-expression. But the attractions of belonging are scarcely all that hold social systems together. Every enduring social structure incorporates special mechanisms to ensure compliance with distasteful requirements. These mechanisms range from cajolery and moral suasion through the lash of market forces and invidious example to physical coercion and, ultimately, elimination of the recalcitrant or incorrigible. For most people, most of the time, such mechanisms work. There may be grumbling or complaints—or indeed people may be so thoroughly inured as to be unaware of pressure to conform. But in either case, "normal" social demands and obligations are usually upheld.

Not always, though. Sometimes latent divisions of interest blossom into open conflicts, and previously accepted rules become points of contest. Some such conflicts widen to entail destruction of property or people—in the form of rebellion, riot, revolution or civil war. These fateful transitions bristle with consequence for ordinary people and for the larger systems in which they act.

Perhaps the most fundamental of such consequences is the disruption of "normal" expectations of peaceful dealings with others. One cannot expect polite behavior from one's fellow theater-goers if a fire breaks out in the hall. One cannot count on accustomed ways of dealing with members of another ethnic or racial group in the marketplace or in the community, if mobs representing the two groups are assaulting one another in the streets. One cannot expect to travel to distant territories if the highways en route are the scene of deadly clashes among rival armies. The uncertainties and curtailments imposed by civil strife are pervasive, going far beyond the immediacies of violent action. Thus Hobbes wrote,

For as the nature of Foule weather, lyeth not a shower or two of rain; but in an inclination thereto of many dayes together; So the nature of War, consisteth not in actual fighting; but in the known disposition thereto, during all the time there is no assurance to the contrary. . . . In such conditions, there is no place for Industry; because the fruit thereof is uncertain. (1968, p. 186)

Large-scale violence, then, generates *desperation,* as people take extraordinary steps to attack persons or property ordinarily left in peace, or to avoid becoming victims of such attacks. Under these circumstances, all bets are off on a wide variety of normal social interactions. For these reasons, civil violence intrudes itself into the imaginations of ordinary citizens and social scientists alike.

In centralized nation-states, civil violence takes on a special, additional significance. Recall Weber's famous dictum: The modern state seeks to maintain a monopoly on the legitimate exercise of large-scale coercion within its territory. Actually, Weber might as well have applied the observation to *all* major coercion, for no modern state is apt to concede the legitimacy of large-scale coercion outside its control. In modern societies, compliance with all kinds of normal civil obligations—both between private parties and between them and government agencies—is subject to ultimate enforcement by state coercion. Appearance of major forms of coercion not sanctioned by the state, whether in the form of mob violence, protection rackets, or private armies, threatens the credibility of government claims to uphold "legitimate" civil obligations. In short, such outbreaks threaten *sovereignty,* a feature of quintessential importance for modern states. Thus civil violence may be rare or common, but it is always in some sense *extraordinary,* a challenge to one of the basic assumptions of civil normality.

State agencies are often participants in civil violence, either as targets or as aggressive agents of coercion. Yet even in highly centralized modern polities, many violent events play themselves out between private parties: rival ethnic or racial groups, embattled religious communities, or contending political or economic formations. All such events fall within the concerns of this book.

Central to these concerns is what has come to be called the Hobbesian question: Where does civil violence come from? What accounts for the transition from co-operative or at least quiescent "normal" civil relations to periods of riot, rebellion, or civil war? No less important, how are we to explain the transition back from strife-torn social states to relatively peaceful, nonviolent ones? What characteristics of governing structures, communication patterns, political participation, moral solidarity, urbanism, grass-roots standards of justice and injustice, childhood socialization, or any of countless other aspects of social life govern such transitions? Beyond the causes of particular violent events and episodes, what are the deeper conditions underlying civil violence *in general?*

This question has an extremely long pedigree in the history of social and political thought. It is sometimes termed "the problem of order," allegedly the most fundamental of all problems facing the social sciences. I avoid using that term in this book, because "order" has taken on such a variety of meanings in social science discourse. But there can be no denying that any account given for civil violence in general must relate to a wide variety of other basic issues in social science, among them the nature of sovereignty, the bases of political participation, and the workings of social control. Most of the major currents in social and political thought since Hobbes's time have contributed something to the debate on the origins of civil violence. Most of the key methodologies current among social scientists today have served as vehicles for arguments on the subject. As much as any other relatively delimited issue, it offers a microcosm of social science thinking.

If the cause of civil violence is an enduring preoccupation of social theorists, the status of social science theories is no less so. What logical form ought such theories to take? How should they relate to one another, and to empirical inquiry? What standards ought to govern the competition of contending theories, and what forms of "progress" can we expect to arise from such competition? Most broadly, what theoretical principles offer the best hope of ordering the results of past inquiries and directing the conduct of future ones? No questions are more central than these to social scientists' view of their enterprise and their roles within it.

Nor are any more deeply contested and unresolved. One symptom of this dissensus—there are many—is the inability of scholars to agree on the essential accomplishments of theoretical inquiry in social science. One cannot easily specify what theorists of civil violence or any other key subject have *established* without danger of dispute by other members of the scholarly community. The theoretical heritage of social science is simply too inconclusive.

Nearly everyone can agree that the works of Hobbes, Comte, Marx, Pareto, Park, and many other giants from our past represent important achievements. The problem arises in specifying what exactly *endures* from their work, and how such enduring contributions figure in some broad pattern of advancing knowledge. The writings of the historic ancestors of present-day social science are full of provocative possibilities and intriguing departures. But a clear line of consensually validated *progress* remains difficult to trace.

How are we to account for this unsettled state of intellectual affairs?

One standard response is to cite the supposed youth of the social sciences. They need more *time,* it is alleged, to attain the rigorous theoretical organization supposedly characterizing the so-called hard sciences. But are the social sciences really so young? Many of their key concerns are those of the classical Greeks; a few of these, including the Hobbesian question, have been subjects of relatively consistent attention for hundreds of years. Surely there has been time to test intellectual limits and possibilities. Perhaps, then, something distinctive about the study of social life—about the logic of the relationships involved or about our interest in those relationships—poses special constraints on orderly cumulation.

There are a number of clues pointing in this direction. One—noted most tellingly by Merton—has to do with the way students first learn social science. One cannot fully grasp the present state of knowledge in these disciplines, it is agreed, without coming to terms with their *classic texts.* Even the most up-to-date student of social stratification, for example, must know something of the writings of Marx. By contrast, one would not expect a modern student of genetics or astronomy to deal with the actual writings of Mendel or Kepler—however much the ideas of these founding fathers are embodied in modern texts of their subjects. Somehow the intellectual structures of social science do not so fully encapsulate the insights of their pasts as in the natural sciences.

Another clue to the difference between social science and the "hard" sciences has to do with *discoveries.* Many decisive intellectual developments in the natural sciences appear to come through critical experiments or other key observations. Members of these fields can often envisage hypothetical future results or observations that would surely represent discoveries in this same sense, should they occur. We have little to compare with this in social science. Although we can point to all sorts of provocative findings and noteworthy research results, it is hard to distinguish anything that could be agreed to be a "discovery." For that term implies a degree of consensus as to the significance of findings simply not characteristic of our fields. Perhaps because we are uncertain as to what we know and how we know it, we are typically divided as to the significance of new findings.

Both these points—the relation of social scientists to their history and the ambiguous status of discoveries—should alert us to peculiarities in the *theoretical organization* of social science. These peculiarities give rise to disputes that involve two issues: What can we actually claim to know about key subjects, and which theoretical doctrines should guide future work? The study of civil violence is no less prone to disputes and ambiguities of this kind than any other domain of social science.

At least we have recently come to appreciate better the complexity of these issues. We no longer take seriously, for example, what might be called the "incremental accumulation" view of social science. In this view, every new fact or finding represents an equal, atomistic step toward increased total knowledge. Thus the overall accomplishments of a field would be in direct proportion to its total of recorded facts, regardless of their intellectual context. This approach obviously makes no distinction between systematic cumulation and sheer *accumulation* of data.

But, of course, not all "facts" or findings or results are, so to speak, created equal. Thanks to Kuhn's celebrated book, nearly everyone now understands what philosophers of science had acknowledged for decades— that the growth of scientific knowledge requires the organizing medium of theoretical structures. Kuhn's famous term for these structures was "paradigms," but others mean similar things when they speak of theoretical "orientations" or "viewpoints" or "perspectives" or "frameworks". There are differences of connotation among many of these terms, and often great vagueness in the way they are used. But they all reflect the idea that no system of inquiry can avoid prior assumptions about what is known and what is not, and about how new information can add to such understandings. Without such organizing principles, scientific inquiry cannot transcend the production of what George Homans has called "just one damn finding after another."

In the past few decades, concern with the intellectual structures, such as paradigms, meta-theories, and theoretical orientations, that stand between social scientists and their subject matter has become pervasive among social scientists. One might almost say an obsession. It is now almost universally acknowledged that such mediating elements in social theory do the following things: They specify what it means to explain or interpret or account for a particular phenomenon or category of phenomena. They provide rules for interpretation or evaluation of empirical material—data, evidence, findings, and so forth. They identify aspects of empirical reality as problematic or unproblematic, as requiring special explanation or as unremarkable. And they offer rules for moving from observation of the empirical world to inference and conclusion. Few students of social theory would still claim that theories consist only of assertions about their subject matter.

Hardly less widespread is the appreciation that the forces shaping these mediating elements are not exclusively intellectual. They are also existential, relating to the cultural context, political identifications, social position, and various other influences in the life of the thinker. What analysts want out of their theories—whether theories of bureaucratic change, or modernization and underdevelopment, or political participation, or of the causes of poverty, or indeed of civil violence—depends on their biographies, their political assumptions, and their social identifications. Hence we should not be surprised that different thinkers, at different historical points and from different social viewpoints, produce widely varying accounts of "the same" phenomena.

These appreciations have been immensely fruitful for our understanding of theory. It is simply indispensable to appreciate that theoretical orientations or paradigms relate to the peculiarities of the thinker and the intellectual community as well as to the nature of the subject matter.

But good ideas can give rise to bad. In some cases, attention to these mediating factors has led some writers to a relativism bordering on solipsism. "Questions of fact—that is, concern with what the facts are," wrote the late Alvin Gouldner with apparent approval, "seem to enter surprisingly little into much social theory" (1970, p. 483). The message here is that changes in social theory are to be understood as manifestations of changing intellectual needs and predilections of the scholarly community. Evidence, research, and empirical investigation are thus epiphenomenal.

No doubt this view has gained some credence from recent studies of the history of science. A number of these investigations have shown that theoretical shifts, especially replacements of one broad theoretical view by another, do not proceed by strictly logical rules. Even in the hardest of the "hard" sciences, the inability of a theory to explain discordant findings may not lead to abandonment of the theory. Nor do newly accepted theories always show superiority in explanatory power over those they replace. To at least some settings, theoretical shifts resemble religious conversion more than they do rigorous proofs to formal logical problems. That is, they represent changes in the importance ascribed by different aspects of reality, rather than straightforward increments in knowledge. In other words, they involve shifts in intellectual *taste* rather than fuller satisfaction of a single enduring taste.

But, carried to its extreme, the view of theoretical paradigms as standing or falling *only* in terms of the degree of satisfaction they afford the thinker, regardless of any objective standard of ability to account for evidence, yields a disastrous prescription for theoretical work. The worldview of a paranoid schizophrenic, after all, entails a kind of theoretical paradigm. The paranoid mind has its own rules for identifying what warrants attention and explanation, for evaluating and interpreting evidence, and for moving from empirical observation to conclusions. Such a world-view presumably is eminently suitable to the special needs and perspectives of the thinker. Indeed, it may even enable the paranoid to account for all sorts of things for which the rest of us can offer no special explanation. Yet most of us, I trust, readily prefer "scientific" systems of interpreting the empirical world to the hermetic world-view of the paranoid. We prefer the former, not despite the rude collisions it affords between theoretical expectations and empirical reports, but because of them.

We want our theoretical views to yield statements about the empirical world that are in some respects *falsifiable*. In using this term, I hardly mean to invoke the entire approach to the subject of falsifiability developed by Karl Popper. I simply hold it a significant and desirable characteristic of social science theories that they not be equally consistent with any and all possible statements about the empirical world. To be empirically falsifiable, a theory should yield statements for which, in principle, contrary evidence might be adduced. Falsifiable theories afford the possibility of organizing research so as to seek potentially undermining evidence. They enable us to envisage evidence compatible with one theory yet tending to cast doubt on another. Perhaps more important, one can *compare* theories in terms of their ability to withstand confrontation with specific potentially falsifying data. If any form of inquiry is to claim *progress*—movement from what all participants could agree were less satisfactory to more satisfactory states—some relatively enduring standard of falsifiability is essential.

Still, Gouldner may have been at least descriptively correct in his assessment. Perhaps the fluidity and inconclusiveness of social theory, much commented on in Gouldner's work, reflects the inaccessibility of these theories to falsification. Perhaps the theories propounded by social scientists are such direct expressions of the existential circumstances of the thinkers that evidence is unlikely to make much difference. Perhaps these theories come and go simply according to their novelty value or the expressive possibilities they offer those who espouse them. Thus, the theories of social scientists would be destined always to resemble fashions in clothing—always changing, but never improving. I find this prospect unappealing and perplexing, but it should hardly be rejected out of hand.

---

To what extent the realities of social theory fit Gouldner's model, or any other, is hardly a matter to be settled a priori. Instead, this book seeks to illuminate these issues through a searching look at the actual unfolding of theories on a single subject. My goal is not only to provide a critical view of what has been thought and discovered, but also to mobilize such observations as bases for more far-reaching conclusions on the possibilities and limitations of social science theories more generally.

Central to all these inquiries will be the question of falsifiability. Do the theories under study admit, if only in principle, of evidence that might tend to undermine them? What would an actual inquiry aimed at seeking such evidence be like? Answering such questions may not be so simple as it might appear. Theories of civil violence typically come to us in language that is indirect, inexact, allusive. The job of teasing out the implications for evidence is highly interpretive. Consider, for example, the following three statements.

the governing class . . . changes considerably in character from the addition to it or the withdrawal from it of relatively small numbers of individuals. . . . That circumstance lends stability to societies, for the governing class is required to absorb only a small number of new individuals in order to keep the subject class deprived of leadership. However, in the long run the differences in temperament between the governing class and the subject class become gradually accentuated. . . . when the difference becomes sufficiently great, revolution occurs. (Vilfredo Pareto, *The Mind and Society* [1935, p. 1517])

Society . . . acts under the influence of a multitude of minor impulses and tendencies which mutually interact to produce a more general tendency which dominates all the individuals of the group. . . . The crowd acts under the influence of such a dominant tendency, unreflectively, without definite reference to a past or a future. The crowd has no past and no future. (Robert Park and Ernest Burgess, *Introduction to the Science of Sociology* [1921, pp. 798–99])

The problem of order, and thus of the nature of the integration of stable systems of social interactions . . . thus focuses on the integration of the motivation of actors with the normative cultural standards which integrate the action system, in our context interpersonally. These standards . . . are patterns of value orientation, and as such are a particularly crucial part of the cultural tradition of the social system. (Talcott Parsons, *The Social System* [1951, pp. 36–37])

Anyone familiar with these authors will agree that these statements are characteristic of their overall theoretical outlooks. Indeed, each encapsulates some of the writer's most distinctive ideas, not just on civil violence but on basic social processes more generally. Yet, perhaps for this very reason, the empirical implications of statements like these are not to be read easily or automatically. Parsons apparently has *some* empirical meaning in mind when he states that "normative cultural standards . . . integrate the action system." But specifying categories of evidence that might serve for evaluation of this statement requires a hard look not just at this passage but also at the broad corpus of his work. The same holds for virtually all theorists examined here. Identification of the key falsifiable implications of their theories will require interpretive assessments of the broad designs of their thinking.

It would be foolish to imagine that any of these theories, even those much more clearly articulated than Parsons's theories, should stand or fall in terms of a "critical experiment" or other single research operation. We now know that theories are never sustained or refuted in such economical ways, either in social science or anywhere else. Theories like those considered in this book simply have too many implications for too many different forms of data to be upheld or destroyed at a stroke. But this should hardly discourage us from seeking broad categories of data, actually established or yet-to-be-discovered, that would tend to strengthen or weaken the credibility of the theory.

The explanations for civil violence considered here are almost as various as social theory itself. This is no accident. A key reason for focusing on the Hobbesian problem is the sheer variety of contributions that it has attracted throughout the history of social and political thought. And it is especially opportune that Hobbes's question has always been so intensely politicized. Some of the "solutions," most notably those of Marx and his followers, have held distinctly revolutionary implications; others, like those of Pareto and Hobbes himself, have seemed to provide justification for authoritarian regimes. It could hardly be otherwise. No account of what holds people in compliance with the "normal" demands of civil life can avoid bearing a strong political charge. The intellectual "paradigms" governing thinking on this subject cannot help but be shaped by deep-going interests, identifications, and needs of the thinkers concerned.

Besides being so politically charged, the Hobbesian problem offers yet another advantage for the purposes of this book: It relates closely to theoretical questions that go well beyond civil violence alone. Theories put forward to account for civil violence closely parallel those adduced to explain revolutions, social movements, and other forms of militant *mobilization*—that is, processes in which people depart from their "normal" lifeways to challenge prevailing power relations and other social arrangements.

But there are good reasons for not extending the mandate of this work to encompass theories of revolution, social movements, and similar phenomena, except as these things play a role in civil violence narrowly speaking. "Theories" of revolution have been expected to account for everything from the ideological origins of revolutionary strategy to the long-term institutional consequences of revolutions. "Theories" of social movements have been expected to offer accounts of movement recruitment, the social interactions of movement participants, and the evolution of movement goals over time. Obviously there are excellent reasons for studying any or all of these subjects. But the fact that so many intellectual tasks are being undertaken makes it difficult to reach clear, summary conclusions on what has and has not been accomplished. By contrast, in examining theories of civil violence, I focus on a more conceptually bounded problem—when and how relatively peaceful relations within polities give way to deliberate, large-scale destruction of persons and property; and conversely, when and how such destructive episodes subside into more peaceful states.

Now some may object that this way of construing the problem under study itself carries a debatable theoretical message. Why should we necessarily focus on the causes and characteristics of active, collective destruction of persons and property rather, say, than on extreme coercion of duress more generally, or on other forms of social conflict? In short, do we have reason to view civil violence as a cohesive, clearly bounded category of phenomena, rather than simply as a congeries of manifestations of diverse other social processes?

In some respects we have reason to do quite the opposite. Most of the key theoretical approaches considered in this book have pictured civil violence as part of some broader social or political process. For Hobbes, civil violence was simply another manifestation of weakness in the life-giving strictures of rulers, along with crime and other private forms of lawlessness. For the turn-of-the-century irrationalists, civil violence was one of many symptoms of "crowd mentality." For Charles Tilly and his followers, civil violence is another manifestation of pursuit of normal collective interest. In all these cases, as in other theoretical approaches considered in this book, the explanation of civil violence is hardly to be distinguished from explanation of the larger processes in which it is held to be embedded.

But for the purposes of this study, these facts offer an opportunity, rather than an obstacle. For views of civil violence as arising from fundamentally different kinds of social processes offer the possibility of contrasting falsifiable considerations about when, where, and in what form to expect it. It is precisely such clashes of empirical expectation that hold particular interest here.

Then there are similar objections to singling out violence as a separate subject matter—objections on ethical or political grounds. Focusing on acts of collective violence, some say, inevitably distracts attention from destruction wrought by inaction or apparently nonviolent action on the part of power holders. Why study the occasional violent acts of crowds, rather than the institutional processes that lead to mass starvation, industrial accidents, or economic underdevelopment, with all the destructive consequences that they entail?

In their most polemical form, these objections characterize the study of civil violence as a retrograde symptom of bourgeois consciousness. Such analysis, Eric Hobsbawn writes, merely reflects the world-view of "the authorities or the upper classes" (1984, p. 10). From the grass-roots, the picture is completely different: for striking mineworkers, for example,

The worst offense would be scabbing, and there would be no substantial moral difference between peaceful picketing, the pressure of public opinion and physically stopping cabs going down the pit. Beating up a scab or two would be relatively venial and might be inevitable, but an uncontrolled riot of the *Germinal* type might be regrettable, and sabotaging the pumps or the safety arrangements would generally be condemned. Some kinds of violence would be classified with non-violent actions, since they would become distinct from them only because of outside intervention in an otherwise peaceful activity. The crucial criterion would be distinction not between force and non-violence, but between different kinds of force and violence, and the crucial variable not the miners' willingness to use force, but the employers' determination to resist strikes and the means they were prepared to use. (1984, pp. 10–11)

Hobsbawn is certainly right on one key point: The seriousness of violence, indeed the extent to which destructive acts are perceived as belonging to a separate category like "civil violence," is a matter of cultural convention. But the interests guiding social analysis, and the analytic categories arising from such interests, need not necessarily be those of participants in the processes under study. Birth, death, and marriage obviously hold endlessly varied meanings to those involved, but this fact should not deter demographers from analyzing statistics on these events for their own purposes.

Collective violence—deliberate destruction of persons or property by people acting together—holds analytic interest from a great variety of perspectives. It is a sign of change or potential change in social arrangements; an indication that strong interests are engaged; a signal that key claims of governments are being challenged. For all these reasons and more, one might legitimately wish to study where it comes from and how, when and where it occurs. Such analytic interests hardly imply an a priori claim that other, related social processes are unworthy of study; surely attention to collective civil violence should not preclude study of other forms of destructiveness or of nonviolent forms of collective action. But neither are these latter pursuits inherently more worthwhile than the study of civil violence. As in all areas of social inquiry, the subject matter can only be justified by the force of the conclusions that result from it.

True, most theories of civil violence have been theories of the origins of grass-roots action, rather than theories of violence by governments or powerful groups. Pareto, Tilly, Traugott, and a few others do occasionally

offer accounts of repressive violence, but these make up a small proportion of all theoretical attention to civil violence. Perhaps the reason for
this bias has to do with the relative frequency of concerted civil violence
initiated by those in power. Perhaps powerful interests in general, and
governments in particular, do not need to resort to civil violence as often
as do less established actors. After all, those on top may more often "win"
simply by not losing, whereas those on the bottom may have to force
action in order to satisfy their needs. Or perhaps collective violence
initiated by the established—for example, government destruction of
shantytowns in present-day South Africa, or company-instigated attacks
against I.W.W. organizers in America around the turn of this century—
has simply not had the attention from theorists that its frequency would
warrant.

   This is not the kind of question that a book like this can settle. Here I
take the major theories of civil violence as I find them. My concern is how
they explain, and how well they explain, what they attempt to explain;
why they do not seek to explain something else is not my main preoccupation. Nor does the agenda of this work—a critical review of the key accounts of when, where, and how civil violence occurs—provide bases for
conclusions on the relative justice or injustice of popular versus officially
sponsored destructiveness.

   In sum, objections to the study of civil violence as if it were a coherent
category of phenomena do alert us to some serious intellectual hazards.
We can assume from the outset that civil violence represents a highly
heterogeneous category, and we have some prima facie reason to suspect
that the various theories under consideration apply more to one sort of
violence than another. Some analysts in the relative deprivation tradition,
for example, have treated statistics on aggregate levels of civil violence as
direct indications of popular frustration with or grievance against governments. But such a view fits badly with the elementary observation that
much popular violence within the polity is directed at nongovernment
targets and occurs among antagonistic racial, ethnic, or communal groups.
Similarly, as noted previously, government agents may as well be perpetrators as targets of violent action: What interpretation does relative
deprivation theory offer for high levels of violence committed by state coercive agents against initially peaceful crowds?

   Civil violence, then, takes a vast number of forms: attacks on governments, attacks by governments, and struggles among nongovernment parties; actions directly tied to the exercise of central power and ones substantially disconnected from it; actions carefully orchestrated in advance,
and ones emerging from the immediate flux of events. It involves contention over issues that are overtly political, as well as those rooted in the

workplace, the neighborhood, the schools, and the place of worship. Nevertheless, many gifted theorists have put forward theories seemingly purporting to account for civil violence *in general.* Without prejudging those claims, I want to examine them in their own terms, and in terms of relevant empirical investigation.

The task, then, is to survey key theories of civil violence, beginning with those of Hobbes and continuing down to the present day. Current disciplinary distinctions, arbitrary as they are, will not matter here; the ideas under examination are from the tradition common to contemporary political science, anthropology, sociology, and other social science disciplines. The theories are taken up very roughly in historical order, and much of the latter part of the book examines theoretically oriented research that has blossomed only since the middle of this century. But as I seek theoretical ideas in their continuity, some chapters follow single themes from their inceptions centuries ago to the present.

My first concern is to assess the empirical content, if any, of each theory. What forms of data, if discovered, would tend to weaken or falsify the theory? What evidence, if any, would reflect on the virtues of this theory versus those of its competitors? What aspects of civil violence or its absence remain unexplained by this theory, and what importance can one attach to such gaps? More broadly, what grounds for choice exist between the theory under examination and its alternatives? Does evidence count among such grounds, or are they more a matter of perceptual style or preference? Pursuit of questions like these obviously requires much interpretation, particularly in extracting empirical implications from texts couched in allusive or abstract language. But such efforts are essential if we are to lay bare the inner workings of social theory.

Besides identifying the empirical implications of each theoretical approach, I consider the relation of each to research. Obviously theories from before the turn of the century were not part of research traditions, although their twentieth-century descendants have certainly generated research. But where research that relates to these various theories has been undertaken, I consider that relationship in some detail. Has research been designed so as to corroborate or refute theory? Or has it more often, as one sometimes suspects, simply served to illustrate the paradigm or conceptual system underlying the theory? Has research generated new theoretical ideas? In short, whatever the relationship *in principle* between the two activities, what effects do research and theory actually have on one another?

Third, for each theoretical approach, I note major existential or cultural forces influencing its acceptance or rejection. I have hardly undertaken a full-scale sociology of knowledge in any of these cases, but often

connections between theories of civil violence and the times in which
they flourish are readily noted. These connections typically concern what
I have called the rhetorical content of theories, including their evocations
of values or interests that make them more or less appealing to potential
intellectual "consumers." No analysis of Pareto could be complete, for example, without consideration of his special appeal to conservative intellectuals during the 1920s and 1930s as an antidote to Marx. This appeal,
incidentally, was closely bound up with the two theorists' explanations of
civil violence. Similarly, it is impossible to understand the ascendance of
political models of civil violence in the 1960s without noting the relation
of these theories to changes in American political life more broadly. It will
be essential to weigh such contextual forces along with immanent intellectual influences in shaping the history of these theories.

Taken together, the results of these inquiries set the stage, in the concluding chapters of this book, for consideration of some fundamental
questions: What has this theoretical tradition accomplished? How have
we learned what we know? What forms of evidence, what theoretical assumptions sustain our claims to such knowledge? What is the relation of
modern, empirically oriented social inquiry to the sweeping ideas of its
classical ancestors? What role has research played in the development of
theory? What styles of inquiry look most promising in retrospect, and
which have led to dead ends? Have theoretical traditions derived significantly from one another, or has each approach begun its task anew? And
most important: Does the sweep of ideas since the time of Hobbes reveal
anything worthy of the name of "progress"? If so, what form does it take?
If not, how is its absence to be explained? Finally, in light of all these
matters, how should we working social scientists alter our expectations of
our disciplines, or change the ways in which we pursue our work?

I can mentally hear objections to this program on two quite different
grounds.

The first is that it is futile to attempt to resolve epistemological problems through empirical investigation. The difficulties of social science
theory, it is alleged, reflect unresolved disputes over the nature of knowledge and the proper strategies for explanation in these fields. The theoretical inconclusiveness noted here merely represents the symptoms of
this disarray. Thus, seeking coherence or direction in these theories is
useless until the underlying philosophical problems are unraveled.

The second objection might be considered the diametrical opposite of
the first: Too much time and energy have already been wasted, it may be
said, in social scientists' obsessive rummaging in their own intellectual
attics. The only way to progress, in this view, is to cease worrying about
the history of social and political ideas. Instead we should get down to

business and find explanations for civil violence that finally and decisively *work*. Once we hit on winning formulas—for this or any other problem— the reasons for past inconclusiveness will no longer matter.

Certainly there is some force in both these charges. Clashes among contending epistemologies and theories of explanation undoubtedly have helped block orderly cumulation. At the same time, many ruminations by social scientists about their own intellectual history have surely only deep- ened the perplexities. But such observations scarcely warrant the skeptics' conclusions. We have no exact idea of the extent to which epistemological and related differences contribute to the current state of theoretical affairs until we look closely at the details of how ideas have actually unfolded. It may well be that some sort of "working consensus" in social science could coexist with all sorts of dissensus on a more abstract plane. After all, dis- putes among historians and philosophers of science over what natural sci- entists actually do have not necessarily blocked everyday business within the scientific disciplines themselves. We need to weigh these considera- tions along with others to judge their importance in social science.

Nor will it do to place our hopes exclusively on the discovery of some new approach that finally "works." For even a superficial consideration of the sweep of ideas on the Hobbesian question suggests that what "works" at one historical moment and for one category of thinkers may appear useless or worse in another context. What we need to know is whether there is enough stability in answers to the Hobbesian question or indeed in interpretation of the question to warrant hope of long-term continuity. This knowledge can only be gained through thoughtful analysis of how we have gotten where we are now.

---

It should be clear that this project springs from a very particular view of that subset of social science bracketed as "social theory." That sub- discipline, I hold, has suffered greatly from often being a hermetic en- terprise, isolated from actual practice of understanding specific subject matters. To be sure, this charge does not apply to all works in this cate- gory. But many of the more turgid contributions to what passes for social theory predictably leave the reader asking a most embarrassing question: What difference could the resolution of issues preoccupying specialists in "theory" possibly make for the actual conduct of inquiry?

This book aims to take a hard look at what analysts of social life actually do when they set out to build theories. I hope to make it plain that the formal pronouncements of social theorists may bear little direct or straight- forward relation to the realities of theoretically oriented empirical in- quiry. Indeed, the relation of the two seems more like that between

Christian doctrines as expounded from the pulpit on Sunday mornings and the realities of everyday life the rest of the week. The two are obviously not unrelated, but only the most naive observer would take the former by itself as a direct guide to the latter. By analyzing the actual conduct of theory-building on a key intellectual problem, I hold, we may hope to narrow the gap between formal doctrines of social theory and the actual practice of our disciplines.

These inquiries, I believe, drive home some important points about social theory, and especially about questions of progress and cumulation.

First, the main theories of civil violence, for all their exponents' undoubted differences in epistemological or metaphysical assumptions, do entail falsifiable implications. With conscientious interpretation, one can envisage empirical inquiry that would tend to support or undermine their credibility. In a few cases, moreover, we can identify important theoretical ideas that have notably succeeded or failed in withstanding confrontation with potentially falsifying evidence.

Second, one can readily imagine systematic progress in overall understanding of civil violence in terms of a comprehensive effort to pursue those ideas that withstand attempts at falsification. It is difficult, however, to point to many actual strands of investigation concerted enough to have resulted in such cumulation. The conduct of inquiry, in other words, has often failed to exploit possibilities for theoretical development that the subject offers.

Third, the most conspicuous obstacles to consensually defined progress in this field are neither lack of epistemological consensus nor failure of methodological rigor. Rather, they spring from the extreme responsiveness of social theorizing to the larger social, cultural, and political contexts of intellectual life. The constant reinterpretations of the question under study, in the face of changing intellectual climates, have played an enormous role in the inconclusiveness of efforts to account for civil violence. This fluidity in intellectual agenda in turn forces us to ask whether the actual practice of social science is more a *scientific* activity, strictly speaking, or more an *expressive* one.

Whether readers will find these interpretations convincing I cannot be sure. What I *am* sure of is the high ratio of provocative, intriguing theoretical ideas on the origins of civil violence to systematic inquiry needed to attain closure on such ideas. At the very least, this disparity between the lofty promise of social inquiry to unlock the secrets of riot, rebellion, and civil war and the considerable inconclusiveness of consensually attested results poses compelling questions for our view of social science.

Almost throughout its history, social science has suffered from poor fit between its performances and the "scientific" model held out for it. These models hold the promise that systematic and rigorous collection of evidence would ultimately produce a coherent body of related truths, consensually acknowledged as such. Yet we now have behind us a considerable history of attempts to make theoretical sense of a great variety of facts. Despite all sorts of successes in delimited areas of inquiry, the intellectual configurations of social science as a whole do not fit the expectations of the original model.

In the following chapters, I intend to take the "positivistic" claims of social science seriously, by subjecting the falsifiable content of theories on a single key subject to searching examination. Where these efforts appear to have succeeded, or to promise success, I want to understand how this has come about. Where cumulative development has been frustrated, I want to know the roots of these frustrations.

What I seek, then, is a more realistic approach to theory; I can think of no more urgent need in modern social science.

*Chapter One*

# Civil Violence as the Outcome of Rational Calculation: Hobbes and His Modern Followers

A full understanding of civil violence surely must deal with the *interests* of participants, and with participants' judgments as to how such interests are engaged in strife-torn situations. For one tradition among theories of civil violence, calculation of self-interest has figured as the centerpiece of any viable explanation. This line of thinking began with Thomas Hobbes and has continued, via utilitarianism, to various approaches flourishing in present-day social science.

## Hobbes

No one has surpassed Hobbes in the clarity with which he articulated the question central to this book. Social life necessarily involves relatively stable complementary and co-operative behavior. Yet any particular set of social arrangements must entail some pattern of advantage and disadvantage to those involved. Unlike bees, ants, and other social animals, human beings are capable of playing an endless variety of different social roles. Hence the enduring question: What particular principles of advantage and disadvantage, of privilege and subjection, will prevail among any particular people? And how will compliance with these patterns be assured from those who would seek a different distribution of life-chances? When do latent conflicts of interest break out into collective violence? When, conversely, do violent situations return to states of quiescence?

In raising these questions, Hobbes was pursuing objectives of an applied sort. He wanted to propound practical advice for rulers about the design of sound polities, and for citizens about their proper roles in such polities. Thus, in extracting and analyzing Hobbes's theory of civil violence from his larger span of concerns, I am using his work in a way he did not intend—much as with other authors considered in this book.

Despite his practical goals, Hobbes's thinking is eminently theoretical. He distinguishes clearly between theories of civil violence *in general* and analyses of the *occasions* of specific episodes. He understands fully that particular instances of violent collective action stem from particular events and circumstances—a quarrel over succession to political rule, for example, or a flare-up of ethnic rivalries. But he proceeds from the assumption that all instances of civil violence must have some distinguishing qualities in common, and that these shared qualities "of those things that Weaken, or tend to the Dissolution of the Commonwealth" would yield to reasoned analysis. "Ignorance of remote causes," he wrote, "disposeth men to attribute all events, to the causes immediate, and Instrumental" (1968, p. 166). Hobbes seeks the "remote causes" of civil violence, of which each immediate cause of a particular event must partake.

Hobbes's theories are always empirically relevant. He seeks to base the normative advice he propounds on observed patterns of individual behavior and institutional process. He encourages us to observe how individuals behave, and to trace the implications of these individual dynamics through their repercussions in collective life. At every stage he leaves his argument open to criticism in terms of its fidelity to observable social realities.

Finally, Hobbes understands that any explanation of civil violence must also be an explanation of stable civil authority. He concerns himself preeminently with situations where forces conducing to civil violence confront a relatively centralized polity. He assumes, although does not use Weber's terms, that governments must retain monopolies on the means of large-scale coercion if they are to remain viable as governments. Thus, for Hobbes, whatever causes civil violence to flare also is a concomitant of government weakness, and vice-versa.

---

Modern social scientists often speak as though the state of social order Hobbes sought to explain was normally an accomplished reality. We would do better to assume that popular acceptance of social order is always somehow unfinished, even in relatively peaceful settings. It is true that riot, rebellion, civil war, and other states of civil strife are generally less prevalent than their absence. But even in the most stable civil societies, compliance with social strictures is incomplete.

In the state of New York, for example, private consumers are accustomed to paying sales tax on consumer purchases made from businesses.

In fact, New Yorkers are no less legally bound to forward to Albany on their own initiative tax on *any* purchase made within the state—for example, on the purchase of a used lawnmower from a neighbor. The state government does manage to enforce this obligation in sales of used cars among private parties by refusing to register these new purchases without evidence that tax has been paid. But for most private transactions no such enforcement mechanism is available. I suspect that most New Yorkers, if informed of their obligations to pay sales tax on private transactions, would simply consider the idea quaint. Yet this law is no less authentic than that on sales from businesses or sales of used cars. Indeed, it is no less authentic than federal laws requiring payment of income tax, something people comply with widely if hardly totally. What accounts for these differences in compliance is surely the varying ability of government agencies to back legal obligation with actual inducements to comply, including effective surveillance and sanctions for noncompliance. To say that the law requiring New Yorkers to pay sales tax on purchases made from private individuals fails because it is held in contempt is to confuse effect with cause. This particular law is held in contempt because it is unenforceable. Hobbes would have understood this in a way that modern theorists of value integration and moral solidarity can not.

In every social system one finds some normative constraints on self-interest that are almost universally accepted, some with which compliance is chancy and disputed, and some that are honored only in the breach. Not all of these more or less successful constraints, of course, relate to obligations between individuals and governments. But whether or not governments are directly involved, not all contracts are kept, not all obligations are observed, not all "proper" procedures are followed. A theory of "social order" must explain why the limits of compliance fall precisely where they do—why the forces underlying adherence are just so strong, and no stronger. Compliance with strictures against civil violence is a subset of this broader category of normative compliance, but a particularly important one.

## The Theory

Hobbes's theory of civil violence begins with his catalog of human "passions"—that is, his assumptions about motivation.

Hobbes is widely known as the expositor of a relentlessly selfish, if not actually bloodthirsty account of human nature. Indeed, most of the passions he details involve pursuit of selfish ends—sensual gratifications, for example, or physical comfort and safety. Many of his key passions are not only selfish but zero-sum, such that one person can only be satisfied by depriving others of the same enjoyments—for example, strivings for status and power. But these are not the only sorts of passions in Hobbes's array. He clearly acknowledges quite different sorts of motives, such as kindness, benevolence, good will, and charity or "Desire of good to another" (1968, p. 123).

Nevertheless, these latter, more generous motives do not figure much in Hobbes's analyses of collective life. Most of the time, Hobbes apparently reasoned, human beings operate in an environment of emotional scarcity. Pursuit of zero-sum goods shunts aside more generous motives; selfish appetites overwhelm the unselfish.

Greatly sharpening the focus on ungenerous motives, in Hobbes's view, was the pervasive uncertainty of the human situation.

Nature hath made men so equal . . . that though there be found one man sometimes manifestly stronger in body, or of quicker mind then [*sic*] another; yet when all is reckoned together, the difference between man, and man, is not so considerable, as that one man can thereupon claim to himself any benefit, to which another may not pretend, as well as he. For as to the strength of the body, the weakest has strength enough to kill the strongest, either by secret machination, or by confederacy with others. (1968, p. 183)

Given the human tendency to overrate one's own powers and claims versus those of others, Hobbes reasoned, this rough equality of human capabilities was a formula for unceasing conflict. Because of the pervasive uncertainty as to others' actions, the only hope of safety may lie in attacking before being attacked one's self. Hence the relentless human quest for power, even when not for its own sake.

In the first place, I put for a generall inclination of all mankind, a perpetual and restless desire of Power after power, that ceaseth only in Death. And the cause of this, is not alwayes that a man hopes for a more intensive delight, than he has already attained to; or that he cannot be content with a moderate power; but because he cannot assure the power and means to live well, which he hath present, without the acquisition of more. (1968, p. 161)

Without some force external to human nature to stem this uneasy pattern, peaceful social life is impossible. Contrary to widespread belief, Hobbes did not envisage this State of Nature—a world without organized social constraint—as marked by constant bloodshed; the "Warre of All against All" of which he wrote was more a situation of pervasive uncertainty and instability.

For as the nature of Foule weather, lyeth not in a shower or two of rain; but in an inclination thereto of many dayes together; So the nature of War, consisteth not in actual fighting; but in the known disposition thereto, during all the time there is no assurance to the contrary. (1968, p. 186)

Thus, even in peaceful moments, security is impossible, and long-term planning out of the question.

> There is no place for Industry; because the fruit thereof is uncertain; and consequently no Culture of the Earth; no Navigation; nor use of the commodities that may be imported by Sea; no commodious Building . . . no Knowledge of the face of the Earth; no account of Time; no Arts; no Letters; no Society; and which is worst of all, continuall feare, and danger of violent Death. (1968, p. 186)

Essentially missing from the State of Nature is the ability to form contracts—that is, any co-operative understandings involving reciprocal obligations. For given the overwhelming force of selfish passions, contractual obligations would not be adhered to in the absence of enforcement mechanisms. In the State of Nature, Hobbes tells us, people have only the laws of nature to guide them; these laws simply dictate that people do what best suits their interests. And it is in no one's interest to adhere to a contract when one's contractual partner cannot be expected to do the same.

Although Hobbes was not totally consistent on the point, he did not necessarily view the State of Nature as a historical reality. At least, such an assumption was not required for his argument. The State of Nature figures more as an ideal type in his thinking, a heuristic extreme case of the total lack of central regulation over human appetites. One cannot understand how much we owe to established political systems, Hobbes was trying to say, unless we consider the alternative of *no* central power at all.

Hobbes's account of our escape from the State of Nature is well known. Human beings renounce private recourse to violence, in effect creating specialists in large-scale coercion in the shape of governments. Governments—sovereigns, in Hobbes's words—then set down their own rules for social obligation, both among private individuals and between individuals and governments, appointing agents to enforce these rules with coercive sanctions where necessary. The existence of a central system of coercion creates an interest among private citizens both in adhering to their obligations to the sovereign, and in keeping contractual responsibilities to other private individuals. The role of the sovereign, Hobbes tells us, is to inspire "Awe" throughout the populace—that is, respect for power greater than one's own. Once this is accomplished, people's interests lie in supporting the "rules of the game" established by the sovereign, which after all make a more commodious and predictable life possible.

Note, in this capsule account of Hobbes's position, the essential elements of theories of civil violence based on rational calculation: Human beings approach their social environments with certain enduring needs or interests; what actions may serve these interests depends on the larger social setting. Hence individuals relentlessly *attend to* the state of the social world and *calculate* how different courses of action may serve their interests. Whether the resulting actions will be peaceful or militant depends on the results of these calculations.

---

Hobbes does not pin his main hopes for compliant behavior on popular internalization of proregime sentiments. The birth of the commonwealth does not transform human nature or individual personalities, but rather alters the conditions under which people pursue abiding drives and passions. Life in the commonwealth, as distinct from that in the State of Nature, offers different contingencies, such that the rational person will find adherence to prevailing norms more attractive than evasion. The establishment of the commonwealth, after all, offers a chance of peace and predictability, and there is no chance whatsoever of these things in the State of Nature. "The Passions that incline Men to Peace," Hobbes writes, "are the Feare of Death" (1968, p. 188); against such well-founded fears, granting compliance even to a highly flawed commonwealth is only rational.

The social contract—that is, renunciation of private recourse to violence through submission to the Awe-inspiring sovereign—was for Hobbes as much an analytical fiction as the State of Nature. Hobbes writes of it as though it were an implicit understanding among those partaking of the advantages of life in the commonwealth, more than as a particular event. It is the kind of understanding that the occupants of a leaky lifeboat might share: All bail furiously to keep their craft afloat, each knowing that all will be lost, should any one slacken his efforts.

The trouble was, Hobbes felt, that citizens' self-interest in following the rules of the commonwealth was less evident to most of them than the interests in keeping the lifeboat afloat would be to its occupants—thus, Hobbes's own self-appointed role of demonstrating to citizens how much they really owed to governments. Under any government, Hobbes tells us, people

attribute all the inconvenience [of their lives] to that forme of Common-wealth; whereas the Power in all formes, if they be perfect enough to protect them, is the same; not considering that the estate of Man can never be without some incommodity or other. . . . For all men by nature provided of notable multiplying glasses, (that is, their Passions and Self-love,) through which, every little payment appeareth a great grievance; but are destitute of those prospective glasses, (namely Morall and Civill Science,) to see a farre off the miseries that hang over them, and cannot without such payments be avoided. (1968, pp. 238–39)

Hobbes's project was to make better citizens and better commonwealths by showing all concerned where their self-interest really lay.

## Some Questions About the Theory

Many modern readers are appalled by the quasi-totalitarian implications of Hobbes's message. But he is nothing if not consistent. If any government is better than no government, or if any strong government is better than a weakened government, then unquestioning obedience to sovereign dictates is no more than rational. Remember, Hobbes claims no other standard of rationality than what lies in the self-interest of each individual. As in the leaky lifeboat, anyone not helping keep the ship of state afloat must be contributing to the undoing of all.

But there is also a much different and seemingly contradictory side to Hobbes's normative prescriptions. Consistent with his extraordinary valuation of order and predictability in social life, he held that adherence to contracts could be right (prudent from the standpoint of the individual's interests) even in the State of Nature. The fundamental law of nature, he tells us, is that "every man ought to endeavor Peace, as far as he has hope of obtaining it; and when he cannnot obtain it, that he may seek, and use, all helps, and advantages of Warre" (1968, p. 190). Peaceful and co-operative behavior conduces to the commodiousness of life, he reasons, and hence serves the interests of the individual whenever they do not expose him or her to danger. Yet such dangerous consequences of norm-abiding behavior are more the rule than the exception in the State of Nature.

For he that should be modest, and tractable, and performe all he promises, in such time, and place, where no man els should do so, should but make himself a prey to others, and procure his own certain ruine, contrary to the ground of all Lawes of Nature. (1968, p. 215)

Similarly, Hobbes holds that *rulers* have a duty—which is to say, an enlightened interest—to foster the productive and rewarding pursuit of self-interest by their subjects. The sovereign is bound to "the procuration of the safety of the people," he tells us, and this means not just "bare preservation, but also all other Contentments of life, which every man by Lawfull Industry, without danger, or hurt to the Commonwealth shall acquire to himself" (1968, p. 376). For the use of laws, Hobbes holds,

is not to bind the People from all Voluntary actions; but to direct and keep them in such a motion, as not to hurt themselves by their own impetuous desires . . . as Hedges are set, not to stop Travellers, but to keep them in the way. . . . the good of the Sovereign and People, cannot be separated. It is a weak Sovereign, that has weak Subjects; and a weak People, whose Sovereign wanteth Power to rule them at his will. (1968, p. 388)

These passages provide a fuller view of Hobbes's overall intent in pro-
mulgating his theories. Although apologists for totalitarianism may draw
comfort from some of his doctrines, totalitarianism was clearly not the outcome he sought from his writings. The way to abundant life for all, he
wanted people to see, lies in recognizing the interests of rulers and ruled
alike in compliance with government authority. If only people will yield to
rulers the unquestioning compliance that is due them, rulers should find
it in their interests to provide the safety and opportunities for pursuit of
private well-being so notably absent in the state of nature. Like many a
self-help writer, Hobbes urges his readers to do well by doing good.

Such, at least, was his intent. The question is, do Hobbes's arguments,
and especially their sociological underpinnings, support his conclusions?
In particular, do his assumptions about human nature and his analyses of
the contingencies of social life sustain his conclusions about ordinary citizens' interests in compliance?

I think not. If rulers are made of the same stuff as the rest of humanity,
why would they necessarily see their interests in strengthening their subjects, rather than exploiting them? Even accepting the contention that a
prosperous and productive populace will often conduce to a strong state,
it is hard to believe, within the constraints of Hobbes's assumptions, that
such considerations will necessarily outweigh rulers' interests in exploiting their basically unchecked power to their own personal advantage.

Similar misgivings apply to Hobbes's arguments for the interests of
ordinary citizens in accepting the rules of the sovereign order. But here
the implications are much more serious for his theory of civil violence.
Undoubtedly, everyone shares an interest in a relatively law-abiding, predictable social order, where contractual arrangements and other long-
term plans have some chance of fulfillment; and, as Hobbes argues, each
individual act of compliance with authority helps strengthen a system that
benefits all. But the most attractive situation, from the standpoint of the
selfish interests that predominate in Hobbes's view of human nature, is a
world where others comply, while one's self does not. Force and fraud are
all the more effective, after all, if one's competitors are constrained against
using them.

In a leaky lifeboat, failure of any one person to co-operate could well
mean the ruin of all. But in the life of the commonwealth, contingencies
are not normally so tightly drawn. The likelihood that one's own support
for law and order would make a noticeable difference in the ability of the
system to produce compliance in one's own interest is presumably remote.
Such a difference would appear likely only in social units much smaller
than the state. Thus a Hobbesian actor—calculating and almost entirely

self-interested—would surely opt for the relatively certain and palpable benefits of opportunism over the abstract and uncertain results of supporting the system to one's immediate disadvantage. In short, Hobbes fails to deal convincingly with the lately celebrated "free rider problem."

## Falsifiability

Again, Hobbes's ultimate objective was to propound practical advice for rulers and the ruled. Yet the theory of social compliance he develops en route to this destination bears some provocative empirical implications, if only we can decipher them. Unfortunately, the falsifiable expectations attributed to Hobbes have typically done scant justice to the real depth of his thinking. Most often he has been interpreted as a simplistic theorist of deterrence, as though he viewed the likelihood of compliance as a direct function of the amount of coercive force available to governments. The implication thus would be,

*Expect compliance with rules upheld by any government to be greater, the larger the numbers of coercive personnel and other coercive resources available to that government.*

This oversimplified implication of Hobbes's theory is in fact easily falsified. Many lightly policed states such as Iceland and Luxembourg enjoy low rates of both crime and civil violence. Conversely, many countries like South Africa or the Philippines, with vast military and police establishments, also have high rates of domestic strife. A number of quantitative studies, analyzing data from large numbers of countries, also tend to cast doubt on the crude deterrence model. Such studies (Feierabend and Feierabend 1972; Gurr and Duvall 1973; Orbell and Rutherford 1973; Muller 1985) suggest that the repressive capacity of regimes is by no means closely associated with civil violence. The difficulties in interpreting results of such correlational studies are discussed in detail in Chapter Seven. For now, we can note that empirical support for this version of Hobbes's theory is scarce.

This simple deterrence model assumes that most or all citizens adhere to normative constraints only for fear of immediate sanction, should they fail to do so. But Hobbes posited a positive interest in compliance with rules of normative co-operation, when conditions of the overall system make it safe to do so. The role of the sovereign was hardly to repress everyone at once, but rather to instill just enough "Awe" throughout the citizenry to tip the balance from a situation where adherence to obligations was unsafe, to one where such adherence lay in the interest of the individual. Brian Barry has put the matter well:

To reduce Hobbes to saying, "Obey the sovereign, or he'll punish you," is to miss the core of his doctrine, which is that you are obliged to obey wherever certain nullifying conditions are absent. Obedience pays because it helps to secure peace, which is the only sure means to personal survival. It pays, *other things being equal,* and it is the state's job to make them equal. . . . If we have to reduce Hobbes to a slogan, it must be something like this: "Obey even when there isn't a policeman, because this contributes to peace: only provided that there are enough policemen around to give you more security than you would get in a free-for-all." And it may be added that since a free-for-all is very, very insecure, the critical level of police protection need not be very high to make it preferable for you to cast your vote by obeying the government's commands. (1968, p. 127)

As I have argued, this position of Hobbes's does not really fit very well with his assumptions about human motivation. For a truly Hobbesian personality, the payoffs of "casting a vote" in favor of normative order would pale versus those of exploiting that order to one's own narrow benefit. But there can be no doubt that this was Hobbes's position. And there is no reason not to seek empirically falsifiable implications from this doctrine.

Unfortunately, these implications are by no means so straightforward as those of the simplistic deterrence version already considered. Here the investigator would want to assess people's *perceptions of* and *beliefs about* their political world and about the effects of their own actions on that world, much more than objective coercive capacity. The resulting empirical expectation might be as follows:

*Expect popular support for government-sponsored social constraints to be greater and civil violence less, to the extent that the general population embraces the following beliefs:*

*That the normative order facilitates fruitful pursuit of one's own private interests, and*

*That exercise of government coercive powers sustains the normative order, and*

*That one's own compliance with the normative order is essential to the ability of government to sustain its coercive capacity.*

Assessing such convictions would be no easy matter. One would have to tap very deep feelings, not necessarily consciously held, about matters on which people would have reason to be less than candid. Moreover, to be true to the distinctively Hobbesian qualities of the theory, one would have to take great care that one's inquiries dealt strictly with the *instrumental abilities* of a regime to protect private interest rather than straying into other, non-Hobbesian reasons for regime support such as identification of the regime with chauvinistic symbols.

Clearly distinctions of this subtlety would exceed the capacities of such familiar data-collecting mechanisms as public opinion polls. Something more like clinical interviews might be necessary. And the practical difficulties of carrying out such interviews on a scale large enough to give confidence about the distributions of these states of mind throughout large populations would be formidable.

On the other hand, one might gain some special insight into these theoretically critical beliefs through close observation of crisis periods. For example, one might identify an episode in the life of a polity when it appeared that the entire population, or most of it, had suddenly lost confidence in the ability of government agents to instill "Awe"—a period in which beliefs in the ability of government to maintain an effective modicum of coercion would collapse. Such changes should yield abrupt breakdowns of compliance, if Hobbes's doctrine is correct. Indeed, we know that such sequences sometimes occur, as in sprees of looting and other crime that occasionally follow power blackouts, police strikes, and other interruptions in central coercive capabilities.

Taking seriously the falsifiable implications of Hobbes's full view yields some interesting and nonintuitive expectations. For example, a regime might secure widespread compliance with normative obligations while retaining few repressive agents and, indeed, exercising very little actual coercion. If people's perceptions of what the regime could accomplish against any potential deviance were decisive, only occasional coercive sanctions against very scattered acts of noncompliance might serve to sustain popular belief in the three points I have cited. A low level of "demonstration effects" might well suffice.

The model of enforcement and compliance thus described clearly does correspond to certain ranges of empirical phenomena. Elementary school teachers and traffic police may realize that their only hope of securing general compliance is to take relatively few but conspicuous disciplinary actions against particularly flagrant deviants. At best, a few such actions *pour encourager les autres* may secure co-operation from large numbers of would-be deviants who certainly could not be all sanctioned at once. These forms of social control strike me as absolutely fundamental social processes. Although he does not make the connection explicit, Hobbes often seems to allude to processes of this kind, as in chapter twenty-seven of *Leviathan*.

But this view in turn suggests some intriguing possibilities concerning transitions between states of compliance and states of rebellion. In an authentically Hobbesian world, it would be quite consistent to imagine a populace entirely law-abiding until a single event brought about a change in perceived ability of the regime to compel compliance. Thus, the failure of government forces to repress rebellion by one disaffected ethnic group, or to protect the property of one upstanding citizen against an angry mob, could theoretically trigger an abrupt and general collapse in confidence throughout the system. If we accept the three-part conditions of compliance derived from Hobbes, we should then expect an abrupt outbreak of civil violence. Obviously, the more Hobbesian actors lose confidence in the ability of governments to protect their interests, the less support the normative order will enjoy—hence, a transition from compliance to contention that could move very quickly.

Such implications place Hobbes in some unexpected theoretical company. The scenario given above bears some striking resemblances to accounts by Parsons and his followers of revolutions and other civil strife as instances of "power deflation." These views, discussed at greater length in Chapters Five and Eight, draw an analogy between civil rebellion and "runs" on banks, where an inordinately large proportion of depositors demand their deposits in cash at once. Under the equivalent political conditions, large numbers of citizens are said to make urgent demands for government action, resulting in inability of governments to make good on "normal" obligations to their citizens.

A more lucid development of this idea comes in Mark Granovetter's "threshold models" of collective behavior, discussed at the end of this chapter. To be sure, Granovetter's spare mathematical model does not address a matter central to Hobbes's concerns: the role of governments in shaping private citizens' calculations of whether adherence to normative dictates or evasion represents a more promising course of action. In Granovetter's language, Hobbes is concerned with how governments shape *thresholds.* The good government is one that keeps its citizens' thresholds high enough so that slight perturbations, such as outbreaks of civil violence or other nonnormative acts, do not touch off chain reactions leading to collapse of civil authority. Changes in distributions of thresholds throughout populations, as they affect popular perceptions of the consequences of noncompliant activity, should correspond to changes in distributions of law-abiding versus other behavior.

I have argued that empirical investigation has a long way to go before it affords systematic conclusions on the falsifiable implications of Hobbes's theory. Yet some sequences of political life clearly fit Hobbes's formulations eminently well. During the late 1970s, Turkey, a formal democracy, became increasingly ungovernable. When the two major political parties became deadlocked on selection of a president, a political stalemate resulted, in 1980, when no legislation could be passed. Perhaps even more serious, forces outside the government were exercising more and more power on their own. Factions acting in the name of both right- and left-wing political elements were taking control of neighborhoods and entire communities; some two thousand people lost their lives in political violence during the early part of 1980. To many Turks, a complete breakdown of central authority seemed imminent.

On 12 September 1980, the military took over. One of the army's first actions after the bloodless coup was to remove some one hundred twenty political leaders, government officials, and trade union leaders from the capital. A conservative military government was formed, and most political activity was proscribed. Martial law decrees banned all strikes, demonstrations, and political meetings; censored the press; and authorized the use of deadly force in pursuit of suspected opponents. During the seven months following the coup, the authorities arrested some twenty-five thousand suspects; nine hundred were convicted of "anarchic action." Four were hanged, and others spent long periods in jail.

How did these coercive gestures affect compliance? Private political violence dropped remarkably, from an estimated total of more than twenty deaths per day before the coup to about two per day afterwards. From all accounts, the main popular reaction was one of relief at the increased safety and predictability of everyday life. Carrying of personal weapons became less common; shopkeepers removed the bomb-proof shutters that had protected their shops. At least in the early stages, the military government seemed to enjoy relieved acceptance from the majority of the population.

From any point of view, this is a Hobbesian story. There are many similar stories: the reduction of popular protest in France under the draconian rule of Louis-Napoleon; the "law and order" *cum* political quiescence under Spain's Franco; or the lack of popular mobilization prevailing under successful totalitarian regimes in the Soviet bloc today. The introduction of conspicuous coercive capacity and the will to use it in troubled political situations often does result in suppression of rebellious activity.

The trouble is, things clearly do not always work this way. Sometimes high coercive capabilities, and even ruthless application of such capabilities, lead only to heightened rebellion. But in these cases, we generally know nothing about the perceptual variables noted previously that may link formal coercive capabilities to actual compliance. Thus, although Hobbes's theory of civil violence appears to be empirically relevant, the systematic empirical work necessary to explore its overall strengths and weaknesses has hardly begun.

## The Scottish Moralists and the Utilitarians

Given the subtlety of his doctrines, it is sad that many present-day sociologists now mention Hobbes only to dismiss him. His name is invoked simply as a reminder of how far sociological theory has come since anyone could believe that *force majeure* alone could account for compliance with distasteful social obligations. Hobbes deserves better. I have already noted that he tells us altogether too little about how the ingredients of political power, particularly coercive might, are translated into popular perception of a regime's ability to protect private interests. And I will argue that his motivational assumptions are indeed unsatisfactory for any theory of civil violence. But students of civil violence have much still to learn from his contributions.

It is all the sadder that shortcomings attributed to Hobbes—often accurately, regarding his restricted view of human motives—have been unfairly extended to important groups of later thinkers who did not in fact share them. These are the Scottish moralists and the utilitarians. Many of these figures drew heavily from Hobbes, particularly concerning his view of calculation in human action. But few if any thoroughly shared Hobbes's insensitivity to human motives of willing attachment to the interests of others, or to abstract principles transcending self-interest.

In fact, skepticism of this aspect of Hobbes's thinking goes far back in the British tradition. Dugald Stewart, writing in 1828, put forth the following reactions to Hobbes's position:

The question with respect to the social or the solitary nature of man seems to me to amount to this, whether man has any disinterested principles which lead him to unite with his fellow creatures, or whether the social union be the result of prudential views of self-interest, suggested by the experience of his own insufficiency to procure the objects of his natural desires. Of these two opinions Hobbes has maintained the latter, and has endeavoured to establish it by proving, that in what he calls the state of nature every man is an enemy of his brother, and that it was the experience of the evils arising from these hostile dispositions that induced men to unite in a political society.

Stewart's adverse judgment of this position was not unusual in his time:

That this theory of Hobbes is contrary to the universal history of mankind cannot be disputed. Man has always been found in a social state; and there is reason even for thinking, that the principles of union which nature has implanted in his heart operate with the greatest force in those situations in which the advantages of the social union are the smallest. (1855, vol. 6, pp. 33–34).

These words could have been written by a number of Stewart's contemporaries. They and their Enlightenment predecessors saw the experience of social living itself as engendering attachments to various values beyond narrow self-interest. These broader interests included both the well-being of others and more diffuse interests in principles of justice and fair play peculiar to each distinct social order.

Such distinctly un-Hobbesian ideas were scarcely less characteristic of

the utilitarians proper. Certainly David Hume, Adam Smith, Jeremy
Bentham, and the two Mills derived much from Hobbes. But with the
possible exception of James Mill, all these figures acknowledged the importance in social action of motives transcending narrow self-interest. Significantly, none of these authors had a great deal directly to say about civil
violence; the question that virtually obsessed Hobbes was much less salient to them. They simply saw a much greater scope for spontaneous co-
operation and fewer areas of inherent zero-sum antagonism in social life.
The reason was not just that they assumed a "natural identity of human
interests," as Parsons alleged (1937). The utilitarians also held that people
were capable of adopting the interests of others, were desirous of the
approval of others, and were sensitive to injunctions of conscience on
matters of abstract principle. As Camic (1979) has demonstrated, the neglect of this aspect of the utilitarian legacy has meant a serious distortion
of our intellectual heritage.

How has this distortion come about? Part of the reason is certainly the
misleading view put forward in *The Structure of Social Action* and subsequent work in the Parsonian tradition. Perhaps another has to do with two
present-day theoretical traditions that derive directly from utilitarianism—neoclassical economics and behavioristic psychology. Both these
disciplines have adopted some assumptions from utilitarianism, above all
the view of behavior as reflecting the individual's summation of potential
costs and inducements. For certain ranges of problems encountered by
psychologists and economists, such a model may well suffice, as it did for
the utilitarians for specific purposes. But to ignore those costs and benefits that extend beyond the narrowest self-interest does little justice to the
original utilitarian model of social action.

## Rational Choice Theory

In the past two decades, via economics, a similarly truncated version of
utilitarian thought has taken an important place in the study of collective
protest and social movements. Rational choice theory is the analysis of interactions of self-interested decisions in formation of collective actions.
Theorists in this vein—mostly economists and political scientists—study
lobbies, social movements, and other purposeful joint efforts to satisfy the
interests of individual participants. This style of analysis rose to prominence in the late 1960s, about the same time as theories treating violent
political action as rational pursuit of group interest. But rational choice
theorists' model of individual rather than collective interest as the mainspring of collective action places them on a theoretical collision course
with virtually all sociological theories of civil violence.

The classic work in the rational choice tradition is Mancur Olson's *The Logic of Collective Action* (1965). It would be difficult to name any work published over the last twenty years in the study of social movements and political contention that has received as much attention as this.

The essentials of Olson's argument are now well known. Many forms of collective action aim at attaining public goods. These are benefits that must be made available to everyone, if they are available to anyone; they cannot be restricted to those who may have exerted themselves to obtain them. Examples are the benefits of national defense, clean air, relief from taxation, or government services to broad groups such as veterans or farmers. When the numbers of interested potential beneficiaries rises above a certain relatively low number—a number that can be determined in terms of the size of the benefits and the costs of the action by each party—it becomes irrational for any individual to participate. For then the likelihood that one's own contribution will make the difference between obtaining and missing the benefit is small, whereas nonparticipants will enjoy the benefits of such collective goods whether or not they shoulder the cost of obtaining them.

Understanding these things, Olson argues, helps account for the un-questionably large numbers of shared interests that never get acted upon. The fact that people share an interest in a particular public good never in itself guarantees that they will join in collective action. For the individual cannot rationally believe that his or her contribution will make the differ-ence between obtaining and missing the benefit. Collective action will not occur in these cases, Olson argues, without selective incentives—that is, inducements that can be administered to or withheld from participants individually according to whether they participate. For farmers seeking federal services through lobbying, the selective incentive might be spe-cial advantages like low-cost insurance or technical advice provided by the lobbying organization to its members only. For workers confronting management in a strike, the selective incentive might be violence against those who break ranks.

The distinctiveness of this view, and its consonance with Hobbes's thinking (as against that of the Scots moralists and utilitarians) should be obvious. For Olson, social action is "rational" only when it gratifies what I call the *divisible interests* of the actor—those interests that one can con-ceive of an individual enjoying even when no one else enjoys them. Con-ceivably, one's interest in breathing clean air might be divisible if satisfied by using a personal gas mask. But desire to see members of one's own religious faith prosper is not divisible in this sense. Olson sees people as motivated by such attractions as wealth and pleasure but not by desire to further abstract causes or interests of broad categories of humanity. If any action is unlikely to produce a sensible increment in gratification experienced by the individual, it would be irrational to engage in it.

Although Olson has little directly to say about collective violence in *The Logic of Collective Action,* his analysis of collective action in general obviously bears on the concerns of this book. Violent actions, after all—including both actions directed at government, like revolutionary movements, and those directed at other groups—are widely supposed to be efforts to secure public goods in Olson's sense. Yet Olson's doctrine would incline one to believe that such actions will not occur on a large scale unless participants are motivated by personal gain distinct from the indivisible collective gains likely to be produced.

This view has attracted a long line of analysts of collective violence, especially those of conservative bent. It underlies Edward Banfield's analysis of the urban insurgencies in American cities during the 1960s as put forward in the chapter entitled "Rioting Mainly for Fun and Profit" in his book *The Unheavenly City* (1968). Other applications of the same thinking derive more directly from Olson's book (Gunning 1972; Silver 1975). In one such study, Gordon Tullock argues that "public good aspects of a revolution are of relatively little importance in determining the decision to participate" (1971, p. 92). Undaunted by the enormity of the implications of these views, Tullock concludes:

In sum, the theoretical argument for the view that revolutions are carried out by people who hope for private gain and produce such public goods as they do produce as a by product seems to me very strong. . . . Revolution is the subject of an elaborate and voluminous literature and, if I am right, all of this literature is wrong. (p. 99)

One might state the falsifiable implication as follows:

*Expect civil violence only where participants stand to satisfy divisible, individual interests—for example, plunder, rape, personal revenge—by their actions.*

Thus evidence of widespread willingness to sacrifice self-interest for some collective good—to risk one's life, for example, pursuing some collective goal without the likelihood of individual reward—would weaken the credibility of the theory. In every instance of violent collective action, the investigator ought to be able to note the special individual incentives drawing people into participation. Thus, the task of *explaining* civil violence would amount to one of showing how such individual inducements come into play at certain junctures and not at others. Self-interest must be assumed to be a constant feature of social life, after all, whereas large-scale collective violence is relatively rare. Fluctuations in regime coercive capabilities or intent might produce the basis for positing one such intervening variable, but this is hardly the only possibility.

What makes Olson's work particularly important is that he posits mechanisms by which large groups may trigger individually self-interested action in quest of collective goods—selective incentives. In the absence of some such devices to link narrow self-interest with shared ends, he would argue, collective action will not occur. "Economic organizations," he writes, in what might be the thematic sentence of his book, "develop special institutions to solve the membership problem posed by the large scale of their objectives" (1965, p. 65).

But Olson uses the notion of economic organizations or economic objectives in a very particular way. He aims to debunk Marx's expectations of class action arising out of perception of common interest, for example, on grounds that individual proletarians would normally have no selective incentive to participate (1965, pp. 107–8). Moreover, the possibility that Marx may have entertained a conception of *interest* different from Olson's leaves the latter unimpressed. "Much of the evidence suggests that Marx was offering a theory based on rational, utilitarian individual behavior," Olson observes, "and if so his theory is inconsistent."

But even if Marx really had irrational emotional behavior in mind, his theory still suffers, for it is hard to believe that irrational behavior could provide the motive power for *all* social change throughout human history. (1965, p. 110)

Again, note the distinctiveness of the position. Behavior not calculated to produce divisible gratifications to individual interests is "irrational," including actions taken to further interests of larger social units or causes. The assumptions are indeed similar to those of Hobbes, and like his they may be fruitful for specific analyses. But as a comprehensive guide to social action, Olson's doctrine flies in the face of reality. People vote, surely knowing that their ballots have little likelihood of changing the outcomes of elections. People enlist in military forces in times of national emergency, certainly aware that they may not live to see the outcome of the struggle. People refrain from littering, even in places they do not expect to have to look at again. People contribute to relief efforts and charities, even when the beneficiaries of these gestures are worlds removed from themselves. To be sure, not everyone eligible to do these things does so in every case. But these behaviors are not rarities; more to the point, they represent bases for widespread and fundamental social processes. It seems strange to bracket such action as "irrational emotional behavior."

Olson's celebrated book shares a quality of other works of special originality—the willingness to carry distinctive ideas to conclusions others had not thought to consider, and indifference to anomalies and inconsistencies that arise en route. Modern rational choice theory, virtually set in motion by *The Logic of Collective Action*, continues to be distinguished by applying assumptions of narrow self-interest to problems of collective choice.

In all of these writings, the refusal to deal sensibly with the existence of motives other than narrow self-interest has been both a fruitful source of new perspectives and a stumbling block.

Perhaps the most notable work to follow in the tradition established by Olson is Russell Hardin's *Collective Action* (1982). Hardin seeks to apply Olson's basic argument under a wider variety of assumptions and to take greater account of motives other than narrow self-interest in the formulation of collective action. To this extent, his arguments are less dramatic and original than Olson's, and also less estranged from reality. For example, he explores the possibility that some collective decision making may be "contractarian"—that is, that people "play fair . . . [and] try to cooperate if others do" (1982, p. 90). The models of collective action stemming from these assumptions obviously differ from those in which participants are strictly Hobbesian actors. Similarly, Hardin explores varying assumptions about the length of interaction among self-interested actors— for example, whether co-operative behavior is more likely among strictly self-interested actors when they expect involvement extending into the future than when their relations are short-lived.

Hardin has even less to say directly about civil violence than does Olson. But he does pursue a theoretical point of central interest here— the satisfactoriness of positing narrow self-interest as the only socially relevant human motive. Hardin acknowledges the existence of "moral" and other "extrarational motivations" (1982, pp. 101–8), but he seems ambivalent about the extent of their influence in collective processes. "Little more than 1 per cent each of blacks, women, and professed environmentalists have contributed to their group's cause in any year," he writes in a typical passage (1982, p. 102). Or, elsewhere he notes that rational choice analysis "helps to understand why half of the eligible Americans do not vote, but it does little to help us understand the other half" (1982, p. 11).

In fact, rational choice theory warrants no particular conclusion about the roughly fifty percent of American voters who fail to vote. Perhaps, after all, their motives are ones of disdain: They refuse to vote to demonstrate their contempt or indifference either to politicians or to the system as a whole. If so, they are acting as "irrationally" as those who vote; no less than the voters, they are imagining that their actions will make some perceptible difference.

Where Hardin does confront evident collective action over issues of high principle, he sometimes seems more inclined to explain away than to explain. In a discussion of the attractions of "participation," he asks, "Are Iranians a loonier race than most?"

More likely they are merely further proof of economists' claim that the marginal value of an experience or good is, other things being equal, greater, the rarer the enjoyment. Iranians suddenly had the opportunity to participate in their nation's history during the late seventies, and they would not have missed it for the world. (1982, pp. 108–9)

This analysis threatens to reduce the forces mobilizing millions of persons over profound and historic issues to the level of those drawing crowds to a traveling circus. Not all forms of participation, not all unusual experiences are equally attractive. Some issues and personalities are seen as sufficiently momentous to demand participation from very large numbers of people at considerable personal cost, including participation in collective violence. The question facing social scientists is what distinguishes these bases for participation from those that move no one.

Hardin's example mixes cause with effect. Iranians sought participation in the events of the revolution because they identified with the issues they saw at stake. Had this not been true, there would have been no great events in which to participate. Analysis of mobilization in terms of the attractions of participation makes little sense of the early resistance of highly committed activists at a time when most saw the Shah's position as unassailable. Their early, exemplary resistance was essential for creation of later events that drew mass participation. Accounting for their actions in terms of rational choice theory is an unenviable task.

Although Hardin's efforts are less doctrinaire and more interesting, Olson himself at least acknowledges the tension between his position and the evident realities of some forms of collective action. His theory, he writes,

like any other theory, is less helpful in some cases than in others. It would take too long here to examine any . . . lobbies with "noneconomic" interests. . . . The theory is not at all sufficient where philanthropic lobbies, that is, lobbies that voice a concern about some group other than the group that supports the lobby, or religious lobbies, are concerned. (1965, pp. 159–60)

This statement amounts virtually to a claim that the theory can be expected to hold only in those conditions where it does in fact hold. If every collective action in which participants were not clearly motivated by selective incentives or some other form of divisible gratification to their narrow self-interests were ipso facto relegated to the "noneconomic" category, Olson's theory would be circular.

In fact, the dynamics of what Olson apparently regards as "noneconomic" collective actions do not differ greatly from those seemingly aimed at satisfying the self-interest of participants. The participation of young women in the antiwar movement during the Vietnam War years, for example, took much the same form as that of young men, although men were presumably motivated by desire to avoid conscription in the conflict, a condition not affecting women. Similarly, one wonders whether the emotional dynamics of support for the Irish Republican Army in Northern Ireland are that different from those underlying its support in the Irish Republic or, indeed, New York City. But then, by Olson's reasoning, none of these mobilizations should have occurred at all, because no one participant could realistically expect his or her participation to affect the shared outcomes.

But probing the logic of Olson's *Logic* eventually gives one the feeling that one is asking the wrong questions—that the theory of rational choice has gone forward on conceptual bases inadequate to its analytical tasks. Specifically, the distinction between "narrow" self-interest—the presumed basis for what Olson would call "economic" action—and other kinds of interest that move people is much fuzzier than rational choice analysts allow. Occasionally someone will insist that everything anyone does is in response to some kind of self-interest, but such usage obviously destroys any utility the notion might have. There has to be some basis for distinguishing between actions taken on behalf of divisible self-interest and others—those on behalf of other persons, for example, or abstract principles.

We distinguish readily enough between the self-interested actions of someone who hoards his resources to purchase choice viands, lavish entertainments, and fleshly delights for himself alone, versus the philanthropic actions of someone who anonymously grants his fortune for good works to the needy in a different corner of the world. But what do we make of the man who makes a substantial donation to, say, his alma mater, on the condition that his son be admitted as a student? This latter case is perhaps less clear-cut. The gift is intended to benefit the son, but most people would probably feel that the father's interests are somehow implicated with the son's. Thus the donation would appear at least partially "self-interested."

Now, one can extend this example into a continuum; consider some further hypothetical gestures by the same donor.

A gift to his alma mater to establish a scholarship fund in his own name, earmarked for young men of the same racial or ethnic background as himself.

A gift to his alma mater to establish a scholarship fund in his own name, earmarked for male and female students of disadvantaged racial or ethnic groups other than his own.

An anonymous gift to his alma mater for any purposes it may see fit.

An anonymous gift to relief organizations for aid to poverty-stricken persons abroad.

These examples illustrate the difficulty—and, I suggest, the futility—of seeking a rigorous distinction between self-interest and other kinds of interest. They illustrate something quite basic about social motivation— that people can and do identify with a variety of interests at varying distances from the narrowest of divisible self-interest. People may devote themselves to the interests of their loved ones; to those they see as sharing some essential characteristic with themselves; to those of persons deemed worthy of compassion, even at considerable social distance; or to those of abstract causes and principles. To try to partition these interests into either-or categories of self-interest versus altruism or philanthropy distracts attention from a reality that has much more nuance. We do not know what causes people to identify with one or another kind of interest, to embrace it as "their own." But we do know that the whole gamut of such identifications does, from time to time, serve as a basis for important collective actions.

To this, one suspects that rational choice theorists might rejoin that collective action on behalf of interests other than divisible self-interest is at most a rare occurrence. Their paradigm of collective action is the lobby, an alliance of self-interested actors in quest of concrete and divisible gratifications to their own interests. Lobbies are the very stuff of everyday public life, they might argue, whereas altruistic movements are rarities.

I doubt that anyone has systematic evidence to support such an assertion. But in any case, the theoretical importance of various forms of collective action is hardly just a matter of their relative frequency. Consider a class of collective actions at some kind of theoretical extreme from lobbies—charismatic movements. Here participants become absorbed in the pursuit of some abstract principle—creation of a world of perfect social equality, for example, or submission to the will of a charismatic leader, or furtherance of revolution. To such ends, participants may neglect narrow self-interest altogether, even to the point of sacrificing life itself. Although they are rare compared with other forms of social action and often die without enduring impact, mobilizations based on this sort of commitment can grow into very powerful social forces indeed, and often give rise to established churches, political systems, and other major social institutions. En route, they are often prolific sources of civil violence. It would be a short-sighted view of collective action indeed that ignored them.

Again, social scientists cannot say much that is precise about when people will come to interpret "their own" interests as embracing larger

groupings or principles. But we do know that perceptions of what constitutes one's own interests are highly fluid and forever being reshaped by
the flux of events. Political process does not simply involve the represen-
tation (or nonrepresentation) of preexisting interests. On the contrary,
much of the drama, and the complexity, of political life stem from ongoing
processes of interest redefinition and from activists' efforts to shape these
processes.

If people's interests were fixed, or influenced simply by calculation,
emotional appeals for support and other forms of exhortation would play
little role in political struggles. Yet professional politicians and other political activists exhort those they judge susceptible to "stand up for the
rights of people like ourselves," or to "show the country that there are still
people who believe in the old-time virtues," or to "reassure those fighting
for the values we hold sacred that they are not alone." These are appeals
to *redefine* one's own interest, to identify with social groupings or with
abstract principles that extend beyond one's self. Such appeals are central
to broad categories of political life, ones involving much collective action.

Thus, Olson is simply wrong when he writes,

in general, social pressure and social incentives operate only in groups of smaller
size, in the groups so small that the members can have face-to-face contact with
one another. (1965, p. 62)

As Gusfield's study (1963) of the Temperance movement and a variety of
other researches have shown, far-reaching mobilizations may occur whose
purpose is mainly to assert status supremacy of the activists. Various political activities having to do with drugs, abortion, the teaching of evolution in public schools, prayer in the classroom, and religious observance
as sanctioned by the government are fundamentally symbolic. That is,
they are struggles over what activities—and hence what kinds of people—
will be publicly defined as righteous, respectable and worthy, and which
will be bracketed in the opposite ways. In America, the McCarthy movement is an archetype of such movements. Political participation tells who
we are and what we stand for—to the world at large and to ourselves.
Thus the stakes are very high, even when they have nothing to do with
the kinds of interests allocated by lobbies and other "economic" action.

Do mobilizations arising out of such symbolic contention lead to civil
violence? Certainly. Much religious, sectarian, racial, or communal violence, for example, seems to be of this kind. Acts like lynchings, mass
rape, and other forms of punishment and humiliation of members of
opposing groups—perhaps victims chosen quite randomly—may be as
much ends in themselves as means to some further end.

A more difficult question is whether movements based on strictly "economic" interests, in Olson's sense, often lead to civil violence. Here I am not so sure. Certainly a variety of narrowly self-gratifying behaviors figure in many violent episodes, such as looting, settling of private scores, even sexual violence. But as I noted previously, motivations for such behavior must be considered more widespread than the behavior itself; thus we require an explanation that will account for when such motives can be expressed and when they cannot. The only explanations known to me are variants of Hobbes's theory. It is clear that such self-interested violent behavior may spring forth when coercive capacities are suddenly neutralized, as in police strikes or in the electrical power failure that blackened much of New York and led to much looting in the summer of 1977. Yet it is equally clear that civil violence and other breakdowns of civil authority are hardly the only or the inevitable results of such conspicuous breakdowns of coercive power. Often they come and go with no interruption of "normal" compliance.

---

At the same time, we can easily identify some forms of mobilization, including some violent ones, for which selective incentives are essential. The easiest cases are actions sponsored by powerful interests where the actual perpetrators are paid for their participation, as in attacks on strikers. By contrast, it is much more difficult to show the role of selective incentives in the outbreak of grass-roots action. For such cases, one must show how selective incentives, absent in peaceful periods, come to take on their potent effects in periods of violence. The logic of Olson's view makes it hard to see how grass-roots activists would be willing to undergo the costs of beginning such action, when the goal was some sort of public good.

The empirical record suggests that militant action can stem from the most various sorts of motives and purposes. In some settings, contra Olson, would-be participants' perceptions of wide support for action in favor of public goods creates greater likelihood of participation, not less (Klandermans 1984). Moreover, various evidence, including that most recently gathered by Muller and Opp (1986), sustains the conviction that *collective* interest motivates militant participation, often in settings where such participation is quite irrational in terms of divisible self-interest. Where Olson misleads, then, is in his insistence on categorical statements about selective incentives. As Hardin prudently concludes (1982, p. 103), the nature of the forces drawing participants into collective action should be determined contextually, through evidence from the particular events and processes under study. This conclusion, although less dramatic than some theorists of rational choice might like, is closer to the realities of the subject.

## Some Other Models

Not all views of militant action as arising from individual calculation assume divisible self-interest as the basis for such calculations. Rational choice theory has had a number of original and provocative applications, including those by Rogowski (1974) and DeNardo (1985), predicated on calculations of collective rather than individual interest. These studies, like others in the rational choice tradition, begin with a small number of spare, plausible assumptions about the considerations that govern calculations of political interest. They then develop the implications of these assumptions to yield empirical implications on the interactions of contending political groupings under real world conditions. Sometimes these include implications for civil violence.

Thus, Rogowski begins with some seemingly simple assumptions about what sorts of governments, other things equal, people will support. They are governments that show the highest likelihood of making the sorts of decisions that the individual would make himself and putting these decisions into effect. Governments that appear most likely to do these things are *rationally legitimate* (1974, p. 43); such governments will be most likely to win public support—again, other things being equal.

Rogowski builds on these points with further assumptions on the perceived ability of groups to contribute to the workability of the social whole. No government will appear workable, he posits, if composed only of members of a social stratum identified as capable only of specialized activities—for example, a caste. By contrast, "any faction whose members know more essential skills will expect to have more influence than one whose members know fewer" (p. 202). In Rogowski's world, factions have what he terms "natural" shares of power, in light of such skill considerations. Political arrangements that do not accord such power in actual practice will be seen as rationally illegitimate. Similarly, "the acquisition by one member of an essential skill thought to be unique to members of some faction or factions of which he is not a member" (pp. 206–7)—a process that Rogowski calls "outward mobility"—bears implications for the viability of governments. Thus,

> Outward mobility always strengthens the political position of the outwardly mobile individuals; and unless existing government grants them an influence that accords with this stronger position, they will perceive that government as rationally illegitimate. (p. 207)

From here, Rogowski develops his main empirical implication for civil violence.

> My own suggestion is that nearly all of history's great revolutions will turn out to have occurred in segmented or mixed societies, to have been preceded by great

expansions of outward social mobility, or by decay of skill bases, and to have been led by outwardly mobile individuals. (p. 263)

To derive such crisp hypotheses, of course, Rogowski has manipulated an extremely spare set of assumptions. The same holds for DeNardo (1985) and other builders of elegant rational choice models. One of DeNardo's key concerns, for example, is to identify the precise public demands by insurgent activists likely to yield maximum concessions from governments; another is to specify how much governments are apt to change their policies to avert various levels of insurgent violence. These formulations could yield valid implications for collective action in the real world, provided that insurgent activists indeed calculate their actions so as to wring maximum concessions from governments, or that governments are indeed interested in changing their political directions to appease insurgent violence. But some insurgent movements prefer to engineer government denial of seemingly reasonable demands, for example, as a means for building sympathetic grass-roots support. And some governments undoubtedly prefer a measure of violent protest, as a pretext for repressive action. Indeed, both Rogowski and DeNardo treat political contention as a means of obtaining policies agreeable to the groups concerned. Yet other theorists of civil violence, such as Pareto, have treated political contention as a struggle of activists for government power as an end in itself, regardless of the content of particular government policies.

For many cases, assumptions like those made by Rogowski and DeNardo are obviously appropriate. But the fact remains that models like theirs must inevitably disregard a host of considerations that other students of militant action have found crucial, ranging from the dramaturgy of individual violent episodes to variation in the logistical ease of mounting insurgency and repression. There is nothing necessarily wrong with such paring of explanatory possibilities; no analysis could proceed very far without some such restrictions. But rational choice models only move from the provocative and intriguing to the convincing by identifying sets of data for which the models provide better accounts than do alternative possibilities. We need more serious efforts to confront the models with such pertinent evidence.

A different kind of theoretical innovation came in Mark Granovetter's threshold model of participation in collective violence (1978). The model seeks to account for the process of central interest to this book—the shift from quiescent to violent collective action, and the subsidence in the opposite direction. The model fits in the Hobbesian tradition in that it assumes behavior is predicated on individuals' calculations of others' behaviors. But its special originality lies in that, unlike most theories of civil violence, it offers explanations based not on what participants have in

common but on differences among participants. In this respect, incidentally, Granovetter's threshold models bear intriguing parallels to his well-
known studies of the effects of network membership in allocation of jobs
and other roles. Both analyses deal with the cumulative effects of different
propensities of individuals to fit into larger social aggregates.

Granovetter's point of departure is an eminently plausible assumption—that the decision of any would-be participant to join in collective
events may depend on the numbers of those already participating. Someone's threshold, then, is the number of others who must be participating
in, say, a riot, before that individual will participate. Some individuals,
one might assume, are prepared to riot even if they have to do so alone;
they can be said to have thresholds of zero. Others would join in only if
everyone but themselves has already done so, and so have a threshold
exceeding ninety-nine percent. Thus, whether a riot will begin and, if
so, how large it will grow should turn on the distribution of thresholds
throughout a group eligible to riot.

Note the absence of any assumption on the nature of the motives leading people to riot. The model is compatible with Hobbesian motivational
assumptions—for example, that more people will join in challenging rules
set down by the sovereign, the less dangerous it appears to do so. But it is
no less compatible with assumptions of an instinct of imitation, a la Gabriel
Tarde. Indeed the threshold model is compatible with the assumption
that the grievances, goals, or motives of participants have nothing in common with one another.

Note, too, that the model need not only apply to violence. As Granovetter and Soong point out (1983, p. 166), the model might as well describe patterns of adoption of birth control techniques or farming methods, departures from social occasions, decisions to emigrate, or other
forms of social behavior where the decision of one individual to act is contingent on the number of others who have already taken the same action.

Thus Granovetter considers a potentially riotous hypothetical crowd of
one hundred persons: one individual has a threshold of zero (that is, he
will riot even in the absence of any other rioters); a second individual has
a threshold of one, a third has a threshold of two, and so forth, up to the
last individual with a threshold of ninety-nine. Given this distribution of
thresholds, the assumptions of the model make the outbreak of a riot involving all participants inevitable. The individual with a threshold of zero
will begin rioting, say, at time $t$, instigating rioting by the individual with
threshold one at time $t + 1$, until the entire one hundred are participating. But note the implications of removing any one individual from this
one-hundred-person population: The riot then cannot spread to those with
thresholds higher than that of the individual removed. Thus if the person

with threshold forty-seven leaves the scene to attend to urgent business elsewhere, none of those with thresholds forty-eight and higher will join in, and the riot will reach its full participation with forty-seven participants. Of special interest to Granovetter and Soong here are the equilibrium conditions implied by various threshold distributions—that is, the number of eventual participants expected under the given conditions.

Granovetter and Soong pursue these and other implications of the threshold idea in a series of mathematical models (1983). They explore, for example, the implications of viewing crowds as samples of distributions of thresholds from throughout larger populations of potential participants. They show the implications of altering the original assumptions so that the participation of some rioters matters more than that of others in shaping the individual's decision to join in. They also explore the possibilities of "ceiling effects," in which individuals decline to participate when certain numbers of others have already participated. Often the mathematical elaboration of these conceptual innovations yield intriguing, quite nonintuitive results—for example, in their examination of the conditions of stable equilibria, or situations where participation rises to a given point and remains constant. Some of their models show two quite different stable equilibria that are both consistent with the same distribution of thresholds (1983, p. 171).

The threshold model is strictly speaking an interaction theory—one in which outcomes are determined by the effects of individuals in shaping one another's behavior as that behavior itself evolves. It is not a theory of how people came to be inclined to participate in the first place. Thus, as Granovetter notes (1978, pp. 1435–37), his model need not be incompatible with other, more conventional theories of civil violence. Such theories typically focus on long-standing characteristics of individuals or groups, characteristics they bring with them to violent affrays, as key explanatory factors. Threshold models, by contrast, do not assume that individual thresholds need be long-enduring; indeed, the fact that riots stop, as well as start, suggests their mutability. Thus, although levels of, say, relative deprivation among would-be rioters might predict levels of tension or overall readiness to riot, threshold distributions among particular crowds or bodies in particular settings might account for the actual outbreak of violence in those spots, or the lack of it.

Granovetter argues that threshold analysis may yield a level of exactitude otherwise impossible in the explanation of violent occurrences.

Since behavior is partially determined by all the usual characteristics studied, it is not surprising that they have some moderate correlation with behavior. But if we take the threshold model seriously, it also follows that correlational studies will miss the dynamics of aggregation and thus be unable to provide more than this moderate level of correlation. In situations where we have, for example, two nearly identical distributions of thresholds which generate very different outcomes, correlational studies making predictions in the usual way from multiple-regression procedures will predict outcomes to be the same. (1978, p. 1436).

Thus Granovetter finds great interest in the findings from Spilerman's (1970; 1971) investigations of urban rioting in black neighborhoods in America during the 1960s. These studies showed that, with certain qualifications, the propensity of a city to experience riots during this time was directly associated with the total black population of the city, more than with various measures supposed to capture other hypothetical causes such as levels of relative and absolute deprivation in these communities. Granovetter holds these results eminently compatible with the threshold model: The larger the total population "at risk," he reasons, the greater the likelihood that crowds will form containing just the right threshold distributions to ignite rioting that, through processes of aggregation, will grow to involve large numbers.

How are we to evaluate the threshold model? It is, after all, a highly abstract view of participatory behavior, an ideal type like the notion of perfect competition or Weber's totally rational action. As in the models of Rogowski or DeNardo, various possible empirical contingencies are ignored in an effort to focus on the workings of a single set of social forces. Yet there is ample unsystematic evidence available to any thoughtful observer that threshold processes are often at work in civil strife. Indeed, recognition of these processes is often implicit in the actions of those seeking to promote or repress various forms of participation. Authoritarian regimes undoubtedly predicate their coercive policies on a determination to keep thresholds high among their people and to maintain levels of actual participation well below such levels. As Hobbes might remind us, raising the costs of being the first to protest is a time-honored technique for preventing any protest from getting off the ground. Conversely, organizers of protest typically seek to persuade would-be participants that their numbers are legion, that support will be forthcoming from all quarters if only a few will take the first step.

But difficulties arise when we seek a more exact correspondence between empirical expectations generated by the model and evidence from actual riotous situations. Whereas the model is elegantly spare and idealized, riots are ragged, chaotic things; applying the threshold model to them presents both practical problems and conceptual ones. The force of threshold considerations would be easiest to judge in cases where there are clear lines between participation and nonparticipation in riotous settings, and where individuals are fully in control of their own allocation to the participant or nonparticipant categories. Some real riots afford these conditions, as when a crowd forms and a few begin throwing stones, leading others to join in. But many riots are deemed to begin, at least in the information available to researchers, when coercive forces fire on crowds, or where scuffles begin as two antagonistic demonstrations meet one another. In these latter cases, the behavior of many, perhaps most individuals in the crowds may not have changed, yet the social construction of their actions may move them from the nonrioter category to that of rioters.

Some of the difficulties posed by these questions of who is participating and who is not are simply practical, though formidable. But note that elsewhere behavior defined as riotous may unfold, not with the aggregation of individual decisions taken but with action binding on whole categories of participants, taken by a single individual. Repressive forces may begin using their weapons on order by a superior officer. Insurgents in well-organized protests may respond to similar signals from their leaders. Where riotous behavior is rehearsed or coordinated in advance, then, the model is apt to be less applicable. Indeed, the model is probably less informative when would-be participants have various sources of information about each other's potential for riotous behavior, apart from actually observing such behavior directly. On the other hand, where actual behavior on the spot is the best or only way for would-be participants to gauge the extent of support their own riotous actions might have—that is, in a Mertonian situation of pluralistic ignorance—threshold processes appear most likely to matter.

The patterns of social communication implicit in the threshold model should spur reflection on some unexpected affinities between Granovetter's model and models of collective violence based on shared excitement or communication of "crowd mentality." The contagion of crowd feelings as proposed by LeBon, Park, and Blumer (see Chapter Three) may be simply another manifestation of the cuing that goes on as people formulate their own behavior on the basis of others' actions. Note that these processes need not involve physical proximity among would-be participants, as indeed the irrationalists and collective behavior theorists specified. People may predicate their participation on actions by others in far distant places, others who are perceived to share the same grievances, interests, or susceptibility to sanction as one's self. In France, the propensity of the provinces to generate their own revolutionary episodes in response to change or threatened change in power in Paris is part of revolutionary mythology; the patterns of such sympathetic insurrections is documented in the case of the Revolution of 1830 (Rule and Tilly 1975). Analysts can profitably dispute whether the actions of those involved in these sympathetic events really turned more on the sharing of revolutionary excitement or the calculation of costs and benefits of rioting. In either case, the events in the capital did apparently trigger action by would-be rioters far removed in distance.

Next consider the durability of thresholds. Nothing in Granovetter's model makes it necessary to assume that thresholds are long-enduring characteristics of individuals; indeed, he makes the opposite assumption. But the model offers greatest promise of predicting or explaining the detail of the unfolding of riotous events if some continuity in the durations of thresholds is assumed. If the distribution of thresholds at time $t$ were sharply different from that at time $t + 1$, and that in turn differs from the distribution at time $t + 2$, then the model affords no definite implications about how and how rapidly the violence will develop. Thus, the processes by which individuals' thresholds shape their behavior and, in turn, activate the behavior of others are unlikely to be described precisely for any population unless it can be assumed that the individual thresholds remain the same until the riot reaches equilibrium. How often can this condition be met? Among all forms of participation, one suspects, participation in violent events is especially attended by strong emotions, including, a fortiori, emotions generated by the playing out of the events themselves. Hence, the possibility exists that events occurring at time $t$ might feed back on the thresholds of would-be participants so as to alter their distribution at time $t + 1$. In this connection, threshold models might stand a better chance of showing close correspondence with data on behaviors other than violence—for example, departures from tedious social events, or adoption of birth control techniques.

Is the model falsifiable? Certainly we know of cases where people protest, to their own cost, quite regardless of the participation of others, or refuse to do so despite the almost universal actions of others. Although it would be consistent to say that the thresholds of these individuals is zero or one hundred percent participation, the model is certainly uninformative here. Perhaps the most pertinent question is not whether or where the model is falsifiable altogether, but how often we can expect the predictions of a threshold model to account for patterns of results in ways no other theory can do. Here I confess to doubts. A host of considerations surely shapes the willingness of any individual to begin participating in any violent affray; thresholds in Granovetter's sense are but one of these. Others might include seeing friends and allies under attack, the flourishing (or besmirching) of sacred symbols, sighting of a particularly detested enemy figure, or the appearance of an especially tempting target. In most empirical situations, I suspect, threshold considerations interact with these confounding influences. Further, thresholds are bound to be difficult to measure, apart from the behavior that they are supposed to explain. Even assuming that thresholds are relatively enduring, one would not expect would-be participants in violent events to be able to provide accurate reports on their own thresholds. Thus it is reasonable to hold that threshold processes are most likely at work in various forms of participation, both violent and others, yet to expect little precise prediction or explanation based on threshold models. Again, prospects for such exactitude appear more promising for forms of participation other than violent action.

The great contribution of the Granovetter model is heuristic. It formalizes and gives increased force to analytic ideas that otherwise would receive only vague lip service. Most important among these is the notion that small differences in interaction characteristics, attributable to chance combinations of actors or circumstances, may account for enormous differences in violent outcomes. Clarification of this point alone is worth dozens of conventional studies of the statistical predictors of participation in violent episodes.

Granovetter's model ranks with a small handful of truly innovative departures during the past two decades in the study of civil violence. It equals in originality, for example, Olson's *Logic of Collective Action*, and it has the virtue of avoiding statements at obvious variance with major bodies of fact, as Olson's contribution does not. Unlike Olson's work, Granovetter's has not yet figured widely in empirical researches. But as often in the unfolding of theories and research, this fact seems to have little to do with the profundity of the theory in question.

----

Much the most direct and fruitful application of rational choice thinking to empirical material on civil violence is Samuel Popkin's *The Rational Peasant* (1979). This book presents a critique of "moral economy" accounts of collective action by peasants—that is, views of peasant communities as bound by traditional moral solidarities. Proponents of such views, notably Scott (1976), explain quiescence of peasant communities in the face of deprivation as a result of mutual support among community members. Militant action occurs, by contrast, when forces outside the village seek to disrupt traditional ways, especially long-standing agricultural practices and village loyalties. Moral economy theories picture peasants as particularly resistant, for such reasons, to incorporation into market economies, where new economic and social ties would weaken traditional village loyalties.

Popkin holds that peasant political action is better understood as a result of rational calculation of narrow self-interest under conditions of uncertainty and oppression. Accounts of communal solidarity and grassroots democracy in peasant villages are misleading, he argues. Both political and economic resources are distributed quite unevenly in peasant communities, with the majority badly exploited by a small minority of landowners and money lenders. Ordinary peasants would be only too willing to produce cash crops for the market, Popkin contends, but their efforts to do so meet with stiff opposition from the dominant local interests, who stand to lose their preeminent position through such changes. Overt rebellion against the rural upper classes is not a practical possibility for ordinary peasants, given their mutual suspicion and their dependence on wealthier neighbors for loans and other support.

Popkin couches his arguments in terms of peasant communities vis-à-vis modern economies *in general.* But his in-depth evidence comes from Vietnam during the nineteenth and twentieth centuries. There, he argues, peasants were indeed normally obliged to compete against one another for their very survival. Through their discretion in lending money and dispensing justice the upper classes were able to thwart any nascent tendencies to collective action by "their" peasants. Any collective effort by those at the bottom to break out of their dependency would have foundered on the temptation of most in that group, often living at the margin of subsistence, to act as free riders. As such, they would continue to enjoy patronage from those at the top while sharing any potential benefits from their overthrow. Villages were indeed closed and unified, as moral economy theorists had argued. This unity, however, was enforced by those at the top so as to sustain their own privilege.

Yet peasant rebellions did occur in Vietnam, culminating in, but not limited to, the one that ultimately stymied American power there. Popkin's account of how the obstacles to collective action among peasants were overcome is ingenious and full of theoretical implications. He describes (1979, chap. 5) four groups that succeeded in orchestrating joint action where none would otherwise have occurred. These were the Catholic Church; the Viet Minh; and two syncretist religious movements, Cao Dai and Hoa Hao. The ideological contents of these four movements could hardly be more diverse. But they shared the ability to inspire and sustain collective action by peasants, including violent action against rural upper classes.

Popkin's account of how this occurred is rich and complex. In essence, he portrays these movements as providing alternate sources of predictability that afforded peasant actors reasonable confidence that their efforts at innovation would not be too costly. Thus, membership in the Catholic Church gave ordinary peasants a reasonable expectation of allies, possibly powerful ones from outside the village, in the event of conflict with their local overlords. Similarly, the Cao Dai movement won its following by championing the rights of peasants in title disputes and other legal struggles with landlords. The Viet Minh sponsored the teaching of literacy to peasants, something actively opposed by the upper classes, so as to enable them to fare better in their economic and legal conflicts with more privileged adversaries. In these and various other ways, these four new forms of solidarity provided mutual support for those who would otherwise take grave risks in any attempt to challenge the status quo.

Popkin interprets these observations in the language of rational choice theory. "Whereas moral economy views of peasant protest and rebellion emphasize defensive reactions against threats to subsistence guarantees, loss of legitimacy for traditional elites, and moral outrage," he writes, "I emphasize political entrepreneurs, incentive systems, free riders, and risk" (p. 245). But though his observations give little support to value integration accounts of civil violence of the sort I discuss in Chapter Five, Popkin's analysis does not rely exclusively on rational choice thinking in the narrowest sense.

True, he accounts for the normal "conservatism" of Vietnamese peasants in terms of their rational determination to minimize individual losses under risky conditions. But the role played by the successful insurgencies, he judges, required some form of dedication that transcended narrow self-interest. Indeed, one of the things that established these four very different solidarities as viable bases for collective action was that peasants perceived movement activists as motivated by something other than divisible self-interest. Grass-roots action in the absence of such outside forces was normally impossible, because peasants would not risk the mutual trust required to co-operate with other peasants they regarded as strictly self-interested. Nor could ordinary peasants normally imagine a viable alternative world that might ensue from successful challenge to established patterns. But the insurgent movements offered cadres motivated by obvious moral commitments to long-term efforts at establishing a better world. "Credibility, moral codes, and visions of the future, then, all affect a peasant's estimate that his investment will either contribute directly to a collective goal or will bring an acceptable return of individual benefits," he concludes (p. 262).

I suspect that Popkin's observations on the microbases of militant collective action could have a wider application. Grass-roots desire for change, understood either as self-interest or collective interest, may remain latent for long periods, given what are perceived as unacceptable costs of mobilization. The translation from interest to action occurs precisely when a small group of activists shows themselves willing to sustain extraordinary costs in the pursuit of fundamental rearrangements. Like the miniscule particles of dust without which water vapor cannot become rain, the minority of dedicated activists has a catalytic effect. Or as Granovetter might put it, a hard core of activists with very low thresholds for mobilization are required to trigger participation by the majority endowed with higher thresholds. Participants in militant action may shade off gradually from the strictly self-interested, through those of mixed motives, to those few willing to make any sacrifice for the desired end. But without at least some of the latter, the action potentials of the former may remain forever dormant.

Theories based on individual calculation have not entered so widely into empirical studies of civil violence as have other theories discussed later. And it is difficult to believe that any of the theories in the tradition deriving from Hobbes can account for certain widely attested aspects of civil violence—notably the indisputable role of various forms of group identification in motivating participation. Yet certain other features of civil violence seem eminently susceptible to analyses along these lines— for example, the sharp outbreaks or cessations of violence occasionally noted in response to changed repressive capacities of governments. More- over, such abrupt "changes of state," to use Granovetter's term, point to some intriguing parallels in the empirical implications of otherwise quite disparate theories.

## Conclusions

Like all the theories considered in this book, theories of civil violence in the tradition of Hobbes account for some kinds of outbreaks much more persuasively than others.

For example, rational calculation on the basis of divisible self-interest offers plausible accounts for participation in violent events once such events are under way. When looting, attacks against members of hated ethnic groups, or destruction of tax offices become widespread, risks and other disincentives to taking part in such action are apt to be much re- duced. Under these conditions, it does not take a rational choice theorist to conclude that destructive action may become rational in a way not true before.

Much more problematic is accounting for the *beginnings* of violent clashes. Remember, theories considered in this chapter assume rational calculation based on relatively enduring interests. The assumption that interests endure and that calculation is rational implies that behavior will not change unless the state of the world changes. Thus, theories of this kind need to account for how contingencies bearing on individuals change, so as to warrant change in their actions.

Granovetter offers a minimalist response to this problem. The only external contingency in his threshold model is the number of relevant others already participating in the action in question. This formulation leaves it open to other analysts to account for what the relevant population of participants will be and what social forces make the individual susceptible to act in the first place.

Other analysts identify more explicit contingencies. For Hobbes, the key focus of individual attention and calculation is the ability of governments to safeguard the private pursuit of self-interest. Thus, perceived changes in government strength are central to Hobbesian accounts of the outbreak or subsidence of civil violence. For Olson, provision of selective incentives plays the analogous role: People act together, militantly or otherwise, when each individual is assured of receiving divisible rewards for participation. For Popkin, the change in contingencies that most conspicuously made it rational for peasants to switch from compliance to militance was the rise of social movements based on motives other than divisible self-interest.

Authentic examples can be found to fit all of these models. Sometimes government coercion works in reducing participation in grass-roots militancy. Sometimes selective incentives—for example, payments to mercenary insurgents—undoubtedly do trigger civil conflicts. Sometimes, as in Vietnam, the appearance of highly committed activists may well spell the difference between passivity and revolt among the downtrodden. But counter examples are not difficult to find, as well—instances where abrupt reduction of government coercive ability has no effect on popular compliance, for example, or where groups mobilize readily without selective incentives. As elsewhere, the great unsolved theoretical puzzle is that of distinguishing where models will apply and where they will not.

*Chapter Two*

# Marx and Pareto

Marx and Pareto are counterweights.

The two theorists shared strikingly similar intellectual concerns: a focus on the relationship between economic and other forms of action; a conviction of the inadequacy of capitalist "rational" behavior as a model for all social action; a desire to debunk ideological pretentions so as to reveal the true, hidden forces governing social behavior; and a belief that insurgent movements serve as indices of fundamental social change.

Yet their political enthusiasms and *partis pris* were often utterly antipathetic, and Pareto has gone down in history largely as an intellectual nemesis of Marx. Marx made it his life work to forge intellectual weaponry for a movement that was to put a definitive end to all social irrationality. Pareto dedicated himself to demonstrating that social movements rarely change what they claim to change, and that irrationality is endemic in social life. Marx's name has been invoked (often with questionable justification) by revolutionary movements around the world; Pareto has been lionized (with still less justification) by fascists. Even among their most sophisticated readers, enthusiasts of one theorist are unlikely to be deeply attracted to the other.

For present purposes, these theoretical antinomies offer a special opportunity. For nowhere do the two theorists' analyses contrast more sharply than in their accounts of militant activism and civil violence. In tracing these differences, my guiding concern will be to identify evidence that, if forthcoming, would weigh clearly for or against either position. Could any findings, any outcome of empirical inquiry lead one to value Marx's theories of civil violence over Pareto's, or vice-versa? Or are their doctrines simply evocations of political tastes and values that must ultimately elude closure on empirical grounds?

## Marx's Project

Marx never sought to propound a theory of civil violence per se. His goal was not a set of scientific principles to explain any and all social phenomena, but a theory of liberation. He wanted to enable engaged thinkers to transcend the constraints of flawed consciousness and hasten the historical break with the miseries and irrationalities of the world as it was. Yet the analysis of militant social conflict in general, and of collective violence in particular, could hardly fail to figure importantly in these efforts.

Does Marx offer us a theory of civil violence at all, then? No doubt some would reject any attempt to distill a specific Marxian theory of any single sociological subject, in the sense of a set of falsifiable statements of where and how the phenomenon should occur. Marxian theory, it might be said, aims instead at *interpreting* the social and political world—at ascribing to events their true significance for human liberation, for example—rather than at predicting or explaining.

But this position is unsatisfactory. Either Marxian analysis assumes some regularities in the working of the empirical world, or it does not. Taking the latter position implies that no particular state of world—no sequence of events, no historical process, no juxtaposition of cause and effect—is any less compatible with Marxian thinking than any other. I do not believe that this is what Marx, or most of his followers, intended. Marxists may not commit themselves to specific predictions on such matters as when the ultimate revolutionary struggle might break out, nor does their theoretical project require them to do so. But Marxist scholarship certainly offers empirically relevant statements about such things as the origins of social conflict, the interactions between material and ideal forces, and the bases of political power. Such statements must designate, however inferentially, some possible findings as plausible and expectable in light of the theory and others as less so.

But the problem is how to derive authentic empirical commitments from Marxist thinking without doing injustice to the intentions of the theorists and the best possibilities of the theory itself. But how can we determine the "correct" Marxist position? By a poll of present-day thinkers identifying themselves as Marxists? By textual exegesis of the classical writings of Marx himself, or perhaps of Marx and Engels together? In the latter case, who is entitled to interpret controversial passages? Or in the former, who really qualifies as an authentic follower of Marx?

One approach that must be rejected from the beginning is to restrict one's efforts to a piecemeal search for "hypotheses" in the classic writings—direct statements by Marx and Engels on causes of or conditions for

civil strife. The problem is not the absence of such statements, although
they are not numerous. Consider for example the following passage, from
an article published in the *New York Tribune* of 25 October 1851; this
appeared under Marx's name but is now thought to have been written for
him by Engels (McClelland 1973, p. 286). The subject was recent revolutionary events in various small German principalities.

When interests are so varied . . . ; when these contending interests . . . are
mixed in different proportions; when . . . there is no great centre in the country,
no London, no Paris, the decisions of which, by their weight, may supersede the
necessity of fighting out the same quarrel over and over again in every single
locality; what else can be expected but that the contest will dissolve itself into a
mass of unconnected struggles, in which an enormous quantity of blood, energy
and capital is spent, but which for all that remain without any decisive results?
(Marx and Engels 1937, p. 11)

There is no question but that these observations imply a theoretical position, and an empirically relevant one at that. The problem is simply that it
is not particularly Marxian. There is little about it that would distinguish it
from theoretical formulations from other traditions. Indeed, the key ideas
in this passage are more characteristic of the thinking of Simmel and
Coser than of Marx.

Our task of identifying positions essentially distinctive of Marxian
analysis can only be done holistically. We need to develop a view of the
place of collective strife in general, and civil violence in particular, within
an overall Marxian model of social process. This approach demands a
grasp of the logic of Marxian thinking on such matters as the nature of
authority and power, institutional continuity and change, and routine and
extraordinary action.

The bases of such a logic are well known. Marxian analysis views every
social whole as a system of domination, in which the special interests of
one social class, or a coalition of classes, are preeminently reflected in established institutions and patterns of social action and culture. The nature
of the domination of the ascendant classes—that is, the bases of their
power in the productive process—sets down constraints over other aspects of social life. In the long run, these constraints override strictly intellectual, cultural, or other "ideal" forces in shaping the course of social
events. Yet the dominant influence of particular classes is bound to be
transient. Countervailing against such influence are revolutionary trends
originating in new social class relations. When prevailing economic forms
have changed sufficiently, change in patterns of authority, obedience, and
political institutions are bound to follow.

These transitions are rarely peaceful. No ruling group relinquishes its
special position willingly; few dominant classes can read the signs that

their hour at the center of the historical stage is over—hence the disorderly, conflict-laden periods in which one ruling system is deposed and another instated. The most dramatic evocation of such transitions in Marx's own writings is the famous passage from the *Contribution to the Critique of Political Economy.*

At a certain stage of their development, the material productive forces in society come in conflict with the existing relations of production, or—what is but a legal expression of the same thing—with the property relations within which they have been at work before. From forms of development of the productive forces these relations turn into their fetters. Then begins an epoch of social revolution. With the change of the economic foundation the entire immense superstructure is more or less rapidly transformed. (1983 [1859], pp. 159–61)

The "social revolution" of which Marx writes includes transformations not only of formal institutions, but also of patterns of obedience and principles of authority associated with them. A most likely concomitant of these changes is civil violence.

Thus, a straightforward but entirely legitimate empirical implication of Marx's theory is as follows:

*Expect high levels of civil violence throughout entire social systems during periods of transition from one form of class rule to another.*

Expect levels of civil strife to vary directly, in other words, with the severity of disjunction between the class interests reflected in key institutions and the prevailing forms of production of material wealth. Or, in more properly Marxian terms, expect the extent of and intensity of civil violence within any social system to vary with the sharpness of the disjunction between *relations* of production and *forces* of production. Look for violent contests, along with many other forms of symbolic and behavioral conflict, as representatives of the old order seek to defend forms of authority that have lost their force in social class relations. On the other hand, where ruling ideas and institutions show a close "fit" with the requirements of class relations, one should expect relatively low levels of strife and rebellion throughout the population as a whole.

All of this is true enough to Marx, as far as it goes. But is the translation of these injunctions into actual steps for empirical inquiry as simple as it appears? What rule does one invoke to determine the closeness of fit between underlying social class relations and institutions of public authority? How does one know when the social class relations and productive forces supporting a particular system of domination have passed their peak?

These questions are not just procedural but have everything to do with the falsifiable status of the theory. It is only too easy to insist retrospectively, regarding a period of dramatic strife, that dominant institutions were out of step with the material reality underlying the actions of the protestors. Can such linkage be made independently of the conflicts it might be invoked to explain? Contemporary Marxists disagree endlessly, after all, over whether to characterize the present status of the Western economies as "late capitalism," as many optimistically do, or whether these institutions still have considerable life ahead of them. The problem, apparently, is not whether social class relations in these societies embody contradictions; Marxists readily agree that they do. The problem is whether such tendencies are strong enough to count as major, life-threatening contradictions, ones that might imminently lead to violent challenge to the established order.

Again, some would insist that these queries miss the point. Marxian analysis need not predict high levels of civil strife, it might be held, but should simply alert us to the role of underlying class conflict in the origins of such strife.

Does this formulation offer any falsifiable expectations? The best I can do is the following:

*Expect any manifestation of civil violence to be contingent on the presence of class conflict elsewhere in the social system.*

But such a statement runs afoul of many of the same problems already considered. What principle could one apply to determine whether a particular violent episode depended for its occurrence on some form of class conflict? Such connections are often intuitively apparent to proponents of the theory, but we need a rule of identification that would yield the same results for skeptics and believers alike. It is only too easy to examine the social setting of any violent period and adduce class conflicts of which the violent events might be symptoms. But could similar conflicts just as well be identified at other, more quiescent periods?

The only way to transcend these ambiguities is through research that would address an array of settings showing varying levels of civil violence. Each setting would have to be evaluated independently in terms of the intensity of class conflict and the level of civil violence prevailing at the stage. By "independently" I mean in such a way that one kind of judgment does not influence the other. Obviously the researcher would face considerable conceptual ambiguity in the two key concepts, especially that of class conflict. For example, should this notion be interpreted to mean manifest conflict such as strikes, parliamentary battles, and demonstrations? If so, the conflicts so reckoned would have to stop short of actual violence, or the theory would be circular. The alternative would be to assess some form of latent conflict of interest among classes. But here the conceptual difficulties would appear insurmountable, for Marxian analysis makes fundamental opposition of interest among classes virtually a universal given of social life.

Independent assessment of levels of class conflict versus those of civil violence is the only really promising avenue for evaluating the empirical implications of Marxian analysis in this respect. Difficult though it would be to agree on the empirical significance of the key concepts, this approach is still infinitely preferable to any alternative. Yet the literature of empirical investigations has few enough studies entailing systematic rating of levels of civil violence within or across particular social systems over time (see, for example, Sorokin 1962; and Tilly and Rule 1965). And none of these, to my knowledge, has sought to match such ratings to assessment of fluctuation in class conflict.

## Small-scale Insurgencies

Discussion thus far has focused on implications of Marxian analysis for civil violence throughout large political systems. But the same theory also suggests implications for militant action by small subgroups.

For example, when a group occupies an *institutional* position inconsistent with its standing in *material relations*, Marxist analysis suggests that that group will be embroiled in conflict. By material relations I mean what Marxists would call relations of production—in short, the role played by the group in question in creation of material wealth. Thus the rise of an ascendant class—for example, the industrial bourgeoisie, as its importance in the economic order soared—would bring conflicts as it inevitably sought political and other institutional weight commensurate with its economic power. Alternatively, a group threatened with loss of its position in the web of material relations would be likely to fight to preserve established prerogatives. Interestingly, Marxists have produced many more analyses of the latter, conservative collective actions than of the former.

An excellent example is *Captain Swing*, by E. J. Hobsbawm and George Rude (1969), a historical investigation of a wave of rural violence that swept Southern England during 1830. I present an account of a typical event.

Beginning on 19 November [1830] the Andover riots lasted for several days. Summing up their results a week after they started, a local magistrate wrote . . . "the Peasantry have not only dictated a rate of wages, not only destroyed all agricultural machinery, and demolished iron foundaries, but have proceeded in formidable bodies to private dwellings to extort money and provisions—in fact, have established a system of pillage." It began with the destruction of a threshing machine in a village near Andover. A prisoner was taken and escorted to Andover jail, where he was followed by a "huge multitude" who compelled shopkeepers to close their doors and bolt their windows and who . . . broke open the prison gates, released the prisoner and carried him in triumph through the streets. . . . On the next day, a large party set out for Tasker's Waterlooo Foundry at Upper Clatford, two miles

away, and demolished its machinery, valued at £2,ooo. "The pretext for this outrage", the Andover magistrates wrote the same day to the Home Office, "was that
the proprietor of the foundry in question has been in the habit of manufacturing
iron work for threshing machines". (pp. 118–19)

Violent attacks on human beings were apparently rare in these events,
though the rioters did often demand money from prosperous farmers and
gentlefolk whose properties they invaded. The recurrent theme was destruction of the technologies of more capital-intensive forms of agricul-
ture, threshing machines above all—devices that threatened the livelihood of the landless laborers who were the main participants. The broad
intent underlying these events appears precisely the same as that involved in the machine breaking in early factories—to preserve traditional
claims of laborers to their work, in settings where change in technology
and its ownership threatened to leave such claims outmoded. In both
cases, shared material interest appears to have been the basis for recruitment to the insurgency.

Such attacks are one manifestation of what E. P. Thompson has termed
"the moral economy" (1971). He means by this people's sense of membership in social and economic groupings with complementary responsibilities to one another, responsibilities enduring over long historical periods.
In the example from Hobsbawm and Rude, these might be the responsibilities of farmers and landless laborers to provide one another with employment and labor. Marxian analysts often invoke sensibilities of this
kind to explain militant action by those, like the landless laborers of 1830,
whose traditional role is becoming outmoded through changing material
conditions.

Such explanations are certainly consistent with the logic of Marxian
thinking. If social consciousness is indeed, as Marxists hold, shaped by
shared experience of collective striving within a class hierarchy, it is no
more than reasonable that people should look to the situations of people
like themselves in the recent past as models for what ought to be in the
present. If people view themselves as part of a stable nexus of dependency knit by mutual claims and obligations, and if such views form their
most profound orienting assumptions about the meaning of social existence, one would naturally expect that violations of such views would give
cause for extreme action.

The rural militants depicted by Hobsbawm and Rude were fighting the
destruction of their traditional class identities. But again, Marxist analysis
also allows for violent self-assertion by groups who are gaining advantage
in class contention. Perhaps the best examples are Marx's own analysis of
the violent assertions of power by the political representatives of rising

industrial capital in France during the period 1848–1851. These bloody events, Marx held, were manifestations of the growing role of industry in French economic life, reflecting the quest of the industrial bourgeoisie for political power commensurate with their weight among the emerging forces of production.

Implicit in Marxian analyses of violent collective contest is an assumption of *calculation*. Militant action, either by dominant or subordinate groups, is most likely when those groups identify a striking, objective chance to do significantly better in the struggle for social well-being, or to avoid doing significantly worse. To assume otherwise would be to imagine that shared material interest was not the key to when and where explosive collective action occurs.

But the *form* of calculation implied here is not identical to that entertained by Hobbes or his modern successors, the rational choice theorists. The divisible, individual interests considered by Hobbes are not to be equated with group interest, nor is the notion of group interest implied in Marxian analysis simply an aggregation of individual interests.

In the recent intellectual enthusiasm for rational choice modeling of every conceivable social process, there have been some heroic attempts to reanalyze strategies of class action along those lines, most fruitfully by Przeworsky (1985) and Elster (1985). These two studies have the virtue of establishing some important points—for example, the contrast between short- and long-term consequences for class actors of following various conflict strategies, or the contrasting payoffs to individuals and groups of militancy versus aquiescence. But both Przeworsky and Elster seem to embrace the sensible conclusion that not all forms of militant action appear oriented to divisible individual gain.

To imagine otherwise would run counter to the logic both of Marx's original analyses and of militant activism itself. As I argued in Chapter One, people identify with the widest range of interests, from selfish, divisible ones to those of causes far removed from or even counterproductive to them. Marx and Engels's assurance to workers that they had "nothing to lose but their chains" was certainly rhetorical flourish. No one familiar with the details of how grass-roots movements begin can fail to note the extreme personal costs often undergone by organizers who embrace the interests of such causes. Any industrial worker in Marx's own time who took on such tasks stood to lose a great deal in terms of narrow, personal interest—a modicum of peace of mind at least, and perhaps much more.

Such forms of self-sacrifice attest to something qualitatively different from an extension of divisible self-interest. Activists identify not only with interests of people somehow like themselves but also with values perhaps not yet realized in anyone's experience. They identify with causes, with the dream of realization of national or cultural identity, for example, or with the pursuit of novel ethical or religious ideals.

But such pursuit of abstract, nonindividual interests may nevertheless be entirely calculative. A particular contribution of Marxist analysis is to alert us to the kinds of collective interest that form bases for such calculations, and to the ways these may differ from narrow, divisible self-interest. For example, George Rude, in his analyses of preindustrial food riots (1972), emphasizes that the crowds typically sold captured bread and grain at what they considered a just price ("*taxation populaire*"), rather than plundering it for their own use. Here, it would appear, the calculations were apparently rational, yet not solely oriented to individual interests; as various analysts have pointed out, food rioters often saw themselves as resisting an antipathetic way of life associated with the encroaching market economy.

Another case for shrewd calculation of shared material interest is E. P. Thompson's analysis of the Luddites.

the term 'reactionary' comes too easily to some lips. For despite all the homilies addressed to the Luddites (then and subsequently) as to the beneficial consequences of new machinery or of 'free' enterprise . . . the machine-breakers, and not the tract-writers, made the most realistic assessment of the short-term effects. (1968, p. 601)

Or as Charles Tilly notes, the destructive efforts of the machine breakers were scarcely ineffective in their own terms; they often preserved employment for years (1979a, p. 94).

Thus, a few more empirical expectations:

*Expect the content of militant collective action to reflect shared class interests of participants—in terms of the targets of action, for example, or of the forms of institutional change or official action being sought.*

*Expect participants in militant collective action to be recruited in terms of their identification with the material interests at stake.*

*Expect the likelihood of militant collective action to vary with the perceived importance of the material issues at stake.*

These statements are hardly free of conceptual ambiguity. How do we distinguish authentic class or material interest from other sorts of interests? How are we to judge whether a particular action really stems from a perception that key material interests hang in the balance?

Such questions are both more difficult than they appear and more important. Fundamental to the distinctiveness both of Marxian analyses and the related theories discussed in Chapter Six is the notion that collective action reflects rational calculation of some form of objective interest. If

this idea has any meaning, it must imply that a reasonable person, survey-
ing the material or political realities of the situation, could specify where
militant action would or would not likely occur.

By contrast, what if the timing of collective violence were governed not
by objective factors but by strictly subjective variation on the part of participants—for example, by transient waves of emotional excitement generated by events reported in mass media or the appeals of charismatic
leaders? For such scenarios, theories based on rational calculation are less
apposite. For here the crucial variable would not be the objective payoffs
available for would-be participants, but rather their internal sense of what
issues are worth acting on, or of the relative importance of various possible
bases for action or inaction. Such accounts of militant action as outcomes of
variation in internal psychic states, considered in Chapter Three, are the
natural theoretical antagonists of Marxian accounts.

Sophisticated proponents of Marxist analysis would probably be happy
to acknowledge that their view tells a great deal about violent clashes between groups whose interests are "objectively" opposed, and little about
clashes, say, between adherents of rival football clubs. In other words,
Marxist analysis is consistent with violent events that reflect "objective"
clashes of interest, but would not lead one to expect such clashes in their
absence.

But this formulation is not without problems. For groups whose interests might be thought to stand in "objective" opposition nevertheless
spend a lot of time *not* engaging in violent contest with one another. Further, if we take Marxian theory seriously, we must believe that clash of
interest is so pervasive that nearly all groups have *something* that might
be worth contesting with various other groups at almost any time. If these
objective clashes of interest are really so pervasive, may not their transition from latent to active status depend on emotional or other "nonrational" dynamics? If not, can it convincingly be claimed that the outbreak of violent events corresponds precisely to participants' calculation
of *the* most rationally propitious moment for action to maximize their
interests?

Let us not hold Marxist thinking to standards more rigorous than those
applied to other theories. There is at least a falsifiable element of the
Marxist position. We might exploit it by seeking to assess the frequency of
violent collective actions that seem to reflect pursuit of some shared material interest versus those where no such interests, by any stretch of the
imagination, seem present. Such an inquiry will certainly face a variety of
ambiguous cases. But if rioting stemming from football homecomings outweighs that originating from such things as subsistence riots and labor

conflicts, then surely some theoretical revision is needed. These difficult but important issues come in for further consideration in Chapter Eight.

## Social Control: A Marxian View

Perhaps discussion has gone as far as it can without a closer look, not at Marxian treatments of particular violent episodes but at the logic of the theory more generally. What broad principles does the theory advance to account for compliance with established authority versus rebellion *in general?*

All but the very simplest societies, Marx held, are marked by division between an exploitative, controlling minority and an exploited majority. The former owe their position to control over the key processes for producing material wealth and well-being; they produce nothing themselves, yet consume in disproportion to their numbers. By contrast, the exploited majority provide the labor that forms the basis for that wealth, only to have what they produce appropriated by the minority. The specific roles and social identities of the members of the two categories, of course, are as various as history itself. Yet despite the endless variety of historical forms of domination and exploitation, Marxian analysis assumes some constants across all class societies. Notable among these is the centrality of class relations as a basis for social conflict and an engine of social change, and the assumption that class domination sets in motion many-faceted patterns of control that reconcile the dominated to their subordinate state.

But the fact that class conflict is endemic in complex societies hardly means that class groupings are always arrayed in active struggle. The only reasonable assumption is the opposite: In most settings, most of the time, class conflicts are neither conspicuous in most people's social perceptions nor objectively responsible for militant action. More often, the endemic fact of class conflict manifests itself in chronic private tensions and antagonisms between representatives of the larger class groupings. Thus, lord and peasant, master and slave, landlord and sharecropper, capitalist and worker collide routinely with one another in pursuing their everyday roles. As long as the economic realities underlying class relations remain relatively static, such private conflicts may never form bases for collective action.

But acquiescence by the majority to the domination of the minority is never "natural," in the Marxian view. Such acquiescence requires forceful applications of influence. The fact of domination always generates processes tending to reinforce the principles and arrangements inherent in that domination and smooth the way for its perpetuation. These processes work to rationalize prevailing patterns of domination, to make them appear natural and inevitable. They may reflect no one's conscious plan; no one may recognize their broad tendency. But the effectiveness of these forces of social control is what determines whether the domination of a particular ruling group will meet with quiet acceptance or violent challenge.

Marx viewed participation in militant collective action as most typically fueled by group interest, rather than divisible, individual interest—or so I have argued. How, then does the transformation occur between the everyday pursuit of private, individual interest and those crucial moments when people risk individual costs on behalf of collective goals?

In his influential *Making Sense of Marx* (1985), Jon Elster agonizes at length about Marx's allocation of explanations between "intentional" and "functional" modes. In intentional explanations, *explananda* are accounted for in terms of the wishes or choices of individuals; functional explanations provide such accounts in terms of needs or requirements of larger social units. Elster finds great virtue in the first and often deplores the second. To me it seems that the energies lavished on pursuing this distinction are not always well spent. Do we always need an account of the exact mechanisms underlying distinctively Marxian processes, in order to profit from the possibilities afforded by the idea for analysis of real-world phenomena? Surely it is of great interest to consider, say, the Marxist notion that dominant religious ideas within any social order, over the long run, tend to reinforce prevailing patterns of class advantage—whether the processes supposed to underlie such a relationship are intentional, functional, or something else altogether.

Accordingly, I know of no explicit Marxian account of how the transformation from pursuit of strictly private self-interest to collective interest occurs. Yet Marxian theory clearly does imply such shifts. The best way to grasp what Marxist thinking has to tell us on these subjects is to consider the overall view of social control it conveys. These processes of control fall into three categories: cultural, economic, and coercive. The shift from motivation by private self-interest to that by militant collective interest grows more likely to the extent that one or more of these processes breaks down.

*Cultural forces* include those often bracketed in Marxian writing as "ideological." They entail all the multifarious influences implied in the famous line from *The Communist Manifesto*, "the ruling ideas of each age have ever been the ideas of the ruling class." The ways of thinking, perceiving, and feeling that Marx had in mind include ethical ideas, political doctrines, religious systems, aesthetic standards—the whole array of ways in which cultures differ in assessing the satisfactoriness of social arrangements. Every ruling group perceives eternal virtue in its own characteristic forms of social action; the "ruling ideas" disseminated by such groups are the generalization or universalization of these principles. Thus, the early industrial bourgeoisie, rising to dominant social position, tended to apply to all areas of social life the standards of deliberate, prudent action and calculation of utility essential to their defining economic roles. Again, Marxian analysts see no need to assume that dissemination of such thought-ways forms a part of anyone's conscious plan. It is simply an inevitable result of the class basis of any particular set of institutions.

The "ruling ideas" entail both attitudinal or evaluative and cognitive elements—that is, both *sentiments,* such as those of active affirmation of the goodness of particular social arrangements, and *assumptions, theories,* and *commonsense precepts* about how the social world works. Much of the force of these latter ideas lies in their ability to obscure possibilities for social change incompatible with prevailing forms of class rule—that is, to sustain the assumption that *things could not be otherwise.*

Marx was not, then, what today would be called a value consensus theorist. He did not believe that *active affirmation* of principles sacred to any particular regime was indispensable to the perpetuation of that regime, though of course he recognized this as one possible mode of domination. The cultural dominance of ruling groups might just as well express itself in the form of massive resignation to unjust fate, or in the conviction that no alternative exists to the evils of the present system, as in active support of abstract values supposed to underlie the system's institutions.

The point is, Marxian analysis pictures regimes as controlling the *meanings* available to people to make sense of their lives. Regimes put forward, in ways both blatant and subtle, understandings of what is worthy and unworthy, significant and irrelevant, possible and impossible in social life. Their success in making these ideas universal and persuasive is an index of their overall hold on domination.

*Economic forces* are a second key element in the Marxian model of social control. These are all the influences based on control by dominant groups over wealth. In capitalist societies these might include the ability to shift investments to an area whose labor force is most compliant, or to force workers to bid against one another in seeking employment. In other systems, economic controls might include the master's ability to determine subsistence levels of his slaves, or the ability of central authorities in what Wittfogel (1957) terms "hydraulic empires" to withhold water for irrigation from peasant cultivators. Human experience is formed, Marx tells us, by the relentless need to wrest a living from nature; members of dominant classes have the ability to set the terms for this struggle on the part of the ruled.

Finally, *coercive processes* of control involve direct physical combat between rulers or their agents and the ruled.

Obviously the key interest of this book lies in conflicts played out in coercive terms. But the Marxian analysis of coercion cannot be understood without taking into account the workings of cultural and economic forms of control, as well. Essential to this analysis is the complementarity of the three forces.

I hardly intend to recapitulate the endless debates over how these forms of social control interact. But it is clear that recourse to coercive measures by rulers, and the use of force by insurgents, are not simply interchangeable with other forms of influence. Large-scale coercion, Marxists argue, is more likely when other processes of influence are failing. When cultural and economic controls work "normally," force is not a conspicuous feature of domination—and, presumably, levels of violent strife are relatively low. In short, widespread coercion most likely indicates that an old regime is desperately resisting its downfall, or that a new system is struggling to be born.

In the classical writings of Marxism, the clearest statements on these subjects come in Engels's *Anti-Duhring* (1962 [1884]). Karl Eugen Duhring would no doubt now be forgotten, if not memorialized in Engels's articulate contempt. A left-wing philosopher and economist and a one-time admirer of Marx, he published series of works identifying in coercion the basis of oppressive political power. Engels's attack was ferocious.

Every socialist worker, no matter of what nationality, knows quite well that force only protects exploitation, but does not cause it; that the relation of capital and wage-labor is the basis for his exploitation, and that this was brought about by purely economic causes and not at all by means of force. (1962, p. 211)

Regime coercion, Engels holds, serves mainly in the breach, when the ideas of the system have gone bankrupt and its economic powers are faltering.

So long as a mode of production still describes an ascending curve of development, it is enthusiastically welcomed even by those who come off worst from its corresponding mode of distribution. . . . And while this mode of production remains normal for society, there is, in general, contentment with the distribution, and if objections to it begin to be raised, these come from within the ruling class itself (Saint-Simon, Fourier, Owen) and find no response whatsoever among the exploited masses. Only when the mode of production in question has half outlived its day . . . it is only then that appeal is made from the facts which have had their day to so-called eternal justice. (1962, pp. 206–7)

Here we find several distinctively Marxist ideas. Regimes have "life cycles" or "natural histories"; they are strong in their youth, and increasingly vulnerable in old age to the infection of ideas and agitation transmitted by their would-be successors. One should expect little active challenge to a regime in its early stages, including little antiregime violence, and more as the system passes its peak.

George Lukacs argues much the same point in his essay "Legality and Illegality." He begins by noting the role of cultural and economic forces in disseminating a view of the invincibility of regimes.

The organs of authority harmonise to such an extent with the (economic) laws governing men's lives, or seem so over-whelmingly superior that men experience them as natural forces, as the necessary environment for their existence. As a result they submit to them freely. (Which is not to say that they *approve* of them.)

Note the distinction here between active support for regimes and a simple sense of their inevitability. Lukacs continues.

For if it is true that an organization based on force can only survive as long as it is able to overcome the resistance of individuals or groups by force, it is equally true that it could not survive if it were compelled to use force every time it is challenged. If this becomes necessary, then the situation will be revolutionary; the organs of authority will be in contradiction with the economic bases of society and this contradiction will be projected into the minds of the people. People will then cease to regard the existing order as given in nature and they will oppose force with force. (1971, p. 257)

Thus for Lukacs, as for other Marxist analysts of civil strife, coercion is apt to take precedence in enforcement of regime dictates precisely where more customary claims to preeminence fail. "The strength of every society," he writes, "is in the last resort a spiritual strength" (1971, p. 262). The more a regime must take recourse to violent repression, the greater the likelihood that the population will question its ability to sustain that repression in the long run. Such doubts, in turn, are likely to spell the final end for a worn-out system of domination.

These ideas from Engels and Lukacs reinforce the view, discussed earlier in this chapter, of history as a series of relatively stable periods of class domination, punctuated by violent periods of transition. Unfortunately, they entail some of the same logical difficulties. How does one know when a "mode of production" should be counted as on its "ascending curve"— apart from reckoning levels of social strife or compliance that one might wish to explain? If the period of ascendancy of any class regime is reckoned in terms of popular compliance with its dictates, then we will never find any regime that faces rebellion during its "ascendancy." If a "stage" of class rule is demarcated as a period between violent episodes, then there will never be violent eras within stages. For this aspect of the theory to be empirically falsifiable, we need clear conceptual rules for specifying the boundaries of "stages," and for identifying when the strength of a class regime is on the rise versus when it is waning. The literature of Marxism is not rich in such formulas.

More broadly, the idea of regime coercion as a sign of failure in other forms of social control is itself highly vulnerable to circularity. This notion, to be sure, is scarcely peculiar to Marxian analysis. Many theories of civil violence picture violent contests between regime supporters and insurgents as evidence that other, more routine forms of control have failed. But as always, we must ask what sort of evidence could possibly support a contrary interpretation. If any civil violence is ipso facto taken as evidence of failure of all other forms of social control, then the doctrine is unfalsifiable. The only alternative would be some reckoning of the success of other forms of control *independent* of whether coercion was also taking place—in other words, in the case of Marxian theory, some rating of the success of economic and cultural controls in their own terms. Such a research strategy would be exacting but hardly impossible in principle. But I know of no effort, either by Marxists or by proponents of other versions of the theory, to develop such an investigation.

## Class Conflict: Private and Public

One characteristic of Marxian analyses that often perplexes non-Marxists is a tendency to see class conflict as responsible for instances of collective action seemingly little related to class issues. Thus, Marxists are apt to account for ethnic antagonisms, nationalist movements, and popular religious enthusiasm as expressions of class interest, albeit flawed or refracted through some form of false consciousness. Such movements and conflicts are often prolific sources of civil violence. Do class explanations of such antagonisms really have a place in the logic of Marxian theory?

I believe that they do. Indeed, understanding that place may help clarify the logic of the theory.

Marxian theory of course views class membership and the conflicts growing out of it as key forces shaping all facets of social reality. Yet class interest, for most people most of the time, manifests itself in pursuit of private ends, as people act out their often antagonistic roles in various social hierarchies. When do these antagonisms become bases for collective action, rather than simply for private tensions? Part of the Marxian answer is known: The cultural forces associated with class domination give rise to ideas that picture certain social forms as righteous, honorable, or simply inevitable. Such notions—for example, the idea of slavery as reflecting natural differences in the God-given capacities of master and slave—are passed from generation to generation as part of enduring patterns of domination. Often such views are associated with concomitant ideas of mutual obligations among solidary groups, along the lines of E. P. Thompson's "moral economy" (1971). Taken together, this complex of assumptions and attitudes determines what people find "normal" in their social environments.

How, then, does mobilization for collective action come about? The logic of Marxian analysis suggests that people mobilize when the world they perceive about them no longer fits the cultural patterns formed by earlier class arrangements. In other words, breach of these cultural standards is a necessary, though hardly a sufficient condition for mobilization. Mobilization means extraordinary action, beyond normal pursuit of self-interest, as people join forces to alter social reality. Mobilization is increasingly likely to the extent that established patterns for satisfying private concerns no longer serve. The occurrence of such situations, in the Marxian view, is virtually built into the nature of social existence, for the standards by which people judge their world are formed out of specific material relations, and these relations are always in the process of change, rapid or not. I do not know of any Marxist writer who has developed this formulation in explicit terms. But these ideas seem more than merely implicit in the works of key figures such as Hobsbawm, Rude, Thompson, Soboul, and Lukacs.

Marxist analysts also typically assume that participants in such mobilization may be unable to give an accurate account of the reasons for their actions, to the world or even to themselves. Hence ideologies or programs of action embodying distorted, flawed, or other-worldly expressions of the tensions that led to mobilization. Marxists consider such distortions especially likely when direct political action against class antagonists appears threatening or unfeasible. Thus, many Marxists would explain early Christianity as a flawed movement of the oppressed, expressing an allegorical protest against the oppression of the lower classes in the Hellenic and Roman civilizations of the eastern Mediterranean. This was originally Engels's argument in "On the History of Early Christianity" (1959). And E. P. Thompson, in a famous chapter of his history of the English working class, accounts for the nineteenth-century Methodist movement as a kind of substitute gratification for working-class populations deflected from direct political action (1968, chap. 11). Less distinguished versions of the same argument are sometimes advanced to account for ethnic, linguistic, or communal strife in places like India, Northern Ireland, or Canada. The theme is the same: militant action apparently stemming from solidarities of ethnicity, religion, national identifications, language, region, or the like is really a "disguised" manifestation of shared material interest.

Does this view yield anything like an unambiguous falsifiable implication? The best I can do is the following:

*Expect, for every mobilization on behalf of religious or other nonmaterial ends, to find some antecedent frustration to the material interests of groups among whom the mobilization occurs.*

But this formulation entails a host of problems. A measure of frustration is implicit in the class experience of virtually any group, at least in the Marxian view. Can we distinguish between more and less frustrated groups? What warrant do we have for attributing to any particular collective frustration a causal role in the subsequent mobilization? How far back in collective experience should one look in making such an attribution? What sense is one to make of the vast array of frustrations that seem to have no such results? I do not see that the literature of Marxism offers persuasive answers to questions like these.

No doubt many Marxians would deny that their theory was meant to yield such definite implications. Not all religious, ethical, or other nonpolitical movements can be ascribed to material circumstances, it might be said. But some instances of such mobilizations give evidence of particularly direct causation in terms of shared material interest.

But such a response comes dangerously close to asserting that the theory should apply only where the evidence happens to fit, while instances of discordant evidence should simply be ignored. Moreover, even in those cases where some analysts would find compelling evidence of material origins to ideal movements, some sticky questions remain—above all, what should be considered persuasive evidence of linkage between mobilization and earlier group frustrations of a material sort? Without some formulation enabling such connections to be made by believers and skeptics alike, the theory is bound to remain unconvincing.

## Some Empirical Studies

Most mobilizations studied from Marxian perspectives do not present the problems of interpretation encountered in the previous section. Most, in fact, focus on contention over overtly political and economic issues. The best of these studies demonstrate that such mobilizations often occur just as Marxian thinking would lead us to expect—that is, as responses to clashes of collective material interest.

Consider a few more notable examples from this literature: Dirk Hoerder's *Crowd Action in Revolutionary Massachusetts 1765–1780* (1977) focuses on a period rich in popular violence. Hoerder shows that colonial crowds typically responded to conservative principles as bases for action—for example, the defense of customary popular rights, or disapproval of excessive display of wealth or privilege by the increasingly affluent upper classes. Here we see "the moral economy" of the time at work—class consciousness as a basis for efforts to forestall unjust innovation. A fascinating feature of Hoerder's work is the glimpse it gives of the narrow line that the colonial upper classes trod in seeking to encourage popular action against the British after 1776, while ensuring that they themselves did not become its targets.

John Foster advances some similar points in his *Class Struggle and the Industrial Revolution* (1974). He examines class relations in three early nineteenth-century English towns: Northampton, South Shields, and Oldham. He sees working-class activism constrained by social-control processes of the broad sorts considered previously: cultural, economic, and coercive. He identifies special pressures by government institutions to prevent autonomous development of working-class culture and hence to forestall growth of militant consciousness and action. For example, he cites stringent licensing efforts directed at keeping that bastion of working-class life, the public house, free of agitation (1974, p. 218).

A more famous study of class militancy in the Marxist tradition is Eric Wolf's *Peasant Wars of the Twentieth Century* (1973). Wolf considers six historically weighty peasant insurgencies: Mexico, China, Russia, Viet Nam, Algeria, and Cuba. He argues that these rebellions occurred where traditional peasant economies and social systems had faced pressures toward modernization and capitalism in general, and from the encroaching money economy in particular. This formulation, again, fits well with the view of lower-class action as governed by a "moral economy." Wolf also has a lot to say about relations between resources available to different would-be insurgent groups and their ability to launch successful actions; success in these rebellions, he stresses, requires that capitalist encroachment on peasant resources and options be less than complete. He argues that even successful rebellion in the countryside cannot be carried through to revolutionary conquest of the entire political system without an alliance between peasants and urban-based activists of some kind.

Yet another celebrated study of peasant violence with Marxist inspirations is *Agrarian Revolution* (1975), in which Jeffery Paige sets out to explain why militant peasant movements in single-crop regions of today's underdeveloped world have taken precisely the forms that they have.

The fundamental causal variable is the relationship of both cultivators and noncultivators to the factors of agricultural production as indicated by their source of income. Thus the theory is based on a strict definition of class in terms of relations to property in land, buildings, machinery, and standing crops and financial capital in the form of corporate assets, commodity balance, or agricultural credit. (1975, p. 10)

Thus, Paige argues that revolutionary movements strictly speaking—those aiming at the total overthrow of ruling classes—arise where landless laborers confront upper classes that have nothing but their claim on land itself as the basis for their domination. By contrast, where landowners also possess significant other forms of capital, such as agricultural machinery essential to the productive process, peasant movements tend to pursue more moderate, less zero-sum goals. Like the other works discussed, Paige's study demonstrates characteristics of violent movements that are distinctive to Marxist thinking—the notion that class interest forms the basis for recruitment of participants in violent actions, and that such actions reflect rational calculation of class interest by participants.

These four studies are simply examples from a rich and extensive literature of Marxian analyses of civil strife; one could cite Hilton (1973), Peacock (1965), Schwartz (1976), or numerous other studies to much the same effect. Of course, such works have a variety of intellectual objectives, not all relating to civil violence. They are written to capture the drift of unique events in a specific period, or to trace similarities in social action across varying situations. But they demonstrate that certain falsifiable expectations distinctive to Marxian theory sometimes withstand confrontation with data that could, in principle, tell a different story. They show, among other things, that mobilization for militant social action may occur along class lines, that the targets of such action are sometimes consistent with shared material interests of the participants, and that rational calculation marks the timing and character of violent actions. These are noteworthy achievements; I return to their consideration in Chapter Eight.

## Trotsky's *History of the Russian Revolution*

Trotsky's *History of the Russian Revolution* (1974 [1932]) commands a special place among Marxist studies of violent civil strife. No more than the authors considered in the previous section would Trotsky have proclaimed his work as an "empirical test" of Marxist theory. Nevertheless, like them, he sought to demonstrate the worth of this theory by showing that it afforded superior understanding of an important series of events. I know of no other study of civil violence that applies Marxist analysis in such detail to the unfolding of violent events.

Trotsky's *History* is not just an account of revolutionary violence followed by transfer of political power. It is an analysis of the unraveling of one entire system of political power and of the beginning of its reconstitution on profoundly different bases. Trotsky sets the scene for his analysis with some typically Marxian assumptions. The actors in his story are social classes, and the violence of their contest stems directly from the ill fit between established institutions and underlying reality of material relations.

Of the period leading up to 1917, Trotsky writes:

Tzarism during this period came into still sharper conflict with the demands of historic development. The bourgeoisie became economically more powerful, but . . . its power rested on a higher concentration of industry and an increased predominance of foreign capital. Impressed by the lessons of 1905, the bourgeoisie had become more conservative and suspicious. The relative weight of the petty and middle bourgeoisie, insignificant before, had fallen still lower. The democratic intelligentsia generally speaking had no firm social support whatever. . . . In these circumstances only the youthful proletariat could give the peasantry a program, a banner and leadership. (1974, vol. 1, p. 13)

Thus Trotsky sets the stage for the definitive power struggle that will ultimately spell the end of domination based on one set of class forces and the rise of its historical alternative. The playing out of the revolutionary drama occurs through the increasingly desperate efforts of the old regime, based on a coalition of class allies basically unsuited to one another, to make its accustomed modes of social control effective. The cultural force of the old order was largely dissipated by the time Trotsky's story began. Popular support for the Czar and the semifeudal order surrounding him was dissolving in the face of a new world whose realities were increasingly industrial and bureaucratic. Economically, the ability of the regime to ensure production and provide a secure livelihood to its people was faltering, particularly as the war with Germany wore on. From a Marxist perspective, of course, failure of these primary control mechanisms is always a telling sign: "One of the chief features of a revolutionary crisis," Trotsky writes, "consists in this sharp contradiction between the present consciousness and the old forms of social relationships" (pp. 115–16).

In a characteristically Marxist position, Trotsky insists that even the inability of the regime to feed its people breeds revolt only when its other claims to domination are failing as well.

The mere existence of privations is not enough to cause an insurrection; if it were, the masses would be always in revolt. It is necessary that the bankruptcy of the social regime, being conclusively revealed, should make these new privations intolerable, and that new conditions and new ideas should open the prospect of a revolutionary way out. Then in the cause of the great aims conceived by them, those same masses will prove capable of enduring doubled and tripled privations. (1974, vol. 2, p. vii)

The "bankruptcy" of which Trotsky speaks results from the exhaustion of the symbols, ways of thinking, and attitudes that sustained the old regime—in short, from the breakdown of cultural controls. Such a loss in conjunction with inability to make economic institutions work promises to leave the regime with nothing other than coercion to weigh against determined agitation from below.

The coercive confrontation between representatives of the old regime and the new hardly occurs in a single decisive cataclysm. Much of the brilliant detail in Trotsky's work lies in his tracing the coercive interactions between the old and new orders. These interactions have their own logic, manifest in the testing of each side by the other and the calculation of future action based on the results of such tests. The old order begins by presenting the appearance, to most of its people, of immutability. As Lukacs suggests in the passage quoted previously, that appearance then erodes through confrontations between regime representatives and those willing to challenge them. Insurgents and their sympathizers, Trotsky is telling us, have to learn how broad their bases of support really are, and how limited the capacity of the regime to make good on its claims through coercion. Coercion becomes increasingly important as a forum for such interactions, as the regime has virtually no other forms of influence at its disposal. Regime adherents and supporters at the same time are learning the limitations of their coercive options, particularly in light of the failing material bases of its class position. Some adherents, seeing for the first time the shakiness of structures they had considered so sound, are reconsidering their loyalties. Thus, key forces realign in the process of militant confrontation.

The writ of the old regime holds longest among its own coercive forces, Trotsky observes, because they are precluded from the kinds of testing experiences available to civilians.

The going over of the army to the insurrection does not happen of itself, nor as a result of mere antagonism. The army is heterogeneous, and its antagonistic elements are held together by the terror or discipline. . . . On the very eve of the decisive hour, the revolutionary soldiers do not know how much power they have, or what influence they can exert. The working masses, of course, are also heterogeneous. But they have immeasurably more opportunity for testing their ranks in the process of preparation for the decisive encounter. Strikes, meetings, demonstrations, are not only acts in the struggle, but also measures of its force. (1974, vol. 1, p. 12)

Thus Trotsky's model of revolutionary transformation involves something more than just a shift of opinion or sympathy from old regime to insurgents—and something qualitatively different. He is describing an evolution in assessments by various sectors of the population of the long-term ability of the old regime to continue to ensure some sort of "normality," versus the possibility of a similar performance by the new. Which side is more likely to deliver, to be capable of making good on its coercive intentions? Nowhere are these tensions more dramatically drawn than in the following passage.

The critical hour of contact between the pushing crowd and the soldiers who bar their way has its critical minute. That is when the gray barrier has not yet given way, still holds together shoulder to shoulder, but already wavers, and the officer, gathering his last strength of will, gives the command: 'Fire!' . . . The rifles waver. The crowd pushes. Then the officer points the barrel of his revolver at the most suspicious soldier. From the decisive minute now stands out the decisive second. The death of the boldest soldier, to whom the others have involuntarily looked for guidance, a shot into the crowd by a corporal from the dead man's rifle, and the barrier closes, the guns go off of themselves, scattering the crowd into the alleys and backyards. But how many times since 1905 it has happened otherwise! At the critical moment, when the officer is ready to pull the trigger, a shot from the crowd . . . forestalls him. This decides not only the fate of the street skirmish, but perhaps the whole day, or the whole insurrection. (1974, vol. 1, pp. 121–22)

These electrifying words convey the sense of standing between two comprehensive systems of social order—one about to breathe its last, the other about to be born. The events Trotsky describes are molecular: They are processes by which single individuals change their way of fitting themselves into larger systems of power and compliance. Yet, Trotsky wants to show, these molecular changes, when aggregated across an entire populatio, make profound differences in what institutional forms of authority are possible. Violent confrontation is the medium in which support for revolutionary patterns of social order is formed.

What theoretical conclusions can be drawn from Trotsky's monumental work? Certainly that a Marxist perspective offers a highly suggestive basis for observing the fine detail of a cataclysmic instance of civil violence, for ordering the many events in the revolutionary tapestry and ascribing them significance. But we must pursue a more specific question: Does any evidence give grounds for affirming the superiority of one theory over others?

Consider an alternative theoretical lens for viewing the same sort of phenomena.

## Pareto's Project

Pareto has been called "a Marx for the middle classes." Especially during the 1930s, he held a strong appeal for conservative intellectuals who sought a deep, "theoretical" analysis of social change and political conflict, yet who could not accept Marxian lionization of the working-class movements. Pareto often heaped scorn on those who spoke for the proletariat, particularly on their claims for the historical significance of their often violent actions. Yet, unlike both Marx and Hobbes, Pareto held no categorical sympathies with either rulers or the oppressed. Insurgent social movements often held the only hope for revitalization of outworn institutions, Pareto argued, and movements associated with the working classes might well play such a role for what he regarded as the effete political systems of his day.

What Pareto consistently attacked was the notion that the ideology of any political activists, whether insurgent or established, represented an accurate guide to their long-term political directions. His obsession, often pursued at tiresome lengths, was to strip away the claims of social activists and to offer instead his own veridical analysis of the forces underlying their actions. Of special interest to Pareto were militant political actions, to which he attributed great importance in the larger workings of political and social systems. Here his theories offer a provocative counterpoint to the significance attributed to collective violence by Marxian thinkers.

Unlike Marx, Pareto did not spawn a tradition of Paretian analyses of political movements and social change. His positions on civil violence and other sociological issues are set down in three voluminous works: *Les Systèmes Socialistes* (Paris, 1902); *Manual of Political Economy* (New York, 1971; originally published in Italian in 1906); and his multivolume tour de force, *Trattato di Sociologia Generale* (Florence, 1916), translated and published as *The Mind and Society* (New York, 1935). Undoubtedly Pareto's political and sociological ideas, as distinct from his influential contributions to economics, would have more currency today had he only mastered his addiction to verbiage for its own sake. He insisted on embellishing every idea with items from classical texts, ethnographic accounts, and the daily press. Yet at the core of these writings are some important sociological ideas—and a distinctive theory of civil violence.

We can begin with Pareto's social psychology. Like other turn-of-the-century thinkers including LeBon and Freud, Pareto was fascinated with the discovery of the unconscious. No analysis of social behavior could be complete, he held, without accounting for forces in social action that the actors themselves could not know about. A distinguished economist, Pareto saw these motives as precisely those that economics, the study of "rational" action, ignored. People typically represent their behavior as "reasonable" steps taken to attain widely understood "reasonable" ends. Yet much social behavior, Pareto maintained, was either an end in itself or a means to some distant end other than that claimed by the actor. Only hard-headed, critical analysis could disclose the true ends governing most of human action.

Various cultures, for example, have more or less ritualized practices in-

volving some form of anointing. Christian baptism is but one of these; in
other social and historical settings, the anointing is performed with milk,
blood, or even excrement. Although a core of social behavior remains
relatively constant in all these practices, accounts given of the reasons for
anointing show the greatest variability, from washing away the taint of
original sin to placating the civic gods. The discrepancy between a consistent core of social behavior and the fluctuating accounts given as reasons
for the behavior indicates that the real reasons are beyond the compre-
hension of the actors.

Pareto does not argue, however, that people never understand the reasons for their behavior.

The field of logical behavior, exceedingly limited in the case of animals, becomes
very far-reaching in mankind. All the same, many many human actions, even today among the most civilized people, are performed instinctively, mechanically,
in pursuance of habit; and that is more generally observable still in the past and
among less civilized peoples. (1935, vol. 1, para. 157)

Still, like LeBon and Freud, Pareto holds that the veneer of civilization
does not go very deep. Even in the most "advanced" societies, many public actions proclaimed efficacious to valued ends are either nonrational
(ends in themselves) or irrational (ineffective to their proclaimed ends).
Political actions, Pareto insists, are among the most heavily encrusted
with these elements.

*Residues* is the name Pareto gives to relatively durable patterns of social action of a nonrational or irrational sort, anointing being an example.
*Derivations* represents the relatively variable accounts produced to make
the behaviors appear rational. For present purposes, we need not look
more deeply into Pareto's account of the residues and derivations, which
is certainly not without its inconsistencies. The critical point is that residues—or more exactly, the tendency to embody particular residues in
one's own actions—are not evenly distributed throughout populations.
Different social groups have different action characteristics, and different
ideologies to account for these characteristics. On these differences, Pareto
predicates his theory of civil violence.

Pareto's classification of six types of residues and their many subspecies
is tedious, and mostly of no concern here. But two types of residues involve
quintessentially political behavior. The so-called class I residues, translated as the "Instinct for Combinations," include the making of "deals,"
such as political log-rolling, clever compromises, and the playing off of
one group against another. Like all residues, these may be justified with
the widest variety of derivations, from the high-minded to the cynical.
What matters is that certain individuals are constitutionally inclined to
engage in these characteristically political activities.

The class II residues, called "Group Persistences" or "Persistence of Aggregates," involve yet another kind of political activity, the application of force. People characterized by these residues are inclined to fight rather than compromise, are ready to risk their lives and well-being against heavy odds, and are willing to use coercion against their enemies once they themselves gain power.

Note that residues are not drives or character traits in themselves, but standardized forms of social behavior. Nevertheless, the inclination to act out such behavior obviously stems from some sort of abiding urges. Pareto clearly views these urges not as genetically given, but as shaped by social experience (1935, vol. 2, para. 1046). Nor are they subject to appraisal in strictly rational terms. Is it better to die for one's party and one's ideals, or to make a deal with the other side and thus avoid bloodshed? Answers to such questions can only be affirmation of existential "taste," or what Weber would term choices of ultimate value (see Pareto 1935, vol. 4, para. 2197; 1971, p. 86).

Crucial for Pareto's theory of civil violence is the distribution of these action types throughout the social hierarchy. Pareto invokes two cross-cutting forms of stratification. On the one hand, he identifies *elites*, categories of people defined by outstanding talent in any branch of activity. Of special interest are political elites, those adept at acquiring and wielding power. Like other sorts of elites, political elites do not necessarily constitute a cohesive group; to varying degrees, they are scattered throughout populations. They are defined strictly by their talents.

Another form of stratification is what Pareto often calls *class*. He does not mean class in the Marxian sense, but interest groupings based on various forms of shared advantage or disadvantage. Pareto takes it for granted that most social systems experience conflict between more and less privileged classes. His particular concern is in the ability of hereditary privileged classes, or aristocracies, to preserve their special advantages over the sweep of historical time. When do aristocracies, and the institutional systems associated with them, manage to deflect challenges from the lower orders, and when do they succumb? The answer to this question turns on the distribution of political elites across classes.

In a position much like Weber's, Pareto holds that the application of coercion is essential in maintaining any kind of organized social life; "force is the foundation of all social organization," he writes (1971, p. 94). No ruling group can expect to continue for long in power without being willing to coerce its antagonists. For "a mere handful of citizens, so long as they are willing to use violence, can force their will upon public officials who are not inclined to meet violence with equal violence" (1935, vol. 4, para. 1575). Thus the distribution throughout populations of political elites of the forceful sort takes on special import. If these people are concentrated in positions involving the exercise of government power, the political system will likely be stable; if not, the excluded are apt to form activist movements, and violent challenges to the government are likely.

Of course, class I residues are also political and include the wheeling-and-dealing behaviors included in the "Instincts for Combinations." Indeed, Pareto specifies that governing is impossible without some measure of these qualities, along with the forceful ones of the class II residues. On the other hand, the conquest of power and the violent steps necessary to set up a line of succession or an institutional system require the forceful residues of class II. Even here, however, an admixture of class I personalities is necessary for planning and co-ordinating the power-grabbing assault. So, the problem is one of the proper balance of political residues among government elites.

Complicating the assessment is Pareto's famous doctrine of shifts in elite qualities over time. Class II residues give way, as elites remain in power, to class I. This means, he affirms, that established elites

decay . . . in quality, in the sense that they lose their vigour, that there is a decline in the proportions of the residues which enabled them to win power and hold it. The governing class is restored . . . in quality, by families rising from the lower classes and bringing with them the . . . proportions of residues necessary for keeping themselves in power. It is also restored by the loss of its more degenerate members. (1935, vol. 3, para. 2054).

Thus the question arises whether the elite is open to new recruits. Slow replacement of class II residues from the outside is desirable from the standpoint of the longevity of the elite. But the aristocracies or other "classes" associated with established political elites may not permit such recruitment. Under these circumstances, those in governing positions tend to display qualities associated increasingly with the class I residues, and decreasingly with the class II.

After a governing class . . . has maintained itself for long periods of time on force and acquired wealth, it may subsist for some time still without using force, buying off its adversaries and paying not only in gold, but also in terms of the dignity and respect that it had formerly enjoyed and which constitute, as it were, a capital. In the first stages of decline, power is maintained by bargainings and concessions, and people are so deceived into thinking that that policy can be carried on indefinitely. (1935, vol. 3, para. 2059)

Under these circumstances, the perpetuation of the old elite is least certain, and civil violence most likely. Activist challengers on the outside, Pareto holds, will recognize the weakness of the regime and before long will attack with a forcefulness that the defenders of the old order will be unable to match.

Revolutions come about through accumulations in the higher strata of society . . . of decadent elements no longer possessing the residues suitable for keeping them in power and shrinking from the use of force; while meantime in the lower strata of society elements of superior quality are coming to the fore, possessing residues suitable for exercising the functions of government and willing enough to use force. (1935, vol. 3, para. 2057)

It seems fair to generalize what Pareto says here about revolutions to other forms of civil violence, as well. The same contention between an established but declining elite and an aggressive insurgent elite that would lead to revolution might well, in less extreme cases, lead to other forms of civil strife.

Now consider the link, in Pareto's theory, between elite activists and their "constituencies"—a key matter in any theory of civil violence. Why do various social groups support one or another elite, and what loyalties do elites bear to their supporters in turn? Clearly Pareto scorns the Marxian notion that the efforts of lower-class activists represent a simple expression of solidarity with the class interests of those they identify with. Such claims on the part of insurgents, he would argue, are simply derivations put forward to explain behavior that has much deeper roots. The quest for power is an end in itself, and those with a taste for this quest are likely to put forth whatever accounts of their actions appear most plausible and expedient.

Assume that the new elite was clearly and simply to proclaim its intentions which are to supplant the old elite; no one would come to its assistance, it would be defeated before having fought a battle. On the contrary, it appears to be asking for nothing for itself, well knowing that without asking anything in advance it will obtain what it wants as a consequence of its victory; it asserts that it is fighting solely to obtain equality between [the upper and the lower classes]. (1971, p. 92)

This passage seems to suggest conscious cynicism on the part of insurgent elites in the choice of ideological appeals. This is not Pareto's characteristic position. He more often writes as though derivations of all kinds had a certain persuasiveness for both their "producers" and their "consumers":

A derivation is accepted not so much because it convinces anybody as because it expresses clearly ideas that people already have in a confused sort of way—the latter fact is usually the main element in the situation. Once the derivation is accepted it lends strengths and aggressiveness to the corresponding sentiments, which now have found a way to express themselves. . . . For the very reason that derivations exert influence only through the sentiments which they stir, persons who are alien to such sentiments . . . find it difficult to appreciate the practical importance of certain derivations. (1935, vol. 3, para. 1747)

Thus, expecting an intense emotional bond between insurgent elites and their supporters is reasonable when the former articulate derivations corresponding to deeply felt sentiments among the latter. Such derivations—for example, "solidarity among the oppressed"—may help the rising elite solidify its support. For all their empirical inaccuracy, derivations concentrate sentiment and intensify the residues associated with them.

But such shared sentiments, however deep, should not be taken as evidence of the action-tendencies of the elite. What influences their behavior is a drive for power, whatever the claims they invoke in the process of its conquest. Pareto admits that the supporters of a rising elite may benefit materially and politically from its success (1971, p. 93). But "the people" never rule in Pareto's world. Once instated in power, one elite acts much like another, consolidating its position and doing as much as possible to retain power indefinitely. In the final analysis, political elites have more in common with one another than any one of them does with those it represents.

## Falsifiable Implications

The attitude Pareto strikes in these analyses is unmistakable. He is the world-weary observer—urbane, detached, yet sometimes melodramatic—who perceives patterns and connections invisible to more engaged intellects. Contending groups come and go on the historical stage, he tells us, all claiming to pursue some special historical mission or to uphold sacred values of one sort or another. Yet the real explanation of their behavior is much simpler. They are simply attracted to power, much like moths to a summer lantern. Although these elites may make history, they do so even less "as they please" than in Marx's vision. For the new political orders that successful elites establish are bound to erode, whether through gradual dilution by new elite elements or from abrupt overthrow from violent, energetic counterelite challengers.

Is this position as distinct in its falsifiable implications as in its political evocations?

Consider two broad expectations from Pareto's theory of civil violence:

*Expect militant collective action, including a fortiori violent action, to be the work of elites.*

*Expect the frequency and intensity of civil violence within any polity to rise in proportion to the length of time an elite has held power without admitting nonelite elements to ruling positions.*

These expectations sound as though one could easily envisage evidence that would tend to falsify them. Yet they may also be interpreted as circular, such that no refutation would be possible. What if one man's elite were the next woman's proletarian vanguard, or the third person's psychological crowd (to use LeBon's term)? What, in other words, if all militant collective action were ipso facto ascribed to the work of elites? Then any imaginable violent episode would count as consistent with the theory. We need, then, an empirically specified definition of an elite, one that would distinguish elites from other social formations that might act in civil violence.

First of all, a Paretian elite has to have some continuity over time. To be distinct from activists recruited on other principles, elites must act together for months or years. They must be guided by some community of interests and goals that are distinct from those of their alleged constituencies. Whether we are thinking of an entrenched or an insurgent elite, in other words, we should be able to distinguish between the actions of the elite—those actually engaged in seeking or wielding power—and those of members of larger strata associated with it.

With this caveat in mind, findings tending to falsify Pareto's doctrine are not so hard to picture. Imagine, for example, a series of kindred violent affrays where the perpetrators are indistinguishable in their actions from the groups in whose name the mobilization is carried out and where those engaged in one episode of violence are not necessarily the same persons as those engaged in subsequent events. In other words, a series of authentic grass-roots actions. Such findings are typical of those reported by Marxian analysts like Hobsbawm and Rude. They do not appear reconcilable with Pareto's theory, unless one could show that elite activists were somehow manipulating and controlling the actual perpetrators of the violence. The Marxian accounts of small-scale insurgencies discussed previously have no hint of any such indication. In larger revolutionary movements such as the Bolshevik party, however, Paretian interpretations are less implausible; there professional revolutionary groups may appear more distinct from their grass-roots constituencies.

I must say that, prima facie, this element of Pareto's thinking does not appear likely to withstand confrontation with potentially disconfirming evidence, at least not as a general theory of civil violence. Of the totality of collective civil strife recorded across countries and periods, too much seems to be of types different from that envisaged in Pareto's theory—for example, communal disturbances, seemingly quite unplanned, among members of different religious, ethnic, or national groupings. One might well identify elites within such groupings. But I suspect that it would be difficult to show that they necessarily inspire and orchestrate the bulk of such seemingly volatile events as the fratricide among Hindus and Moslems in India at the time of the partition.

Pareto's position would be stronger if considered to apply to violent activisms aiming directly at influencing or capturing state power. Pareto does not explicitly specify this range of phenomena, but most of his examples of violent collective action seem to be of this kind. One can imagine an investigation reviewing periods of high civil violence directed at state power, sifting the backgrounds of these events for evidence that the violent action was performed or orchestrated by an empirically defined elite. Again, care would be necessary to distinguish elite action from all political activism. One would have to show that those responsible for violent affrays were socially different from those they claimed to represent; that they did act with self-conscious cohesion and continuity over time; and that the consistent goal of their actions, whatever the activists themselves may have thought, was the seizure of state power. Such an investigation would be exacting to carry out but scarcely impossible in principle. Yet I know of no attempt in this direction.

A distinctive feature of Pareto's elites is that they seek power for its own sake. Elite actors, both entrenched and insurgent, are motivated by different ends from their supporters. What potentially falsifying evidence might be sought with which to confront this view? Findings that the leadership of insurgent movements urged their followers to continue the struggle for full political power when the latter appear ready to settle for "half a loaf" would be consistent with Pareto's position. On the other hand, findings that both leadership and rank-and-file followers tended to return to political inactivity once more moderate goals were met would tend to falsify Pareto's theory. Note that Lenin's doctrine on the role of the vanguard party in activating and orchestrating mass action is really closer to Pareto's model than to any idea of Marx's—for example, in its insistence that only an elite is apt to grasp the long-term goals of revolutionary action.

The second empirical expectation cited previously derives of course from Pareto's famous theory of elite circulation. As elsewhere in Pareto's theories, there is real danger of circularity here. The problem has to do with the concepts of *insulation* of entrenched elites, versus their openness to recruitment from the outside. How do we recognize a closed elite when we find one? Clearly no group of individual power holders can expect to remain in place longer than their own lifetimes; in this sense, all elites circulate. Short of this form of elite self-perpetuation, the ultimate closed elite would be an endogamous clique of male and female power holders who are self-reproducing both in the demographic and the political sense—that is, who never accept successors who are not their own offspring. Clearly, this is not what Pareto had in mind when he wrote of closed elites, either.

What Pareto certainly was thinking of was a situation in which established elite roles—that is, positions involving the exercise of established power, whether or not associated with a particular office—are always filled by members of a restricted social category. Examples might be an aristocracy, a group of "establishment" families, or the families of Communist party members in the Soviet bloc. Note Pareto's distinction between an established elite (those actually engaged in the exercise of state power) and what he called a privileged *class*. The latter is always a much larger category. Pareto's theory only makes sense if we envisage a symbiosis between the two categories, such that the smaller elite is continually replenished by new members from the more inclusive upper class.

Such, then, is Pareto's view of a "closed" elite. But questions remain. If the elite admits only members of the privileged class, what about admission to this class? Consider two possibilities: Admission to the elite only for offspring of the privileged class, and no new members ever admitted to this class; and admission only from this class, but admission to the class itself relatively open. Would the second case still count as a "closed" elite? As far as I can tell, Pareto does not give a clear answer to this question. Yet he does acknowledge (1902, p. 10) that even formal aristocracies normally experience considerable infusion of new blood over a period of generations. The case of a thoroughly closed elite must be rare indeed.

So, the role of this privileged "class" from which the elite of power holders is drawn takes on great importance for the theory. To be falsifiable, it has to incorporate definite commitments as to what rate of assimilation of new members to the privileged class should count as *insulation* versus *openness*. Perhaps even more urgently, we need specification of how broadly that class may be defined. Would the "middle class" of the United States count here? Presumably not, because Pareto seemed to have in mind a relatively small minority of total populations such as hereditary aristocracies. But the ambiguity of this definition threatens trouble for the theory, because the boundary of the class can so readily be shifted to make the theory impervious to falsification. Imagine an army coup against a civilian government, a common and often violent occasion for change of power in present-day third world countries. A Paretian might hold such events consistent with the theory, with the military representing an excluded counterelite claiming power from a weaker established elite. Typically there are some differences between the social backgrounds of army officers and those of politicians. Yet by another standard, both groups may be part of a small privileged stratum within the larger populations of their countries. There is always danger of shifting the definition of the privileged upper class to exclude those who challenge established power holders. Thus challengers ipso facto become counterelites, and the theory becomes circular.

Similarly, what would Pareto have made of the challenge to the British political "establishment" by the early Labour Party? If the Labourite leaders of, say, 1945 were defined as outsiders to the British upper classes, then their arrival to power might be taken as the assimilation of new elements to the existing elite. Had the Labourites led a movement to seize power through some violent, noninstitutional channels, a proponent of Pareto's theory would no doubt interpret these actions as the predictable consequence of exclusion of a rising elite. Again, it is hard to specify a case that would falsify Pareto's theory of elite circulation. Because no group of entrenched power holders can ever be expected to wage violent challenges against themselves, every challenging group can be defined as an excluded elite.

I believe that Pareto's notion of elite circulation as the basis for a theory of civil violence is unfalsifiable in the terms given in Pareto's writing. The boundaries of his concepts of elite and class are simply too elastic. Perhaps major surgery, and some sort of conceptual prosthesis, could make the theory unambiguous enough to serve as the basis for actual empirical investigation. But such additions to the theory would necessarily be theoretical contributions in their own right, for Pareto's own theoretical pronouncements clearly promise much more than they deliver in this respect.

## Conclusions

Think back to Trotsky. His absorbing account dramatizes not only the events of the Russian revolution, but also the imprint of theories on our understanding of such events. A major participant in the riveting struggles he describes, Trotsky shows little doubt that his account demonstrates the superiority of Marxist analysis over other interpretations. He obviously feels that he has seen the momentous events more profoundly, more accurately than those lacking the special theoretical lens of Marxian analysis. In this respect, he has much company, distinguished and otherwise. Every thinker attracted to an overarching theoretical view can sense a special "fit" between that view and any slice of reality that catches his or her interest.

For many thinkers, seeing one's theory "fit" is reason enough for accepting the theory, indeed for preferring it to others. But for purposes of this book we need a more rigorous standard. If one embraces any theory on the grounds that it "fits" evidence that might as well support a variety of other theories, the choice is more a statement about one's own inner world than about a shared, exterior one. Hence, the concern of this work to identify expectations that admit in principle of evidence that might tend to falsify them, yet are clearly distinctive to the theory.

By this standard Trotsky's *History* is a work that demonstrates the organizing powers of a comprehensive theoretical view, without always strengthening the credibility of the theory. One can appreciate nearly all of his acute factual observations øn the events he recounts, and indeed accept them, without regarding the work as a vindication of a Marxian theory of civil violence in the rigorous sense required here. One can accept, for example, that the old regime was increasingly forced to rely on coercive inducements during the revolutionary period because of the failure of cultural and economic forms of control; or that a major dynamic of the revolutionary period was a growing popular disbelief in the ability of the regime to make good on its coercive intentions. One can accept Trotsky's telling accounts of face-to-face confrontations between popular forces and forces of order. One can accept all these invaluable observations, yet still remain agnostic about their relation to a distinctively Marxian theory of civil violence.

What if the *History of the Russian Revolution* had been written by Pareto, rather than Trotsky? The tone and the *partis pris* would have been different, to say the least. But most of the factual observations, including those highlighted in the previous discussion, could remain in place, fitting into a larger Paretian interpretation. There can be no doubt that the Bolsheviks and other activist formations fit Pareto's definition of an insurgent elite, for example. They were, after all, specialists in getting and using power, and they capitalized on popular dissatisfaction with the old regime, just as Pareto would expect. And, Pareto would argue, the exigencies of attaining and wielding power figured much more heavily in the activists' behavior than the demands of their declared "constituents," both before and after the revolution.

Indeed, the facts reported by Trotsky might also "fit" passably well the analyses of a Hobbesian observer. Consider the electrifying passages describing the coercive interactions of crowds and armies. For Trotsky, of course, these are microscopic records of the unraveling of one form of class authority and the spontaneous creation of another. But the Hobbesian might claim a more parsimonious interpretation: What these scenes describe is the process by which ordinary citizens determine which of two would-be sovereigns really has the stronger claim on that role. Calculation is taking place, as Trotsky observed, but it is calculation not of class interest but of individual advantage. People are calculating which of two systems of sovereignty—one struggling to stay alive, the other struggling to be born—is most likely to provide the safety they ultimately desire for their own private pursuits of self-interest. Once a clear winner emerges out of the flux of events, a Hobbesian might argue, most people will accept the winner as sovereign and return to the private pursuits of self-interest that sovereignty affords.

There are problems with a Hobbesian interpretation. Trotsky's accounts are full of grass-roots actors actively challenging the regime, out of hatred for its actions and its social bases. Sometimes they are even willing to risk their lives in hopes of bringing that regime down. These are not the actions of ordinary citizens in the Hobbesian world, who do not rebel unless they see some divisible, personal interest in doing so. Hobbes's citizens are more likely simply to wait and watch to determine which would-be sovereign is more likely to provide safety for their private pursuits. Yet on the other hand, if Hobbesian assumptions cannot readily explain why ordinary people would be willing to run the risks encountered by Trotsky's demonstrators, it is by no means clear that class identification a la Trotsky need be the explanation. Trotsky constantly interprets the mass mobilization of ordinary folk against the Romanoff regime as evidence of class solidarity. But ordinary Russians shared various nonclass interests in ridding themselves of a regime that was endangering their safety and survival through its ruinous economic performance and its disastrous war policies. Although Trotsky convinces us that ordinary people mobilized at considerable risk to overthrow the czar, more evidence is needed to conclude that class identification was the principle of selection to this mobilization.

I hardly think that the facts given in Trotsky's *History* suffice to give either of these alternative theories a decisive edge over Trotsky's Marxian view. The point is simply that that distinguished work demonstrates the organizing power of a theory without affording judgment on the satisfactoriness of that theory versus other contenders, at least where civil violence is concerned.

The other studies in the Marxian tradition that I have discussed are less ambiguous in this context. The works of Hobsbawm and Rude, Hoerder, Foster, Wolf, and Paige all address data that relate to falsifiable expectations of Marxian theory. All show congruence between interests specific to class groupings and the content of militant action. The targets of violent mobilizations, the recruitment of participants, and the character of the repressive response in these events all correspond to expectations of Marxian theory, and much less so with those derived from other notable theories of civil violence. Thus, they offer grounds for choice among various theories of civil violence, rather than simply a loose "fit" that a variety of theories might well share.

---

Still, we need to consider what studies of this kind cannot tell us, as well as what they can. The investigators undoubtedly began their work by identifying instances that showed prima facie indications of militant class action. One might imagine an adherent of Pareto's doing the same thing—scanning the historical record to find an authentic instance of decay of ruling qualities among an "insulated" elite, and determining that the regime involved did indeed fall victim to violent movements from below. Such a discovery would then obviously provide a suitable vehicle for illustrating the strengths of the theory.

This strategy has a long and not unrespectable tradition. One must start somewhere in fitting theory to evidence, and the best place to start may be those cases where the fit is best. But this strategy, in its nature, cannot tell us much about how widely the theory applies. For this we need a method that will select cases for study where the theory ought to apply, then determine whether empirical expectations are indeed falsified.

Again, many adherents of Marxian or other theories must view such an approach as unduly rigorous, or simply irrelevant to the virtues of their chosen theory. Theory, they might argue, earns its keep by affording penetrating interpretation of inherently important events or periods. The fact that the theory may appear inapplicable here or there is simply of no interest.

There is no logical reason why Marxian, Paretian, or any other style of analysis might not apply in some settings and not others. Indeed, on nothing more than intuitive grounds, I suspect that virtually every theory of civil violence ever propounded could be shown distinctly superior to all others for at least one case. But there is something unsatisfying about building theories that apply only in settings that cannot be anticipated in advance. An insight that holds only for certain special cases is not very exciting *unless* we can specify in advance what those cases will be. Perhaps what Weber said of the materialist theory of history holds for theories in general: They are not conveyances to be taken and alighted from at will.

So, what of the theoretical antinomies between Marxian and Paretian analyses of civil violence? If exponents of the former have an advantage to date, it lies largely in their identification of an array of cases that clearly tend to lend credibility to their theory at the expense of others, Pareto's included. We know, in other words, that there are at least some episodes where clashes of material interest lead to significant civil violence, where calculation of such interest shapes the timing and character of the militant action, and so on. But again, without some sort of systematic attention to a variety of situations where this or any theory might apply, questions are bound to remain. There is no way of knowing whether the findings of Marxian investigators are a reliable guide to what other investigators might report, or a tribute to a special gift for ferreting out instances that fit the theory.

Why are systematic efforts at assessing the relative strengths of theories so rare? One obvious reason is that the large-scale collection and organization of empirical materials for such a study are costly in money, time, and self-discipline. But another answer has more to do with the intellectual appetites that lead people to social inquiry in the first place: Investigators simply derive strong satisfactions from locating and reporting evidence that fits their chosen theories. For most of us, setting out to find data that give the strongest possibility of falsifying our theories has about as much appeal as strangling our own children in the crib.

*Chapter Three*

# Collective Behavior:
# Civil Violence as Social Devolution

Hobbes was not the only theorist to picture civil violence as the antithesis of "normal" social process. For a group of European thinkers at the turn of this century, riots, revolutions, and other manifestations of "crowd mentality" involved the unraveling of constraints essential to all civilized social life. I call these thinkers—Tarde, Sighele, and LeBon—the irrationalists. Transformed and Americanized by Robert Park, their doctrine became the theory of collective behavior, which shaped social scientists' views of collective violence and other changeful social processes for more than four decades.

## The Irrationalists' Doctrine

In the closing decades of the nineteenth century, western European intellectuals sensed profound rumblings from below. Instead of exhibiting steady movement toward heightened civilization, their societies seemed in danger of destruction. Modern social forms had, to all appearances, brought rampant individualism, crime, urban degradation, moral breakdown, and, most disturbing of all, militant left-wing agitation. The Paris Commune offered a horrific view of "normal" society torn apart and stood on its head by these ferocious forces. For conservative and moderate thinkers, these trends seemed to threaten not just specific political arrangements and institutions, but civilization itself.

From social theorists these developments demanded a "scientific" analysis. Who were the revolutionists? How could apparently law-abiding, "reasonable" populations so abruptly be transformed into raging, wanton mobs? What qualities of the people, of the times, or of situations made such things possible? What, in short, caused these outbreaks of destruction and retrogression, and what could be done to prevent them? In asking such questions, these theorists were entertaining an authentic version of Hobbes's original problem.

The irrationalists' answer to Hobbes's question was eminently sociological: The excesses of crowd behavior arose from a certain intensified, emotional influence from one's fellow human beings. As LeBon wrote,

> By the mere fact that he forms part of an organized crowd, a man descends several rungs in the ladder of civilisation. Isolated, he may be a cultivated individual; in a crowd, he is a barbarian—that is, a creature acting by instinct. He possesses the spontaneity, the violence, the ferocity, and also the enthusiasm and heroism of primitive beings. . . . he allows himself to be impressed by words and images— which would be entirely without action on each of the isolated individuals composing the crowd—and to be induced to commit acts contrary to his most obvious interests and best-known habits. An individual in a crowd is a grain of sand amid other grains of sand, which the wind stirs up at will. (1960, pp. 32–33)

Contrast this theme of the irrationalists to those of Durkheim. In this comment on suicide, he was reacting to much the same sort of moral breakdown perceived by the irrationalists.

> The only way to remedy this sickness is to provide social groups with enough stability to enable them to hold the individual more firmly, and to enable the individual to hold to them in turn. The individual must feel himself more solidary with a collective being which has preceded him, which will survive him, and which envelopes him at every turn. (1897, pp. 428–29)

Both Durkheim and the irrationalists posited a system of controls imposed by civilization, yet threatened by disruptive psychological influences of one sort or another. For the irrationalists the problem was seen as stemming from too much social influence, whereas for Durkheim there appeared to be too little.

Three central figures developed the irrationalists' position, all apparently under the influence of the conservative historian of the French Revolution Hyppolyte Taine. They were Gabriel Tarde (1843–1904), Scipio Sighele (1868–1913), and Gustave LeBon (1841–1931). Tarde and LeBon were French; Sighele was Italian. LeBon's work is much the best known among American social scientists, perhaps because his key work *The Crowd* was available in English as early as 1916. LeBon does not appear to have originated the distinctive ideas shared by the irrationalists, but his skills as a publicist contributed enormously to their propagation.

I call this group the irrationalists because their theory of crowd action stressed its discontinuity with the "rational" action forms supposedly characterizing "normal" social life. For them, crowds acted on deep and often unaccountable impulses little affected by critical judgment. These views of the irrationalists formed part of a much broader intellectual current in the decades just before and after the turn of the twentieth century. This view focused on the newly discovered realm of the unconscious. Besides crowd action, hypnosis, mental illness, and the lives of primitive peoples were seen as manifesting such hidden but potent forces in human behavior.

The early psychoanalytic movement clearly drew from these same inspirations. Freud commented at length on the writings of LeBon, McDougall, and other theorists of crowd action in *Group Psychology and Analysis of the Ego* (1921). Freud basically accepted LeBon's contention that crowds acted on deeper, less rational bases than normal, well-socialized individual actors. He saw crowd process as manifesting weakened super-ego function and consequent regression to primary forms of thought. These were the same thought forms he identified in neurotic symptoms, dreams, and the behavior of children and primitive people.

The irrationalists also had much in common with their Italian contemporary Pareto, another figure fascinated by the unconscious. They shared his conviction that the formal doctrines of revolutionaries were no guide to the true cause of mass action. The violent, impulsive character of the crowd was not to be understood in terms of the insurgents' objective interests, or by their doctrines, but as manifestations of shared instincts or impulses that disclose themselves under the special conditions of mass action. Unlike Pareto, the irrationalists had no well-developed theory of elites. But they joined him in believing that any long-term coherence in popular action, especially in the coordination of political violence, was only possible through elite direction.

What was the irrationalists' essential answer to Hobbes's question? The cause of civil violence, as they saw it, was the breakdown of rational control over human behavior through the spread of what one might call "crowd mentality." Implicitly, popular violence could never be a reasonable reaction to real needs or conditions. Violence was hardly the *only* symptom of crowd process, but the irrationalists apparently believed that no civil violence occurred without the influence of "the crowd."

In crowd situations, the excitation caused by the physical or psychic proximity of others triggers extraordinary and pathological mental processes. As Sighele wrote:

The effect of number is to impart to all members of a crowd a sense of their sudden, extraordinary and uncontrollable power, such that no one can judge or punish their actions; and this assurance leads them to commit acts which they [individually] condemn, feeling them unjust. (1892, p. 93)

The irrationalists typically emphasize that the change in the behavior of crowd participants is most often for the worse—that the crowd is more likely to be destructive, hateful, or unjust than generous, constructive, or noble.

Although the idea is not thoroughly developed in any of their writings, the irrationalists evidently associate the "normal" and "rational" direction of behavior in everyday life with the cumulative intellectual influence of civilization. Such critical abilities are best exercised by the isolated individual. The influence of the crowd is apt to bring on a regression, the irrationalists' description of which sounds much like Freudian accounts of primary process thinking in neurotics and children. As LeBon delicately puts it:

Among the special characteristics of crowds there are several—such as impulsiveness, irritability, incapacity to reason, the absence of judgment and the critical spirit, the exaggeration of the sentiments, and others besides—which are almost always observed in beings belonging to inferior forms of evolution—in women, savages, and children, for instance. (1960, pp. 35–36).

Yet no one is immune from the influence of the crowd. All three of these writers emphasize that even the most cultivated, civilized actors are vulnerable. Tarde quotes (1893, p. 361) with approval the Latin proverb, "The senators are good men; the Senate, a vicious beast." As for Freud, the critical spirit, and the restrained patterns of social action that flow from it, are delicate, developed tortuously over a long civilizing process, and easily upset.

What triggers crowd action? Above all, physical proximity to others. The shared experience of reacting to a single source of stimulation, or sharing a strong emotion, almost irresistibly draws the exposed individual into the crowd state. "It is a universal law of all intelligent life," Sighele writes (1892, p. 56), "that the display of an emotional state touches off the same state in he who witnesses it." Yet the crowd mentality and the processes of contagion by which it spreads need not occur only through physical proximity. The sharing of impulses and degradation of critical faculties characterizing crowd action may also occur through contagion from remote sources, through rumor, individual contacts, or the mass media. This separation of "crowd process" from "crowds" in the ordinary sense of the word takes on special importance in the work of Park and his followers.

Under the sway of the crowd mentality, almost anything can occur. People's wills are no longer their own; the ends they pursue are not their "normal" ones. In the malleable state of crowd excitement, participants are apt to follow the most whimsical suggestion or, more likely, the exhortations of the determined agitator. Thus revolutions, insurrections, and other forms of crowd violence have nothing to do with the real interests or needs of the participants. The fury of the crowd may take a direction in one instance quite contrary to that taken in the next. Through such irrational, destructive processes, the irrationalists melodramatically warn us, great civilizations break down.

Sighele and LeBon add a significant twist to their theory on this point. Those at the very bottom of the social heap, they hold, are especially vulnerable to the bacillus of social contagion. "Criminals, madmen, the offspring of madmen, alcoholics, the slime of society, deprived of all moral sense, given over to crime—these compose the greater part of the revolutionaries," wrote Sighele (1892, p. 104); LeBon echoes him at countless points. The authors do not systematically reconcile this stance with their assertion that virtually everyone is subject to crowd influence; but in many passages they imply that many less "evolved" social types, such as women and criminals, rarely rise in their mentality above the level of the crowd. Such views of the rebellious crowd have a long history in conservative thought.

Whatever one thinks of the irrationalists' theories, the political significance of these ideas hardly requires interpretation. They dismissed the notion that crowd action might be a response to authentic interests or needs. Like Pareto, the irrationalists discounted the intellectual content of revolutionary claims and doctrines altogether. Thus, the only reasonable response was forceful containment of the infection before it reached epidemic proportions.

The irrationalists considered the opportunities for mass action to be rising. Urbanization, decreased traditionalism, population movements, changing occupational structures, and, above all, the rise of mass communications made the contagion of crowd mentality ever more likely. Along with the ideas of Ortega y Gasset, the irrationalists' doctrines on these points helped to form the basis for mass society theories of civil violence and for studies of mass communication.

## Collective Behavior Theory

The irrationalists' key writings on crowd action were published between 1890 and the onset of World War I. By the 1920s, the center of gravity in this theoretical school had shifted to the New World, where it has remained. The figure ultimately most important in this intellectual contagion was Robert Park, whose writings inaugurated the long-lived "Chicago School" of collective behavior studies. But other figures initially commanded as much attention as Park with their adaptations of the irrationalists' ideas.

E. A. Ross's *Social Psychology,* for example, introduced American students and scholars to these ideas in 1908. Influenced above all by Tarde, Ross added little that was new to the irrationalists' account of the origins of militant collective action. Like them, he explained both crowd action and social movements by the communication of emotional stimuli through intensified forms of social interaction. Like them, he feared such influences as a threat to progress, a notion dear to his Midwestern heart, as Vidich and Lyman have shown (1985). "Essentially atavistic and sterile," Ross wrote, "the crowd ranks as the lowest of the forms of human association" (1908, p. 57). Again, like the irrationalists and their exemplar Hyppolyte Taine, he saw in the formulation of crowd action an irrational suggestibility. Ross seems to have made it his personal mission to administer mass intellectual vaccinations against crowd thinking to generations of dangerously impressionable undergraduates at the University of Wisconsin.

Another work exerting much influence in America during this period was William McDougall's *The Group Mind* (1920). Influenced by the irrationalists and other European sources, McDougall in effect sought to resolve the apparent contradiction between the positions of LeBon and Durkheim—that is, the view of collective influence as intellectually and socially repressive versus collective influence as constitutive of everything civilized. So far as his theory of civil violence was concerned, McDougall again differed little from the irrationalists, portraying crowd action as suggestible, inordinately emotional, and destructive.

The irrationalists' ideas also influenced other important early twentieth-century works relating to civil violence: Everett Dean Martin's *The Behavior of Crowds* (1920), L. P. Edwards' *The Natural History of Revolution* (1927), and Richard LaPiere's *Collective Behavior* (1938). But none of these writings rivaled in originality or enduring impact the work of Park.

Park had spent his sociologically formative years during the period 1899–1903 studying in Germany with such figures as Simmel and Windelband. The work of the irrationalists helped form the basis for his doctoral dissertation, *Masse und Publikum,* recently published in English as *The Crowd and the Public* (1972). On his return to the United States, Park wove his reworking of the irrationalists' ideas into the famously influential *Introduction to the Science of Sociology,* authored by him and Ernest Burgess (1921).

It may seem strange that Park took this key role in shaping theoretical perspectives or paradigms; many social scientists remember him more as founder of a research tradition than as a theorist. But as Lewis Coser has observed:

Park himself, although very much concerned with accurate social reporting and description, saw his major contribution in the development of a set of concepts that would allow systematic classification and analysis of social data. (1977, p. 357)

One might view Park's enterprise as one of conceptual "mapping" of the subject matter of sociology. The fundamental shapes and contours of the field were noted and classified, leaving it to later students and followers to chart the terrain in more detail. In this respect, his approach had much in common with that later undertaken by Parsons.

Concern with the conditions of civil violence versus co-operation and cohesion was central to Park's overall theoretical view. His famous classification of four basic social processes—competition, conflict, accommodation, and assimilation—points to what Park considered a central tension in social life, stasis and institutional continuity versus institutional breakdown and change. The social forces conducing to the former effects he bracketed as *social control;* those innovative or changeful processes arising from failure of social control he termed *collective behavior.*

Collective behavior, as Park conceived it, was a most inclusive rubric, encompassing all sorts of innovative or nonnormative social processes. These ranged from rebellions, riots, and panic-driven stampedes to the activities of social movements to shifts in public opinion and taste in dress, clothing, and speech. Park's notion of collective behavior (or *social unrest,* its preliminary form) was much the same as what the irrationalists had described as crowd behavior; Park drew freely from their ideas on these subjects and acknowledged his debts readily.

But Park broke with the irrationalists on a key point of evaluation, for he did not share their generally gloomy view of collective behavior. Even in its violent forms, Park seemed to believe, collective behavior might be an altogether positive transitional element. As he and Burgess wrote:

Social unrest may be, therefore, a symptom of health. It is only when the process of disorganization goes on so rapidly and to such an extent that the whole existing social structure is impaired, and society is, for that reason, not able to readjust itself, that unrest is to be regarded as a pathological symptom. (1921, p. 926)

It would be difficult to overestimate the influence of Park's writings on collective behavior for the treatment of civil violence and other changeful social processes in North American social science. Much of this special influence arose from the often unacknowledged theoretical content implicit in the concept itself. Because of this heavy theoretical baggage, one can identify those who have used the concept in Park's original sense as constituting a distinctive theoretical strand. Some key works in this line of succession from Park and Burgess include Herbert Blumer (1957a), Ralph Turner and Lewis Killian (1957; 1972), and Kurt and Gladys Lang (1961).

## The Concept of Collective Behavior

Park and Burgess described collective behavior as

the behavior of individuals under the influence of an impulse that is common and collective, an impulse, in other words, that is the result of social interaction. (1921, p. 865)

Note that the social behavior arising out of social interaction is contrasted with behavior directed by customary or institutional standards. Park and Burgess underline this distinction when they write:

Society . . . moves and acts under the influence of a multitude of minor impulses and tendencies which mutually interact to produce a more general tendency which then dominates all the individuals of the group. . . . The crowd acts under the influence of such a dominant tendency, unreflectively, without definite reference to a past or a future. The crowd has no past and no future. (1921, pp. 798–99)

Here we note intellectual debts both to the irrationalists and to G. H. Mead. Like the former, Park and Burgess see crowd process as discontinuous with "normal," institutional social life, the product of atypical psychic states. From Mead, the authors seem to have developed the idea that these special states arise from processes of intensified interaction. Again like the irrationalists, Park and Burgess hold that "crowd" behavior need not take place only in crowds in the conventional sense.

The followers of Park and Burgess have adopted definitions of collective behavior that correspond closely with this approach. For Blumer (1957b, p. 130) collective behavior is social behavior that "lies outside of this area of cultural prescription. . . . it is concerned with large group activity that comes into being and develops along lines that are not laid out by pre-established social definitions." For Turner and Killian (1957, p. 4) collective behavior is characterized by "spontaneous development of norms and organization of society." For Kurt and Gladys Lang (1961, p. 14), "the unorganized collective pattern . . . is a collective psychological phenomenon whose course is governed by impulse, sentiment, and the direct interaction of personalities rather than by objective structure." Thus, for all of these writers, collective behavior is that social behavior not specified in the "official rules" of social life. It is emergent, improvised, a departure from the social script. Collective violence is simply one of many forms of such departures.

All these writers would no doubt agree with Park and Burgess in identifying collective behavior as the result of failed social control. For Park and Burgess, these forces in principle include both moral constraint and the coercive influence of state power (1921, p. 786). But the moral forces seem to bulk much larger in their thinking: "legislation and the police," Park and Burgess write (1921, p. 786), "must, in the long run, have the support of public opinion."

Other writers in the collective behavior tradition follow Park and Burgess in this respect, explaining episodes of collective behavior in terms of symbolic changes among the participants rather than, say, by shifts in coercive power relations. For Park and Burgess, the weight given to moral authority in social control seems to reflect an early influence of Durkheim and Sumner.

Another important theoretical influence in the formation of collective behavior theory in America was symbolic interaction. The development of episodes of collective behavior was seen to involve exchanges of new attitudes and innovative definitions of situations. Such symbolic exchanges among participants appeared to American thinkers an essential aspect of the "contagion" of collective behavior. Sometimes they emphasize the circular or self-amplifying quality of these interactions. As Blumer writes:

One gets a clue to the nature of elementary collective behavior by recognizing the form of social interaction that has been called *circular reaction*. . . . the interstimulation assumes a circular form in which individuals reflect one another's states of feeling and in so doing intensify this feeling. It is well evidenced in the transmission of feelings and moods among people who are in a state of excitement. (1957a, p. 170)

Here again, we see the influence of G. H. Mead, as well as that of the irrationalists. The contagious process is identified as "social unrest" by Park and Burgess (1921, p. 54); "milling" by Turner and Killian (1957, p. 58; see also 1972, pp. 12–18); and the development of a "common mood" by the Langs (1961, pp. 119 20). Many case histories of collective behavior episodes represented by these authors concentrate on the special, atypical, intensified periods of interaction supposedly triggering the event.

## A Viable Concept?

Consider the concept of collective behavior itself. Does it really make sense to bracket such disparate things as changing hem lines and the storming of the Bastille within the single rubric of nonnormative behavior—and then to explain such events in terms of the weakening of normative forces?

On the surface, such a position seems incredible. The culturally standardized scenarios of such standard collective behavior events as lynchings, demonstrations, race riots, and social movements—what Tilly and his followers call "repertoires" of collective action—appear to attest directly to rich normative content. If such events and processes did not follow some socially standardized expectations, how is it that we do readily recognize their recurrent and characteristic features? Moreover, does not the moral indignation implicit in these challenges to existing social patterns itself indicate a normative reference, shared at least by the active participants and most likely by many passive supporters as well? Surely similar points could be made concerning nearly all of the social phenomena included in standard treatments of collective behavior, both violent and nonviolent.

Or perhaps not in quite every case. Some instances among those usually treated as collective behavior appear to entail a nearly complete abandonment of normative restraints. Panics—mass flights from a perceived source of danger, as on the battlefield or in a burning building—seem to approximate this extreme, as participants forget all obligations and commitments in an effort to save themselves. Recent research (Quarantelli 1977) has shown that such complete breakdowns in co-operative norms are the exception rather than the rule in situations of extreme danger. But there do seem to be at least a few instances of collective behavior that devolve into every-man-for-himself sequences.

A defender of collective behavior theory might thus see great significance in panic as an extreme case. Collective behavior, it might be held, is an ideal-typical category; panic simply represents its most extreme form, the "pure case" of collective behavior. If social processes designated as collective behavior are not absolutely free of normative guidance, they at least represent departures in the direction of this extreme.

Park and Burgess take a position consistent with this interpretation when they acknowledge different degrees of lack of normative organization in crowd phenomena.

The crowd "in being," to use a nautical term, is dominated by an impulse to achieve a purpose that is common to every member of the group. Men in a state of panic, on the other hand, although equally under the influence of the mass excitement, act not corporately but individually, each individual wildly seeking to save his own skin. . . . If the "organized crowd", "the psychological crowd", is a society "in being", the panic and the stampede is a society "in dissolution". (1921, pp. 33–34)

Indeed, for Park and Burgess this distinction forms the basis for a life-cycle account of collective behavior.

There is at first a vague general discontent and distress. Then a violent, confused, and disorderly but enthusiastic and popular movement arises. Finally the movement takes form; develops leadership, organization; formulates doctrine and dogmas. Eventually it is accepted, established, legalized. The movement dies, but the institution remains. (1921, p. 874)

So far, so good: Different forms of "collective behavior" entail different mixtures of normative and nonnormative elements. But does this formulation enable us to point to any qualities common say, to social movements, lynch mobs, revolutionary actions, Luddite machine breaking, and American race riots that mark such events as *distinctively* less norm governed than "normal" activities not considered collective behavior? Is the planning that goes on among social movement activists any less norm-oriented than that taking place in a boardroom? Was the machine breaking of the Luddites less normative than the innovation of factory owners in attempting to instate the machines? Or was the Luddites' action perhaps even more consistent with social precedent? In short, does collective behavior theory offer any really distinctive explanation of civil violence?

Turner and Killian sought to meet such problems by adopting a slightly different distinction between collective behavior and "normal" behavior.

As crowd behavior develops, there is communication of mood, imagery, and a conception of what kind of action is appropriate. These are *emergent*, not traditional. While they are related to the past experiences and previously held norms and attitudes of the participants, they constitute new products of the interaction in the particular situation. (1957, p. 83)

It would be hard to dispute this statement in its own terms. Crowd behavior undoubtedly does entail fluctuating imagery of the situation and novel notions of "appropriate" action. But then, so does "normal" life in the family, in church, in the marketplace. Even in bureaucracies, those most rule-ridden institutions, only a simpleton would assume that rules can be interpreted without regard to emergent climates of opinion and perception, within and outside the organization.

Turner and Killian further seek to distinguish collective behavior in terms of the ways in which existing norms are interpreted and selected as bases for action.

The attitudes that are expressed in the crowd are those which, while being sanctioned in the culture of the crowd members, are ordinarily limited in their expression. But situations arise in which conflicting attitudes can no longer be reconciled, and attitudes that have previously received only limited expression are more fully expressed. Thus it may be said that the basic condition out of which crowd behavior arises is one of cultural conflict, of a breakdown of normative integration; it is not a condition of *absence of culture*. (1957, p. 84).

Those statements certainly mark a shift from the position of the irrationalists, and a most reasonable one. Indeed, Turner and Killian here offer an important corrective to certain statements both by Park and Burgess and by Blumer. The latter, for example, wrote that the crowd is "spontaneous and lives in the momentary present," and "has no heritage or accumulation of tradition . . . no conventions, established expectations, or rules" (1957, p. 180). Such statements do not fit the most elementary observations of crowd events.

But although accurate, the characterization given by Turner and Killian still does not suffice to distinguish between collective and "normal" behavior. Surely nearly all social behavior entails identifying special issues or concerns as central to the "definition of the situation"; surely this always means that other possible approaches or definitions must be de-emphasized. Few if any social interactions proceed only in predetermined steps, like a computer program; most involve the actors' choosing which rules to invoke in justifying their own actions and which normative obligations to focus on in their demands of others.

## Falsifiable Implications

Are the theories of Park and the irrationalists empirically relevant? Do they point to expectations of evidence distinct from those that might derive from other theories? The core of the doctrine, it would appear, is the linkage of violent crowd action to a special crowd mentality or some other form of socially altered consciousness. If there were a falsifiable implication here, it would go as follows:

*Expect little if any collective violence without independent evidence of crowd mentality on the part of participants.*

The problem, of course, is to specify what should qualify as evidence of "crowd mentality," independent of the militant action supposed to follow from it. It will not do simply to count any crowd action as ipso facto evidence of some special group mentality, for then the argument becomes circular. We need a conceptual rule for analysis of empirical situations that distinguishes between "crowd mentality" and other forms of group process.

The use of the concept of *contagion* in the explanation of collective behavior lends itself to similar abuse. No doubt various ideas, issues, emotions, and other ingredients of collective behavior episodes can be traced through processes of contagion from origins elsewhere. But so, of course, can various ideas, issues, and emotions figuring in "normal" social behavior. One would not explain the actions of a violent group of demonstrators by reference to respiration, even though demonstrators must certainly breathe if they are to demonstrate. Similarly, contagion is not germane to the explanation of collective behavior unless and until it can be shown that the workings of contagion in these cases are somehow different from its workings elsewhere.

One such attempt is apparent in a passage from Kurt and Gladys Lang in which they attempt to identify "stresses" in social systems liable to give rise to collective behavior.

In general, such stress occurs at points in the society where there are either no clear norms or no shared expectations, that is, where organization is lacking, is ill defined, or has been disrupted. These points may be thought of metaphorically as "gaps." (1961, p. 16)

Fair enough. By showing where "normal" behavior is apt to be interrupted, one seeks to put theoretical meat on the skeleton of collective behavior concepts. But without empirical specification of what constitutes a "gap," specification independent of what is to be explained, the circularity is simply extended. We can only infer the existence of a "gap" retrospectively—not a logically satisfactory situation.

As I argue later, these difficulties in specifying the special character of "crowd action" or "collective behavior," or the situations likely to produce it, have always plagued this doctrine. But these are not the only falsifiable implications that the theory yields. Others include the following:

*Expect* collective decision-making processes *leading to collective violence to be especially marked by suggestibility and openness to innovation.*

*Expect the* ends *of violent collective action to be unpredictable and discontinuous in relation to the participants' other, "normal" interests and goals.*

*Expect* participants *in violent collective action to be disproportionately deviant, isolated, low in social status, or otherwise poorly integrated into solidary social relations.*

The empirical states highlighted here are no doubt more accessible to such investigation than "crowd mentality" or "strains" leading to collective behavior. With a bit of editing and interpretation, these expectations could readily form bases for empirical inquiry. The *ends* of crowd action, for example, are often noteworthy at the time; hence, they may be recorded and available for future study even if no researcher is on hand for the original events. Assertions that the actions of crowds are discontinuous with participants' "normal" lives would be falsifiable in light of such data. Here inferences are hardly simple. The very existence of a concerted group means that the participants have a degree of power that they are apt not to have on their own. If powerless people seem to adopt new interests when acting collectively, it may be simply because they for once have the chance to do something about interests they felt all along. Still, the matter is highly researchable.

Similarly, the social identities of *participants* in collective behavior are susceptible to study, though not so readily as their actions. Are the participants in crowd violence disproportionately drawn from the "dregs" of society? Are the associations between crowd participation and crime, deviance, and mental deficiency empirically demonstrable? Do social movements attract disproportionately those without stable social identification? All these questions point directly to possibilities for empirical investigation.

Yet it is striking how slow research was to appear that might confront these expectations with potentially falsifying evidence. Most of the studies launched by members of Park's theoretical tradition served more to illustrate key concepts than to pass judgment on these expectations. One of the few empirical studies that actually appeared to influence the development of the theory, the historian Crane Brinton's famous *Anatomy of Revolution* (1938), was not carried out from Park's theoretical viewpoint at all.

Brinton argued that four great historical examples of revolution—the English, American, French, and Russian—showed striking parallels in terms of their evolution and eventual consequences. Of special interest to collective behavior theorists was Brinton's identification of growing tension throughout social systems as revolutionary tendencies grew, followed by gradual reequilibration as a new institutional order established itself. Here, Park's followers felt, was vindication of ideas like *intensified interaction* as prelude to collective violence and eventual institution of collective behavior impulses.

Thus, we see Brinton's influence in Rex Hopper's widely cited study "The Revolutionary Process: A Frame of Reference for the Study of Revolutionary Movements" (1950). Brinton presents what one might call a composite portrait of the development of revolutions. The "natural history" or life-cycle sequence of revolution that he presents clearly owes much to collective behavior theory: There is a "Preliminary Stage of Mass (Individual) Excitement, the Popular Stage of Crowd (Collective) Excitement and Unrest, the Formal Stage of Formation of Issues and Formation of Publics, and the Institutional Stage of Legalization and Social Organization." But Hopper makes no attempt to evaluate the fit of this scheme with any systematically gathered data on actual revolutions.

By contrast, consider Guy E. Swanson's "A Preliminary Laboratory Study of the Acting Crowd" (1953). Deriving his concepts and concerns directly from collective behavior theory, Swanson set out to create an analogue of the crowd situation in his laboratory. He created twelve three-member groups of undergraduate subjects and gave each group a novel task to perform, one that required improvisation and co-operation. The experimental group had its behavior during the tasks monitored at once; the control group was given an opportunity to practice the task for ten minutes before the trial, which was measured and recorded. Swanson's rationale was that the "no practice" groups more closely approximated the interactions of what collective behavior theorists term "the acting crowd."

Swanson reported finding that the experimental group was less skeptical (more suggestible, in his interpretation) about the suggestions and ideas of their coplayers; communicated more frequently among themselves; directed more communications to their groups as a whole, as distinct from individual others; showed greater stability of certain forms of role behavior; expressed fewer "self-oriented needs" than the control group; and were less satisfied with their coplayers than members of the control group.

Swanson interprets these results as confirming certain of the special characteristics attributed by collective behavior theorists to crowds. In most cases it appears that there is a simpler explanation: The experimental group was simply showing the effects of inacquaintance with the task and with each other. Indeed, the experimental situation lacked some of the key characteristics of crowd situations. The participants undertook a task prepared for them, rather than ends arising out of their own internal process. The distance separating the participants in Swanson's laboratory and the suggestible, volatile crowd participants evoked by LeBon appears considerable.

One of the few other contributions dealing directly with collective behavior theory on the formulation of crowd action comes from Richard Berk (1974a). A critic of the collective behavior tradition, Berk reported field observations of a crowd engaged in antiwar demonstrations on a university campus. The crowd contained members of various political tendencies, each of which naturally attempted to influence crowd symbolism and actions in its preferred direction. Berk observes that the actions of these groups appeared entirely "rational"—that is, calculated to be effective in winning the maximum support. He considers this finding as tending to cast doubt on collective behavior theory.

Of course, many other studies also cite the "rationality" of crowd action, without attending as much as Berk to the inner details of any single scenario. One wonders whether supporters of collective behavior thinking would regard their findings as telling. Perhaps a Blumer or Swanson would find—in the event reported by Berk, for example—unnoted evidence of failed rationality or of the emergence of new norms. The literature on these subjects has simply not fostered a sufficiently intense exchange to force proponents and critics of collective behavior theory to specify what data, precisely, they would consider sufficient to weigh for and against their positions.

Another empirical study in the collective behavior tradition is "Zoot Suiters and Mexicans: Symbols in Crowd Behavior," by Ralph Turner and J. Servace. The authors surveyed references to Mexicans in the *Los Angeles Times* during the period leading up to that city's anti-Mexican riots in 1943; these events were called "zoot suit riots" at the time. Turner found that, as the riots approached, newspaper references to "zoot suiters" rose, whereas other references to Mexicans bearing less emotional and negative connotations declined. The zoot suit had become a symbol or code expression for the "bad" Mexican, even though it appeared that few of the Mexican youths involved in the riots actually wore the notorious outfit.

Turner and Servace give their central hypothesis as follows: "overt hostile crowd behavior is usually preceded by a period in which the key symbol is stripped of its favorable connotations until it comes to evoke unambiguously unfavorable feelings" (1956, p. 12, italicized in original). Certainly such symbolic revision appears to have occurred in this instance. Exploring other outbreaks of collective violence for similar patterns would be interesting, though that possibility obviously exists only in those events that have a long "gestation" before the outbreak. As in the Swanson study, the findings here do not appear to provide special support for any assertions peculiar to collective behavior theory. Still, demonstrating that such symbolic processes may play a role in the origins of violent episodes is worthwhile. Other theories of civil violence simply have much less to say about such matters than does the collective behavior tradition.

Another distinctive and potentially falsifiable element in this theoretical tradition is its emphasis on *contagion* coupled with *irrational thinking and action* in collective or crowd behavior. Here we have a number of empirical studies.

One of the most noted of these, Hadley Cantril's *The Invasion from Mars* (1940), reported reactions to Orson Welles's famous 1938 radio drama depicting the invasion of earth from outer space. This broadcast was so persuasive that many listeners took it for a news report and spent hours anticipating their imminent doom. The fact that the broadcast could easily have been checked with more reliable sources of information, such as local newspapers, was quite lost on the approximately twenty-eight percent (1940, p. 58) who took the broadcast as news. Cantril's subsequent survey analysis showed that better-educated listeners were somewhat less liable to accept the broadcast as authentic; there was some evidence suggesting that worry about world conflicts during this pre–World War II period may have enhanced the contagion. Cantril makes no mention of the theorists discussed in this chapter, but his study clearly demonstrates the input of an emotional milieu on perception and reasoning.

Another well-known study, D. M. Johnson's "The 'Phantom Anesthesist' of Mattoon: A Field Study of Mass Hysteria" (1945), reports a rash of attempted "gassings" of residents of this small city in Illinois during September 1944. These events at first received considerable and serious attention by local authorities and the press. Although there evidently was no intruder pumping gas into the homes of Mattoon residents, there were many reported sightings of the furtive figure. A number of residents, all women, experienced physical symptoms of gas inhalation. Public credulity in the attacks dropped off abruptly after a few weeks, and with it the reported gassings.

Another study of contagion, "Diffusion and Collective Belief in a Collective Delusion" by Nahum Medalia and Otto N. Larsen (1958), differs from the previous two studies by citing collective behavior theorists. Here the object of contagion was the observation of pits in the windshields of Seattle automobiles during the Spring of 1954. These reports also gained credence through extensive coverage in the press, which peaked and then fell off in a matter of about four weeks. Competent analysis of the windshield pitting made it clear that what was being observed was nothing unusual, and the newspaper reports ceased. The authors note, however, that belief in the phenomenon seems to have continued among the Seattle public, even after the press had lost interest.

The most thorough and illuminating of sociological studies of contagion is *The June Bug*, by Alan Kerckhoff and Kurt Back (1968). In this study of an epidemic of fainting and other physical symptoms among workers in a Southern textile factory, the influence of collective behavior theory is again clear. The outbreak affected at least sixty-two workers, all but three women, out of a workforce of nearly one thousand. These sixty-two were seriously enough ill that they sought medical attention or stopped work; others appeared to have experienced symptoms without showing outward signs. The events were attributed to bites from a mysterious insect but were in fact psychogenic. Kerckhoff and Back conducted a detailed survey analysis in an effort to account for the pattern of who was affected. They found that workers experiencing certain empirically specifiable forms of strain in their work and domestic roles were disproportionately likely to experience the contagion. Social networks also played a pattern in the contagion; in fact, either unusually high levels of strain *or* embeddedness in networks where others experienced the contagion raised the likelihood of a worker's being affected.

These studies of contagion warrant our attention because they show limited support for certain of the original contentions of the irrationalists.

In some instances, the effects of milieu do alter people's reality testing, enabling them to turn fantasy into fact and indeed even into physical sensations. Contagion is not an unreasonable term for the transmission processes at work here, and the forms of contagion involved are indeed different from the "normal" spread of social ideas and attitudes. Proximity is not necessary for such effects. It does not appear that events of this kind are common—for example, in comparison with such forms of collective behavior as social movements or riotous demonstrations; nor has evidence been reported that such states of altered consciousness are ever involved in collective violence. But they do occur.

## Mass Society Theory

In discussion of theories descended from the irrationalists, *time perspective* has received insufficient attention. The original inspiration of Tarde, LeBon, and Sighele concerned direct and immediate exchanges of social stimuli among coparticipants in crowds. Thus, they focused on cause-effect sequences lasting no longer than the intense interactions alleged to produce violence and other typical forms of crowd action. But the irrationalists soon expanded their view to include observations on more abiding social structural conditions held productive of crowd stimuli, such as mass communications, social dislocation, and the decline of traditional social forms more generally. The two theoretical elements have not always coexisted gracefully with one another and, in the years since the irrationalists, have often developed under separate intellectual auspices.

The more strictly structural view of the production of militant social movements became mass society theory. This view took its inspiration from the irrationalists, Ortega y Gasset, and other antidemocratic turn-of-the-century figures and held enormous influence until the 1960s. According to it, irrational social movements incubated the bacillus of crowd action and preserve and extend its effects over time. For left-leaning as well as for conservative analysts, Hitler and Stalin appeared to fulfill the baleful prophecies of Sighele and LeBon concerning the malleability of rootless publics under bombardment from sophisticated mass propaganda. George Orwell, C. Wright Mills, Emil Lederer, and Hanna Arendt, among many others, partook of this view. To be sure, they differed in matters of detail; but all shared the perception that violent social movements sprang disproportionately from the ranks of the socially dislocated. Such persons, it was held, were easy prey for manipulation by distant and cynical elites.

This long and influential tradition of political analysis received quintessential expression in William Kornhauser's *Politics of Mass Society* (1959).

This work sets down the implications of mass society theory for the origins of civil violence in their clearest and most strictly sociological form.

For Kornhauser, "mass" political behavior is participation in movements and activities that seek sweeping and extreme goals and operate outside the established channels of institutional politics. People are vulnerable to being drawn into such movements to the extent that they lack intermediate ties to large social institutions. "Within all strata," Kornhauser writes, "people divorced from community, occupation and association are first and foremost among the supporters of extremism" (1959, p. 73). Or, elsewhere: "People are available for mass behavior when they lack attachments to proximate objects. When people are divorced from their community or work, they are free to reunite in new ways" (1959, p. 60). For Kornhauser, the "good" society is plainly the society where all political strivings are expressed through the medium of established institutions, and in modest, incremental steps.

Civil violence results when people inadequately embedded in institutionalized political life seek political ends directly. As Kornhauser writes,

Violence in word and deed is the hallmark of the mass movement uncommitted to institutional means. Mass behavior, then, involves direct, activist modes of response to remote symbols. (1959, p. 46)

Thus, we have an authentic response to Hobbes's original problem: In modern, complex societies, "mass" politics is the cause of civil violence, and "normal" or institutionalized politics safeguards stable civil sovereignty.

In one sense, this last sentence is virtually unfalsifiable. Because the modern state seeks to monopolize the exercise of large-scale coercion, any popular violence must of necessity be the work of those "uncommitted to institutional means."

A more important element of Kornhauser's theory, however, is falsifiable—the notion that "mass" political activities and hence civil violence are disproportionately the work of the socially isolated. This idea, which receives much emphasis in Kornhauser's work, derives directly from the tradition of the irrationalists. But the trouble with this falsifiable implication is that it is almost certainly false. As Marx and Wood point out in their thorough commentary (1975, p. 392), "Recent literature has generally shown . . . that membership in secondary or even primary groups can *facilitate* recruitment to political movements that are radical or reformist in nature." In addition to the six studies they cite, other forceful evidence can be found in Lees and Tilly (1975), Logan (1978), Pinard (1975), and many other studies. Indeed, in a field of inquiry where theoretical ideas often come and go without confronting potentially falsifying evidence, it is hard to think of another influential idea that has received such wide refutation. Somewhere there may be violent social movements or crowd actions that attract social isolates. But in those movements studied systematically, participants in what Kornhauser might call "extremist" activity appear at least as well connected with institutions of neighborhood, community, and polity as nonparticipants.

Kornhauser's noted book, published in 1959, seems to have been both the definitive synthesis of mass society thinking and, ironically, the last of its theoretical line. The disdainful view of militant activism conveyed in the work became so unappealing to most social scientists by the 1960s that it simply attracted no more defenders.

If one were to trace any later articulation of mass society thinking as related to civil violence, it might be in Samuel P. Huntington's *Political Order in Changing Societies* (1968). To be sure, Huntington's reasoning there gives no indication of being especially influenced by Kornhauser or the irrationalists—at least, no more than by the great variety of other sources cited in this wide-ranging work. But Huntington does share with mass society theorists the key idea that militant collective action results from a combination of political passions and weak or absent institutional channels that might afford their "orderly" expression.

Like many a conservative theorist, Huntington holds that such restraining political institutions are slow to grow. That is why the politics of developing countries are so violent—because of the scarcity of institutions that might provide more orderly, less destructive outlets for newly released political energies. Effective institutions, he tells us, have the following characteristics:

They are *adaptable* (rather than rigid): "The more challenges that have arisen in its environment and the greater its age, the more adaptable [an organization] is" (p. 13).

They are *complex* (rather than simple): "A political system with several different political institutions . . . is much more likely to adapt. The needs of one age may be met by one set of institutions; the needs of the next by a different set" (p. 19).

They are *autonomous* (rather than subordinate): "A political organization that is the instrument of a social group—family, clan, class—lacks autonomy and institutionalization" (p. 20).

They are *coherent* (rather than disunited): "An effective organization requires, at a minimum, substantial consensus on the functional boundaries of the group and on the procedures for resolving disputes which come up within those boundaries" (p. 22).

These statements obviously do more than just imply a theory of civil violence. Presumably we should expect polities made up of institutions evincing adaptability, complexity, autonomy, and coherence to be relatively peaceful, whereas others should be more subject to collective violence.

But these variables obviously require much more exact specification, if the argument is to escape circularity. "A highly developed political system has procedures to minimize, if not eliminate, the role of violence in the system," Huntington tells us (p. 21). But if adaptability, complexity, autonomy, and coherence—in short, those things that mark political systems as "highly developed"—are taken ipso facto as conditions that could never be associated with militant action, then the theory becomes unfalsifiable and uninteresting.

One does wonder about groups like the Palestine Liberation Organization and the Irish Republican Army. They seem to embody at least a measure of Huntington's four institutional qualities, yet still to participate in a good deal of violent action. Perhaps Huntington would insist that they are just not adaptable, or coherent, or complex, or autonomous *enough*. But then the question of how to judge the relative measure of these crucial qualities without allowing judgments to be influenced by what the theory seeks to predict would become paramount. As Zimmermann's thorough and thoughtful study shows (1983, pp. 109–18), attempts at empirical investigation of Huntington's assertions have not yielded great support for them.

## The Decline of Collective Behavior Theory

"Collective behavior is one of the most unworked of our research areas," wrote Anselm Strauss (1947, p. 352) in a dismayed review of the literature more than twenty-five years after Park and Burgess published their famous *Introduction*. Some ten years later Herbert Blumer (1957b, p. 127) drew much the same conclusion: "The field of collective behavior has not been charted effectively." About the same time, William A. Westley (1957, p. 33) noted the "almost complete absence of empirical studies and . . . the consequent highly speculative nature of the major theories" in the field. In 1961, Kurt and Gladys Lang wrote (p. 545), "professional sociologists . . . have never regarded the empirical investigation of the collective dynamics of mass society as either especially rich or promising in results." Finally, in an article published in 1972, Richard Berk, a critic of collective behavior theory, cast doubt on the accuracy of traditional collective behavior depictions of crowd process (1972b). He suggested that such inaccuracies may have perpetuated themselves through lack of systematic confrontation with actual data on crowds.

I see no reason to disagree with any of these views. The longevity of

collective behavior thinking in the mode initiated by Park was extraordinary. For four decades, along with mass society theory, it was virtually the
only theoretical lens available to North American social scientists for
viewing changeful and conflict-ridden social processes. Yet it seems to
have owed much of its dominance to the theoretical and research vacuum
in which it persisted. As I have tried to show, the limited empirical research undertaken in direct response to the Park tradition unearthed few
results not equally compatible with other theoretical views. Later chapters of this book will examine more deeply this apparently loose fit between theories and research associated with them.

   By the mid-1960s, the dominance of collective behavior thinking was
decidedly on the wane. Works from altogether different theoretical traditions—for example, Smelser (1962), Rude (1959), Tilly (1963), and Gurr
and Rutenberg (1967)—were demanding and receiving much scholarly attention. Often these theoretical directions brought with them vigorous
new research programs. In addition to this sudden proliferation of alternatives, a number of critics began attacking newly noticed weaknesses in
the theory. Most often these critics, including Couch (1968), Berk (1972b),
Quarantelli (1970), and Gamson and McEvoy (1972), found fault with the
picture of riotous or rebellious behavior as "abnormal" or "disorganized."
Instead, analysts were beginning to see in crowd action evidence of purposeful response to collective interests and continuity with "normal" social life.

   Along with the theoretical reexamination of collective behavior came
objections in more strictly political terms, direct attacks on the allegedly
conservative bias of the theory. Perhaps the best example is Currie and
Skolnick (1972). Though their ultimate target is Neil Smelser, Currie and
Skolnick begin by taking aim at the tradition of the irrationalists. And they
contend that the antidemocratic elements of this tradition remain in the
thinking of Park and his followers.

Perhaps the most fundamental of these biases is the implication that collective behavior is in some sense "irrational" behavior. This bias may be traced in LeBon's
distaste for the mystical loss of individuality and civilized behavior in the "crowd",
and reaffirmed in modern "riot control" manuals, as well as most contemporary
social-scientific approaches. In line with the emphasis on irrationality, collective
behavior has usually been seen as destructive and, in most treatments, inappropriate and distasteful. (1972, p. 61)

Currie and Skolnick were hardly alone among analysts of social contention
in voicing these sentiments.

   Clearly Currie and Skolnick's charges as applied to the irrationalists are
accurate. In their application to Park and his American followers, how-

ever, the case is not so clear. True, Park and Burgess and Blumer did depict crowd action as less organized and more impulse-governed than other action. But as other, previously quoted statements indicate, they viewed collective behavior as a potentially progressive process by which new and more satisfactory social forms developed. If Park and his followers regarded collective behavior "disorganized," they also considered a measure of disorganization sometimes a positive thing.

These attacks brought some articulate responses. In an important article, Gary Marx (1972) raised some penetrating questions on the newly discovered "purposefulness" of crowd action. He notes that crowds and riots seem to vary in the extent to which they entail "a critique of the social order and the belief that violence will help bring about needed social changes" (p. 50). Among his targets are certain positions of Charles Tilly and his followers considered in Chapter Six.

Although Marx persuasively argues that some critics have gone too far, he seems to agree that some basic conceptual distinctions from the Park tradition need revising. Indeed, I believe he is pointing to what proves to be a central issue in the viability of collective behavior theory, the principle of demarcation between collective behavior and other social processes. Other commentators had already begun to note the difficulties in specifying such a demarcation (Janowitz 1964, p. 115). Soon concern over this question was to become intense.

The first sensitivity to the importance of this question comes in Turner and Killian (1957), where they picture collective behavior as characterized by "emergent norms" rather than "the absence of culture." Similar reservations about the distinctiveness of the category comes in statements by Lang and Lang (1968, p. 557; 1970, pp. 109–10). Indeed, in a survey article, Turner made an even more radical break.

Careful examination of a wide range of collective behavior reveals few instances that are not specifically justified by their participants on the basis of some extant social norm and which cannot be shown to have some continuity with tradition. (1964, p. 383)

And he adds, a bit later,

It is altogether possible that . . . no special set of principles is necessary to deal with the subject matter. (p. 384)

In the second edition of their *Collective Behavior*, however, Turner and Killian seem to return to a more conventional position, describing their subject as behavior "governed by norms that are not envisaged in the larger society and that may even modify or oppose these broader norms" (1972, p. 5).

Concern over the distinction between collective behavior and the rest of social life seemed to intensify during the 1970s. Building on Turner and Killian's "emergent norm" idea, Weller and Quarantelli (1973) sought to characterize the subject in terms of the novelty both of the norms and the social structures involved. They offered a map of the conceptual possibilities (1973, p. 676), presented here as Figure 1. The authors define collective behavior as that located in the northwest, southwest, and southeast cells of the diagram, plus a fourth type that "involves emergence in neither dimension, but occurs when previously dissociated systems of norms and relationships are integrated with each other into a collectivity" (pp. 676–77).

Weller and Quarantelli consider it a key virtue of their approach that it offers a "positive" definition of collective behavior, rather than one couched in terms of the absence of norms. Gary Marx makes a similar effort at a new principle of demarcation (1980, p. 270), suggesting that collective behavior be defined as:

a. behavior not specifically defined in the traditional culture such as much fad behavior or innovative behavior in disasters . . .
b. behavior defined in the culture but which is prohibited . . .
c. behavior directed toward institutionalizing alternative forms of action.

These authors, like others concerned with establishing a more reasonable delineation between collective behavior and other social behavior, point out that their new categorizations include certain things not previously regarded as collective behavior. In developing these conceptual boundaries, they seek to avoid embarrassment inherent in drawing extreme contrasts between "collective" and "normal" behavior. However, the new views seem to contain so much of what otherwise would be considered "normal" social life that the revised concept begins to lose interest for us. Some element of innovation, after all, is ubiquitous in social life. As social theorists have recently been insisting (see Giddens 1979, especially his chap. 2), everyday life always involves recreation of social rules and conventions. Notwithstanding the observations of a few social scientists, social life rarely if ever consists simply of acting out some preordained "social script." Elements of novelty, improvisation, opposition, and normative redefinition appear as essential social processes—as much in the family, in the church, or in the boardroom as in the rioting crowd. Any conceptual net designed to catch the traditional subject matter of collective behavior is thus apt to bring in as well an enormous catch of the most variegated social processes, including above all the most ordinary.

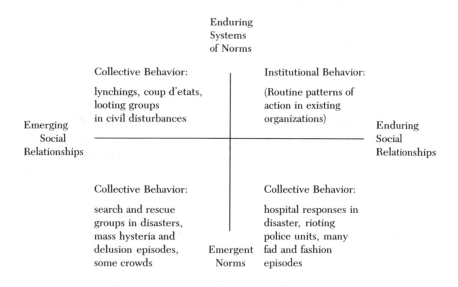

Figure 1.

There are two questions before us. First, is there any reasonable conceptual standard to distinguish collective behavior from the rest of social life? Second, and more central to the concerns of this book, can the theory of collective behavior so defined yield any viable explanation of the causes of civil violence?

These two questions are closely linked. Distinguishing the irrationalists' position from the very beginning was the idea that the violence of crowds was attributable to distinctive, identifiable, social and psychological states. They portrayed the differences between these abnormal states and others in crude, black-and-white terms. Since Park, their followers have sought to back away from this extreme contrast, while still including the innovative and rebellious processes of the crowd in some sort of distinctive category. But the harder the search is pressed, the more difficult it becomes to find a satisfactory principle of demarcation.

Surely there is something ironic about this concern with saving the *concept* of collective behavior. The term was originally put forward to designate a category of phenomena whose conceptual unity was considered apparent. Now that unity appears more obscure, and analysts resort to increasingly tortuous rules to propound a conceptual rule that will include the changeful social processes of original interest. But in the newly

suggested categories, the original foci of interest—riots, social movements, crowd activities, and so forth—represent only a small part, along
with many more "ordinary" social processes.


## Conclusions

In 1981, the Nobel Prize for literature was awarded to Elias Canetti, the
first Nobel laureate widely identified in the press as a sociologist. North
American sociologists greeted the award with an outpouring of apathy. In
1962, Canetti had published *Crowds and Power,* a study of the experience of group membership deriving much from the tradition of the irrationalists. For Canetti, the notions of LeBon and his contemporaries provide a guiding metaphor for exploring individual and group identity. His
inquiries are, if possible, even less oriented to confrontation with potentially falsifying evidence than those of the irrationalists themselves.

But the slack response of North American sociologists to Canetti's work
and to its ultimate recognition seems not to have stemmed from its scarcity of empirical implications. Canetti was simply a proponent of theoretical views that had abruptly lost their central role in the study of militant
social action. By the 1960s, collective behavior thinking, and a fortiori the
notions of the irrationalists and mass society theorists, had lost their attraction as a lens for viewing civil violence.

Part of the reason for this shift clearly involved matters of fact and evidence. Views of crowd action as purposeless and of participants in such
action as socially disconnected simply did not accord well with accounts
that were swelling the empirical literatures on these subjects.

But these now-unconvincing views of the irrationalists and mass society theorists did not characterize the analytic tradition derived from
Park. Perhaps the key insight of this tradition was that special emotional
or interactional states played a distinctive role in the generation of collective violence and other crowd action. For analysts in this line, the problem was to specify those qualities of interaction and communication that
ultimately led to violence.

By contrast, the theoretical views that eclipsed collective behavior
thinking during the 1960s (discussed in Chapters Six and Seven) invoked a
different *time perspective.* For these political and psychological theories,
the origins of civil violence lay well before the interactions that actually
framed the violent episodes. Implicitly if not overtly, analysts in these insurgent traditions treated interactional contingencies as epiphenomenal
to the "real" causes of civil violence, which they saw as abiding social conditions that inclined people to social contention in the first place.

In one respect these critics clearly had a point. Collective behavior theorists had never succeeded in specifying what kinds of special interactions should be expected to lead disproportionately to militant outcomes. For Park and his followers, it was a matter of faith that the investigator, by becoming immersed in the flux of events leading to a dramatic crowd episode, could apprehend something special about the interaction without which the event would not have occurred, or would have unfolded in a significantly different fashion. Unfortunately, the nature of that "something" has never been specified in empirically relevant theoretical terms.

But the fact that no one has made this specification hardly warrants the conclusion that none is there to be made. On the contrary, elementary observation of contentious collective episodes suggests that interaction may well help determine whether particular events will turn in militant directions. In a careful study of strikes in a large industrial plant, for example, three British researchers (Batstone, Boraston, and Frenkel 1978) show how such things as a casual conversation between shop stewards, or the timing of a crucial meeting, may make the difference between a strike and no strike.

Similarly, there can be little doubt that the spread of emotional stimuli may have causal weight in its own right in sparking violent action. The violent episodes that followed news of the assassination of Dr. Martin Luther King in 1968 are simply the most dramatic recent examples from American life. Clearly the communication of highly charged emotions figured in the origin of these events. To be sure, these attitudes would not have existed apart from enduring contention between blacks and whites. But that contention would not have led to these particular losses of life and property without the spur of a single highly charged event.

---

Proponents of the theories that displaced collective behavior and mass society thinking in the 1960s have particularly stressed the assumption of *rationality* in their positions. By contrast, the theories discussed in this chapter are assumed to bracket contentious social action as irrational.

In fact, this contrast is oversimplified. It is true that the irrationalists and mass society theorists wrongly characterized the ends of militant collective action as radically estranged from participants' everyday, "normal" interests. But in their appreciation of this insight, analysts have overlooked a valuable insight from the collective behavior tradition: that the *experience* of participation in collective events may change crucial purposes and perceptions on the part of participants.

As I noted in Chapter Two, the assumption of rational calculation is a meaningful analytic tool where the interests fueling action are relatively enduring. But where interests grow or are redefined through the *experi-*

*ence* of group contention, the effects of calculation become hard to trace. If the nature of the good to which action is oriented is constantly changing, it is hard to be sure what action may result from participants' calculations. It would be rash indeed to assume that such processes of redefinition, in which propensities for action change in the course of social experience, play no role in social contentions leading to violence.

Instead of locating the origins of militant action in enduring structural or attitudinal conditions long prevailing among participants, theories in the tradition of Park seek those origins in the flux of events immediately leading to the violent outbreak. Yet the two approaches need not be exclusive, and sophisticated analysts ought to be able to find ways of using them complementarily, as Klandermans (1984) has done. Perhaps this view has suffered from guilt by association; perhaps rejection of the political implications of some ideas of the irrationalists and mass society theorists has led to unwillingness even to consider the role of group process in shaping violent contention. But whatever the cause, the result is too categorical. Violent episodes undoubtedly are contingent on interaction and shared emotion. We simply have been unable to specify the nature of these contingencies in the form of broadly applicable, falsifiable statements.

*Chapter Four*

# Durkheim, Weber, Simmel, and Coser

This short chapter, like the last, considers the transmission of theoretical ideas on civil violence from Europe to North America.

Durkheim and Weber could hardly be more central to the European heritage of American sociology. Neither put forth an explicit theory of civil violence. Both, however, had important things to say about the nature of authority, the bases of conformity and obedience, and the role of social movements and other dissident actions in social life. Conscientiously considered, their positions on these subjects yield implications for the concerns of this book.

Simmel's case is quite different. His ideas on conflict in general point directly to empirically relevant statements on civil violence. And he was blessed with an articulate exponent in Lewis Coser, whose *Functions of Social Conflict* (1956) brought his ideas into the mainstream of American sociological thought.

## Durkheim

Durkheim's lifelong intellectual mission can be encapsulated with an economy possible for few thinkers of his stature: He sought to establish the indispensability of strictly social influences in ordering individual experience and regulating individual strivings, and to chart the forms taken by these social influences. This was both an intellectual and a practical project for Durkheim. Sociologically, Durkheim was determined to demonstrate that pursuit of individual appetites, unchecked by strictly social influences, was bound to prove disastrous both for the individual and for the social system. Preeminent among life-giving social influences was the moral authority of society as a whole. Concomitant of Durkheim's intellectual project was his determination to place the need for moral reorganiza-

tion on the public agenda of France and the other industrial societies of
his time.

The importance of society as a forceful moral unity transcending the
individual is central to virtually all Durkheim's works. This theme shapes
and suffuses his discussions of sociological methodology, suicide rates,
educational policy, utopian socialism, religious change, and various other
subjects. Although he rarely touched directly on collective violence, his
analyses of the political and social strains in advanced societies put forward in *The Division of Labor in Society* are more than just suggestive of
a theory of the subject.

Durkheim's central argument in that work is perhaps the most widely
known of any in the history of the discipline. The long evolution of human
societies, he argued, entailed increasing specialization of social roles,
along with growth in the sheer size of populations. The moral unity possible in smaller, earlier social systems was jeopardized as members of
complex, modern systems lost the experience of intense interaction with
and dependence on their fellows. Only informed planning could restore
the conditions necessary for moral unity. Yet such unity, so urgently required (and so conspicuously lacking) in advanced societies, should not be
produced forcibly.

We cannot adjust these functions to one another and make them concur harmo-
niously if they do not concur of themselves. . . . What gives unity to organized
societies, however, as to all organisms, is the spontaneous consensus of parts.
Such is the internal solidarity which not only is as indispensable as the regulative
action of higher centres, but which also is their necessary condition. (1960 [1893],
p. 360)

Durkheim regarded the grave, and indeed violent, social conflicts associated in France and elsewhere with class struggle as symptoms of this
broad moral failing. He takes this position explicitly at various points,
both in *The Division of Labor* and elsewhere. Struggles over the distribution of social wealth and advantage, either between workers and capital
or between rival political forces, reflected the lack of a superior authority
to prescribe duties and protect the rights of the parties. In one of his lec-
tures on moral education, for example, Durkheim gives his standard diag-
nosis of the modern era as characterized by "revolutionary and critical"
tendencies resulting from relaxation of traditional authority.

This is the origin of the anarchic aspirations which, conscious or not, manifest
themselves today, not only in the sect of that name, but among those diverse doctrines which, though opposed on other points, share a common estrangement
from any form of regulation. (1938, p. 62)

For Durkheim, as for Hobbes, violence was simply an ultimate symptom of the failure of regulative processes constitutive of society itself. The key difference between the two doctrines, of course, lay in the nature of the central source of restraint—essentially moral for Durkheim, essentially coercive for Hobbes.

Is there a falsifiable empirical expectation implicit in this view? If so, it might be as follows:

*Expect levels of violent collective conflict to vary inversely with the intensity of ordinary citizens' attachments to moral principles underlying major institutions.*

The obvious question is, how do we assess such master levels of moral solidarity? Durkheim tells us nothing in this connection as regards political violence. But perhaps we would not stretch a point by taking rates of such things as suicide, participation in civic ceremonies, or compliance with requirements of taxation and other patriotic duties as indices of the overall strength of public morality.

———

Durkheim's identification of moral weakness as responsible for social strife in modern societies has recently come into question (Abercrombie, Hill, and Turner 1980). These authors hold that Durkheim's real explanation for cohesion in advanced industrial societies lies in the division of labor, rather than in states of moral solidarity. The extreme dependence of different individuals and sectors of society on one another, as they see it, is the force that ensures cohesion. "Durkheim explains the coherence of modern society not in terms of common values," they write, "but by reference to the interdependence of members of a society. The structure of social relations compels people to depend on one another, thereby promoting a solid form of integration" (p. 168).

This statement is misleading, though the confusion stems partly from some labored qualities of Durkheim's own arguments. Durkheim does hold, in *The Division of Labor,* that solidarity based on appreciation of differences represents the "normal" moral state of advanced, highly specialized societies. What marks Durkheim's argument as tendentious is the fact that these "normal" conditions appear the more conspicuous by their absence, the more highly differentiated the social system. The advanced division of labor in these settings was an accomplished fact; missing was the moral force, indispensable for setting the terms of co-operative social relations, that was supposed to accompany it. Advanced division of labor might be one necessary condition for organic solidarity in modern social systems; but it could hardly have been the condition whose absence was blocking co-operative, harmonious relations in Durkheim's time. Thus the remarks in the concluding paragraphs of *The Division of Labor:*

But if the division of labor produces solidarity, it is not only because it makes each individual an *exchangist,* as the economists say; it is because it creates among men an entire system of rights and duties which link them together in a durable way. . . . If economists have believed that it would bring forth an abiding solidarity, in some manner of its own making, and if, accordingly, they have held that human societies could and would resolve themselves into purely economic associations, that is because they believe that it affected only individual, temporary interests. (1938, pp. 406–7)

Durkheim, of course, advocated revival of the corporation as a means of combating the host of disintegrative conditions including violent strife. Such a measure would have involved change in social structure. Yet these arguments, too, show that moral solidarity represented the key missing ingredient for the containment of such strife.

The term *corporation* is no doubt best left untranslated, as any English counterpart is apt to be misleading. The corporations of the Middle Ages were guilds, but the modern institutions whose creation Durkheim sought clearly had to be much different. Durkheim had in mind some comprehensive form of occupational association that would encompass all members of each occupation or profession throughout the nation. In ways never adequately explained, such bodies were to participate in setting the terms of service for their members, dealing directly with central planners of the state. The solidarities associated with these arrangements were supposed to preclude the strife and anarchy associated with economic life at the turn of the twentieth century. The plan is remarkably utopian, especially for a figure of such rigorously positivist views as Durkheim. Yet the importance Durkheim ascribed to the scheme shows that although structural arrangements could support desired forms of moral solidarity, the presence of the latter was the final, indispensable element for regulation of grave social conflicts in modern societies.

Another thoughtful study of Durkheim's theoretical account of social strife is by Mark Traugott (1984). Traugott takes exception to the disparagement of Durkheim's contributions on this subject in recent writing on collective action—notably Charles Tilly's essay "Useless Durkheim" in *As Sociology Meets History* (1981). To characterize Durkheim's interpretation of militant collective action as a simple result of moral breakdown is unjust and misleading, Traugott contends. Such a view, often taken by Tilly and others, "runs contrary [to Durkheim's] consistent emphasis on the importance of social solidarity for successful collective action" (1984, p. 323). Such a view, Traugott argues, "is no more valid an extrapolation of the Durkheimian perspective than models based on Marx [*sic*] concepts of alienation and immiseration which, taken out of context, justify the use of absolute deprivation as a predictor of rates of collective action" (1984, p. 323).

These formulations, Traugott holds, focus attention on the most dubious and least fruitful implications of Durkheim's thinking for collective action, while ignoring highly pertinent insights from the same work. The more useful ideas are Durkheim's formulations on the role of intense group feeling in the mobilization of concerted action and the importance of symbols, rites, and collective celebration in such mobilization. Traugott quotes Durkheim's statement characterizing periods like the French Revolution as "creative epochs" and noting:

It is, in fact, at such moments of collective ferment that are born the great ideals upon which civilizations rest. The periods of creation or renewal occur when men for various reasons are led into a closer relationship with each other, when reunions and assembles [*sic*] are most frequent, relationships better maintained and the exchange of ideas most active. (1984, p. 326).

Traugott accurately notes that Tilly and his collaborators have themselves documented celebratory sequences in crowd action that sound very much like Durkheimian *rites* and collective representations.

All this is correct as far as it goes. As Traugott points out, Durkheim never states in so many words that fluctuations in civil disorder should be inversely correlated with fluctuations in indices of moral solidarity. Nevertheless, one must not forget that Durkheim attributed social strife to the alleged lack of moral solidarity in industrial societies; and collective violence certainly represents a signal instance of the sorts of strife he had in mind.

The fruitful conclusions that Durkheim might have drawn on the role of moral solidarity in fueling militant collective action run in a collision course with the relentlessly *holistic* cast of Durkheim's overall theoretical approach. For Durkheim, the force of moral authority was always associated with but a single moral system extending throughout society. Unlike Weber, he stubbornly refused to consider that different elements within a single population might respond to the most various and indeed antipathetic moral imperatives. Still less did he consider that individuals might experience conflicting loyalties arising from codes of conduct that could be equally moral in reference and equally social in origin. For Durkheim, moral force could proceed only from a single, consistent set of standards binding equally on all members of society. Hence the sharp (and false) alternative pervasive in Durkheim's thought between acceptance of moral direction, on the one hand, and disintegration, disruption, conflict, and self-destruction, on the other.

Thus the quotation from Durkheim given above by Traugott can be fitted into Durkheim's overall theoretical view only by ignoring some of the most basic facts about the historical period of which he writes. To refer to the great revolution of 1789 as entailing "collective ferment . . . born of the great ideals upon which civilizations rest" glosses over the fact that these events entailed life-and-death conflicts between partisans of "great ideals" fundamentally opposed to one another. Conversely, to posit but a single system of moral reference as accounting for all compliant, cooperative behavior within a population leads to equally unsatisfactory conclusions—to wit, the lumping of collective rebellion and individual nonconformity arising out of strong ethical impulses with purely self-interested or pathological acts of deviance. Lewis Coser has said it best.

Durkheim was forced to assume that the major social norms generally express the sentiments of the total society. He never seriously entertained the idea that they might only express the sentiments of a special stratum within it. If it is assumed a priori that the major social norms express the sentiments of the total collectivity, then one cannot recognize conflicting norms within a society; one cannot take cognizance of clashing views; one is unable to understand . . . that certain subordinate social strata may accept a norm only because it is imposed on them by violence or because they passively submit to it, whereas it is the genuine expression of moral sentiment only of a superordinate stratum. (1960, p. 218)

To be true to his overall theoretical vision, then, Durkheim must interpret violent collective action as a manifestation of weakness in the larger moral organization of society. Holding in abeyance this holistic cast of Durkheimian thought, one may of course identify Durkheimian processes of rites or collective representations in the militant social action. But Durkheim has little to tell us about when and where such upsurges of militant group solidarity occur, or how these solidarities are formed. To this extent, Tilly is right: Durkheim is simply not very useful in building a theory of civil violence.

Steven Lukes, in his magisterial intellectual biography, describes Durkheim's public debates in 1905 with Hubert Lagardelle, a leading revolutionary syndicalist. Lagardelle took the position that the prevailing order in France had no place for the working classes, either morally or politically. Only by destruction of the entire system could a new and better world be born. Durkheim's rejoinder was predictable in light of his theory.

Man's intelligence should precisely have as its overriding aim the taming and muzzling of these blind forces, instead of letting them wreak destruction. I am quite aware that when people speak of destroying existing societies, they intend to reconstruct them. But these are fantasies of children. One cannot in this way rebuild collective life; once our social organization is destroyed, centuries of history will be required to rebuild another . . . we must avoid acts of destruction that suspend the course of social life and civilization. (Lukes, 1973, pp. 543–44)

The equation of civilization with co-operation and violence with "blind forces" represents a quintessence of Durkheim's thinking on the social origins of civil violence. This holistic view is the authentic and immediate ancestor of the value integration doctrines of Parsons and his followers discussed in Chapter Five.

## Weber

Weber's overall sociological program differed profoundly from Durkheim's, both in his view of the nature and possibilities of sociological inquiry and in his beliefs on the role of sociological insight in generating directions for human action. For Weber, models of sociological understanding based on natural science were illusory. The regularities sociologists could reasonably seek were not the invariant laws pursued by natural scientists, but empirical generalizations, painstakingly built up through historical and cross-societal comparison.

Weber had no general theory of civil violence—that is, he was unwilling to cite conditions always necessary for the occurrence of violent collective action, or to offer generalizations as to what settings, groups, or issues are most likely to produce such action. It is not just that Weber, like Durkheim, wrote little about violence per se. It is that, unlike Durkheim, he largely eschewed categorical assertions about what had to be or what could never be in social life. His generalizations were more retrospective, more provisional. He wanted to know what forms of religious belief most often occurred with what principles of social stratification, what kinds of military organization went with what forms of state organization, which economic forms and religious beliefs conduced to change and which to stagnation. Perhaps no other sociologist has ever amassed so much of the scholarly capital required for such generalizations. When Weber did, occasionally, note a historical trend that might be extended to future instances, as in his conclusion that rational action forms tended to prevail in competition with traditional and other forms of social action, the statement carried authority.

American students of sociology often absorb a skewed version of Weber's thinking. For Weber is often taught as an intellectual counterweight to Marx. Thus, where Marx is interpreted for students, often too crudely, as a unicausal materialist, Weber is made to play the role of the theorist of ideal interests. Such treatment is hardly fair to Marx, and even less so to Weber. In fact, Weber would hardly rule out any of the characteristic causal connections made by Marx and his followers, including the role of class struggle in shaping political institutions; the importance of class membership in determining political participation; and the influence of material forces on ethics, ideology, aesthetic taste, religious belief and the like. Where Weber took leave of Marx was not in his willingness to entertain such connections in particular cases, but rather in his unwillingness to ascribe ultimate causal importance to any one category of social forces. Weber was simply determined to consider the widest possible array of associations and connections. Besides subscribing to explanations based on characteristically material considerations, Weber offered his readers explanations based on administrative forms, religious ideology, military arrangements, technological constraints—a whole gamut of historical possibilities. If sociology were religion, then we would have to classify Weber as a pantheist.

Part of the overemphasis on Weber's concern with ideal elements in social action no doubt also stems from his attention to the meaningful dimension of social life. He did of course characterize the world of shared meanings as the distinctive subject matter of sociology. But participation in mutually meaningful interaction hardly indicated support for the principles underlying social arrangements.

'Consensus'. . . . exists when expectations as to the behavior of others are realistic because of the objective probability that the others will accept these expectations as 'valid' for themselves, even though no explicit agreement was made. The reasons for such behavior on the part of others are irrelevant for the concept. . . .

. . . Persons linked together through a consensus may deliberately violate it, just as 'associates' may disregard their agreement. As the thief . . . orients his action to the legal order by concealment, so a disobedient person may 'agree' on the facts of power by resorting to subterfuge. Hence consensus must not be taken for 'satisfaction' of those adhering to it. Fear of dire consequences may bring about 'adaptation' to the normal meaning of oppressive rule. (1968, p. 1378).

In short, Weber was far from being a value consensus theorist along Parsons's lines. He characteristically avoids categorical commitments as to the nature of the investments people must share in the meaningful orders in which they participate.

True, Weber formulated the famous characterization of modern states as claiming a monopoly on exercise of legitimate coercion within their boundaries. No doubt some readers have seen this statement, along with his famous typology of legitimate authority, as an indication that Weber held moral support for state institutions indispensable for popular acceptance of established power. But Weber's actual discussion is in fact highly nuanced and qualified on these points.

'Every state is founded on force,' said Trotsky at Brest-Litovsk. That is indeed right. . . . Of course, force is certainly not the normal or the only means of the state—nobody says that—but force is a means specific to the state. . . . In the past, the most varied institutions—beginning with the sib—have known the use of physical force as quite normal. Today, however, we have to say that a state is a human community that (successfully) claims the monopoly of the legitimate use of physical force within a given territory. (1946, p. 78)

Note that this characterization of the modern state is given in ideal-typical terms; it is not an assertion of the empirical indispensability of legitimacy for acceptance of the writ of the state. Weber follows the preceding passage with a brief review of his typology of the bases of legitimate authority. He then comments:

It is understood that, in reality, obedience is determined by highly robust motives of fear and hope—fear of the vengeance of magical powers or of the power-holder, hope for reward in this world or in the beyond—and besides all this, by interests of the most varied sort. (p. 79)

None of this is to suggest that Weber doubted the potential efficacy of popular support derived from ideal interests as a force for compliance with established authority. Popular identification with political leaders and institutions as embodiments of deeply held principles, either of a religious or other ideal nature, could weigh heavily in favor of popular acceptance of state dictates. But Weber simply never portrayed such support as indispensable for the avoidance of civil strife. Nor did he ascribe the kind of causal primacy to religious or other ideal sentiments later envisaged by value integration theorists. In his studies of China and India, for example, he notes the manipulation of religious beliefs by ruling interests as means of domesticating rebellious populations and the suppression of religious heresy as a technique for forestalling political rebellion (1951, p. 223). Ideal sentiments, for Weber, were often but one link in what might be long chains of causation, and not necessarily the first.

Like many other observers, Weber was well aware of the frequency, if not the virtual inevitability, of *claims* by rulers of moral support from their people. Unlike others, however, Weber declined to attribute any *necessary* weight to these bases for civil peace, as against a wide variety of other forces that he considered. Unlike Durkheim in particular, Weber appreciated acutely that ideal sentiments could actually fuel violent breaches of civil peace, as in disputes over which interpretation of "the mandate to rule" ought to prevail.

As David Beetham has noted,

The absence of the concept of legitimacy in an explanatory capacity in Weber's political writings becomes less surprising . . . once the point of its use in his his-

torical sociology is recognized; its purpose is to provide an organising and differ-
entiating principle, and a means for identifying a complex of elements in particular systems of rule (patrimonial-bureaucratic, leadership-bureaucracy) rather than
to serve as a tool of explanation for the rise and fall of regimes. (1974, p. 258)

Along with his ideas on legitimacy, Weber's most distinctive contribution to our understanding of civil violence comes in his analyses of charisma. Earlier theorists could hardly have failed to notice the intense mobilizations of human energy that from time to time break out on behalf of
innovative religious, political, or other values. But Weber called attention
to the special characteristics of charisma as a kind of sociological and historical wild card, asserting itself without warning, systematically undermining more established claims on human loyalties. Charismatic appeals
always demand direct response to the highest authority imaginable: the
will of God, ethical perfection, the dialectic of history, the honor of one's
ancestors, or whatever. In their nature, such claims are always disruptive,
revolutionary, and discontinuous with established loyalties and obligations. Social action stemming from charismatic appeals is a prolific source
of civil violence.

But what causes charisma? Are charismatic innovations simply random
mutations in the genetic inheritance of culture? Or is there some way of
identifying populations and social settings particularly "at risk" to such innovations? Modern functionalist writers have sometimes claimed to ascribe
susceptibility to charismatic appeal to one or another form of "strain" or
deformation in "normal" social relations. Such arguments are enormously
problematic; they suffer from the almost irresistible temptation to identify
"strain" as present in situations where it would never have been noticed,
had it not been followed by charismatic outbreaks. Yet one cannot deny
that some settings, such as the "burned over region" of western New York
State during the early decades of the nineteenth century, have been prolific in charismatic movements out of proportion to the numbers of their
inhabitants. Weber, however, has no concept of "strain" and no formula
for suggesting where charismatic authority will assert itself. Charisma
thus remains a *deus* or *diabolus ex machina*—a potent source of social
innovation and strife but finally unaccountable in its origins.

## Simmel and Coser

Simmel is nothing if not distinctive. For him, the essential subject matter
of sociology was not constraints born of social facts, as with Durkheim, or
the world of interpretive meanings, as with Weber, but *social forms*. Following Kant, Simmel viewed the empirical realities of social life as shaped
by the constraints of a basic and universal logic of social relationships.

This logic—perhaps the exact term should be *socio-logic*—set down constraints and possibilities that register across the widest varieties of social contents. Thus, we have Simmel's famous analysis of the fundamentally different character of relationships of two versus relationships of three—for example, in the possibility of alliances in the latter. The dynamics so identified hold whether the parties are lovers, family members, coworkers, bureaucracies, or nation-states. Simmel's sociology, then, aims at a particularly far-reaching kind of generality. These theoretical aspirations properly claim our interest when applied to matters of conflict and violence.

Simmel's contributions on this subject are mainly found in his *Conflict* (1955), the English translation of a chapter from his *Soziologie* (1908). True to his larger intellectual project, Simmel there sought to trace patterns of social conflict that inhere in the eternal nature of the conflict relationship itself. Consider, for example, his observations on the intensity of intragroup antagonisms, or in Simmel's words, "hostility whose intensification is grounded in a feeling of belonging together." He writes of

hatred . . . directed against a member of the group, not from personal motives, but because the member represents a danger to the preservation of the group. . . . the two parties hate each other not only on the concrete ground which produced the conflict but also on the sociological ground of hatred for the enemy of the group itself. Since this hatred is mutual and each accuses the other of responsibility for the threat to the whole, the antagonism sharpens—precisely because both parties to it belong to the same social unit. (1955, p. 49).

Needless to say, such conflicts over the very identity of a group—for example, as to who should be included in the definition of American, Jewish, or Communist—may generate much civil violence.

Undoubtedly Simmel's contributions on conflict and violence would be a much less salient part of his intellectual heritage, if not for Lewis Coser's articulate amplification of these ideas in his famous *The Functions of Social Conflict* (1956). Coser cast the essential ideas of Simmel's *Conflict* into succinct propositions, and suggested some empirical fields in which they might apply. Of these sixteen propositions, three relate particularly directly to collective violence. For example:

In groups that appeal only to a peripheral part of their members' personality . . . conflicts are apt to be less sharp and violent than in groups wherein ties . . . [involve] the total personality of their members. In effect, this suggests that conflicts in such groups as Rotary Clubs or Chambers of Commerce are likely to be less violent than in groups such as religious sects or radical parties of the Communist type. (1956, pp. 68–69)

Coser's propositions lend themselves especially directly to falsifiable expectations. In this proposition, the expectation is as follows:

*Expect higher levels of violence in conflicts, the more the antagonistic parties claim total loyalty or involvement from their membership.*

Similarly, another of Coser's formulations holds that

The interdependence of antagonistic groups and the crisscrossing within such societies of conflicts, which serve to "sew the social system together" by cancelling each other out, thus prevent disintegration along one primary line of cleavage. (1956, p. 80)

Conflict patterns are said to contribute to stability of group life to the extent that allies in one conflict are apt to be antagonists in another, or in inverse relationship to the extent that various conflicts pit the same parties against one another, as women against men, Left against Right, or an older generation against a younger. Thus,

*Expect more violent conflicts, to the extent that various instances of conflict within a single population reproduce the same lines of antagonism.*

Finally, a third of Coser's observations states that when antagonists view one another as embodiments of impersonal forces, struggles are apt to be more intense.

The consciousness of speaking for a superindividual 'right' or system of values reinforces each party's intransigence, mobilizing energies that would not be available for more personal interests and goals. (1956, p. 112)

Hence, a third expectation is as follows:

*Expect more violence, to the extent that participants perceive the issues at stake in terms of abstract values transcending the specific case.*

All these expectations readily suggest programs of empirical inquiry that might ultimately strengthen or undermine the credibility of the theory. Had researchers taken up such a task when *The Functions of Social Conflict* was published, we would now no doubt have a relatively well-documented verdict on Simmel's theories.

Although *The Functions of Social Conflict* soon assumed an eminent place in American and world sociology, it did not play this kind of role initially. The book appeared in 1956, a time of notable social quiescence in America and corresponding inattention to conflict among American sociologists. In his thoughtful introduction, Coser commented wryly on the contrast between this state of affairs and the intense interest in social conflict in the formative years of American sociology at the end of the previous century. Although the book was well reviewed, Lewis Coser tells me, sales remained modest for several years. Then, with the explosion of agitation and conflict throughout American life in the 1960s, *The Functions of Social Conflict* became a sociological best seller. At the time of this writing some thirty years after its publication, the book continues to sell and has been translated into many foreign languages. Yet still, the work gave rise to nothing resembling a Simmel–Coser tradition of conflict studies. Indeed, though Lewis Coser has continued to write about conflict throughout his subsequent career, the later writings have not followed an especially Simmelian mode.

Wherein, then, did the influence of this landmark book lie? Raymond Mack, writing of the book in most appreciative terms in 1965, noted "hordes of footnotes to it," yet acknowledged that it seemed to have been "heeded by no one" (p. 389). Mack seems to have been referring to the scarcity of direct reverberations of Coser's book in research. Yet the citations to the book to which Mack refers suggest that the book was "heeded" in a quite different way. Although the matter is difficult to document fully, my own impression is that citing *The Functions of Social Conflict* became for years a kind of token acknowledgment of what many sociologists took to be "progressive" attitudes on the social conflicts of their own time. From reading the sociological literature of the 1960s and 1970s, one retains a kind of composite portrait of ways in which authors set a theoretical context for their own concerns: They begin by noting consensual influences as fundamental constituents of social life (typically with a reference to Parsons), then follow with a statement that conflict is also worthy of sociological attention, usually citing Coser. Citing *The Functions of Social Conflict* seems to have been a way of showing that one's sociological consciousness had risen above the level of the 1950s, as Coser characterized it in his introduction to the first edition of the book.

*The Functions of Social Conflict* appeared in a near theoretical vacuum concerning conflict and violence. For decades, theories deriving from the irrationalists had been the only theoretical lens available to American sociologists for analyses of civil strife, Marxism having been substantially excluded from academic sociology. Thus, the work attracted considerable attention simply by being a kind of theoretical cynosure for those who wished to affirm that conflict and related phenomena were worthy of sociological attention. Yet this hold on the American sociological imagination seems to have had nothing to do with the ability of the theories articulated in the work to account for any particular body of empirical phenomena or solve any research puzzle. Surely this observation offers some important lessons for our understanding of theoretical change in social science.

I return to these issues in Chapters Eight and Nine.

# Chapter Five

# Parsons and Value Integration Theory

This is a sociological legend.

Once upon a time, the tale goes, social theory lay in the oppressive grasp of narrow doctrines named positivism and utilitarianism. Under the spell of these views, nearly everyone assumed that social behavior entailed only the pursuit of narrow self-gratification—for example, physical comfort, sensory pleasure, or status superiority. This sterile doctrine led thinkers into all sorts of errors, anomalies, and intellectual dead ends. The worst was the inability to account for people's support of concerns, causes, or principles beyond their self-interest. Throughout the nineteenth century great minds struggled to free themselves from this doctrine, always with inconclusive or unsatisfactory results. The final break came only through the birth of a new approach to sociological theory, based on recognition of human commitments to abstract principles transcending self-interest. This doctrine, which forms the basis for all modern society theory, is known as value integration theory.

The hero of this tale of course is Talcott Parsons, and the theoretical revolution came with publication of *The Structure of Social Action* in 1937. Parsons's theories clearly did reshape American sociological thinking to an unprecedented degree. They set down a comprehensive conceptual map of the concerns of the sociologist, placed those concerns in historical perspective, and provided a wealth of general ideas in a discipline otherwise afflicted by "dust bowl empiricism." They offered an account of the linkages between individual action and large social institutions, one of the key historical problems of all sociological theory. And they provided a theory of the social forces sustaining compliance with the constraints of organized, co-operative social life. Parsons's theories are the most distinctively American response to Hobbes's problem.

Thus we have a prime example of the central subject matter of this work, a comprehensive theoretical vision embodying a theory of civil violence. Assessing this contribution is no easy task. For one thing, Parsons's early works have few direct comments on civil violence. But a more serious problem is Parsons's writing. Straightforward, empirically relevant statements are scarce. Instead, his theories seem to unfold according to rules of their own, with things like "action elements" and "media interchanges" combining, transforming themselves, dropping in and out of the analysis according to principles seemingly known only to the author. The language is above all allusive, full of references to assumptions and distinctions not spelled out. One unfortunate result has been a widespread tendency to regard Parsons's theoretical world as a self-contained entity, something like a religious or aesthetic taste, to be accepted or rejected according to inclination, but not subject to reasoned judgment.

I hope to improve on this response. It is surely not true, as some (Gibbs 1972) have suggested, that Parsons's key ideas are entirely without empirical reference. I seek to show that the doctrines of value integration must have some sorts of falsifiable implications for the origins of civil violence. I intend to sketch a variety of these implications and assess the weight of available evidence—often fragmentary and unsystematic—that applies.

In short, I aim to treat the doctrines of Parsons and his followers as bases for yet another empirically relevant theory of civil violence.

## The Historical Departure

We must start with *The Structure of Social Action*. There Parsons began the project that occupied him throughout his long and prolific career—analysis of large-scale social structures and institutions "from the ground up," through the actions of individual participants in these systems. Parsons's theory of action is an attempt to create a comprehensive repertory of the forces bearing on human social behavior. From this "general anatomy" of social action, Parsons would proceed to specify basic constraints and principles at work in larger social units. Note from the beginning the generality of his ambition, not just to trace the forces shaping social behavior or social institutions in a particular class of settings, but to describe fundamental characteristics of all social action and social systems.

Parsons viewed nineteenth-century social theory as largely dominated by utilitarianism. In this view, social action was characterized by four key features: "atomism, rationality, empiricism and randomness of ends" (1937, p. 60). By the first three of these terms, Parsons seems to mean (1937, pp. 58–59) that people seek to accomplish their purposes as efficiently as possible, in light of calculated assessments of opportunities and obstacles present in their environment; dispassionate scientific inquiry is given as a paradigm of all social action in these respects (1937, p. 58).

The last of these four defining tenets of utilitarianism is the crucial one—the "randomness of human ends." Parsons attributes this position to the utilitarians through an extraordinary chain of reasoning: "For the failure [of the utilitarians] to state anything positive about the relations of ends to each other can then have only one meaning—that there are no significant relations, that is, that ends are random in the statistical sense" (1937, p. 59). This characterization of the utilitarians is repeated at various points throughout the work (pp. 237, 327, 451).

How could human ends be random "in the statistical sense"? Taken literally, this statement would mean that one could never anticipate the goals, motives, or interests of any one person by acquaintance with those of others. No serious social theorist of any school would take such a position. Perhaps what Parsons means is that people do not naturally seek common or complementary ends, that co-operative behavior can occur only "by accident," where selfish ends happen to complement one another.

A close reading does suggest that at least part of Parsons's meaning is the idea that the utilitarians viewed human action and motives as narrowly self-interested—that what in Chapter One I called *divisible* self-interest was the only kind of interest weighing importantly in social action: "For in so far as men's ends are genuinely random," Parsons writes, "it follows that, given the rationality of their action, others are significant to them *only* in the capacity of means and conditions to their own ends" (p. 327).

Hobbes, whom Parsons idiosyncratically counts as a utilitarian, is treated as the key spokesman for this view (1937, pp. 89–94). But Hobbes, Parsons declares, also saw the problem it entailed: If people only cared for their own narrow gratifications—pleasure, safety, eminence, and so forth—how could they accept the constraints essential to any organized social life? Why, under these circumstances, would anyone refrain from plunder, fraud, or murder, if such acts promised a chance at a more gratifying existence? "In any society," Parsons writes, "there must obviously be some mechanism by which are settled the relative claims of different individuals to command over disposable scarce nonhuman resources" (1937, p. 235); it was Hobbes's great achievement to have defined this fundamental problem.

But Parsons holds Hobbes's solution unsatisfactory. Renunciation of private force in favor of a sovereign posits a "momentary identity of interest" in mutual security (1937, p. 238) that is incompatible with Hobbes's view of human motivation. If human ends are really "random," Parsons seems to be saying, why would people not constantly be slipping out of their obligations under the social contract? No coercive order could possibly be so thoroughgoing as to obviate all such attempts. How then, he wonders, is it possible, "still making use of the general action schema, to solve the Hobbesian problem of order and yet not make use of such an objectionable metaphysical prop as the doctrine of the natural identity of interests?" (1937, p. 102).

Parsons holds that this question dogged all thinkers who followed Hobbes in the utilitarian and positivistic traditions. True, he acknowledges, others did not perceive it so vividly. Locke, for example, saw human interests as more mutually compatible than did Hobbes. Locke's position was "more reasonable" than that of Hobbes, Parsons notes mystifyingly, but less "theoretically penetrating" (1937, p. 97). Later members of the utilitarian tradition adopted other unsatisfactory solutions to Hobbes's problem in their turn; they posited various social forces as constraining social action so as somehow to stave off the "breakdown" of any system based on "random ends." Examples are Malthus's concern with population pressure and the Social Darwinists' focus on competition for survival (1937, pp. 102–25). Even Marx is fitted into this pattern; in a truly extraordinary passage (p. 110), his thinking is treated as "a version of utilitarian individualism." In ways never adequately explained, these themes are seen as attempts to solve Hobbes's original problem. What was fatally missing in all these attempts was precisely what Parsons sought to establish: "normative thinking."

Unfortunately, "normative thinking" is another key concept of Parsons whose exact meaning is unclear. "For the purposes of the present study," Parsons writes, "the term normative will be used as applicable to an aspect, part or element of a system of action if, and only insofar as, it may be held to manifest or otherwise involve a sentiment attributable to one or more actors that something is an end in itself, regardless of its status as a means to any other end" (1937, p. 75). Taken literally this statement could mean that a lecher's pursuit of sexual gratification would represent normative thinking, provided that his lust were indeed an end in itself. Hobbes, of course, held that people pursued such things as status gratifications and power as ends in themselves. Surely this is not what Parsons means by "normative." He seems to mean behaviors aimed at pursuit of some sort of collective state, as distinct from strictly divisible interest. By collective I mean ends relating to states of the social system as a whole, such as justice, harmony, or conformity with the plans of God. Throughout *The Structure of Social Action*, Parsons regularly juxtaposes "normative" action to pursuit of the "random ends" allegedly envisaged by the utilitarians.

By the end of the nineteenth century, Parsons argues, the difficulties of social theory stemming from failure to acknowledge the role of normative principles were acute. Marshall, Pareto, Durkheim, and Weber, straining at the limitations of positivism and utilitarianism, began to embrace elements of normative thinking in their theories, often without realizing or acknowledging what they were doing. Thus Marshall's ideas on the changing character of human wants as a result of the growth of economic prosperity is seen as a revolt against utilitarian assumptions of purely "random" wants. Similarly, Parsons sees great significance in Pareto's discussions of the interests of "society as a whole," in Durkheim's concern with ritual and collective representations, and with Weber's attention to the special normative content of early capitalism.

All of this sets the stage for Parsons's famous synthesis. The solution to Hobbes's question, he writes,

> involves a common reference to the fact of integration of individuals with reference to a common value system, manifested in the legitimacy of institutional norms, in the common ultimate ends of action, in ritual and in various modes of expression. All of these phenomena may be referred back to a single general emergent property of social action which may be called 'common-value integration'. (1937, p. 768)

Thus the christening of value integration theory—the result of the definitive "breakdown of the positivistic tradition in its transition to a voluntaristic theory of action" (1937, p. 719).

What are we to make of this historic conclusion? It is hard to grasp Parsons's claims without a clearer conceptual inventory than he provides. Let me try to suggest one.

First, it is easy enough to identify a category of human ends or interests that might be bracketed as strictly self-regarding and divisible. These are goals consisting strictly of enhanced states of one's own self, excluding even gratifications like group pride that can only be experienced by being shared with others. Physical comfort, sexual pleasure, and avoidance of disease and pain are perhaps the purest cases, with individual status gratification and power for its own sake a close second. These seem to be what Parsons has in mind when he speaks of "random wants," and they correspond roughly to what people mean in everyday English when they speak of "selfish interests."

To such interests, one might contrast a category of interests in abstract principles. Sometimes people exert themselves to attain moral perfection, total self-control, complete honesty, or communion with the divine. These interests may be strictly private or widely shared. Such interests may be selfish or not, in that they may or may not be pursued to the exclusion of others' interests.

Next, consider a subset of this second category: interests in those abstract principles the pursuit of which presumes co-operative and complementary behavior from others—equal justice under the law, for example, or support for the monarchy, or devotion to the principles of caste. Such principles cannot reasonably be adhered to privately. One cannot uphold legal universalism, a particular line of royalty, or the sanctity of Brahman ritual except as part of a pattern of behavior in which others participate. Although these interests are experienced by individuals, they can only be realized collectively. Let me call interests of this kind *collective values.*

In *The Structure of Social Action* Parsons ignores the second of these two categories, posits an either-or distinction between the first and the third, and claims discovery of the latter as the long-awaited solution to Hobbes's problem. The utilitarians and positivists, he seems to be saying, never understood that people had interests in the abstract principles underlying social institutions—or indeed interests in other people except as means to their own gratification. Thus utilitarianism and positivism actually obscured the key subject matter of sociology, the shared value orientations underlying all enduring social structures and making possible all cooperative social behavior (1937, p. 768).

It is striking how widely these claims were accepted and how long the acceptance has endured, given their variance with the facts. Parsons's characterization of utilitarianism *arguably* applies to Hobbes, though many Hobbesian scholars (for example, Lamprecht 1940; Barry 1978) would dispute even this. But as I argued in Chapter One, it is a seriously inaccurate portrayal of the Scottish moralists and the utilitarians. Indeed, one can find explicit and detailed appreciation of collective values in the works of eighteenth-century social theorists such as Montesquieu and Hume, not just of the role of such considerations in individual action, but also of their importance in sustaining social institutions.

Further, such key utilitarians as Bentham and J. S. Mill were acutely sensitive to the role of concerns transcending narrow self-interest in the formulation of human action. As Camic (1979) has shown, Parsons's work does systematic and fundamental injustice to this important category of thinkers. Bentham, because of such misinterpretations, is often considered wholly mechanistic and hedonistic in his view of human nature. Yet his *Introduction to the Principles of Morals and Legislation* treats the moral and religious "sanctions" as among the "four basic sanctions of social life," and deals at length with human sensitivity to such nonhedonic considerations as the opinions of others and the forces of conscience (1948, esp. pp. 24–28; see also, on this point, Plamenatz 1963, pp. 1–3). In fact, Bentham and other key figures in the utilitarian movement are hardly even named in *The Structure of Social Action;* their work is inaccurately characterized without being discussed.

Similar peculiarities abound in the lengthy treatments of Marshall,

Pareto, Durkheim, and Weber that make up the bulk of the work. In each of these studies, Parsons fastens relentlessly on those elements of the writer's views showing similarities with his own ultimate value integration position, while deemphasizing other themes and assertions even to the point of distortion. The distortion is least serious in the case of Durkheim, who accords moral solidarity virtually as much importance in the containment of grave social conflicts as does Parsons. In Pareto's case, by contrast, the distortion is acute.

For Pareto, the distribution of residues within any population was perhaps its crucial sociological characteristic. Residues correspond to propensities for different forms of social action. Thus, some elements within a population may share inclinations toward sexual prudery, whereas others have an affinity to wheeling and dealing or political compromises—just to take two of Pareto's favorite cases. Entire social systems may be characterized in terms of the distributions of residues prevailing within them.

Parsons sees (1937, p. 210) in Pareto's notion of residues something corresponding to ultimate values. Indeed, the patterns of social action that correspond with Paretian residues do imply the existence of something like ultimate values. For such patterns represent ends in themselves rather than means to other ends; they are at least to some extent the product of social experience (rather than being given genetically, for example); and their distribution varies within and between populations. In short, both ultimate values and the shared impulses corresponding to residues involve some uniformities in the long-term directions of social action. But the question is, can such uniformities be supposed to have the crucial effect of overriding endemic conflicts of interest that would otherwise lead to breakdowns of social cohesion, including civil violence?

Parsons makes much of the fact that Pareto discusses (1937, pp. 243–44) the concept of *utility of a collectivity as a whole,* as distinct from the aggregated private utilities of its members. As Parsons sees it, the mere fact that Pareto entertains this concept points to the identification of the sentiments underlying the residues of a particular population with a set of common ultimate ends. Such common ends are in turn taken as the key force leading to acceptance of civil authority and avoidance of civil violence.

All of this is authentic Parsons. But it amounts to intellectual mayhem when offered as an account of Pareto's position. Pareto was above all antiholistic in his theory of civil violence: He saw the crucial conditions for forestalling and limiting violence within the polity as lying in the correct adjustments of contrasting psychic elements within the population, rather than in the universal sharing of single psychic states. The critical question was not, in other words, whether uniform residues are held strongly enough throughout a polity, but whether those endowed with political residues, especially the more forceful sort, in fact held state power. True, similarity between political elites, inside government or not, and their supporters in terms of residues espoused would enhance solidarity between leaders and followers. But Pareto never treated the containment of political violence as primarily a matter of moral solidarity throughout entire populations.

Pareto could hardly be more explicit in insisting that government effectiveness in forestalling and repressing violent challenges depends on the presence of just the right action tendencies among the political elite—versus those of the potentially opposing counterelites. Foremost among the qualities essential for ruling (and likely to lead to open strife if found too widely among the political "outs" rather than the "ins") was facility in recourse to force and fraud. Such qualities are hardly what should be required in a government basing its authority on grass-roots moral support.

Yet on this point Parsons writes,

Except where forceful coercion is employed as a means of enforcing commonly accepted rules, as by the state, which does not seem to be prominent in Pareto's treatment, the appearance of either or both [force or fraud] on a considerable scale may be considered a symptom of lack of social integration. For, on the one hand, the 'lions' have occasion to use force mainly against persons or groups that do not share their faith—hence insofar as the faith is shared in common by the whole community the occasion does not arise. On the other hand, considerable limitations on the use of fraud appear to be indispensable conditions of stable social relations within the community. (1937, p. 291)

This breathtaking statement almost defies comment. What we see here is not just selective emphasis, but a 180-degree alteration of Pareto's essential theory of civil violence and social cohesion. To suggest that government coercion as a means of securing compliance with "commonly accepted rules . . . does not seem prominent in Pareto" could hardly be farther from the truth. And, of course, Pareto held that fraud and clever compromise, if performed competently, should and did play a major role in ensuring political stability and forestalling violence.

In the end, Parsons's interpretations of the four main authors are marked by the same sorts of ambiguities as the discussion of Hobbes and utilitarianism. If Parsons's contention were simply, as he often seems to imply, that these four figures acknowledged the role in social action of commonly held ultimate values transcending narrow self-interest, then his hundreds of pages of exposition represent massive overkill. Pareto, Marshall, Durkheim, and Weber readily acknowledged that considerations of collective value played a role in social action; such acknowledgment hardly represented an innovation in relation to the ideas of the utilitarians and earlier writers. But if Parsons means to claim (as he often seems to do) that these writers posited attachment to collective values as sine qua non for all acceptance of social constraint, and hence for avoidance of civil strife, then he far outstrips any evidence he cites.

Yet if these interpretations are peculiar, there is something even more peculiar about the intellectual strategy of *The Structure of Social Action* as a whole. For if it were the author's purpose simply to establish the role of normative considerations in social action, a seven hundred page excursus through intellectual history would hardly be necessary. One might simply point to any number of readily noted facts: the fact that people take the trouble to vote, and even seem to derive satisfaction from doing so, despite the unlikelihood that their particular vote will make a difference in the outcome. The fact that members of monarchical—or democratic, or authoritarian—societies often show approval and support for the sorts of institutions they know best. The fact that supporters of a particular principle—for example, freedom of expression for unpopular ideas—often support such principles even when it costs something for them to do so. The fact that people do not murder, rape, or steal whenever the threat of coercive force is absent. Any number of such observations might well have sustained the conclusion that people often act in response to concerns transcending their narrow, divisible self-interest.

## Degrees of Commitment

What exactly does Parsons mean to establish? Does he simply seek to show that collective values *matter* in individual social action? Or does he have some more forceful message about the role of such values?

It is difficult to draw an unambiguous answer to these questions from *The Structure of Social Action*. At some points, Parsons seems to portray common value integration as a very sweeping constraint on social behavior indeed.

A common system of ultimate values precludes the identification of the concrete ends of individual action with the random wants of utilitarianism. The conception is rather that of long, complicated interwoven chains of intrinsic means-end relationships culminating in relatively integrated individual systems of ultimate ends, each of which in turn is to a relative degree integrated in a common system. This common system is related to the subsidiary intermediate sector of the chain in various complex ways formulable for present purposes mainly (1) as supplying the ultimate end of each chain and (2) as forming the source of the moral authority of institutional norms. (1937, p. 465)

Taken literally, this statement would offer a truly extraordinary view of human action. It would portray common, collective interests or values not just as *part* of the ends of human actions, but rather as constituting *all* of such ends. It would suggest that people strive to eat, sleep, and earn money—that is, pursue "subsidiary" or "intermediate" ends—only as means to the accomplishment of goals of the society as a whole. There are some real examples of such dedication, such as the political activist or religious ascetic who lives only for some intensely valued higher goal. But this hardly seems a plausible picture of human social action in general.

But Parsons concludes this passage with an ambiguous qualification.

But the common value system is never the source of all elements in the concrete immediate ends of the intermediate sector. There are other elements of various kinds, many of which may be held to have centrifugal tendencies. Hence . . . the necessity for control of these interests is understood. (1937, p. 465)

What can this mean? Parsons seems to be acknowledging the obvious, that people strive after things other than what I have termed collective values. Yet he also implies that commonly held, collective values are the only long-term ends of human action, and that other, more private and shorter-term ends are disruptive to the stability of social systems, or at best neutral. Devotion to commonly held collective values, in other words, appears as the only influence among the forces shaping social action that conduces to acceptance of social constraint.

To assess these claims, we need to think in terms of the relative weight of different interests or ends people pursue. How important are collective values among the other forces shaping human action? What *costs* are people willing to undergo to pursue such values and how do these costs compare with those accepted in pursuit of other interests or values?

Consider an extreme form of successful value integration, a social system where common values or interests were of overriding importance to all participants. People would be willing to endure any cost—for example, to renounce any conflicting personal interest—in order to contribute to the realization of the Kingdom of God, or to World Revolution, or to the perfection of a community based on sharing or equality.

Real social groupings approximating this extreme do exist, in the form of charismatic movements, total-commitment sects, and others of what Lewis Coser (1974) has called "greedy institutions." Such bodies tend to deny their members pursuit of any private interests or idiosyncratic values. Participants are expected to devote their entire energies to furtherance of common goals. There can be no doubt that the sort of value integration prevailing in such groups does have the effect of suppressing what Parsons calls "centrifugal tendencies." Moreover, such groups mobilize energies that would never be available to less committed groups. The first Christians, the Mormon followers of Brigham Young, the early Bolsheviks, and the adherents of Jim Jones would certainly never have gotten as far as they did without something approximating total commitment to collective values.

But does such intense individual commitment ever underlie behavior throughout entire societies? I believe not. Perhaps the closest any entire society ever comes to this extreme is in wartime. Then common commitment to eventual victory may result in willing suppression of discordant interests, with industrial disputes, consumer demands, and ethnic conflicts being set aside for the duration of the conflict. But this is not the normal state of any social system.

For most people most of the time, collective values simply take their place among a variety of interests, of which they are by no means the most compelling. Even the intense fixation on collective values noted in charismatic movements does not seem to endure. Such bodies do not usually survive a single generation in their original, intense form. If they manage to avoid dissolution, they seem to do so by undergoing some form of what Weber described as routinization of charisma. This entails institutionalization of what had been overriding social values so that they occupy a portion of the followers' concerns, rather than their entire existence. Thus in due course we find formerly charismatic movements evolving into groups of people who are devoted to their families, avocations, occupations, and so forth, *and* to their membership in church, party or the like. In many movements, this evolutionary process is marked by a growing division of labor between a full-time staff and rank-and-file supporters no longer expected to devote their total energies to the cause. Compensation of the full-timers with pay, rather than simply with the rewards of righteousness, enables them to vary the personal interests they can gratify, as well.

In one passage in *The Structure of Social Action*, Parsons seems to agree that deep commitment to common values is atypical; he does not mean to imply, he writes, that

concrete societies are in general even approximately perfectly integrated . . . or that their members are normally, the majority, conscious that there is any system of common ends. But whether this system be explicit or implicit, whether integration be closely or only distantly approached, does not affect the theoretical importance of this theorem. . . . A concrete example which comes relatively close to the experimental conditions of the theorem is that of the Calvinists of Geneva in Calvin's own time who might be said to be pursuing the common end of establishing the Kingdom of God on Earth. But this is unusual. (1937, p. 248)

Here value integration is portrayed simply as an ideal type, a theoretical extreme rarely approached in real societies.

But later in *The Structure of Social Action*, Parsons seems to treat value integration not just as an ideal type, but rather as a life-giving condition that must be present in any viable social order.

The actions of the members of a society are to a significant degree oriented to a single integrated system of ultimate values common to these members. More generally the value element in the form both of ultimate ends and of value attitudes is in a significant degree common to the members of the society. This fact is one of the essential conditions of the equilibrium of social systems. (1937, p. 707)

In the concluding pages of the book, he adds:

The solution to the power question . . . involves a common reference to the fact of integration of individuals with respect to a common value system. (1937, p. 768)

The obvious question is, just what does a "significant degree" of commitment to common values, or a "common reference" to such values, entail? What degree of force should such commitments entail? What sorts of evidence should be taken to indicate the levels of such commitments? In short, if commitment to common values really makes the difference between the Hobbesian world of unbridled conflict and the orderly cooperation of civil society, must not this commitment entail the harnessing of very considerable social energies?

Some of Parsons's followers think not. Some hold that Parsons's idea of value integration amounts simply to some sort of common reference point for social interaction (Bourricaud 1981, pp. 263, 277) rather than a forceful constraint on the interests of the parties. Common values would thus be more like a common language—something necessary for orderly social process, but not a constraining force in any way comparable, say, to the forcefulness of Hobbes's sovereign.

But this response hardly resolves the dilemma in Parsons's formulation. If he asserted simply that most people do observe some considerations transcending their own divisible interests, and that total commitment to such values represents a kind of theoretical extreme case, then hardly anyone could disagree. But this uncontroversial position is also unremarkable and uninformative; it would hardly provide a plausible basis for explaining how social systems manage to constrain profound inner conflicts of the sort that may give rise to civil violence. On the other hand, if Parsons sees people's commitments to collective values as sufficient to restrain the real "centrifugal tendencies" that threaten to overcome social constraint, then his position becomes more interesting but less plausible. These tendencies include conflicts between loyalties to one's party or ethnic group and those to dominant institutions, or solidarities with class, region, family, status group, or race—in short, all the many contending commitments that can and do give rise to civil violence. Either people's commitment to collective values is seen as sufficient to override these centrifugal tendencies, or one must search elsewhere for a solution to Hobbes's problem.

If Parsons's value integration doctrine yields a falsifiable implication for civil violence, then, it would be roughly as follows:

*Expect high levels of civil violence (along with other challenges to so-cial constraint) wherever shared commitment to collective values is weak or absent throughout a population.*

The difficulty with this formulation lies in specifying evidence that would count for the presence of such value commitments, other than the compliance that such commitments are supposed to explain. I have ar-gued that, for value commitments to matter enough to weigh against all the "centrifugal" tendencies that Parsons suggests they overcome, such commitments would have to be very strong forces in individuals' lives in-deed. Apart from such special cases as charismatic movements, evidence of such intense commitment in everyday life seems to me rare.

I argued in Chapter One that people identify with, and act on, a wide range of interests other than narrow, divisible self-interest. But what I have called shared collective values—widespread commitments to prin-ciples underlying key social institutions, that is, Parsons's integrated value systems—are a small subset of the first category. The latter include at-tachment to one's own ethnic or racial group, to one's family, or to the principles animating insurgent social movements—that is, a whole gamut of action commitments that may as well result in challenges to institu-tional authority as support for it. What Parsons needs to show is that those principles underlying major established social institutions enjoy some ex-traordinary, overriding support among all the interests and values that an-imate ordinary people's participation in social life. I believe that, had this idea come across more clearly, its implausibility would have been recog-nized at once.

"People may value democracy," George Homans once remarked in skepticism of value integration theory, "But do they value it as much as their dinner?" The question is apt. For a few people, colletive values are or can be of overriding importance, even in the absence of coercion, propa-ganda, or manipulation; one thinks of those who stand up to repressive regimes, even at the cost of their lives, in lonely witness to principle. But most people are not potential martyrs, even for principles they sincerely embrace.

## Some Alternatives

Parsons's value integration doctrines did not go altogether unchallenged even at the height of his influence; although the amount of serious criti-cism to which they were subjected was not great. In a classic article, Den-nis Wrong (1961) cast doubt on the linkage posited by Parsons between the workings of the Freudian superego and compliance with the strictures of institutional authority. Nothing we have learned from Freud, Wrong held, suggests that *all* the constraints of social life are internalized within healthy adult personalities. Most individuals, in other words, are simply not such staunch defenders of the principles underlying the institutional orders around them.

Other critics have taken a different line of attack. They have argued that value integration cannot plausibly explain social cohesion in many settings because of the absence of shared culture linking rulers and the ruled. Thus Abercrombie, Hill, and Turner (1980) seek to demonstrate the cultural distance between nobility and lower classes in Medieval Europe. Critics also like to point to societies characterized by strong ethnic or racial divisions, like South Africa, where long periods of relative political quiescence evidently could not result from cultural consensus. Similarly, a number of studies (Mann 1970) have examined opinion surveys to show that statements supposedly reflecting fundamental value attitudes do not receive wide and consistent support from members of the general public in today's industrial societies.

These are important arguments, but I feel that they concede too much to the value integration position. Even where participation in a common culture is apparent, I argue, the *force* of collective values in constraining people from violent collective action is doubtful.

The flaws in the value integration account have been overlooked, I suspect, because of the plausibility of one element of the argument. Nearly everyone would agree that some forms of wrongdoing cannot be prevented other than by inner checks. People plainly do not commit child abuse, petty larceny, extortion of sexual favors, and various other reprehensible acts whenever they can escape coercive consequences for doing so. No system of social control relying only on coercive measures to control such behavior would have much chance of success. Such observations seem to lead many to accept value integration as an explanation of social compliance *tout court*.

But it will not do to lump the processes leading to collective civil violence a priori with all other forms of "deviance," to assume that all forms of behavior officially bracketed as "wrong," from incest to militant political activism, must respond to the same controls. As I noted in the Chapter Four, Durkheim took this position, or came very close to taking it, in attributing the violent political conflicts of his age to failed moral authority. But Durkheim was blind to the fact that the political impulses leading to militant activism might well reflect competing moral sensibilities, rather than the absence of any such guidance.

Some forms of "nonnormative" behavior are largely private, shielded from easy scrutiny from the outside world—certain forms of lying, littering, many forms of deviant sex activity, or theft from one's close associates. Here strictly internal controls are apt to be the most important. Other forms of proscribed behavior, by contrast, are inherently more public and require coordination of many actors. Militant collective action is a prime example. Here opponents of the action, either governments or competing activist groups, have many more means at their disposal for raising the costs of such action.

LeBon was perhaps the last to treat collective violence as an unreckoning outpouring of emotion with no purposeful coordination. Since then, most analysts have acknowledged that riots, demonstrations, and aggressive crowd actions require coordination and entail costs to participants. These constraints affect the likelihood of civil violence. The costs to the perpetrator of incest, littering, or certain other forms of deviance are apt to be strictly moral, and the coordination required with other actors, minimal. Outside forces, especially governments, can much more easily raise the costs of collective violence, however, and greatly increase the difficulties of coordination.

It is striking how little this point is appreciated, and not just among Parsons's followers. "Rulers are always few in number," Bendix writes, "and could never obtain compliance if each command had to be backed up by a force sufficient to compel compliance" (1976, p. 250). Like many analysts, Bendix assumes a situation where the ruled stand poised to act together against hated policies of the rulers. Yet it is precisely this unity of sentiment and readiness to act that challengers of political regimes often find hard to develop, and rulers easy to forestall. The latter may, as Tilly and his followers would point out, act so as to prevent the mobilization of protest. They may profit from lack of communications among would-be challengers, such that ignorance prevails as to the depths and nature of support for collective action. Or they may concentrate their forces, so that the first to challenge must undergo, and be seen to undergo, extraordinary cost. Through processes like these, rulers may prevent the build-up of united sentiment and common perceptions among the ruled, and thereby forestall challenge to their positions. There may be strength in numbers, as the saying goes. But what Bendix and many others fail to note is that numerical superiority may have little impact without the ability to act in concert. And such action may be subject to significant costs.

To judge from the works of Parsons and his followers, disintegration of political regimes results almost automatically from lack of moral support among the ruled. In fact, processes leading from popular disaffection to active challenge are far from self-evident. We need to know much more about them, yet thus far we have only a few sociological straws in the wind. Tilly and his followers have taken a few tentative steps toward measuring levels of repression and reckoning its exemplary effects (for example, Snyder and Tilly 1972). Granovetter has developed models of participation in rebellion in which the willingness of some to participate is contingent on the participation of others (1978). Whatever the eventual results of these departures, the effort itself is important. There is good reason to suspect that many instances of what appears to be willing acceptance of dominant political institutions may conceal significant potential for revolt. In such cases regimes may simply have mastered, or blundered into, situations where all the potential challengers remain ignorant of the possibilities for political alternatives. Such ignorance may arise from rigorous repression of occasional challenges, or from curtailment of demonstrations, public declarations, and other gestures that would indicate depth and nature of potential support. Again, if the dissatisfied enjoyed the benefits of some sort of group mind, or some other special technique for acting in unison, rebellion would be much more common. But these are utopian possibilities.

Collective perceptions of the feasibility of revolt can change rapidly. Michael Mann (1973, pp. 45–55) has reviewed a number of such sequences, which he characterizes as "explosions of consciousness." In these events, industrial workers who had previously been resigned to their conditions mounted wildcat strikes with fervor unanticipated, apparently, even by themselves. Some of these events took place in France in response to the student uprising of 1968, itself an unanticipated "explosion." The unfolding of events like these suggests processes that Granovetter calls "change of state," in which propensities for action that in some sense had always been "there" manifest themselves suddenly. Why they occur at some points and not others remains an almost complete mystery. I return to these issues in Chapter Eight.

Value integration thinking, with its emphasis on deep-seated, slow-changing moral commitments to the social order, can tell us little about such transitions. Indeed, Parsons and his followers typically take their theory for granted, counting mere acquiescence as prima facie evidence of deep moral support for the stable regime. Such thinking obviously precludes the identification of political apathy as an important source of stability, which it undoubtedly often is. Inability to envisage viable alternatives to the prevailing regime, or despair about attaining such alternatives, may contribute greatly to the stability of political systems, a possibility not credited by Parsons and his followers. In his famous article on American voting behavior, Parsons illustrates the point as he describes the formulation of voting decisions.

The 'issues' are in general too numerous and specific to provide a focus, the individual can directly 'care' about only a minority of them, and the chances are good he will disapprove of his candidate's stand on some. Furthermore, his own action can have only little decisive effect on the outcome . . . and the direct effect of the outcome on his own personal interests is usually slight.

In this situation the individual seems to vote, other things being equal, with the people whom he most directly feels to be 'his own kind', who are in social status and group memberships like, and hence like-minded with, himself. (1959b, pp. 96–97)

Parsons goes on to characterize the "act of faith" implicit in such voting as "symbolically appropriate."

Parsons obviously regards the situation described here as one of moral solidarity between the electorate and the prevailing political system. The former have only a hazy idea of what is at stake but give a trusting nod just the same to those they consider most likely to do the right thing. In fact, what Parsons is describing could as well be characterized as political apathy so deep-going that voters' choice of political candidates means little more to them than their choice of brands of beer. One might well attribute moral solidarity to the relations between voters and politicians where all concerned agreed that great issues and vital interests were at stake in electoral politics. In such settings, voters may indeed see their chosen representatives as upholding sacred principles or vital interests; indeed, they might be prepared to accept costs for expressing their support far in excess of the costs of voting. But in the situation described by Parsons, voters are unclear as to what their leaders stand for and what difference their election is apt to make. Either they are comfortable with any outcome of the political process, or they see no way in which anything they could do could make them less uncomfortable. Both of these possibilities may be entirely conducive to political stability. But they bear little relationship to moral solidarity or value integration.

## Institutionalization

Parsons consistently offers a qualification to his views on value consensus as a sine qua non of compliance with authority. Values, he holds, simply set down broad directions for social action. They do not result in concrete, working social arrangements unless *institutionalized*.

Values cannot control society by mere "emanation." Their institutionalization involves their specification through a series of levels of function and situation. (1961b, p. 55)

The idea seems to be that any collective value or set of values admits of a range of different social practices or norms. Institutionalization is the process by which specific codes of action come to be accepted as the appropriate ways of putting the broad directions given in values into practice.

One encounters this formulation frequently in Parsons's writings (e.g., 1960, p. 172). To my knowledge, no one has called attention to its logical peculiarities. It is much as though a chemist were to insist that phlogiston were indispensable for combustion—provided only that sufficient fuel, oxygen, and ignition temperatures were also present. It is obvious that general ideas and sentiments about what is desirable in social life do not by themselves yield concrete agreements as to how people should arrange their affairs. After all, the sharpest sorts of conflicts, including many violent ones, surround attempts to specify what social practices should be considered to serve broad ideals or principles people claim to hold in common. Presumably some norms would be incompatible with some values under any circumstances, such as norms of unrelenting hedonism vis-à-vis values of self-denial and other-worldliness. But many principles that would seem to qualify as instances of Parsonian values—for example, the desirability of innovation and progress or the equality of citizens before the law—admit of the most various sorts of concrete social arrangements. Yet alleged consensus on the ultimate values is somehow supposed to ensure the ultimate solidity of particular social arrangements.

The American Civil War was clearly, among many other things, a dispute over the institutionalization of values such as "freedom," "liberty," "democracy," and "federalism." Similarly, many clashes between militant student groups and civil and university authorities during the 1960s and 1970s turned on what practices should institutionalize such values as freedom of expression and equality of opportunity. Such values were certainly professed by all parties to the troubled situations. I hardly wish to argue that these conflicts have been *only* disputes over abstract principle; obviously sheer clashes of interest played an enormous role as well. The point is, apparent consensus among the parties on ultimate values did not afford bases for forestalling grave conflicts, including violent ones. What sense is there, then, in asserting that solidarity in popular affirmation of ultimate value principles is the "real" cause of social cohesion, if only such solidarity can be properly "institutionalized"?

Similarly, conflicts between free-enterprise liberals and socialists can be seen as struggles over institutionalization of the values of democracy. Do democratic principles find their fullest expression where democratic participation extends to the allocation of economic resources? Or is "true" democracy best realized where capitalists retain freedom to allocate wealth as they see fit? Clearly the potential for bloodshed is enormous in conflicts growing out of such differences; clearly, too, the "ultimate value" involved admits of no unique interpretation. Bases for resolving or containing such conflicts short of civil violence, when available, do not lie within the values themselves.

Does it *add anything* to assert that such conflicts are really over implementation of commonly held values? What evidence can be given for the existence of such values? In what sense do struggles over "institutionalization" represent efforts to put into practice some principle that contestants really agree upon? This idea would be falsifiable only if one could point to some range of circumstances in which any kind of institutionalization of norms, and hence any social cohesion, was quite impossible, due to lack of underlying value consensus. Value consensus would be a *necessary* condition for acceptance of social constraint (and for peaceable social cooperation), but not *sufficient* in the absence of institutionalization of concrete normative arrangements. The category of social systems *without* value consensus, in other words, should contain no peaceful, co-operative cases.

The trouble is, the corpus of Parsonian work provides no satisfactory empirical criteria for establishing the existence of value consensus, apart from the cohesion supposed to arise from it. We simply do not know how to distinguish, on any empirical ground, between situations where grave conflicts arise from lack of shared collective values, and those where effects of such values are blocked by lack of institutionalization.

Because of this profound logical ambiguity, any outbreak of civil violence, or any other form of serious conflict, can be attributed to lack of institutionalization, without reflecting on the doctrine of value consensus itself. The fact that people are at odds with one another over what social arrangements to support is, after all, by definition evidence of lack of institutionalization. The status of value consensus as sine qua non for social peace becomes unfalsifiable in principle.

Consider Parsons's account of the Supreme Court Decision of 1954 outlawing public school desegregation.

Institutionalization means some order of integration of the normative complex in question in the more general one governing the system as a whole. . . . Thus the doctrine of "separate but equal" proved to be dubiously integrated with the rest of the American system of constitutional rights formulated on the basis of the constitutional rights of "equal protection of the laws." It can thus be said that the 1954 decision of the Supreme Court was a step in institutional integration, or at least that this was the primary problem before the court. (1961a, p. 225)

Note that the legal struggles mentioned here were part of a much broader pattern of social conflict, one productive of much civil violence. If Parsons's formulations have anything distinctive to tell us about the origins of social strife, it is that these conflicts occurred because of some kind of "poor fit" between segregated institutions and moral sentiments prevailing more broadly in American life.

Yet in what sense are these conflicts, violent and otherwise, *explained* by such "dubious normative integration"? Segregated institutions had been present in America for generations. Surely the specific timing of the desegregation conflicts of the 1950s cannot be traced to the fact that people somehow happened to notice the "dubious integration" of such arrangements for the first time. The question is, when did such matters become subject to contest, and why? As McAdam (1982) has shown, the answer lies in such conditions as changing alignments of political and electoral forces, shifting distributions of black population among the states, and the changing economic position of black Americans. The struggles ensuing from these changing power equations did indeed relate to the institutionalization or normative integration of the roles of black people in the larger institutional order. But again, what does this characterization add to our understanding of the forces that brought these conflicts to the fore, then later caused them to subside?

I have tried to show that commitment to common values is neither a necessary nor a sufficient condition of civil peace. To be sure, popular belief that a particular institution represents the realization of a "good" principle will likely enhance support for that institution. But many other social forces also sustain compliance with institutional constraints, even in the absence of popular support. Indeed, apathy or depoliticization of potentially conflictual issues may represent a more reliable basis for stable civil authority than value commitment. Social units marked by intense value commitment mobilize great energy while consensus endures. But such movements are notoriously prone to factionalism through disputes over the proper interpretation of the overriding values, as the history of charismatic religious, political, and ethical movements demonstrates.

I do not know what the response of supporters of value integration theory will make to these skeptical observations. But one part of this response will certainly be that I have misunderstood Parsons's position Parsons never imagined, it may be said, that value integration in real societies would resemble such things as charismatic movements or total-commitment cults. Instead, it might be argued, the role of values is much subtler; they work, it may be said, only in conjunction with a myriad of other social forces.

But if Parsons's theory is empirically relevant at all, we need unambiguous answers to some simple questions: What evidence is there for the strength of shared values in shaping the actions of ordinary actors—versus the effects of all the various interests, principles, loyalties, and goals that tend to countervail against such values? Are there any empirical grounds for believing that such values are of sufficient force to outweigh, under normal conditions, competing influences of the sort that lead to civil violence? Which social phenomena, and particularly which ones relating to civil violence, can be explained by positing the existence of value consensus that could not more readily be accounted for by other theoretical assumptions? These are elementary questions; I do not see that proponents of the doctrine have provided answers to them.

## Value Integration: 1940–1982

Parsons's thought continued its remarkable evolution for some four decades following *The Structure of Social Action*. Yet value integration remained the key unifying theme throughout the later work.

In the 1940s and 1950s Parsons took a strong interest in psychoanalysis. Here, he felt, was an account of the mechanisms by which shared values were transmitted from generation to generation, and by which they became invested with the deep emotional significance that he attributed to them. The psychoanalysts had seen psychosexual development as leading to identification with the parents' personalities; for Parsons the end point was internalization of the ultimate values current in the culture. For Freud, of course, it was the superego through which society exerted its constraints upon the individual. Parsons agreed.

The place of the superego as part of the structure of the personality must be understood in terms of the relation between personality and the total common culture, by virtue of which a stable system of social interaction on the human levels becomes possible. (Parsons, Bales, and Shils 1953, p. 18)

Note Parsons's reaffirmation of commonly held values as essential to any enduring social system.

But Parsons held that Freud did not go far enough in emphasizing the incorporation of social standards and sentiments within the individual personality.

It does seem that Freud's view was too narrow. The inescapable conclusion is that not only moral standards, but *all components of the common culture* are internalized as part of the personality structure. (Parsons, Bales, and Shils 1953, pp. 18–19)

It is hard to imagine a more emphatic affirmation of the value integration idea.

Growing out of Parsons's psychoanalytic ideas was his rediscovery of social interaction. Writings of the early 1950s emphasized the role of social actors in socializing and resocializing one another toward established normative patterns. In this view, each actor is assumed to have a stake in "normal"—that is, the institutional—patterns of social behavior, such that another's deviation brings a corrective response.

Conformity as a direct mode of the fulfillment of his [the actor's] need dispositions tends to coincide with conformity as a condition of eliciting the favorable and avoiding the unfavorable reactions of others. (1951, p. 38)

An eminently suitable doctrine for America in the 1950s.

In these writings, too, common value integration is taken as an essential condition for the viability of virtually any social system.

This integration of a set of common value patterns with the internalized need-disposition structure of the constituent personalities is the core phenomenon of the dynamics of social systems. That the stability of any social system except the most evanescent interaction is dependent on a degree of such integration may be said to be the fundamental dynamic theorem of sociology. (1951, p. 42)

Thus, a view of social interaction as a self-policing system of adherence to common values.

Congenial to this view of society as governed by self-correcting processes was Parsons's assimilation of the next major theme from outside sociology—cybernetics. Beginning in the 1960s, Parsons came to see in social systems the same sorts of steady-state mechanisms noted by Wiener in various natural and artificial systems. Here, too, the role of value integration in regulating social systems remained central; cybernetic processes were the mechanisms by which the effects of common values were assured.

The basic subsystems of the general system of action constitute a hierarchical series of such agencies of control of the behavior of individuals or organisms. . . . The personality system is . . . a system of control over the behavioral organism; the social system, over the personalities of its participating members; and the cultural system, a system of control relative to social systems. (1961b, p. 38)

Thus, commonly held values, as the key element of culture, are pictured as exerting what Parsons sometimes called a thermostatic control over the whole of social life.

Along with the cybernetic theme came the elaboration of Parsons's famous four-function model of social life. Since at least the 1940s, Parsons had espoused the functionalist notion that every major social institution made its particular contribution to the viability of the social whole. Now he came to picture every social system—from entire societies to small, face-to-face systems like the family—as embodying four functionally distinct domains. These are the adaptive, goal-attainment, the integrative, and the latent pattern-maintenance functions—corresponding very roughly to the political, economic, legal, and religious sectors of social life. The latter, locus of common ultimate values, was seen as exerting cybernetic regulation over other systems. Within that pattern of regulation, however, the various functionally specific subsystems of society each had subvalues corresponding to their special contributions to the whole.

This scheme figured importantly in yet another new theme in Parsons's writing—social evolution. Having in 1937 consigned Spencer to the attic of intellectual history, if not the dust bin, Parsons in the 1960s took up a renewed interest in this writer and his ideas. The overall evolution of human societies, Parsons now saw, was characterized by increasing institutional differentiation along the lines of the functional subsystems and, by this same token, growing adaptivity. This latter concept was interpreted as efficiency in pursuit of broad directions of collective strivings—that is, in the realization of shared ultimate values.

## Civil Violence as Power Deflation

Parsons rarely confronted the issue of civil violence directly in his writings until the 1960s. Then he published a famous series of studies (1961a, 1963a, 1963b, 1964) depicting political power as a "medium," and deriving from this view many conclusions on coercion and rebellion within the state. Of all Parsons's writings, the media studies are perhaps the most obscure. But many see in them Parsons's definitive solutions to Hobbes's original problem.

Each of the four functional subsystems, Parsons held, has its distinctive "medium." The most widely recognized of these is money, peculiar to the economic (or adaptive) subsystem. No less authentic a medium, however, is power, peculiar to the goal-attainment or political system. Activities of each subsystem are supposedly governed by the ebb and flow of its particular medium. But Parsons holds that media cannot function effectively without consensus among participants. This consensus has to do with shared confidence in the strength of the medium itself.

For money, the nature of this confidence is variously described. Sometimes he suggests that confidence in the backing of currency by some trustworthy standard of value, like precious metal, is the essential thing (1963b, p. 237). Elsewhere, the confidence he envisages is that in the fundamental health of banking institutions or the productivity of the economy, such that depositors are willing to entrust them their funds (1964, p. 45). In either case, the idea is apparently that people will not participate in the larger systems of interaction (the economy) unless they are confident that their money is "worth something." But if this confidence prevails, the monetary system affords advantageous individual and collective undertakings that would otherwise be impossible.

So, too, for power. Power arises when people entrust their confidence in the future actions of those designated as political leaders. Like money, power circulates (1961a, p. 53). It flows from followers to leaders, where it forms the basis for binding decisions. The flow is completed by the "returns" of these decisions to grass-roots participants in the polity, in the realization of collective political goals. Modern electoral systems represent the most advanced institutionalization of the power medium, Parsons argues, for votes are numerical expressions of support directly equivalent to money. But his discussions taken as a whole suggest that the same principles apply even in less evolutionarily advanced political systems, where participants must rely on other means to indicate their support of their leadership (1961a, p. 53).

This amounts to a social contract theory. Institutional authority, as for Locke, Hobbes, and Rousseau, becomes possible through grants of confidence by the governed to rulers. But note something distinctive about this contract. Parsons stresses that coercion must play no part in creation of the consensus, and that the mandate of the ruled can be withdrawn without threatening the entire system. Indeed, Parsons's position here is doubly consensual: First, institutionalized power can only arise within the "moral community" required for the existence of "every relatively established politically organized society" (1964, p. 34). Second, fluctuations in the power wielded by specific incumbents results from variations in the "deposits" of political confidence entrusted by supporters.

Parsons stresses the superiority of his position over "zero-sum" conceptions of political power proposed by Mills, Lasswell, and others (1963b, p. 231). In Parsons's view, power can benefit some participants within a political system without harming others; indeed, when the power "deposits" grow, in the form of widespread confidence in the efficacy of the political system, all participants stand to benefit. Just as a stronger economy may create greater wealth for all, so may a stronger system of "political banking" afford more effective decision making and action on behalf of the polity as a whole.

Parsons carries the parallels between economy and polity still farther. If power is like money, he reasons, then the role of force in political life must be analogous to that of monetary metal in economic life. Just as the "gold standard" or some such monetary criterion provides the ultimate basis for confidence in that system, the state's ability *in extremis* to mobilize coercion to enforce its dictates provides the basis of public confidence in the political system. When confidence in either the monetary or political system is widespread, participants do not normally demand frequent demonstration of the ultimate "backing" of the medium. Users of currency, for example, do not demand silver or gold for their paper notes or bills. Similarly, when confidence in the political system is high, political power seems to work "automatically," without the necessity for actually applying coercion; because all assume that coercive capacity is there, its use is not often necessary (1964, pp. 52–53).

But where political confidence has grown, it may also decline. Abrupt loss of public faith in power holders may result in something equivalent to a "run on the bank." In such cases, a claim of any one political interest

may, of course, be met. On the other hand, if it is not met or if the difficulty of meeting it creates a question of the capacity of the system to meet its general obligations, it *may* (not necessarily must) motivate other units to present demands they would not otherwise have presented *at this time*. (1964, pp. 63–64)

And such sequences may give way to civil violence.

In such a vicious circle process, there will be a tendency toward the use of force, in terms both of threat and counter-threat and in the terms of warnings. (1964, p. 69)

This is *power deflation,* in which opposition to government claims requires the authorities to back such claims with increasing application of actual coercive force. For Parsons and certain influential followers, power deflation is an essential element in the outbreak of civil violence. Chalmers Johnson, following Parsons closely, bases his *Revolutionary Change* on this idea.

The one condition that contributes most deeply to a revolution is *power deflation*—the fact that during a period of change the integration of a system depends increasingly on the deployment of force. (1982, p. 93)

Johnson affirms that, under normal social conditions, commonly held values assure acceptance of civil authority. Violent political challenges to any regime are taken as evidence that power has "deflated," that the government no longer enjoys moral support from its people and thus has only force to rely on to achieve compliance. Once a government loses legitimacy, in Johnson's view, any minor strain can topple it (1982, p. 94).

What are we to make of these most abstract and sweeping arguments? Do such rarefied concepts as "media" and "power deflation" relate to any empirically falsifiable theory of civil violence?

Perhaps the best way to start any assessment is not with the problems but with the more positive points. Parsons's imaginative analogies between power and other "media" do imply several sound observations.

1. Power certainly need not be a zero-sum phenomenon. The ability to organize concerted action by large numbers of people may indeed afford accomplishments that leave all participants better off. Thus comparisons may well be made among various social systems, as Parsons suggests, in terms of the total power for concerted action that they afford.

2. When power is well entrenched, it may indeed seem to work "automatically," such that those who exercise it and those who respond to it may scarcely notice that it is being exerted. Indeed, the application of

power is normally most effective when nobody involved needs to be convinced of the potential effectiveness of power holders' claims.

3. Finally, the perception that supposed power holders are unable to make good on their "normal" claims may indeed contribute to further erosion of that ability. This is no more true for those who hold institutional power than for power holders in any number of other settings, from organized crime to the family. No doubt some power hierarchies are toppled through abrupt collapse of confidence in their ability to enforce customary obligations.

One can imagine citing empirical findings to demonstrate that processes like the three described here do, in fact, occur. But for other elements of Parsons's media arguments, I am not so sure. His statements on the ways in which power comes to be entrusted to power holders are truly remarkable.

Interest groups, including government incumbents, are never content to operate in terms of "naked power", but always attempt to legitimize their claims in terms of the public interest. However imperfect the integration may be, this concept's weight is far from negligible in a moderately stable political system. (1961a, p. 68)

In a later study he asserts that political supporters

entrust their stakes in and interpretations of the collective interest to an impersonal process in which binding decisions are made without the members' being in a position to control them. (1964, p. 46)

There *may* be interest groups somewhere who never make claims without justifying them as on behalf of "the public interest"; there *may* be political supporters who provide backing to their favored leaders with absolutely no strings attached. But to offer these statements as theoretical pronouncements on the formation of political power in general is truly extraordinary. To quote Brian Barry on some related ideas of Parsons, "The breathtaking naivete of these remarks provides a remarkable glimpse of the way in which Parsons actually sees the world" (1968, p. 155).

Parsons's supporters might well respond to such objections as follows: True, political support may sometimes be provided for venal sorts of reasons, for example, in exchange for favors. But the support granted in such circumscribed exchanges never permits the freedom of action necessary for really flexible exercise of power. Parsons does in fact characterize conditional political support as the equivalent of barter, in unfavorable contrast to "political banking" where stores of public confidence are available, without restriction, for "investment" by responsible public officials (1961a, p. 68). The best that can be said for this argument is that it ignores the effectiveness of the political "horse trading" and "log rolling" that often result in the cumulation of vast and virtually unrestricted power.

Part of the difficulty of Parsons's position is the vagueness of his idea of political support. Perhaps because he believes that no regime can continue without widespread moral support from those under it, he takes the merest signs of acquiescence as evidence of deep political commitment. His article in the book *Voting* treats the vote of the most apathetic voters as "an implicit act of faith in the necessary relinquishment of control of their affairs to leadership" (1959b, p. 96). Yet what is being relinquished in such instances? Should the interest of the voters in question drop one iota, so that they remain home from the polls, they will be no better or worse off than if they had voted. Similarly, Parsons's idea that voters' participation in elections involves their transmitting a "medium" to elected officials has no empirical reference. This part of the theory offers no falsifiable statements that might not just as well be offered by a quite different theory.

Let me suggest a drastic interpretation of these arguments on the formation of political power and its "flow" back and forth between leaders and followers: that they are most fruitfully read not as a sociological doctrine at all, but as a normative exhortation of how power ought to be formed. I suggest that Parsons simply set down his own convictions about these matters, his own belief that power ought to be accorded by supporters largely as carte blanche to their leaders, for example, or that for every unit of support given to leaders, equivalent units of political outputs should be forthcoming to the populace. For again, these are not empirical notions; one can conceive of no evidence that might be adduced to refute them. Far from establishing "an exact parallel between money and power" as he claims (1964, p. 46), Parsons offers us a series of analogies that shade off from what is to what, in his view, ought to be.

But perhaps a theory of civil violence can nonetheless be salvaged from the more empirical elements of these theories. The most promising of these is the idea of power deflation, as derived from Parsons and developed most notably by his disciple Chalmers Johnson.* The main falsifiable implication of this doctrine might go something as follows:

*Expect heightened levels of civil violence when the power of institutional power holders is deflating.*

Note that this statement refers only to civil violence associated with the workings of state power. Let us therefore exempt from consideration here strife played out strictly between nongovernment forces, for example, ethnic conflicts where governments play no role. For interactions be-

---

*It has always seemed to me that what Parsons and his followers call power deflation should rightfully be power *inflation*—a situation where larger and larger amounts of the relevant medium (power) are required to secure compliance previously attained by smaller expenditures. But I follow their usage in this book.

tween governments and activist groups on the outside, then, we will expect more violence, and perhaps revolutionary change, where power is deflating.

But can any empirical meaning be given to the notion of power deflation, apart from the phenomena it is supposed to explain? If any outbreak of civil violence is taken as evidence of power deflation, then the concept obviously cannot explain civil violence.

A more promising alternative would be to define power deflation as a moral state of society, or rather the polity, as a whole—much like Durkheim's idea of anomie. Indices of power deflation in this sense might include various nonviolent forms of resistance or indifference to government authority, such as refusal to pay taxes or accept decisions of the courts. One might then mount an investigation to determine whether the likelihood of civil violence across a variety of instances was associated with fluctuations in such indices of moral support.

The problem would be to establish connections between civil violence and the moral attitudes of something close to an entire population, rather than simply to discontent among specific groups well positioned to articulate and act on such discontent. Johnson fails to do this in *Revolutionary Change*; he gauges power deflation by the strength of challenges to governments from aggrieved or ambitious activist groups. In fact, I know of no successful empirical effort to demonstrate linkages between civil violence and authentic indices of moral solidarity from below. To be sure, we have empirical studies predicated on the assumption that any enduring political institutions must necessarily reflect strong grass-roots moral support from the populations who live under them (Bendix 1978). But such studies do not undertake the exceedingly difficult task of adducing actual evidence of such moral feeling on the part of the populations concerned. The demands of such research are most exacting. The only evidence I have seen reported on these matters is negative—Tilly's studies showing poor statistical association in France between collective violence and such presumed indices of moral solidarity as crime or suicide rates (Tilly, Tilly, and Tilly 1975, p. 81).

There is no reason to doubt that some outbreaks of civil violence result from something like loss of moral confidence in the regime. Recent civil disturbances in Islamic countries, for example, have obviously had much to do with dissatisfaction of some sectors of the population in the moral and religious posture of elites. Whether these clashes can accurately be described as reflecting a moral state of the society as a whole, rather than an opposition between rulers and specific religiously oriented sectors within the population, remains to be shown. But there are simply no grounds to believe that all breaches in the state monopoly on coercion require a moral explanation. The evidence for changing moral states as essential preconditions to such events is lacking, whereas the availability of other explanations, such as changing balances of coercive forces, is often abundant.

Finally, note that many outbreaks of civil violence—indeed, the beginnings of some revolutions—occur in response to heightened repression or other extraordinary demands from governments against their people. That is, they begin with the opposite of what has been described as "power deflation." One obvious example is the American Revolution. There is no reason why cycles of violence must necessarily start at the bottom. To such observations a defender of the power deflation doctrine might respond that the *nonnormative* violence really began with first grass-roots response. But such a position so thoroughly insulates the doctrine from falsifiability as to deprive it of all sociological interest.

## Smelser's Theory of Collective Behavior

Until the media studies, Parsons himself had written rather little on civil violence, or indeed on social conflict. Yet throughout the decades following publication of *The Structure of Social Action* (1937), Parsons's thinking was acquiring increasing influence among American sociologists as a theoretical lens for viewing the most diverse subject matters. Playing essential roles in this dissemination of Parsonian influence were Parsons's eminent students. Neil Smelser, perhaps more than any other of these influential exponents, sought explicitly to demonstrate the applicability of Parsons's thought to new sociological domains. One of his efforts to this end, *Theory of Collective Behavior* (1962), has become the most influential book on collective behavior ever published in America.

Smelser is explicit, in the opening pages of the book, about his aim in writing it—to substitute categories and terms of analysis drawn from Parsons for alternative theoretical ideas then prevailing in the study of collective behavior. Until the publication of Smelser's work, these prevailing ideas were overwhelmingly drawn from the tradition of LeBon and Park. Smelser takes the *concept* of collective behavior as his subject matter directly from Park, instead of focusing attention on "collective action" or "social movements" or "revolution," as other theorists might have done. "Collective behavior is analyzable by the same categories as conventional behavior," Smelser writes.

The two differ, to be sure. At one hypothetical extreme, collective behavior involves a collective redefinition of an unstructured situation; at the other extreme, conventional behavior is the working-out of established expectations. (1962, p. 23)

Smelser identifies the "fundamental components of social action" as consisting of values, norms, "mobilization into organized roles," and "situational facilities" (1962, p. 32). For any kind of concerted social behavior to take place, in other words, participants must first share common values, then find norms through which to realize such values, agree who is to play which roles within this normative structure, and finally put these understandings to work in some concrete setting. Collective behavior occurs when any of these elements is disturbed. Moreover, the nature of collective behavior is determined by the nature of the interrupted or distorted action element.

Any redefinition of a component of social action necessarily makes for a readjustment in those components below it, but not necessarily in those above it. . . . Changes in basic values entail changes in the definition of norms, organization and facilities. Changes in norms entail changes in the definition of organization and facilities, but not values. (p. 33)

And so on. Alterations in people's ultimate values, the most important basis of social behavior, lead to profound rearrangements in social behavior, whereas alterations of the physical setting in which action takes place, at the other end of the continuum, lead to more limited changes.

Smelser is much more explicit about what his theory is supposed to accomplish than is Parsons. He seeks to explain:

What determines whether an episode of collective behavior *of any sort* will occur? What determines whether one type *rather than another* will occur? (p. 12)

To this end, Smelser develops his well-known "value-added" scheme for analysis of the determinants of collective behavior. This scheme reflects Smelser's desire for an alternative to the then-prevailing views of the followers of Park, particularly to the "natural history" of the origins of events (1962, p 18) The value-added stages are conditions that must be met—in their appointed order, Smelser emphasizes—before any instance of collective behavior can occur. The form taken by each determinant in turn constrains the gestating episode, until it ultimately manifests itself precisely in the form required by all its antecedents.

The value-added stages, in their sequential order, are (1962, pp. 15–17): First, "structural conduciveness"; the setting in which behavior takes place, in other words, admits of some form of collective behavior and not others. Second, "structural strain," "an impairment of the relations among and consequently inadequate functioning of the components of action" (p. 47); as Smelser uses the idea, this seems to mean unwillingness or inability to adhere to institutionalized patterns of action. Third, "growth and spread of a generalized belief," something that "identifies the source of the strain, attributes certain characteristics to this source, and specifies certain responses to the strain as possible or appropriate" (p. 16). Fourth, "precipitating factors," or a triggering event, like an arrest in a ghetto neighborhood that sets off rioting. Fifth, "mobilization of participants for action," or the first beginnings of actual collective behavior. Finally, the "operation of social control"; not quite commensurate with other stages, these are social processes at work at all stages to inhibit and contain collective behavior both before and after it takes place.

*Theory of Collective Behavior* devotes a chapter each to five major types of collective behavior. They are the panic, the craze, the hostile outburst, the norm-oriented movement, and the value-oriented movement. Each corresponds, in Smelser's view, to the breakdown of an increasingly higher-level component of social action. In each of these long chapters, Smelser delves widely through the English-language literature on collective behavior for examples to illustrate the applicability of his scheme. In the chapter on panic, for example, he states,

The first and most determinate condition for panic is structural conduciveness. To assess this condition we ask: . . . What are the opportunities for escape? Are the major social rewards—such as wealth, power, or prestige—freely disposable, or are they "locked" into the social structure in a way that prevents rapid and panicky withdrawal? (p. 133)

He goes on to discuss such things as stock market panics, tulip manias, and flights from burning buildings as constrained by structural conduciveness and other value-added stages.

Smelser's book demonstrates that the conceptual scheme he adopts can *organize* the literature on collective behavior. But that is not a key concern here. We need to know, instead, whether his theory affords the possibility of confrontation with discordant evidence. For example, does it make sense to entertain the following expectation?

*Expect no collective behavior of any kind in the absence of preexisting structural strain on the part of participants.*

Such an expectation is either unfalsifiable or vacuous. Smelser defines collective behavior as that which contravenes institutional or normative ways of doing things (p. 8). Because structural strain is defined as disposition to contravene institutional normative patterns, it is impossible to imagine collective behavior that does not entail structural strain. To be sure, investigators may seek, and find, sources of discontent whose presence helps to account for an episode of collective behavior; but under Smelser's definitions, collective behavior without *some* form of structural strain is logically impossible.

On close examination, the value-added scheme is riddled with similar difficulties; no empirical findings that might be adduced could conceivably refute it. Indeed, the occurrence of the six value-added stages is implicit in the definition of collective behavior itself. The fact that a riot, a revolution, or a panic takes place, for example, makes it apparent that the social setting must have shown "structural conduciveness." Likewise for "generalized beliefs": all social behavior, innovative as well as institutional, presumably requires some sort of definition of the situation. "Growth and spread of generalized beliefs" appears simply to mean that participants must have some common perceptions of what is occurring and what to do about it. Precipitating factors, mobilization of participants for action, and the working of social control all by the same token are things that have to have occurred if something fitting the definition of collective behavior is to take place. Indeed, with the exception of "structural strain" and "the workings of social control," all the value-added stages appear to be necessary conditions for *any* form of social behavior, innovative or routine.

The value-added scheme does make one important heuristic contribution. It alerts us to the fact that, for any instance of collective behavior to occur—or indeed, for any other behavior—a variety of necessary conditions must be fulfilled. The fact that people are in a militant frame of mind, for example, may result in no unusual action unless they agree on targets for corrective action. Or, the fact that given circumstances have produced innovative action in the past have no bearing on the future if new actors view the same circumstances from different perspectives. This way of thinking is an important corrective to the notion that collective behavior or any other social phenomenon results from a single "cause" that, once specified, leaves it firmly and permanently accounted for. Thus, in his well-known study of the rise and decline of the Social Credit Party in Canada, Maurice Pinard (1975) shows the joint dependence of participation in the movement on poor economic conditions (which he identifies as structural strain), organizing efforts (identified as mobilization for action), and a variety of other value-added conditions.

Smelser's discussion of the value-added stages, then, does direct attention to various matters that may indeed make a difference in the way collective behavior manifests itself. "Look for the thing that people are dissatisfied with," Smelser in effect tells us; "its characteristics will have something to do with the kind of action that results." Or, "pay attention to the beliefs guiding the action you are studying; they are bound to affect what people do."

Such statements are just barely falsifiable. If the nature of what bothered people proved to have nothing whatever to do with their resulting actions, then this statement would be cast into doubt. But Smelser avoids any commitment that would increase the falsifiable content of these formulations. He does not tell us, for example, how much structural strain should be sufficient to produce collective behavior, only that there can be no such effect without at least some of it. And, again, because collective behavior is by definition that which contravenes institutional social patterns, the existence of strain seems implicit in any action leading to such behavior.

In some instances, like the protest movement studied by Pinard, one may indeed link particular forms of protest with objective conditions whose responsibility for participants' *experience* of strain has been established—for example, high prices or unemployment. In such cases, fluctuations in the objective condition may be shown to cause fluctuations in participants' experience of strain. But the absence of such an obvious objective condition would hardly represent a falsifying case. In other instances of collective behavior, strain might well arise from changes strictly internal to the minds of participants. Members of a community that never objected to saloons before, for example, might experience strain over their presence as a result of their conversion to temperance. If we take Smelser at his word, strain is anything that might move people to engage in collective behavior; the absence of any particular *objective* condition cannot be interpreted to mean that strain was lacking.

Nor does Smelser offer any falsifiable statements on what kinds of strain lead to what kinds of collective behavior.

> Some structural strain must be present for one or more types of collective behavior to appear. Which type or types depends on the progressive accumulation of the other determinants in the value-added process. We should not attempt to establish particular causal connections between a single kind of strain and a single kind of collective behavior. (p. 49)

No doubt every social *explanandum* is shaped by the joint forces of all the conditions necessary for its occurrence. But this statement is simply not very informative. We need Smelser to provide a rule specifying how much strain and other predisposing conditions are necessary to count as fulfilling the conditions of his theory and how we are to recognize such things independently of the effects they are supposed to produce. Otherwise, it is impossible in principle to imagine evidence that could count against his theory.

Even more perplexing is Smelser's contention that the various stages of the value-added process must be activated in the order given above (1962, p. 19). He acknowledges that a given stage—for example, generalized beliefs—may exist long before collective behavior occurs. But, he insists, "In the value-added process . . . we must distinguish between the *occurrence* or *existence* of an event or situation, and the *activation* of this event or situation as a determinant" (p. 19). The passage shows that he is stressing this difference to distinguish the value-added approach from its theoretical competitor, the "natural-history" approach developed by Park's follower Edwards (1927). But what empirical meaning is to be attributed to this notion of "activation"? If the roof falls in on a crowded department store and people run in panic to the exits, how can one say that the "formation of generalized beliefs" followed "structural strain," or preceded "precipitating factors?" It would appear that the sequence exists only as part of the definition of the concept, or not at all.

Another key theoretical element of Smelser's argument is the classification of forms of collective behavior. Here the stamp of Parsons's thought is especially plain. Does the Parsons–Smelser view embody falsifiable implications more profound than those derived from other theorists? Does characterizing a category of events as value oriented, for example, really provide new information about the force of values in social behavior?

Not really. What Smelser gives us might more modestly be described as a classification of nonconforming or innovative behavior in terms of duration or scope. Value-oriented social movements are efforts to alter fundamental practices, views, or institutions, such as American capitalism; norm-oriented movements aim at narrower innovations, such as antiabortion agitation. Hostile outbursts are short-lived attacks on persons or property, briefer and more limited than the preceding two. Of course, there are ambiguous cases like the famous Free Speech movement at the University of California, Berkeley, which began as a norm-oriented movement yet gave early promise of becoming something much more sweeping. But the real problem has to do with the relation between applications of the classification and the underlying theory. Does it really add anything to our understanding to call especially far-reaching social movements "value oriented"? Does the use of this notion in analysis of actual episodes in any way substantiate the relation between collective values and social action posited by Parsons or Smelser? Indeed, does any element of Smelser's theory disclose empirical relations that would not be anticipated otherwise? I think the answer is negative in both cases. The tenets of value integration theory are assumed in the construction of the classification scheme, rather than subjected to potentially discordant encounters with evidence. The possibility of applying the scheme to data in such a way as to draw critical conclusions about the theory is nil.

This conclusion runs contrary to the impressions conveyed in early passages of the book, where discussions of components of social action and complex diagrams seem to suggest empirically manifest causal forces (see especially Smelser's second chapter). Such forces seem to be implied in statements like Smelser's remark that "any redefinition of a component of social action necessarily makes for a readjustment in those components below it, but not necessarily those above it." Yet he adds,

It should be kept in mind that this is a statement of the *logical* or *theoretical* relations among the components of action. It is a statement of what changes follow, necessarily and by definition, from modification of one or another of the components. (p. 33, emphasis in original)

In other words, if a value-oriented movement *is* a value-oriented movement it must entail disturbance of the "lower" components of action. Yet, Smelser continues:

This is not to say that *empirical* modifications at the lower levels do not ever constitute conditions of structural strain which initiate higher-level changes. This last problem, however, constitutes a set of issues separate from the simple logical relations among the components. (p. 34, emphasis in original)

Given these qualifications, it would seem that we are left with just one important falsifiable implication—namely, that one should never encounter a "value-oriented" movement or other form of collective behavior based on disruption of a higher-level action component that does not entail alteration of "lower levels" of social action. But because things like value-oriented and norm-oriented movements are defined so as to include shorter-term behaviors—for example, blocking the entrance to a building or refusal to pay taxes—there is no possibility of falsification here, either. The scheme is impervious to evidence.

In the closing pages of his work, Smelser provides a conspectus of his theoretical claims and their relations to evidence; it is worth examining in detail.

The master proposition is found in Chapter IV: People under strain mobilize to reconstitute the social order in the name of a generalized belief.

And a few paragraphs later he continues:

How do we decide whether to accept or reject such a statement? What kinds of data do we examine?. . . .

A critical issue to be posed for any proposition before it can be called a scientific principle is: Can we find evidence that would lead us to reject the proposition? In connection with our analysis two types of negative evidence can be found: (a) Situations in which one or more necessary conditions (e.g., strain) are absent, but in which a collective outburst occurs. . . . (b) Situations in which one or more necessary conditions are present but in which the collective outburst does not occur. . . . For those situations in which we find strain but no collective outbursts, then, we must ask if other necessary conditions are absent. If one or more of them is absent, the presence of strain without a collective episode does not constitute negative evidence. If, however, strain *and* all the other necessary conditions are present, but no outburst occurs, this is negative evidence. (1962, pp. 385–87)

Smelser need not worry about anyone's producing negative evidence of this kind. The very conception of these necessary conditions (the value-added stages), along with that of the phenomenon to be explained, makes it impossible to imagine encountering the latter without being able to identify the former. Smelser's theory of collective behavior is an elaboration of a definition. It provides a showcase for empirical materials studied under the rubric of collective behavior, much as do the theories of Park or other theorists. But it brings us no closer to an empirically falsifiable account of the causes of militant collective action.

## Value Integration as an Empirical Doctrine

If ever a "theoretical framework" or "paradigm" can be said to have shaped the perceptions of generations of sociologists, value integration is surely a case in point. Since *The Structure of Social Action*, the idea has grown nearly universal that, in Parsons's words, every "relatively established 'politically organized society' is clearly a 'moral community' to some degree, its members sharing common norms, values and culture" (1964, p. 34). So pervasive has this notion become that it appears to be embraced by many who acknowledge little association between their views and those of Parsons. I have sought to show, in this chapter, that Parsons's allusive and vague formulations make it very difficult to attribute specific empirical meaning to this doctrine, and that the falsifiable interpretations that might be made of it are either unconvincing or unremarkable. Yet even those who disagree with these conclusions must surely acknowledge that the empirical implications of value integration theory for analysis of political conflict and civil violence have not received much critical attention. Instead, the "theoretical framework" from which these implications arise has taken on a life of its own: accepted by many, rejected by some, but in any case rarely confronted with potentially disconfirming evidence.

All of this raises questions not only about our understanding of civil violence, but about our understanding of social theory. What standards would Parsons himself hold out for the acceptance or rejection of broad theoretical doctrines like his own?

Parsons's accounts of what principles should warrant acceptance of his theories are infrequent. And his efforts in this direction range from the diffident to the sweeping. At some points in *The Structure of Social Action*, for example, his claims seem most modest.

The action frame of reference is certainly one of those in which certain of the facts of human action can be for certain scientific purposes adequately described. It is not the only one of which this is true, but the critical results of the study show that, for certain purposes, which cannot but be considered scientifically legitimate, it is more adequate than any of the alternative frames of reference. (1937, p. 756)

This is hardly an overweening assertion; Parsons might simply be telling us that his favorite route to Cape Cod from Cambridge is more scenic, though others may be more direct.

Yet this low-key assertion strikes a contrast to more emphatic claims from his later writings—for example, his claim in *The Social System* that value integration represents "the fundamental dynamic theorem of sociology" (1951, p. 42). Is there any way of reconciling such seemingly different views of the accomplishments of this line of thinking? Or is acceptance or rejection of Parsons's world-view really just a matter of choosing one among many "adequate" ways of looking at things?

In a reflective passage at the close of one of the "media" articles, Parsons acknowledges "an inherent arbitrariness" in his view of power: "I have defined power and a number of related concepts in my own way," he observes, "which is different from many if not most of the definitions current in political theory" (1963b, p. 258). The justification for this approach, Parsons argues, lies in its compatibility with "a gradually developing organon of theoretical analysis and empirical interpretation and verification"— his own, no doubt. The special virtues of this "organon" are reflected in the ability to

illuminate a range of empirical problems which were not well understood in terms of the more conventional theoretical positions—e.g., the reasons for the general egalitarian pressure on the evolution of the franchise, or the nature of McCarthyism as a process of political deflationary spiral. (1963b, p. 258)

Here he seems to be referring to two earlier studies. One accounts for the rise of electoral systems as an evolutionary development affording greater efficiency to societies in pursuit of collective goals (1960, chap. 5). In the other, he explains McCarthyism as an instance of "power deflation," in which growing demands that public officials constantly prove their fundamental loyalty (as a kind of "hard currency" of political life) restricted the uncritical trust necessary for effective governance (1955).

The analogies between political power and money and other circulating media are indeed intriguing. But to take such parallels as bases for claims on how power, or any other social process, must work in general is something else entirely. The McCarthy period did entail sweeping decline of faith in government, with accompanying difficulty of mobilizing political support. But one might equally well describe this period as an attempt by Western and rural interests in the Republican Party to destroy the power bases of their rivals in the Eastern establishment—in other words, as an old-fashioned, zero-sum struggle over power. It is hard to see what evidence would support the claim that political power is "really" non-zero-sum, or that zero-sum relations must be a special case of the non-zero-sum type.

If evaluations of social theory were really to be made through analogical methods, the result would be strange indeed. Warfare, it is often remarked, is much like chess. One can pursue the analogies at length. Yet no account of war that failed to do justice to the differences between the two—for example, in the consequences of losing—could be considered adequate. Similarly, no account of the origins of civil violence or any other aspect of social life should satisfy us unless considered in the light of critical comparisons to other accounts, particularly concerning forms of evidence that might help choose among the alternatives. The failure to offer such critical comparisons, or indeed to acknowledge their importance, leads to the grave shortcomings of value integration as the basis for a theory of civil violence.

*Chapter Six*

# From Collective Behavior to Collective Action: Charles Tilly and Political Theories of Civil Violence

The 1960s brought far-reaching changes in theories of civil violence. Collective behavior and mass society thinking in the line of descent from the irrationalists and Robert Park abruptly lost ground to sharply different views. Prominent among the intellectual insurgents were political theories of civil violence. The key figure in this movement was Charles Tilly, the sociologist and historian now teaching at the New School for Social Research. With primary attention to the extensive writings of Tilly himself, this chapter offers a collective intellectual portrait of this theoretical line.

The distinctiveness of the accounts of civil violence offered by this view is hard to mistake.

First, the political view of civil violence sees militant action as *purposeful and rational*—that is, oriented to achieving authentic and enduring ends of those involved. This observation holds equally for government and nongovernment participants. Thus, a dramatic contrast to the view of the irrationalists and mass society theorists of crowd or mass action as unaccountable in relation to "normal" social action. Moreover, political analysts see militant action as framed in terms of *collective interest*. Note the contrast here to theories of the sort discussed in Chapter One, where a calculation is in terms of *individual interest*.

Similarly, these theorists view civil violence as highly *continuous* with other social action. Indeed, violent action is simply a phase in other forms of collective action, caused by the same forces that move people to other, "normal" assertions of collective interest. Here the theory strikes a contrast to value integration assumptions that violent collective action arises from special states of moral weakness or failed legitimacy. For similar reasons, political theories of civil violence picture participants in such action as representative and well integrated members of the groups on whose interests they act.

Third, political analysis of civil violence is *antiholistic*. In contrast both to value integration and relative deprivation theories, it identifies the origins of violent action not in individual states widely shared throughout entire populations, but in *juxtapositions of interest and opportunity among contending subsets of populations*. Whole populations do not "rise up" in violence here, but instead particular groupings come to blows with particular others over particular issues.

Finally, political theories of civil violence are, of course, *political*. The issues most likely to move people to contentious action are those bound up with the prevailing struggles for power within the polity. Variation in the issues animating political life as a whole will bring variation in levels and kinds of civil violence.

## The Intellectual Pedigree

Although it strikes a distinct contrast to views previously prevailing in American social science, the political view of civil violence has a long intellectual lineage.

One key influence is Marxism. Both the classical writings from the nineteenth century and modern authors such as E. P. Thompson, Eric Hobsbawm, and George Rude helped shape the thinking of Tilly and his followers. True, neither Tilly nor other authors considered in this chapter espouse certain of what some would consider distinctively Marxist assumptions—for example, that class struggle must ultimately lead to a world where both conflict and the state itself disappear, or that all large-scale social conflict must somehow be a disguised manifestation of class conflict. What Tilly and his followers do share with Marxism is something much more important and fruitful. First, the notion that collective violence, and large-scale collective action more generally, occur where important collective interests hang in the balance. Second, the conviction that the forms, settings, and terms of collective violence, as much as other forms of collective conflict, depend on the larger structures of social life.

Another central influence in Tilly's thinking was P. A. Sorokin, Tilly's brilliant and eccentric teacher at Harvard. Fortunately the intellectual inheritance from Sorokin was selective: Not his theory of revolution (1925)— which derived substantially from the doctrines of the irrationalists—nor his stratospheric theories of historical change from *Social and Cultural Dynamics* (1937), but rather certain of Sorokin's historical *methods* became a key part of Tilly's research strategy. Specifically, Tilly refined Sorokin's strategy of assessing internal conflict through systematic *enumeration* of violent events, taking inspiration from the third volume of *Social and Cultural Dynamics*.

Many analyses, especially those of historians, have focused attention on collective violence in proportion to its historically evident *results*. This plausible strategy leads to ignoring or minimizing events that engaged many participants and entailed much strife at the time, yet left few institutional changes. At the same time, it inevitably encourages exaggeration of relatively small-scale events that triggered, or appeared to have triggered, major historical developments. By contrast, Tilly sought to apply the same techniques of identifying and recording violent episodes, regardless of the significance historians subsequently assigned to them. This approach speaks directly to the concerns of this book, which deals not so much with the historical consequences of civil violence, but rather with its setting and origins.

Yet another intellectual current feeding into political theories derives from pluralistic models of political life as developed by figures like Robert Dahl. This is ironic. Nearly all political theorists of civil violence have argued in opposition to classical pluralism, particularly against the view of democratic political systems as open to the needs and interests of all elements of the population. They hold that whereas some groups within the polity exercise preponderant political influence, others are virtually or entirely excluded from it. Indeed, for Tilly and others violence appears as an alternative to institutionalized political influence—the voice of the politically voiceless, the ultimate, and often effective, insistence of the deprived on being taken into account. Yet the analysts considered in this chapter have adopted an assumption characteristic of their antagonists— the view of political life as composed of contending parties, each representing the interests of different sectors of the population.

Such ideas were pervasive at the University of Michigan, where Tilly carried out research and trained many students from 1969 to 1984. Tilly's scholarly contemporaries at Michigan included William Gamson, Jeffrey Paige, Mayer Zald, and a number of other students of social contention. Together, this prolific group had a very considerable effect in shaping a strictly political view of social movements and militant collective action.

Finally, both Tilly and his many fellow analysts of violent contention as political phenomena no doubt shared a diffuse sensitivity widespread in social science and history since at least the 1960s—a desire to get close to the specific events and lives that compose big historical processes. Against the abstractions of more stratospheric theorists, they sought to document the gritty, rude pushing and shoving that go into social change. This turn of mind has given rise to a whole generation of historical and social analysis "from below," in which Tilly's own works play an essential part.

## Tilly: The Development of His Position

Tilly's interest in civil violence began with his doctoral research, completed under the direction of George Homans and Barrington Moore. The subject was the guerrilla warfare in western France that flared against the revolutionary government in Paris during the early 1790s. Ultimately published as *The Vendee* (1964b), this work has probably been read more by historians than by social scientists. Indeed, it established Tilly as a key figure in "the new history"—the study of historical subjects through demographic, sociological, and economic attention to grass-roots populations. And although *The Vendee* is a more strictly historical work than most of Tilly's subsequent writings, its analyses prefigured many of his later theoretical positions, for example, in his view of violent action as arising directly from grass-roots patterns of social organization. Tilly began his theoretical career, then, with a more detailed acquaintance with a major instance of civil violence than had been true for most sociologists before him.

In two important early essays, "Queries on Social Change and Political Upheaval" (1963), and "Reflections on the Revolutions of Paris" (1964a), Tilly began a wide-ranging critique of existing theories of civil violence. Here he attacked arguments attributing political upheaval in general, and violence in particular, to breakdowns in established moral solidarities. Tilly noted two forms of this argument. One was the mass society version as discussed above (Kornhauser 1959); the other derived more from theories of political and economic "development" (Olson 1963). The latter pointed to rapid social change, particularly industrialization, as a cause of violent political protest and conflict. In contrast, Tilly argued, periods characterized by the the most rapid urbanization and industrialization have often been the least turbulent, whereas relatively stable periods have frequently been turbulent (1963, p. 26). Nor did misery itself appear to spur rebellion; many of the most chronically miserable groups were never heard from on the stage of violent action. More likely, Tilly argued (1963, p. 30), the immediate cause of violent protest was abrupt imposition of suffering, rather than sheer misery.

Finally, Tilly scores the various "scum of the earth" theories of participation in violent events. Referring to participation in the insurrections of 1848, he comments:

The evidence suggests that most of the insurgents had formed substantial attachments to one or another of the city's subgroups, had undergone a fairly extensive socialization to the city's way of life, and had perhaps simultaneously received a political indoctrination. . . . Maybe attachment to some kinds of groups *facilitates* rebellion; maybe intensive political socialization normally preceded participation in insurrection. (1963, pp. 34–35)

It would be hard to overemphasize the significance of this last statement as a theme for the outpouring of Tilly's writings to follow over the following decades.

In 1964 Tilly began an ambitious study of social change and political upheaval in France, funded by the National Science Foundation. Covering the period 1830–1960, it aimed at many of the same questions raised in "Queries." Following in Sorokin's methodological footsteps, the plan was to collect systematically all reports of violent incidents available from a daily reading of the French press and a systematic scanning of archival sources, regardless of how, or indeed whether, historians had treated such instances. The ultimate goal was to link the total "production" of violence with other fundamental social, economic, and political changes in a modernizing society (Tilly and Rule 1965).* This study, elaborated from time to time and later extended to Britain, has continued down to the present. The labor-intensive nature of the work has made it a training ground for many graduate students in history and sociology.

Detailed research reports were slow to emerge from the French study, however. During the late 1960s Tilly continued to refine his theoretical position in a series of articles, drawing occasional examples from the accumulating materials on France. In one of the most important of these articles, "The Modernization of Political Conflict in France," written in 1969 but published several years later (1972a), Tilly sets another standard theme—the *normality* of collective violence. "No tragic chasm separates violence from non-violence," he notes, and adds some pages later:

Remember that group violence ordinarily grows out of collective actions which are not intrinsically violent—festivals, meetings, strikes, demonstrations and so on. Without them, the collective violence could hardly occur. People who do not take part in them can hardly get involved in the violence. The groups engaging in col-

*Though I collaborated in two works with Charles Tilly, in this chapter I seek to reconsider the ideas of Tilly and his many followers and collaborators from as fresh and independent a viewpoint as possible.

lective action with any regularity usually consist of populations perceiving and pursuing a common set of interests. And collective action on any considerable scale requires coordination, communication and solidarity extending beyond the moment of action itself. (1972a, p. 74)

Thus, collective violence is seen simply as another form of collective action, oriented to the same purposes that contending groups pursue in "normal" conditions.

The rootedness of civil violence in "normal" social relations is a theme that recurs in nearly all of Tilly's writings on the subject. Collective action of any kind, he argues, requires a sense of entitlement or justice on the part of the aggrieved, and such a sense can only arise out of ongoing group life. Thus he writes in "Do Communities Act?"

Why do groups ever make claims on other groups? In general because some or all of their members believe the group a) needs resources currently controlled by another group, in order to pursue an established collective objective, b) has the right to those resources. The basis for that right might range from a general principle (such as freedom to assemble without harassment) to a specific, established usage (such as villagers' long-established opportunity to glean in a landlord's fields once the harvest is in). (1974a, p. 14)

This intensely normative view of civil violence could hardly strike a deeper contrast to the theories considered in Chapters Three and Five. In many of these formulations, collective violence was as discontinuous with normal social process as the onset of an epileptic fit.

This normative view has formed the basis for Tilly's typology of change in historical forms of collective violence. In a number of articles, including "The Changing Place of Collective Violence" (1970) and "Town and Country in Revolution" (1974b), Tilly envisages three basic types of collective action: primitive, reactionary, and modern. *Primitive* actions are those of autonomous communities prior to growth of the centralized state; they include such things as feuding among adjoining villages and fights among rival bands of craftsmen. *Reactionary* violence, second in the historical sequence, represented the resistance of previously autonomous groups to encroachments from the national state and economy. Food riots were one classical form; others were machine breaking, peasant occupations of enclosed common lands, and violent community resistance to conscription (1969, p. 40). The flourishing of reactionary violence varies from country to country, Tilly argues, according to the timing of the growth of the state.

Ultimately, however, the state wins; local communities are absorbed in national systems of political and economic power. But collective conflict does not end with the rise of the state; it simply takes on new forms. Thus Tilly writes of the characteristically *modern* forms of contention:

The deliberate attempt to seize control of the state qualifies. So does the demonstration, or the strike, which leads to a violent encounter. They differ from the
reactionary forms of collective violence in several important ways: in pivoting on
attempts to control, rather than to resist, different segments of the national structure; by normally involving relatively complex special-purpose associations rather
than communal groups; through a greater articulation of objectives, programs and
demands. (1969, p. 41)

So the struggle among contending groups continues; but the setting and
the stakes, as well as the contenders' identities, have changed.

In the new, national forum, however, the game becomes more complex. There are more possible alliances and oppositions, and new forms of
gain and loss. Some groups on this new stage have power to use the government for their own ends, whereas others are excluded from such opportunities. Tilly's model of the polity as associated with the modern state
is as follows:

If there is an organization which controls that concentrated means of coercion, it is
a *government*. . . . any group that collectively applies resources to influence the
government . . . is a *contender* for power. Some contenders have routine means
of making claims on the government that are accepted by other contenders, and
by agents of the government; collectively, such contenders make up the *polity*
related to a particular government; individually we call them *members* of the
polity. Jointly (but usually unequally) the members control the government. Contenders that do not have routine, accepted means of making claims on the government are not members of the polity; they are *challengers*. (1974b, p. 279)

Tilly develops this model of the polity from about 1969 on. The model is
vague on some key points, and there are slight variations in different versions. Some statements, for example, make it sound as though governments have no interests of their own, but only act as a resultant of the
forces of influential members. Elsewhere (1978, pp. 52–55) Tilly treats
agents of state power as purposeful actors in their own right. While Tilly
has continued to rely on this latter model of the polity, he has lately abandoned the primitive-reactionary-modern typology in favor of simpler
categorizations.

Tilly posits that collective actors will assert their interests especially
vigorously when political power is "up for grabs." Thus, peaks of violence
are the expected accompaniment of what he calls "entries and exits from
the polity," that is, points at which power distributions are being rearranged. For similar reasons, the polity model leads to the expectation
that *repression works*. Collective actors stay at home, in other words,
when governments or other forces make action too costly.

Unfortunately, these political accounts of the timing and intensity of
violent protest are not easy to weigh against other theoretical possibilities

in actual confrontation with empirical evidence. One of the few efforts by Tilly and his followers to engineer such a confrontation comes in an article by Snyder and Tilly (1972). The authors, drawing on data from their enumerations of collective violence in France, seek to assess the relative strengths of political versus relative deprivation models by correlating indices of civil violence during the period 1830–1960 with measures of both hardship and political variables. The former included measures of such things as prices of food and manufactured goods; political variables were measured by such things as arrest rates and years in which elections occurred (a dummy variable). The hardship variables show consistently low associations; the political variables, in some cases, stronger ones.

The methods of the study came in for strong criticism from Charles Halaby (1973). Halaby points out flaws in various measures used in the study—for example, the use of absolute prices as indices for hardship, rather than figures on the rate of change in prices that might better have captured a sense of relative deprivation. In fact, methods of the kind used by Snyder and Tilly are inexact in relation to the demands of the theory. The very idea of using aggregated national data for measuring hardship, political activity, or violence, which are bound to be experienced or produced locally, is less than ideal. But the measures used by Snyder and Tilly are of much the same sort used by the most sophisticated proponents of relative deprivation at the time at which they wrote. Participants in the debate on relative deprivation, in the years following, have refined their methods considerably, so that the effects of their variables are measured at the individual level. But we have no studies that directly compare the powers of these more refined versions of psychological theories to account for the timing and intensity of civil violence with those of political theories.

Some of Tilly's most explicit statements on the polity model appear in his studies of two revolutionary years in France, 1830 and 1848. There he and his collaborators (Rule and Tilly, 1975; Lees and Tilly 1975) examined data developed in the French study in relation to the historical transfers of power in those years. The data show considerable violence *after* the revolutionary transfers, as the new governments apparently sought to extend their control throughout the polity. In 1848, these postrevolutionary contests climaxed in the famous "June Days," in which the revolutionary forces that took power in February bloodily consolidated that power. In 1830, as well, the aftermath of the revolution was at least as violent as the period leading up to it. Both these cases seem to fit the logic of the polity model, as Tilly interprets it–that is, they appear to show heightened "testing" of the new government by other contenders until its repressive capacities are established. Similarly, during periods of intense governmental repression, as after Louis Napoleon's coup in 1851, levels of collective violence were considerably reduced (Tilly, Tilly, and Tilly 1975, p. 61).

The study of 1848 also provided support for political arguments on participation in collective violence. Lees and Tilly join Marx in their interpretation of the period between February and June of that year. The bourgeois forces who had led the revolution turned on the working-class Parisians who had been their allies, and ultimately expelled them from any claim on power. Lees and Tilly's analysis of the records for those captured in the insurgency shows them to be typical members of the Paris working class. There seemed no reason to believe that either deviants or social isolates were disproportionately represented.

In Tilly's view, most revolutionary transfers of power are the work of coalitions—in his language, partnerships among various contenders within the polity, possibly including both members and nonmembers. Usually the winning coalition is unstable. Obviously, allies are useful in the effort to expel old power holders, and troublesome once power is won. But the displacement of entrenched power holders does not occur at once. Drawing from Trotsky's *History of the Russian Revolution,* Tilly (1978, pp. 190–94) envisages periods of dual or multiple power, in a kind of revolutionary interregnum. During this period there is no single authority over the government apparatus; different elements of state power are controlled by various old and new members of the polity. But dual or multiple sovereignty does not last long. After February 1848, mutual testing, claims, and counterclaims among the parties presently led to clarification and consolidation of new power relations and reestablishment of a single power center.

In writings of the mid- and late 1970s, Tilly sought to systematize his treatment of collective action within the polity. Perhaps the most systematic of all these efforts is *From Mobilization to Revolution* (1978). "The analysis of collective action," he writes there, "has five big components: interests, organization, mobilization, opportunity and collective action itself" (1978, p. 7). Interests, Tilly acknowledges, are a slippery notion (1978, pp. 60–61); one must decide whether to impute interests or to let people "speak for themselves" in this respect. In practice, Tilly most often seems to regard interests as "natural" or inherent in actors' social structural position, especially their class position.

But if interests are often taken for granted, organization, resources, mobilization, and opportunity definitely are not. These are the variable determinants of collective action. If a particular category of people is unorganized, it has no hopes of pursuing its interests; indeed it may be unaware of them, or even of its own collective identity. If the group is organized, it may still be unable to mobilize resources to realize its interests.

Mobilization is defined as "the process by which a group acquires collective control over resources needed for action" (1978, p. 7); resources are described as "labor power, goods, weapons, votes and any number of other things, just so long as they are usable in acting on shared interests" (1978, p. 7). Even well-mobilized groups may be unable to take advantage of resources at their command without the proper political opportunities, such as weakness of regime incumbents or propitious coalitions with other challengers. Everyone who has participated in a social movement or grass-roots political activity has an intuitive sense of how groups attempt to mobilize resources to profit from political opportunities.

All of these formulations, of course, go naturally with Tilly's view of the purposefulness of collective action. Ambitious political actors, far from being the volatile subjects of manipulation characterized by LeBon and Sighele, husband their resources and act with great calculation. As Tilly puts it,

1. Collective action *costs* something.
2. All contenders count costs.
3. Collective action brings benefits, in the form of collective goods.
4. Contenders continuously weigh expected costs against expected benefits.
5. Both costs and benefits are uncertain because (a) contenders have imperfect information about the current state of the polity; (b) all parties engage in strategic interaction. (1978, p. 99)

One kind of evidence for these propositions, Tilly might argue, is that such calculations *work;* militant actions, from machine breaking to strikes, do often yield the results that their participants seek.

Like Barrington Moore and many other historically minded students of social institutions, Tilly regards current social and political arrangements as precipitates of collective action of the past. In an earlier study, he noted:

Men articulate, advertise and sometimes achieve their interests through conflict. That includes violent conflict. Ordinary Frenchmen, by rioting, force the authorities to hold down the price of bread. The great demonstrations and sit-down strikes of the 1930's did solidify the place of organized labor in the structure of power. Mass action did help produce significant transfers of power in 1789, 1830, 1848, 1870 and 1958. (1972a, p. 93)

In recent years Tilly and his collaborators have extended their data gathering to Britain, taking note not just of violent events but also of other forms of collective action. A significant additon to Tilly's conceptual ar-

mory during this period has been that of *repertoires* of collective action
(1979b). The repertoire consists of the forms of collective expression available to a particular group at a particular time. Like other cultural items,
from child-rearing techniques to food-getting technologies, the list of expressive forms so available is always limited; people simply do not know
how to do all of the things that in principle they *might* do. The classical
food riot was a central item in the repertoires of rural France until the
mid-nineteenth century; it dropped out when a changing power equation
rendered it ineffective. The tarring and feathering, the "rough music" or
disrespectful popular serenade, and the hanging in effigy were staples of
the nineteenth-century repertoire in Britain and America; they have not
entirely left us. The lynching seems to have dropped out of the twentieth-
century American repertoire—I hope that few will mourn it. The sit-in,
on the other hand, is a twentiety-century invention, and one wonders
what insurgent actors in recent decades would have done without it.

Tilly's idea of the repertoire implies a limit to purposefulness and calculation in collective action. Protest groups may weigh the costs and
benefits of different courses of action, he implies, but not all possible solutions are equally available to them. Like inventions in the usual sense,
items of repertoire may remain in use simply because no one can think of
something better. If collective protest is rational, it also shares at least
some of the inherent conservatism of other cultural patterns.

## Other Political Contributions

Tilly has hardly been the only analyst to view militant collective action as
a political process, though his position is the most comprehensive.

William Gamson is another important figure here. His early studies of
community and national political conflicts in America articulated a reasoned skepticism of pluralist positions. In his celebrated *The Strategy of
Social Protest* (1975), Gamson set out to examine the experience of insurgent social movements: When did the voiceless succeed, through collective action, in making their voices heard in the councils of power? In a
research design of elegant straightforwardness, Gamson drew a sample of
fifty-three from the universe of American social movements recorded during the period 1800 to 1945. These fifty-three were coded according both
to organizational and strategic characteristics of the movement, and in
terms of its success or failure. The results suggested much about the ability of collective action to advance grass-roots interests. Gamson determined, for example, that movements stood a better chance of success
when their goals did not include total elimination of competing groups
from the political scene, and that groups with more bureaucratic move-

ment organization tended to do better than those with less. Of particular interest here was that groups using or advocating violent means to their goals stood a better chance than the nonviolent.

Strictly speaking, Gamson's study does not seek to explain the occurrence of collective violence or social movement formation. He takes it for granted that collective action represents purposeful activity oriented to attainment of authentic collective interests. This is congruent with Tilly's position, and one of Gamson's key findings reinforces a central contention of Tilly: In the long view, violence often works in advancing collective interests.

Another noteworthy use of these same assumptions is by John McCarthy and Mayer Zald. In an influential article (1977), they treat the rise and decline of social movement activity as market phenomena. Their dependent variable is the success of "social movement organizations," or activist cadres with the skills and contacts necessary to mobilize grass-roots actors in pursuit of causes. Social movement organizations, McCarthy and Zald argue, act like businesses competing for markets. The "markets" in this case are elite sponsors, such as foundations, government granting agencies, and affluent contributors, who provide the resources necessary for mobilization. Thus popular discontent is assumed; what varies is the funneling of resources to movement specialists who give such discontent expression. The argument is most persuasive when taken as a description of the vicissitudes of civil rights, black power, and other movements of America in the 1960s and 1970s. But to what extent they intend their analysis to be generalizable is unclear.

Jenkins and Perrow (1977) develop a similar position on the role of elite sponsorship in their study of farm workers' attempts to mount collective action. The authors compare an early wave of organizing attempts in the 1940s and 1950s with a later organizing drive in the 1960s and 1970s. The first failed; the latter achieved some success. Jenkins and Perrow present evidence that firmer alliances with political forces of established power, including national church denominations and liberal foundations, and shrewder political action on the national political scene, accounted for the success of the more recent efforts.

A work more directly concerned with the causes of collective violence is Oberschall's *Social Conflict and Social Movements* (1973), a comprehensive statement on social movements, drawing heavily from the ideas of Tilly and other students of mass mobilization. Oberschall is particularly critical of mass society explanations of social movements. By way of antidote, he analyzes such diverse collective actions as African independence movements, the struggles of black Americans, and the Hungarian revolution of 1956. His concern is with resources available to insurgents and their mobilization. He places special importance on the role of established networks of social affiliation as a resource for collective action. One of his most distinctive assertions is that contests where lower-class insurgents are well organized but insulated from social ties with superordinate groups are more likely to take a violent form than where, as under classical feudalism, ties of loyalty or other contacts cross the lines of privilege (1973, p. 122). This combination of lower-class cohesion with group isolation, Oberschall contends, characterized the riotous situations in American urban ghettos in the 1960s.

This ghetto violence, and the history of social movements by and on behalf of black Americans, have been the subject of much attention from social scientists. Two important contributions to this literature in the political process vein are *Ghetto Revolts* by Joseph Feagin and Harlan Hahn (1973) and *Political Process and the Development of Black Insurgency, 1930–1970* by Doug McAdam (1982). The former is a study of the ghetto violence itself, arguing for a political view of these events. McAdam's work is an overview of the history of black political struggles in America, analyzing changes in the movement's fortunes in terms of resources, mobilization, and political opportunities. Both works have much to teach us about political theories as applied to specific data, as we shall see.

---

These are but a few of many empirical studies inspired by political views of militant collective action. Notwithstanding much variation among them, all share the crucial assumption that such action stems from pursuit of authentic and enduring collective interests, and that such interests are formed through the predictable constraints of social structure. Thus, the ethos of these studies is clear enough. But can we distill from that ethos a core of falsifiable statements that might provide the basis for comparing the political view to its theoretical alternatives?

## Political Theories: Rhetoric and Evidence

The burgeoning of political thinking among students of civil contention is perhaps as close as social science comes to an authentic "paradigm shift" in Thomas Kuhn's sense. Although proponents of other theoretical orientations had begun to experience misgivings about their positions—for example, Turner (1964a)—the innovators were not converts from other traditions. Nor were the new ideas exactly responses to discovery of strikingly new data, for the empirical material they focused on had always been there for any researcher who cared to look. If the evidence presented by Tilly and others on the purposefulness of violence was a discovery, it was a discovery whose time had arrived. How are we to account for this new theoretical perception of civil violence?

Surely the explanation must take account of the broader social and cultural context in which social scientists were working. As Gamson (1975, pp. 130–43) has thoughtfully pointed out, the 1960s saw some profound changes in the emotional associations of popular agitation. For writers of the 1950s, those associations were heavily influenced by totalitarian social movements of the Hitler and Stalin eras, and by the illiberal excesses of McCarthyism. The irrationalists, of course, evinced much the same reaction to working-class agitation of their times, especially the Paris Commune. But by the 1960s, a new generation of social scientists was responding, mostly sympathetically, to protest movements of blacks and university students. A theoretical view of movements and social contention as irrational, retrograde, destructive forces would no longer do. Thus, the analytic shift heralded by political process thinking was also a moral redefinition of the subject matter.

If the subject of this book were art or literature, we might leave matters at this. But theories in social science purport, at least implicitly, to capture a reality that transcends the values and interests of particular thinkers. Social science makes little sense without a basis in consensually validated evidence strong enough to withstand shifts in cultural and intellectual climates. Do these theories appeal to falsifiable statements that suggest clear alternatives to other views of civil violence?

I believe that they do. True, we can expect no single, elegant experiment or investigation that of itself would yield a definitive verdict on any of these theories; historians and philosophers of science have long since acknowledged that theories rarely change this way in any field. But we can envisage broad categories of evidence that, on balance, would tend to sustain or cast doubt upon various theoretical approaches. For most theories of civil violence, the distinctive falsifiable implications fall in three broad categories: those having to do with *participation* in violent episodes; those having to do with the *timing* and *location* of collective violence; and those dealing with the *form* and *purposes* of militant action.

1. *Participation.* Among the positions most often assailed in political accounts of contentious action have been what I call "scum of the earth" theories of insurgent participation. These are the doctrines asserting that participants in popular protest are either deviant—criminal, insane, or otherwise pathological—or socially dislocated or isolated. Against these arguments, Tilly and others have contended that popular protest, both

violent and otherwise, is a "normal" outgrowth of other popular collective action, and that participants are apt to be typical of the social groups whose interests the protests represent. Thus,

*Expect participants in insurgent collective action to be roughly typical of the groups whose interests are represented in these actions, in terms of their occupational and other social roles and their involvement in standard social networks.*

Evidence actually assembled thus far favors the political view. Some of the most systematic studies have been by Tilly and his collaborators, notably the study of participation in the events of 1848 (Lees and Tilly 1975). But equally persuasive studies have been done of ghetto rioting in America, depicting participants as typical residents of the neighborhoods involved (Fogelson and Hill 1968; Caplan 1970). George Rude (1964) reports similar patterns for the nineteenth-century French and British uprisings, while John Logan (1978) presents data on worker participation in twentieth-century protest movements in Spain also showing militants as well-established members of their communities. Many other studies could be cited to the same effect. Of course, even the variety of studies that have made this point may not be conclusive. Perhaps somewhere, sometimes deviants and isolates indeed have their day in popular protest; but systematic research has yet to record such facts.

2. *Timing, Magnitude and Location of Violent Events.*    Like other students of collective violence, political analysts have had much to say about when and where violence occurs. In Tilly's case, a particular contention has been that violent actions normally arise out of standard, nonviolent forms. Indeed Tilly, more than other analysts in this category, particularly downplays the analysis of violence as a special category of phenomena. The forces that move militant actors to purposeful destruction of people and property, he insists, are the same as those that lead to other forceful collective action. Thus,

*Expect most episodes of civil violence to be outgrowths of nonviolent forms of collective action.*

Here one can identify a variety of supportive examples: peaceful demonstrations that turn militant, confrontations between strikers and police that flare into violence, or a public rally attacked by police or political opponents. Such examples obviously fit well with the broader view of violence as purposeful activity.

But contrary examples are also easy to come by. The classical American lynching seems to have represented a self-contained violent scenario of its own. Many terrorist actions, both those of insurgents and of state coercive agents, appear to have violence as their main element. Many communal riots, from those in India at partition to those in American ghettos in the 1960s, seem to have begun and ended as violent actions; Feagin and Hahn (1973, p. 142) emphasize this point with regard to the American events.

Determining which path to civil violence is taken more frequently is impossible without enumeration. To date, Tilly's research offers the only form of data collection systematic enough to provide answers, and none of the analyses published so far have included quantitative comparisons of self-contained versus other forms of violent action. Perhaps these reports from the Tilly study are still to come.

A second theme of political arguments that ought to bear falsifiable implications has to do with the moral claims supposedly underlying violent actions. In Tilly's view (1974a, p. 14), collective actors press their claims violently under the conviction that the resources they seek are rightfully theirs. Such right may be identified either in some revolutionary ideology of entitlement or in conservative notions of traditional group prerogatives. This idea has much in common with the positions of many Marxist analysts of popular protest—for example, Thompson (1971) and Moore (1978)—as well as reverberations in the writings of value integration and relative deprivation theorists. Thus,

*Expect higher rates of violent collective action from groups who experience a sense of rightful claim to the contested resources or prerogatives than those who do not.*

But the falsifiable implications of this view are a good deal more elusive than they might seem. What form of data should count as evidence that people view their actions as having such justifications? Human powers of rationalization being what they are, people can find some justification to offer for nearly any contested behavior. If the argument is to have force, we need further evidence that those in question did feel or logically ought to have felt moral entitlement, apart simply from the fact that they acted.

In practice, such evidence is difficult to develop. One may well show that groups losing traditional prerogatives, such as the use of common lands, often attempt collective actions to resist such loss. But such ac counts have to be interpreted in conjunction with any evidence on instances where such loss is accepted without violent resistance and cases where groups mount offensive claims in the absence of any special moral justification. Without sensitive use of such difficult-to-assemble material, the argument remains unproven.

Another set of falsifiable implications of political theories have to do with the *timing* and *intensity* of violent events. Tilly and his followers have frequently argued that collective violence peaks at times of political activity more generally, and especially when fundamental changes are taking place in distribution of power. Thus,

*Expect high levels of militant collective action at times when the stakes, in terms of threats to and opportunities for objective political interests of the groups involved, are particularly high.*

This expectation, rich in theoretical significance, finds a good deal of support in Tilly's empirical investigations. Mappings of levels of collective violence over historical time (for example, Tilly, Tilly, and Tilly 1975, pp. 57–59) shows peaks of violent activity corresponding to peaks of political conflict and nonviolent change. Such findings create a presumption in favor of political theories of civil violence. Concomitantly, they encourage skepticism of interpretations based on moral breakdown or crowd contagion, unless such states can somehow be viewed as themselves associated with political struggle. But again we need a more thorough search for negative cases. Are there instances where major shifts in power level, perhaps without the conspicuous signals of a change of government institutions, pass without violent accompaniment? Are there peaks of violence, in France or anywhere else, unaccompanied by power shifts? I return to these questions later in this chapter and in Chapter Eight.

Finally, political theories offer some important ideas of *mobilization* and *resources* in the generation of collective violence. Indignation and suffering, it is argued, are much more widespread than collective action; to explain the latter, one must pinpoint not the emotional states underlying it but variations in the objective circumstances that favor or inhibit action. Thus,

*Expect no militant collective action except where participants are endowed with a modicum of resources and a minimal degree of mobilization.*

This argument, too, is vulnerable to circularity. It is most persuasive when, as in the article by Jenkins and Perrow (1977), differing outcomes of collective action at two otherwise similar junctures are explained by variation in available "resources." But if resources are defined so broadly as to mean virtually anything that enhances the success of collective action, deriving falsifiable statements will be impossible. Any collective action, after all, may be considered prima facie evidence that some sort of resources existed, if only the "resources" of collective concertedness or determination necessary to mount the action. Similarly, the fact of collective action might be taken as evidence that the actors in question were "mobilized." Like Smelser's "structural strain," mobilization might be virtually defined as a concomitant of action. Obviously such reasoning will not do. To be sure, such lapses need not be inherent in the notion of mobilization. But we do need specification of how much mobilization or resources should count as fulfilling the requirements of the theory. Or, short of this, we need to compare the outputs of civil violence by more or less mobilized or resourceful groups, other conditions being equal. And for either of these things, we need precise specification of the empirical criteria for assessing resources and mobilization.

Both the hazards and the strengths of reliance on such concepts as resources, mobilization, threat, opportunity, and other key theoretical tools of theorists considered in this chapter are evident in Doug McAdam's *Political Process and the Development of Black Insurgency, 1930–1970* (1982). McAdam argues that success and failure in this struggle are explicable in terms of three factors: "political opportunities"—that is, conditions in the larger political environment creating receptivity to black demands; "indigenous organizational strength"—viable institutions or other networks of co-operation among blacks; and "cognitive liberation"—the willingness of the embattled population to believe in the possibility of success through collective action. He contrasts his analysis to what he calls the "classical approach" to social movements—theories predicated on "normative breakdown," "structural strain," or "shared excitement"—and to what he sees as McCarthy and Zald's assumption (1977) that successful social movements require elite sponsorship.

McAdam proceeds historically, considering each notable change in the political fortunes of black Americans and their movements. Like many other authors, he attributes the political and economic nadir of blacks at the end of last century to their abandonment by the Republican party—that is, "unfavorable political opportunities." Gradual improvement during the early decades of this century is attributed mainly to a rise in the economic condition of blacks; McAdam especially emphasizes the importance of population movements from impoverished rural areas to cities and the rising strength of independent black institutions, colleges, and churches. These changes count as sources of "indigenous organizational strength." Progress in the 1940s and 1950s is ascribed largely to the concern of national political elites for their standing in the eyes of third world countries—that is, political opportunities—whereas the successes of the early 1960s are seen as stemming from growing conviction among blacks that progress was possible—that is, to "cognitive liberation." Deterioration of movement strength after the mid-1960s is laid to internal conflicts within the movement, or declining indigenous organizational strength, and to a less sympathetic national environment, or declining political opportunities.

McAdam's work deepens our understanding of the systemic forces shaping the position of blacks in American life. It also illustrates some ambiguities in political accounts of militant action. It is difficult to draw falsifiable commitments from the explanatory factors he invokes. His position seems to be that major developments in the fortunes of blacks have resulted from one or the other of the three key explanatory influences. Yet there seems to be no way to know which of these three should take on explanatory force in which setting, except in retrospect. This fact itself need not be fatal, provided that the analysis entails a search for potential "negative cases"—instances where change in one of the factors brought results contrary to what would be predicted.

But McAdam does not always alert us to such possibilities. In the absence of such steps, any argument like his risks what I call the "working backward" fallacy. This lapse is common to theories of civil violence invoking "relative deprivation," "structural strain," or other similarly vague explanatory principles. The analyst locates an effect that calls for explanation, then searches in the immediate or more distant past for evidence of one of the posited explainers. Because at least some of such broadly defined conditions as "relative deprivation" or "structural strain" are present in most social systems most of the time, the chances of success in this search are good. For similar reasons, McAdam's account sometimes fails to persuade us that the particular form of organizational strength, cognitive liberation, or political opportunity that he invokes *ought* to be crucial precisely where it is invoked.

3. *The Ends of Collective Violence.*     Perhaps the most distinctive of all political process assertions on the causes of violence have to do with its purposefulness. Here the contrast to other views is at its sharpest: Instead of marking a break with everyday life, collective violence is simply the pursuit of enduring collective interest by unusual but potentially effective means. What evidence bears on the accuracy of this characterization?

In one sense of the term, very little collective violence can be considered "rational" or "purposeful." As Mancur Olson's celebrated book (1965) has shown, the costs to individuals of participating in actions to obtain "public goods" are liable not to warrant the benefits involved. But clearly this is not the kind of rationality that Tilly and his followers have in mind. The purposes pursued in collective action are themselves collective. In the political view, people mobilize for the interests of those like themselves, even at risk to individual advantage. Obviously collective actors must also pursue strictly individual interests in some spheres of their lives, and neither Tilly nor his followers tell us much about when and how the shift from individual to collective orientation arises. But collective purposes are clearly what these analysts see as the mainspring of collective action. Thus,

*Expect the objectives and targets of militant collective action to reflect pursuit of long-term collective interest of the groups represented in the action.*

One of the most vivid and persuasive aspects of Tilly's studies is the historical examples he produces to illustrate such purposefulness. Typically such accounts dramatize the utility of collective action for the position of the group involved—for example, by the destruction of industrial machinery by workers whose livelihood it threatened, or the efforts of left-wing activists to bring down conservative governments.

But examples can also be produced of very different sorts of violent action. News of the capitulation of Japan in 1945, for example, triggered a tidal wave of celebratory but highly destructive violence in the streets of San Francisco. Civilians and military personnel started with jubilant patronage of the city's many bars. From there, action moved to vandalism against downtown businesses and public buildings. Extensive street fighting broke out. Simply being abroad became dangerous; men were attacked and women raped apparently at random. At least eleven deaths were counted, along with about a thousand injuries (*San Francisco Chronicle*, 18 August 1945).

Such events are no less authentic examples of civil violence than the purposeful, calculative actions described by Tilly and his followers. Yet they show no obvious orientation to collective political interests; their episodic, spontaneous quality better fits the accounts of the irrationalists.

Perhaps events of this kind are rare; major wars end only once in a great while, after all. But what makes matters even more complicated is the wide array of violent actions that seem to lie in between the extremes of spontaneity and total calculation. Consider, for example, *Ghetto Revolts* (1973) by Joseph Feagin and Harlan Hahn, a study of the urban rioting by black Americans in the late 1960s. Acknowledging their debt to Tilly, the authors interpret these events as acts of political purposefulness.

Black Americans had not been successful in achieving their principal objectives through the political process of voting, parties, or machine politics. Nor had they fulfilled their goals through rhetoric or non-violent activities such as sit-ins and demonstrations. Given the presence of a coalition of white interest groups unwilling to restructure the extant pattern of racial subordination, to growing numbers of black Americans the prospects of achieving major advances through non-violent tactics must have seemed increasingly dim. . . . The ghetto rioting that erupted in hundreds of cities represented a concerted attempt to achieve political objectives that had not been gained through other means. (1973, p. 43)

Feagin and Hahn go on to evoke a wealth of material in support of their purposeful view of the ghetto events. They particularly stress public opinion studies, including their own, that they feel reflect on the political intent of the rioters and the understanding of that intent by the black community.

Interviews after the 1965 Watts riot indicated that substantially more than 30 percent accepted or condoned the riot. Specifically, 43 percent of the men and

35 percent of the women there felt the riot would help the black cause, while 23 percent and 19 percent, respectively, felt it would hurt. When asked about its main effects, nearly 60 percent of the sample thought the main effects would be very or somewhat beneficial, with only one quarter saying the main effects would be very or somewhat harmful. (1973, p. 134)

The authors report similar results from a number of other surveys done in the aftermath of riots. They also note certain reports of selectivity in riot damage, according to which black-owned businesses and other "friendly" targets were spared by the rioters. And they cite the strong repressive response to the uprisings by prevailing political powers. All of these things, Feagin and Hahn claim, show the political intent and significance of the events.

But interpretation of this evidence is not exactly straightforward. As C. Wright Mills (1940) and others have argued, people attribute motives both to others and to themselves according to inner assumptions as to how the world works. Thus it would not be surprising to find that those who hoped for political results, or who found a principled collective purpose in the riots morally acceptable, might offer political interpretations of participants' motives. Nor is it surprising to note that outsiders critical of blacks' demands—for example, Banfield (1968, chap. 9)—explained the events more as opportunism than anything else. Indeed, one of the studies reported by Feagin and Hahn shows that ghetto residents' own view of the origins of the riots were closely related to their favorability to the rioters' actions (1973, p. 274).

The difficulties of these interpretations demand reconsideration of some basic ideas. What do Tilly and his followers *mean* by their assertions that collective actors weigh potential costs and benefits to collective interest in shaping their militant actions? Surely it would be too much to expect that such actors really take account of *every* conceivable course of action they might follow, ascribing quantitative values to its plusses and minuses in terms of long-term strategic goals. But the logic of Tilly's position does lead to the falsifiable expectation that participants in militant action will choose strategies likely to bring improvement to the interests of the groups represented in the action—and that such interests can meaningfully be reckoned in terms of some objective analysis of the well-being of those involved.

This expectation seems reasonable enough, yet other empirical expectations are no less plausible. Perhaps, for some forms of action, the long-term, strategic consequences matter rather little to participants, compared to the inherent satisfactions of acting. Perhaps, in other words, the strictly *consummatory* rewards of inflicting pain on one's enemies or of destroying a hated symbol suffice to motivate violent action. To take such a view, one need hardly deny that the targets of militant action will be objectively antipathetic to the interests of the actors. One need not accept the irrationalists' view, in other words, that the ends of crowd action are infinitely malleable. Nevertheless, people may attack either to accomplish long-term, instrumental ends or to savor the intrinsic satisfactions of assailing what they hate. But this latter possibility is not what one would infer from political theorists' statements of the rationality and cost-benefit wisdom underlying militant action.

Thus, in the American ghetto uprisings, the predominant forms of activity were destruction of local businesses, attacks on coercive forces and fire crews, and widespread looting. It is difficult to attribute concertedness to these actions, or to see in them results of calculation of the costs and benefits of these as against other possibilities. As Feagin and Hahn and others have pointed out, the overall effects of the riots for the black communities were mixed at best. Some new resources flowed into these neighborhoods as a result. But the communities also suffered material and human casualties of riot control and experienced a hardening of majority public opinion apparently resulting from the riots. Although demonstrations and moral appeals for majority support had proved disappointing to movement activists, it is difficult to see in the violent actions of the rioters a shrewd calculation to attain collective political goals by other means.

Certainly the ghetto revolts attested to blacks' hatred of white institutions and their representatives. But one detects in the violent events little attempt to uphold alternative norms or to create new institutions. The collective action involved in the ghetto riots seems worlds apart from the *taxation populaire* imposed by participants in preindustrial subsistence riots. There, the rural poor often seized foodstuffs not strictly as plunder, but for sale at what they held to be a "just price."

By contrast, the central events of the ghetto uprisings—the looting, the destruction, the attacks on "agents of order"—make more sense as ends in themselves than as means to other ends. It is hard to see concertedness or calculation behind them. Similar events broke out in New York under rather different political conditions, after all, when a widespread power blackout in 1977 left the powers of social control at a disadvantage. Participants in the earlier riots may have felt, either while rioting or in retrospect, that they were "teaching a lesson" to their antagonists. And movement leaders did all they could to maximize political gains from the events and minimize losses. But neither Feagin and Hahn nor any other analyst I know has suggested that the ghetto revolts were organized in advance. Indeed, organized movements on behalf of blacks such as CORE and SNCC seem not to have gained a significant foothold among urban ghetto dwellers during this period.

## The Polity and the Ends of Collective Action

Ambiguities surrounding the purposes of ghetto riots compel deeper attention to some underlying theoretical questions. If collective violence within the state is purposeful, as Tilly believes, what kinds of purposes are involved? What interests, in other words, are to be attributed to participants in public contention? These questions can only be answered through a closer look at his model of the polity. For it is within the polity, according to Tilly, that the interests fueling modern collective violence are thrashed out.

Besides the version quoted previously, Tilly and his collaborators have offered many statements of his model of the polity. A fuller example is the following:

> For any population, we may ask whether there exist one or more organizations controlling the principal concentrated means of coercion within the population. Such organizations are *governments*. We may then enumerate all groups within the population which . . . collectively apply resources to the influence of a certain government. They are *contenders* for power with respect to that government. To the extent that a contender can routinely lay claim to the generation of action or yielding of resources by agents of the government, the contender is a member of the *polity*. . . . Some groups are not contenders, and some contenders (which we call *challengers*) are not members of the polity. . . . Every polity establishes tests of membership, and all polities include among such tests the ability to mobilize or coerce significant numbers of people. . . . The life of the polity . . . consists of (a) the routine application of resources to the influence of the government by members of the polity; (b) attempts by non-members (ordinarily resisted by members in collaboration with agents of the government) to influence the government, including attempts to gain membership; (c) an ongoing series of contests, ranging from parliamentary maneuvering to street fighting, among members of the polity. . . .
> Because of the testing process by which contenders acquire or lose membership, collective violence tends to increase when the membership of the polity is changing rapidly. (Rule and Tilly 1975, pp. 55–56)

As always with Tilly's arguments, one can find many instances that fit the pattern snugly. The French revolutions of 1789, 1830, and 1848 *did* entail bids for participation in power by representatives of interests previously excluded. These revolutions were indeed followed by further violent confrontations that could be described as "testing" among the survivors of the revolutionary transfers. Moreover, as Feagin and Hahn or McAdam would no doubt argue, many violent and nonviolent collective actions of the black movement in the 1960s and 1970s—for example, the demonstrations by black activists at Democratic National conventions—plainly represented efforts at establishing claims on national power.

But one must not judge any model simply by the cases it fits best. For this model and others, one must ask, What sort of empirical world would clearly *not* be compatible with this view? Here one answer would be a world in which militant collective action is the work not of activist representatives of enduring interest groups, but rather of evanescent groupings that formed and died away in response to more transient social influences. I see no reason for rejecting such possibilities out of hand. The fact that some groups do mobilize to fight for their interests repeatedly over long periods, as they clearly do, hardly warrants the conclusion that other instances of collective violence may have more strictly episodic origins.

Then, some statements by Tilly and his followers, like the one above, come close to suggesting that all collective action is oriented to political objectives on the *national* political stage. Yet this surely must not be the intent, as Tilly's empirical writings document many strictly local contentions, even within highly centralized states.

Thus, one may reasonably ask whether it adds to clarity in understanding the origins of civil violence to think of such action as the work of activists representing sharply bounded, enduring interest groups. How would one identify the "contenders" in any particular polity? Who are the members, and who are the challengers? How many "members" are there, say, in present-day America? Ten? One hundred? As many as the number of high-priced lobbyists in Washington? How many contenders? As many as the number of grass-roots political action groups? Is the American Medical Association a member? If so, what about the American Neurological Association? Are *women* members of the polity? This category of the population does mobilize resources, after all, often with significant results. And if women are members, what about men? What about migrant farm workers, welfare mothers, Vietnam veterans, and other relatively powerless groups that still mobilize and influence national political action under at least some conditions?

Readers sympathetic to Tilly's view of the polity will no doubt feel that these queries demand a degree of specificity from the model that is inappropriate. But that is just the point. The essential logic of the model requires sharp boundaries where political reality offers shadings-off and nuances. One can certainly distinguish among more and less powerful groups, but such an effort would identify continuous gradations more than clear distinctions between "ins" and "outs." Moreover, the standing of any particular group, and the public response to its activist representatives, depends not only on enduring power distributions, but also on the immediate political situation at the time of the action. Black activists, for example, got a much better response from power holders in America during the immediate shock after the assassination of Martin Luther King,

Jr., than before. Nor, finally, is the division of the polity into "contenders" with fixed identities always useful, because groups considered solidary at one point may so split and recombine within fairly short periods as to form quite different casts of characters.

In a series of penetrating studies of the Parisian "June Days" of 1848, Mark Traugott (1980a; 1980b; 1985) has thrown strong theoretical light on relations between group membership and participation in militant action. The June Days were the last desperate, violent stand of the lower-class activists whose participation in revolutionary events the previous February had helped bring down the regime of Louis-Philippe. In Marx's writings, these insurgents appear as the activist representatives of the Parisian lower classes more broadly. Their opponents in the Mobile Guard, recruited by the government precisely for the purpose of putting down such rebellion, Marx castigates as members of the *lumpenproletariat*.

Traugott shows that the Mobile Guard, far from being drawn from the dregs of the Parisian population, was strikingly similar in social origins to the June insurgents. Both were overwhelmingly made up of artisans. The key difference between the groups, Traugott persuasively argues, had to do with the treatment the February government had meted out to the two during the months leading up to the revolution. The Mobile Guard were paid, housed, and outfitted by the regime, albeit haphazardly. The insurgent workers, on the other hand, were largely members of the National Workshops, first sponsored by the February regime as a sop to working-class interests, then increasingly ignored and finally disbanded.

Perhaps it should be no surprise, under these circumstances, that the unemployed workers revolted whereas the Guard supported their government patrons. Yet Traugott's account reminds us that a wide variety of influences other than social origin shape participation in militant action. In analyzing American university conflicts of the 1960s and 1970s, no one would interpret mass arrests by police of student radicals drawn from upper-middle class families as an action by working classes against national elites, notwithstanding the social origins of participants on the two sides. Similar caution should prevail in interpreting activist forces like the June Days insurgents as *the* representatives of the social groups from which they were drawn. As Traugott points out (1985, p. 173), the Paris working classes as a whole gravitated by the end of 1848 to support of Louis Napoleon in the presidential election of that year—notwithstanding the Marxian view of that figure as a kind of protofascist. Even in June, support for the insurgents was by no means universal among the Paris lower classes. Surely such observations should inspire caution about linkages between the interests of broad sectors of populations and the activism of particular militant groups.

Thus there are serious questions about the relations between activists and the divisions of populations they are supposed to represent. Tilly ordinarily views participants in collective actions as representative members of the social categories whose interests the actions express. These interests are usually seen as inherent in that group's position in society. But such assumptions are not universal among analysts of collective action. Pareto, for example, considered the professed interests and social identifications of political activists illusory. Although he would no doubt accept Tilly's view of the polity as a coalition of "in" groups warring with "out" groups, he would set little store by the profession of any activists to attachment to the interests or program of a particular part of a population. Political activists of all stripes, regardless of the bases of their support, share with each other an appetite for power and some talent for pursuing it. What they share with their supposed constituencies, according to Pareto, is much more superficial.

Pareto's theory, then, diverges from Tilly's view of militant action as a direct expression of the interests of larger, enduring social groups. As I noted in Chapter Two, few if any case studies have explicitly sustained Pareto's position on the role of elites, as against grass-roots figures, in animating collective action. But then, few researchers have specifically searched for evidence on this score. Tilly and his collaborators have provided many *illustrations* of militant activism as direct expression of group interest. But perhaps other forms of violent action stem from more Paretian processes. The Nazi movement, for example, certainly drew more support from some social groups and strata than from others. But are its goals and strategies, especially the violent ones, better understood as direct expressions of grass-roots interests, or as efforts by a cohesive group of determined activists to pursue power for its own sake?

Here I think Pareto has a point. The relations between the alleged "constituencies" of participants in violent action and the long-term purposes of the activists themselves need not always be so direct as Tilly's model might lead us to believe.

A more difficult decision, even when the identifications and interests of actors seem clearest, concerns whether actions should be interpreted as *instrumental* or *expressive*. Is crowd activity a means to a more distant end, or is it an end in itself? The difficulty in analyzing events like America's ghetto riots of the 1960s lies largely in the fact that the two forms of action often blend into one another.

No one would deny that many politically oriented crowd events are essentially expressive. Indeed, Tilly and his collaborators have provided some of our most vivid accounts of such events. Many elements of the repertoires that Tilly discusses—from nineteenth-century burnings in effigy to such modern extravaganzas as street theater or mock political trials—appear to attract participation mainly through the promise of the emotional satisfactions of being part of the action. To be sure, the inherent satisfactions offered by such events are highly politically *relevant,* for example, in the symbolic humiliation of hated political opponents. And the events are often organized as devices for mobilizing resources of participation or financial contributions. But for many participants, the attractions of such events are the inherent ones of expressing solidarity with the in-group and antagonism to its enemies. They are consummatory more than instrumental, more like Durkheimian rites or collective representations than means to more distant ends.

But if nonviolent collective actions often have this quality, may not violent collective actions, too, represent ends in themselves? Tilly implies that this proposition may be true at least of the "primitive" forms of collective violence. These recurring communal brawls and violent rivalries among guild associations seem, as he describes them, unrelated to the exercise of political power. And such brawling-for-the-sake-of-brawling appears to have its modern counterpart in the contentions of youth gangs, or the fighting among partisans of opposing high school athletic teams, or even the boisterous destruction until recently attending football "home-comings" at America's state universities. Like the VJ Day riots in San Francisco noted previously, such events give every indication of being ends in themselves, rather than calculated, instrumental acts.

Anticipating objections of this kind, Tilly responds:

I do not mean that the sequences I have described are the *only* ones that produce collective violence, just that they are the most regular and reliable. . . . Conventional combats among teams, communities, youth groups, or schools sometimes fit the pattern of 'testing' violence, but more often escape it; they, too, operate on a small scale, within large restrictions. Drunken brawls, private vengeance, festival madness, impulsive vandalism, all reach a dangerous magnitude now and then. What is more, the frequency of conventional combats, brawls, vendettas, and so on undoubtedly varies with the basic conceptions of honor, obligations, and solidarity which prevail within a population. Nevertheless, I would say that in populations under the control of states all these forms account for only a small proportion of the collective violence which occurs, and change far too gradually to account for the abrupt surges and recessions of collective violence which occur in such populations. The chief source of variation in collective violence is the operation of the polity. (1978, pp. 181–82)

So, nonpolitical violence is a small proportion of the total, and "the operation of the polity" accounts for most variation in the level of collective violence under the modern state.

But these critical notions of "political" versus "nonpolitical" violence and of "the operation of the polity" are not so transparent as they may seem. Again, collective violence may be highly politically relevant without being calculated to strategic, instrumental ends. Among the common features of popular violence in India immediately following the assassination of Prime Minister Gandhi in 1984 were attacks by Hindu crowds against individual Sikhs. It appears that the most isolated and helpless were often victims of these actions—for example, beggars singled out by crowds for stoning or burning. In some important sense, these actions were expressions of enduring conflicts of interest between the Hindu majority and the Sikh minority within the national polity. But one would stretch a point to claim that all such local acts of persecution could have been calculated to advance long-term, strategic collective interests. Some may have promised to the actors instrumental payoffs not apparent from newspaper accounts. But surely many were what they appeared to be— acts that gave expression to outrage and desire for vengeance, consummatory rather than instrumental performances. I suspect that much civil violence meets this description, but we will not really know how much until systematically enumerated samples like those assembled by Tilly and his students are analyzed along these lines.

More broadly, the fact that there are strong associations between changing power relations at the political center and levels of popular violence leaves unresolved the nature and direction of causality involved. Undoubtedly Tilly and his followers are right that much popular violence represents a response to threats and opportunities emerging out of central (or indeed local) power struggles. But we cannot reject the possibility that some violent periods and episodes themselves trigger rearrangements among power holders that would not have taken place in the absence of violence from below. Indeed, in some circumstances a single precipitating event may cause both popular violence and redistribution of interests in the polity as a whole. Such was the case, at least briefly, in America's response to the assassination of Dr. Martin Luther King, Jr. When people become sufficiently aroused to wreak deliberate destruction on a large scale, change in power relations at the center may well follow as a calculated response by professional politicians. Yet the violence that leads to such changes may be experienced by those who act it out as consummatory rather than calculated and instrumental.

Taking these observations seriously calls into question some of the distinctness of political models of civil violence, particularly in relation to collective behavior theory in the Park tradition. In Tilly's world, violence is a sign that people see such important collective interests at stake that they are willing to take extraordinary risks in hope of important gains. In this view, emotion is virtually epiphenomenal; at most, outpourings of anger are symptoms of rational perceptions of high political stakes. But if we accept that much popular violence, including much of the most horrendous, is consummatory rather than purposeful, new theoretical possibilities arise. Under this assumption, the association of changing power relations with violent popular action may stem from the need of political figures to respond to carnage for its own sake, rather than from the success of strategic efforts on the part of participants. Thus, emotion itself, such as the intense outpourings of feeling triggered among Hindus by the assassination of Mrs. Ghandi by Sikh bodyguards in 1984, may be a cause of civil violence in its own right. Shifts in power relations among elite representatives of the groups involved may well be more the effect than the cause of such emotional processes. A phrase like "the operation of the polity" may thus mislead, if taken to suggest that the only rewards fueling popular participation are those of strategic advantage.

Consider an alternative model of militant action within the polity. Like Tilly's, the following refers to interactions between central powers and popular action in centralized states.

1. At any point in the life of the polity, there are a changing set of interests around which significant segments of the population may mobilize.

2. These interests cannot be automatically predicted from the structural positions of various population groups, but are defined by the groups experiencing them. When such "vital interests" emerge, however, the groups concerned are apt to perceive them as matters essential to their own symbolic or literal self-perpetuation. Examples might be the right to control the education of the next generation, or the right to traditional occupational roles.

3. Collective action in support of such interests may be either expressive or instrumental—an end in itself, or a means to some longer-term end. In any particular collective action, the two are apt to be mixed.

4. The *proximate* causes of violent collective action are often, though not always, the receipt of new information. Examples might be rumors of insults to cherished group symbols, or reports of violence against members of the group, or news of a weakening of the central powers' coercive abilities.

5. Collective actors do calculate costs and benefits of their actions at least enough to avoid overwhelming repression and to seize evident political opportunities. But where collective actions represent ends in themselves rather than means to other ends, the sheer fact that an action takes place may make it "profitable" to the participants.

6. The frequency and intensity of collective action, including collective

violence, is associated with threatened and accomplished applications of central political power in the following ways:

(a) Collective action demands response from central power holders by challenging their interests, especially their interest in controlling the official means of mass coercion.
(b) Actions by state power holders trigger collective action by offering threats and opportunities to what activists define as their vital interests.
(c) The same developments may simultaneously cause both applications of central power and popular collective action, as when the assassination of Martin Luther King, Jr., sparked both federal legislative activity and street rioting.

Is this tentative model at all preferable to Tilly's? Like his, this one is vague on a number of important points—for example, how one would reckon "major applications of political power." At the same time, as far as it goes, it appears to fit the data presented by Tilly and his collaborators, as well as much else of what is known about political violence. Perhaps the main difference between this model and Tilly's is the agnosticism here as to the kinds of purposes animating collective action and the relation between the structural position of groups involved in militant action and the interests reflected in their actions.

## Conclusion

There is no need to wrestle these issues to the finish at this stage. I return to them in the concluding chapters.

For now, let me simply acknowledge the enormous contributions of Tilly to our understanding of civil violence. More than any other author, he has provided a comprehensive view of political violence as a regular outgrowth of social structure. In rich historical detail he has shown how the conflicts built into different forms of social organization yield characteristic forms of popular mobilization. And he has demonstrated the linkages between change in such standard forms of collective action and broad patterns of structural change. He has linked the life of central political institutions with the mobilization of peripheral groups, and shown how these mobilizations leave their historical precipitate in the form of new institutions and other enduring social arrangements. These insights have inspired a new look at popular mobilization. And this new look brings us far beyond the anxiety-distorted view of the crowd offered by Tarde, Sighele, and LeBon.

*Chapter Seven*

# Relative Deprivation and
# Related Psychological Theories

No doubt most "folk theories" of civil violence are psychological theories. "When people are pushed too far, they explode," one hears; or "When you trample on people's basic sense of right and dignity, they're bound to strike back." This extension from individual experience to collective process has held as much appeal for certain social scientists as for non-specialists. Many students of militant collective action have focused on shared psychic states of indignation, resentment, or frustration as the essential cause of popular rebellion and civil strife. Most influential among these theories have been those identifying the causal psychic state as *relative deprivation*.

One could trace the pedigree of these theories back at least as far as Aristotle. *The Politics* advances a kind of relative deprivation theory of revolution: "Both democracy and oligarchy are based on a sort of justice, but they fall short of absolute justice," we read; the result is that "either side turns to sedition if it does not enjoy the share of constitutional rights which accord with the conception of justice it happens to entertain" (1958, p. 204). But the *locus classicus* of relative deprivation analyses of civil upheaval is a passage from de Tocqueville's *The Old Regime and the French Revolution*.

Patiently endured so long as it seemed beyond redress, a grievance comes to appear intolerable once the possibility of removing it crosses men's minds. For the mere fact that certain abuses have been remedied draws attention to the others and they now appear more galling; people may suffer less, but their sensibility is exacerbated. (1955, p. 177)

This chapter was written by James Rule and Steven Finkel; another version of it is published separately (Finkel and Rule 1986).

These early statements embody the essential elements of the theories considered in this chapter. They posit a standard of comparison by which people evaluate their circumstances, along with an aggressive response when people see the crucial standard violated.

What we call relative deprivation theories are quite a heterogeneous category. The greatest variation lies in the standard of comparison posited to govern individual action. In some versions, this standard may be the perceived state of some social category or group. People's view of this reference group (it might consist of those like oneself, those with whom one feels special rivalry, or individuals or groups chosen by virtually any other criterion) determines the level of relative deprivation or gratification. In other forms of relative deprivation thinking, the origin of the crucial standard for comparison lies strictly within the individual's inner psychic world. Thus people's levels of relative gratification or deprivation may be governed by individual or shared notions of well-being at some past point, or by some other level of expectation fixed without regard to any particular outside group. One early ancestor of this strand of relative deprivation thinking is Dollard's frustration-aggression theory (1939). Strictly speaking, this theory does not involve relative deprivation because Dollard's notion of frustration did not entail a principle of comparison. But if the notion of frustration is replaced with an idea like "frustration in the pursuit of expected just deserts," explanation of aggression based on frustration becomes a relative deprivation theory.

In Dollard et al. (1939, p. 7), frustration is defined as "an interference with the occurrence of an instigated goal-response at its proper time in the behavior sequence." Later authors introduced *attitudes* explicitly into their formulations, and with them the emphasis on comparison levels, expectations, and individual conceptions of justice and entitlement. James C. Davies defines the essential causal process in social-psychological terms, as violent outbreaks are triggered by dashed hopes and aspirations when "a prolonged period of economic or social development is followed by a short period of sharp reversal" (1962, p. 4). For Ivo and Rosalind Feierabend, the key explanatory concept was "systematic frustration" stemming from "specific characteristics of social change" (1972, p. 109). For Ted Robert Gurr, the critical state, which he identifies as relative deprivation, is the "discrepancy between . . . value expectations and value capabilities" (1968a, p. 37). All of these formulations picture aggression of one kind or another—including revolution, political protest, civil war, and social movements—as resulting from the various forms of frustration.

Since the mid-1960s relative deprivation has shared center stage among theories of civil violence with political theories of the kind discussed in

Chapter Six. Indeed, the two theories seem to have risen to prominence on the same intellectual and cultural currents. Both appeared on the scene at the time when civil violence was unexpectedly intruding itself into the consciousness of Americans in general and social scientists in particular. And both seem to have offered a more agreeable explanation for the rise of protest by blacks and others than that offered by moral disintegration or mass society theories. Like the political theories, relative deprivation viewed the rise of popular agitation not as a symptom of social breakdown but as an inevitable, perhaps even normal response to unfulfilled promises of fair treatment. For many, relative deprivation theory promised to explain the rising demands of embattled social groups in terms of universal human longings for justice and equity.

## The Essence of the Theory

Much of the appeal of these theories no doubt lies in their claims to generality. Theorists in this tradition have sought to anchor their accounts of dramatic historical events in forces as basic and universal as any in human nature. Dollard and his colleagues, founders of modern empirical studies in this line, were particularly sweeping in their claims.

The occurrence of aggressive behavior always presupposes the existence of frustration and . . . the existence of frustration always leads to some form of aggression. (1939, p. 1)

Later thinkers have not been so categorical on the first point, but they still tend to picture aggression as a necessary consequence of frustration. As Ted Gurr wrote in 1970,

the primary source of the human capacity for violence appears to be the frustration-aggression mechanism. . . . If frustrations are sufficiently prolonged or sharply felt, aggression is quite likely, if not certain, to occur. . . . The frustration-aggression mechanism is in this sense analogous to the law of gravity: men who are frustrated have an innate disposition to do violence to its source in proportion to the intensity of their frustration. (pp. 36–37)

Relative deprivation theories are fundamentally atomistic. They view the overall likelihood of collective violence as the sum across large populations of individual levels of undeserved frustration, indignation, or perceived injustice. Thus, one individual's aggressive propensities are accorded as much weight as those of the next. Indeed, the logic of the theory implies that intense frustration by a few should yield rebelliousness equal to moderate frustration on the part of many, though this implication has not been pursued.

Note the deep antimony between these atomistic assumptions and those in the Marx–Pareto–Tilly tradition. These latter theories posit economic or political power as essential in generating or suppressing violent collective action; here the point is to identify *differences* in the abilities of different groups to act on their interests or political sentiments. The atomistic idea of a direct translation from discontent, deprivation, or indignation to militant political action runs in a theoretical collision course with these assumptions. And these strictly theoretical differences give rise to contrasting methodological predilections. Relative deprivation theorists are more likely to measure total outputs of violent behavior throughout entire populations, whereas their more politically minded antagonists more often seek explanations for violent actions of specific elements or groups.

Relative deprivation thinking shares some affinities with theories in both the Hobbesian-utilitarian and value integration traditions. Indeed, similarities between the psychological theories discussed in this chapter and present-day rational choice theories like those of Mancur Olson and Russell Hardin are marked. Both see militant political action as arising from actors' individual assessments (conscious or not) of their own actual well-being versus other possible states.

Both traditions share with value integration thinking the assumption that variations in collective militancy must correspond to individual sentiments aggregated across populations. For value integration thinkers, the crucial psychic states are ones of moral support, rather than satisfaction or dissatisfaction more broadly. But if one views perceived moral obligations to governments as leading to, or resulting from, indignation, frustration, or deprivation, the two approaches become relatively compatible.

Sharply contrasting to the logic of relative deprivation analyses is the theoretical position of the irrationalists discussed in Chapter Three. For them, the explanation of collective violence lay in characteristics of *settings* and *forms of interaction* rather than of individuals or regimes. Here the alternatives—explanation by characteristics of participants versus those of situations—are as dramatically drawn as in the contrast between atomistic and holistic theories.

---

Among all theories of civil violence, relative deprivation theories may be the most appealing initially: The idea that people rebel in response to perceived injustice is hard to dismiss, for social scientists and lay observers alike. Yet relative deprivation theories are deceptive in their apparent simplicity. For explanations based on such theories to be both falsifiable and informative, some exacting specifications are required.

First among these are assumptions on the relation between various specific comparison standards that people may hold and their overall tendency to rebel. Undoubtedly most people have *some* standards of justice, equity, or maximum tolerable frustration that, if violated, increase the likelihood of *some* exasperated response. But is it necessarily true that individuals "scan" their overall social environments and arrive at a single "summary" state of its acceptability on all counts considered together? And if such summary states exist, do the aggressions that they cause necessarily take a public or political form?

Alternate assumptions are equally plausible. One might imagine that different forms of frustration govern aggression, according to the broader social context. For example, dissatisfaction with perceived corruption in high places might lead directly to riotous action in some situations, whereas in others the same individuals might be moved to violence by the performance of the economy or the difficulty of getting plumbers on weekends. One implication of these assumptions would be that aspects of regime performance that generate dissatisfactions leading to revolution might prove quite different from those aspects of performance governing support for or opposition to the next regime.

Similarly, relative deprivation researchers often have assumed that people's overall, summary states of frustration will result in violence directed against authorities. Again, other assumptions are no less plausible. Much violent action is directed not against governments, after all, but against members of antagonistic ethnic, racial, or religious groups. Why assume that people direct their antagonism against the perceived sources of their frustrations? Perhaps in some settings—populations marked by high levels of political or psychodynamic repression, for example—frustrations in public life lead to aggressions in the private sphere. Perhaps people beat their dogs, their children, or supporters of rival soccer teams, rather than representatives of the polity. Or perhaps aggression against governments or social out-groups is the result of frustrations experienced in the private sphere.

Then there is the issue of time. Most empirical investigations in the relative deprivation tradition have proceeded from the assumption that deprivation states identified as responsible for aggressive action are relatively enduring. True, some authors such as Gurr (1970, chaps. 1 and 2) acknowledge other possibilities. But researchers have typically assumed that the key states leading to rebellion must have lasted at least long enough to afford investigators the chance to measure them.

The reason why alternatives to the standard assumptions in these cases do not have much place in relative deprivation studies is not that they are inconsistent with the kernel of the theoretical idea. Nor are they implausible in themselves. But taken seriously, such assumptions would vastly complicate the task of empirical inquiry, if not actually scuttle it. If people respond to different standards of comparison or justice at different moments, and if these standards are subject to abrupt change, empirical investigation of the psychic states might have to be done virtually simultaneously with the behavior they cause. For students of civil violence, this prospect is inconvenient indeed.

Perhaps even more tellingly, if crucial standards were seen as highly mutable in this way, theoretical interest would shift from the standards themselves to the forces governing their change. The most compelling question would be, "What brought these particular standards to the fore at this particular moment?" Why do particular sets of dissatisfactions get mobilized as bases for particular violent actions, as against all the other shared perceptions or reactions that might guide public behavior? Thus, the theoretical agenda would begin to look more like that implied by collective behavior theory than that entertained by relative deprivation analysts.

Relative deprivation thinking is perhaps even more susceptible than other theories considered here to being interpreted in ways that are cirular and hence unfalsifiable. Any form of violent collective action, after all, represents evidence that someone was dissatisfied about *something;* all behavior shows an effort to alter some situation in some way, either within one's self or in the outer world. Relative deprivation explanations of violent behavior, by this token, must entail something more than pointing to whatever made people unhappy enough to rebel.

Accounts linking episodes of rebellion to specific frustrations or dissatisfactions without citing a comparison principle that makes such experiences intolerable might be called *absolute deprivation* explanations. They are not necessarily devoid of meaning. To note that a particular rebellion would not have occurred, had the participants not been hungry, underrepresented, or resentful may be both accurate and informative. But such observations are not *theoretical* unless they aim at specifying a range of cases in which, whenever specific conditions are encountered, rebellion ensues. And social scientists can point only too readily to cases where people go hungry, are underrepresented, or are exploited and still do not rebel.

Again, the *standard of evaluation* governing militant behavior might be based either on some outside reference group or on a remembered or imagined condition of one's self or those like one's self in the past, or indeed some much more abstract criterion. But it must be shown that this standard is held with relative consistency over a specific period, such that its violation results in rebellion whereas its satisfaction leads to peaceable action.

Meeting these conditions is both conceptually subtle and methodologically complex. Comparisons of adequacy, justice, deserts, and the like enter into formulation of all sorts of everyday and extraordinary behavior. But the question here is whether *specific standards* can be identified that are (1) shared widely throughout a population, and (2) held in such a way that militant behavior results when they are not met, such that (3) one can distinguish between participants and nonparticipants in civil violence in terms of whether the relevant standard is satisfied. This is a large sociological order.

Consider some forms of militant collective action that are clearly *not* susceptible to meaningful relative deprivation explanations—for example, aggressive political actions in response to the emergence of new collective *opportunities*. Imagine a situation where representatives of an activist political group take to the streets in response to newly perceived political weaknesses on the part of their opponents. Actions born out of sheer desire to seize the whole political loaf by those previously satisfied by half may involve nothing at all like relative deprivation. Similarly for events based on the emergence of *new* interests or attitudes among militant activists. If people are suddenly seized by new-found religious enthusiasm and begin attacking fetishes of other faiths, unveiled women, or those who travel on the Sabbath, relative deprivation becomes highly ambiguous as a source of explanation. To be sure, the militant actors in these cases are responding to a world that somehow fails to meet their standards of acceptability. But one could say as much for any violent action. Cases like these do not show the workings of a standard held consistently over time, and governing whether violent participation will or will not occur.

Most published researches in the relative deprivation tradition do not bring the reader this close to the mechanisms and conditions of violent action. By far the most numerous published studies have focused on aggregate behavior. These studies seek to measure some objective condition hypothetically responsible for variation in psychic states of deprivation or satisfaction widespread throughout the population. They then attempt to gauge the association between such variation and variation in militant action. Such studies reflect the following empirical expectation:

*Expect levels of violent behavior to vary directly with levels of objective social conditions believed to be frustrating.*

The difficulties with this formulation will come in for detailed discussion; still, we will hold, consistent failures to falsify such expectations would at least warrant intensified interest in relative deprivation explanations.

But much greater interest should attach to falsifiability of the doctrine in individual terms—that is, to expectations like the following:

*Expect participants in violent events to be high in self-reported or otherwise individually evinced relative deprivation; and expect those low in relative deprivation not to participate.*

This latter expectation is much more exacting as a basis for research; only a small minority of published studies address it.

But now we are well ahead of ourselves. Relative deprivation thinking has generated the largest array of empirical investigations of any theory of civil violence; let us consider them in detail.

## The Unfolding of Relative Deprivation Research

The first empirical investigations of the relationship between deprivation and collective violence took their inspiration from the original frustration-aggression notions of Dollard and his Yale colleagues. One classic study is that of Hovland and Sears (1940), who found high correlations between lynchings in the American South and various indicators of economic performance such as per-acre value of cotton. The authors explained the findings in frustration-aggression terms. Poor economic performance or recession would serve as a general frustration by "blocking individual goal-directed behavior." This frustration supposedly finds its outlet in lynchings of blacks (rather than some other form of violent action) for two reasons. First, the actual sources of the frustration (landlords, merchants, politicians) are in "protected" positions, and hence actions taken against them would most likely be punished. Displacing aggression onto blacks would have no similar repercussions. Second, many of those lynched were already arrested or were being sought for a crime, and thus they had already acted as a type of "frustrating agent" for society.

Research invoking more explicitly the temporal and intergroup comparisons of relative deprivation theory began in the early 1960s, with the publication of James C. Davies's now well-known study, "Toward a Theory of Revolution." Davies contended that revolutionary events (including failed revolutions) were attributable to popular dissatisfaction generated by a "prolonged period of rising expectations and rising gratification" followed by a short period of sharp reversal, during which the gap between expectations and gratifications quickly widens and becomes intolerable (Davies 1962, p. 6). Davies discussed three revolutionary events: Dorr's Rebellion in early nineteenth-century Rhode Island, the Russian revolution of 1917, and the Egyptian revolution of 1952. In a later study (1979), he offers a similar analysis of the U.S. Civil War, the Nazi revolution of 1933, and the rebellions of U.S. blacks in the 1960s. In all instances he identifies a rising crescendo of enhanced need satisfactions, followed by a sharp reversal.

The argument is an authentic species of the relative deprivation genus.

The comparison standard put forward by Davies is not an outside "reference group," of course, but a standard based on people's subjective expectations of what they could or should be able to anticipate. Gurr (1970, p. 53) would characterize the pattern described by Davies as "progressive deprivation." Like other writers on relative deprivation, Davies does not specify which members of the populations in his examples experience the needs he has in mind. But it seems apparent that the need states he posits are meant to be felt by the great majority of the populations concerned.

Troubles begin when one seeks to trace the particular needs held responsible for revolutionary action. Like other proponents of relative deprivation theory, Davies appears to favor needs that either are conspicuously well documented, like the price of basic foodstuffs, or that fit the pattern required by his theory. More rigorous specifications are needed as to what needs should *matter* in generating revolutionary action. Without such specification, needs appear to be selected to fit the requirements of the argument. In Davies's discussion of Dorr's Rebellion, for example, the long upward trend of increasing need satisfaction is identified with the increasing prosperity of the textile industry, on which a large proportion of the population depended. But the final "sharp reversal" precipitating the violent outbreak turns out to be the frustration of demands for popular suffrage in the state. Other analyses by Davies (1979, for example) show similar shifting of needs identified as crucial for prediction or explanation of collective action.

Again, for any large, heterogenous population one can imagine various standards or needs, held by various sectors of the population, the violation of which might conduce to protest or revolt. But for empirical inquiry to sustain the credibility of relative deprivation theory, we need some reason to believe that the *particular* needs identified by the analyst *ought* to be the ones to govern rebellious action. It will not do simply to work backward from the observed fact of rebellion until one identifies *some* need that appears conspicuously unfulfilled. Such a strategy can never fail, and hence it can never really succeed in informing or persuading us.

Appearing not long after Davies's original study were a series of works by Ivo and Rosalind Feierabend and their collaborators (1966; 1969; 1973). These researches entailed improvements over some of the obvious methodological limitations of Davies's work, including the small number of cases and lack of systematic sampling procedures. The key causal variable here was still an inferred psychic discrepancy between expectations and realities. The Feierabends constructed an index of "systematic frustration" aimed at capturing the degree to which social conditions induced individual frustration through an excess of "want formation" compared to "want satisfaction." Both concepts were indexed by aggregate measures for entire societies—want satisfaction by such things as number of physicians and caloric intake per capita, want formation by such things as rates of literacy and urbanization. Data were collected and analyzed for some eighty-four polities of varying degrees of socioeconomic development for the period 1948–1962.

To the extent that their scheme was theoretically informed, the Feierabends' key influence seems to have been modernization and mass society theories, for example, that of Lerner (1959). They view the modernization process as a race between inculcation of needs and social capacities to satisfy them. At various levels of modernity, and with various rates of change in those levels, needs and capacities should be sorely out of balance. At these times, most likely at middle levels of modernity under rapid economic change, systematic frustration should be highest. The result should be high levels of social instability.

The results of the studies showed mixed support for these hypotheses. There was a strong relationship between indices of systematic frustration and instability, and nations with high rates of economic change showed the highest rates of instability as well. But these nations were not always, as predicted, in the middle ranges of modernity, and there was no curvilinear relationship in general between modernity and social instability. Instead, a fairly strong linear correlation was found, such that low modernity corresponded to low stability, and high modernity to high stability. When one other variable, the level of coerciveness of the regime, was investigated, a curvilinear relationship was found. Nations using extremely high and extremely low amounts of force or repression suffer the least instability, whereas those at middle levels experience the most. Together, these four factors—systematic frustration, level of modernity, rate of economic change, and regime coerciveness—explained over half the variance in social instability during their years of study.

Appearing first in the mid-1960s, the Feierabends' studies won much attention. In 1966, they were awarded the Socio-Psychological Prize from the American Association for the Advancement of Science. But their methods showed a number of flaws to which multivariate studies in the relative deprivation tradition have been notably susceptible. Perhaps the most serious was the assessment of "want formation" and "want satisfaction." Could one really have confidence that the quotient of these two figures, derived from aggregate statistics, really captured a level of dissatisfaction for entire populations so fundamental as to govern participation in violent collective action? Did one have the right to assume that the sectors of the population characterized by such quotients would necessarily be those involved in political activity? Perhaps more important, what a priori grounds were there for classifying, say, literacy as a source of social wants, rather than as a concomitant of their satisfaction? Perhaps even more than in other studies based on aggregate data, heroic assumptions were required to link the statistics indexing objective conditions throughout nations with states of mind of their politically active citizens.

Basically, the key index of want formation divided by want satisfaction amounted to a measure of industrial development. Even if one accepted that this measure did indeed characterize some overall need state throughout the majority of the population, other explanations could well be given for the significance of the resulting associations. Industrializing nations, after all, occupy a special place among the nations of the world. They are apt to have shorter traditions of national identity than the world's industrial nations, and to have had both their borders and their major social and political institutions recently imposed on them from outside. These circumstances alone would more plausibly account for high rates of political instability than the explanatory factors put forward by the Feierabends.

Finally, because the Feierabends made little use of multivariate techniques, the independent impact of each of their primary variables is open to question. When such models were employed, the high intercorrelation of the variables prevented reliable estimation of individual effects. Systematic frustration, perhaps for this reason, was not found to affect significantly levels of civil violence within nations once other variables were entered in full statistical models (Feierabend and Feierabend 1972). In addition, even the multivariate models estimated by the Feierabends were extremely limited in scope. There is almost no inclusion of factors, except regime coerciveness, that might mediate between the frustration-modernity variables and civil violence. In a statistical sense, the absence of these factors may produce biased estimates of the effects of variables that are included. More important, though, these absences indicate a lack of a fully integrated theory of civil violence, one that would outline both fundamental conditions that give rise to aggressive behavior, and forces that diminish or amplify those basic impulses. Thus, although later scholars have drawn substantially on the Feierabends' pathbreaking work, that work marks only the beginnings of multivariate, deprivation-based models of civil conflict.

Ted Robert Gurr's multination studies of civil conflict in the 1960s followed shortly after the Feierabends' first publication. His work represents a quantum leap in conceptual and methodological sophistication. The point of departure is still the concept of relative deprivation; indeed, Gurr's elaboration of its precise components and forms is a major part of his accomplishment. The various forms of deprivation—progressive, aspirational, decremental—and their scope determine the magnitude of anger throughout a population, and serve as "instigating" variables in the model of civil conflict (Gurr 1970, pp. 47–53). Gurr also carefully delineates a series of mediating factors that augment or dampen political violence, and that in themselves explain a substantial amount of variation in cross-national civil conflict. These mediating factors are grouped into three general categories: "normative justifications for violence," such as evident traditions of violent conflict or ideological commitment or belief concerning regime legitimacy; "utilitarian justification for violence," such as the belief in violence as an effective means of obtaining political goals; and "structural" factors, such as the balance of coercive forces between the dissidents and the state. Taken together, these sets of factors are employed in complex multivariate models to explain variations in both overall political violence among one hundred fourteen nations in the 1960s and in subcategories of violence that Gurr labels "turmoil," "conspiracy," and "internal war."

As in past research, deprivation itself was indexed through aggregate statistical measures. Gurr does distinguish between "long-term," or persisting deprivation, however—measured through indices of economic discrimination, political separatism, and the like—and "short term" deprivation, tapped by such things as trends in export values and inflation rates. Measures of the mediating factors were obtained from statistics such as the past frequency of coup attempts (conflict traditions), party system stability (institutionalization), and military personnel per ten thousand adults (regime coerciveness).

The results of Gurr's analysis provide strong support for his overall model, but mixed support for the specific role of deprivation in influencing civil conflict. In early works (Gurr 1968a), the model as a whole explains a very large sixty-five percent of the total variance in political conflict across the sample. However, the deprivation variables did not account for the greatest proportion of this total: persisting deprivation accounted for twenty-four percent and short-term deprivation for twelve percent, whereas mediating factors termed "social-structural facilitation" accounted for almost fifty percent of the total variance explained. In later works (see Gurr and Duvall 1973), long-term deprivation still exerts a strong impact on civil conflict, but the most important predictor turns out to be a complex interaction term between long- and short-term deprivation and past conflict traditions. In addition, other mediating conditions such as legitimacy, economic development, and external military intervention exhibit strong impact as independent regulators of overall civil violence.

Thus, although deprivation assumes theoretical primacy in Gurr's view, "deprivation" variables in his equations do not show the largest associations with levels of civil strife. In additive models, they explain much less of the variance than the mediating variables, and in interactive models, the distinction between deprivation background variables and mediating conditions itself has been diluted. Hence, the implications are less than dramatic. Nevertheless, the work of Gurr does show that aggregate deprivation measures do exert some impact, even after controlling for a host of factors that largely had been ignored in earlier works.

Like that of the Feierabends, Gurr's work evoked both considerable respect and a measure of skepticism about concepts and methods. The high proportions of variance accounted for in his equations made a striking impression. Yet the variables contributing to these large values posed certain ambiguities in theoretical interpretation. For example, does it make sense to code multiplicative values of "political discrimination" (Gurr and Duvall 1973, p. 146) as a direct measure of deprivation? Or might such a value equally well be an index of the potential for active group contention that plays a central role in the political theories discussed previously? Similarly, in this same study, does the number of religious bodies within the polity ("weighted by their coexistence") represent a plausible measure of deprivation? Or would it make more sense to assume that the sheer number of religious faiths has no significance for deprivation, independent of the larger social and political context?

Some of the predictors in fact seem almost concomitant with Gurr's dependent variables. Among the "conflict traditions" reckoned as contributing factors to total magnitudes of political conflict (rather than as direct measures of deprivation) we find "relative scope and success of internal wars 1850–1960" and "frequency and success of coups, 1900–1960." High associations here basically affirm that polities with recent histories of turbulence tend to remain that way. And here, too, there are questions of contextuality. As Zimmermann notes (1980, pp. 58–59), for example, Gurr's measures of extent of internal transportation systems as indicators of "dissident institutional support" would make more or less sense, depending on whether revolt were urban or rural.

Most important, as in the works of Davies and the Feierabends, are questions on the use of aggregate measures for assessing psychological states. Deprivation and other key variables such as legitimacy are fundamentally social-psychological, relating to expectations, evaluations, or temporal comparisons that can only be manifest within individuals. None of these states is ever directly measured. What is shown with these types of aggregate cross-national analyses is simply that "the conditions which are assumed to bring about deprivation are positively correlated with violence" (Palmer and Thompson, 1970, p. 292); little evidence is provided of the linkage between these objective conditions and felt psychic states. But if the explanation for variation in the level of civil violence is really psychological, should not evidence produced to support the explanation itself be psychological?

## Further Empirical Studies

The idea of seeking confirmation for relative deprivation thinking in aggregate data, then, is inherently flawed. Yet the attractions of this strategy are not surprising. Imagine that an investigator were to demonstrate a close and durable association between militant activities carried out by a particular group and fluctuations in some variable that appeared to have inherent significance for the well-being of that group, such as its mean income. Such a finding would at least create a compelling basis for further inquiry to specify the connection. Relative deprivation would certainly present the most promising potential explanation for such a connection in the absence of another hypothesis.

Thus, we should scarcely blame relative deprivation theorists for seeking the associations they have sought. Because those concerned with explaining behavior by large numbers of individuals usually find it much more feasible to examine aggregate data than individual data, this possibility is likely to be chosen first. Nothing demonstrates this attraction so well as the response of American social scientists to the racial conflicts of the 1960s in their own country.

1. *Aggregate analyses.*    When urban rioting by black Americans broke out in the 1960s, relative deprivation explanations seemed obvious to a number of social scientists (Pettigrew 1969; Geschwender, 1964). Black Americans, it appeared, were responding to a social existence that fell below their standards of justice and equity. Hence, a researchable implication: If the rioting was indeed a response to perceived injustice and inequality, one should expect those locations characterized by greatest injustice or deprivation to show the greatest propensity to riot. From such reasoning sprang a host of ecological studies based on aggregate statistics from samples of American cities at that time.

In an early study of some two hundred thirty-nine riot events between January 1964 and May 1968, Downes (1968) reported high positive associations between certain measures of objective deprivation, such as city-wide unemployment, education levels, family income, and proportion of sound housing units, and the occurrence of riots. But other scholars took exception to the Downes study, arguing that the theory of relative deprivation holds that black-white *differentials* in such measures should be the instigating factors to the riot, not simply overall measures of citywide objective deprivation. Further, Downes had essentially compared the percentage of deprived versus nondeprived cities that experienced riots; he had made no effort to discover which deprivation measure was most significant, or even if the differences found could be due to some outside factor not included in his analysis. After correcting for these deficiencies,

Ford and Moore (1970) discovered only weak and equivocal relations between measures of deprivation and riot occurrence or intensity. Several of
the measures, such as the income of nonwhite families, were actually
positively correlated with riot occurrence, meaning that cities with objective conditions more favorable to blacks actually were more riot prone.
This finding has been replicated in several later studies, demonstrating
that *objective* levels of deprivation need not be closely associated with violence (Jiobu 1974; Lieske 1978). Remember, however, that occurrence of
riots where black living standards are objectively better need not be incompatible with a relative deprivation or rising-expectations explanation.

    In a series of methodologically sophisticated multivariate studies,
Spilerman (1970; 1971) showed that various measures of deprivation had
little or no effect on riot occurrence after other variables were taken into
account. Spilerman analyzed data on all instances of substantial racial violence among 673 cities in the contiguous United States with populations
exceeding 25,000 in 1960. He examined the effects on the frequency of
racial disorder of a variety of community characteristics, ranging from
rates of population change to city population per city council member.
A number of the variables were designed to tap relative deprivation, for
example, the ratio of nonwhite family income to the white equivalent. In a
multivariate regression model, Spilerman found that only two variables
were of substantial importance in predicting riot occurrence—the total
size of the nonwhite population, and a dummy variable indicating whether
the city was in the South, where riots had been less frequent.

    Spilerman argued that his findings do not disprove or eliminate rela-
tive deprivation as a potential explanation; they simply suggest that city-
wide variations in deprivation have no impact on citywide variations in
riot occurrence. The riots may have been a response to nationally felt
black deprivation. Spilerman's studies did suggest, though, a kind of
"critical mass" process by which cities were more likely to experience
riots, the larger the population at risk.

    Spilerman's findings, however, did not go unchallenged. Morgan and
Clark (1973) analyzed data from forty-two U.S. cities where riots occurred
in 1967. Although largely agreeing with Spilerman concerning the causes
of riots, they found different determinants for their severity. In these
models, certain variables identified as indexing levels of grievances among
black populations, such as housing inequalities between the races, showed
strong effects. In another study, Lieske (1978) showed that after removing
the effect of Spilerman's main explanatory variable, nonwhite population
size, a substantial portion of the remaining variance could be explained
through what he deemed indicators of black well-being. These included
black divorce rates, black illegitimacy rates, and political factors across

the cities, such as the type of city government structure and the extent of school segregation.

Spilerman rebutted the Morgan and Clark study with a more extensive analysis (1976) of some three hundred twenty-two riot incidents from 1967 and 1968 that he rated carefully according to severity. Contrary to Morgan and Clark, he still found that nonwhite population and regional location were the key determinants of severity. Spilerman thus reaffirmed his earlier position that national stimuli and conditions, rather than local ones, were largely responsible for the riots. Neither did any other interpretation of the causes of urban racial rioting in this country enjoy clear support. But with these types of analyses, conclusive evidence *against* relative deprivation theory was impossible *in principle*. Again, only studies of psychic states themselves can show how such states relate to action, or fail to do so.

2. *Individual-level analyses.* Some field studies of individual attitudes and perceptions also followed quickly from the riotous events of the 1960s. Random samples of the general populations in the riot cities of Detroit and Newark were conducted by Caplan and Paige (1968). In addition, several other researchers chose both random and purposive samples of rioters and nonrioters in Cleveland, Los Angeles, and Waterloo, Iowa (Crawford and Naditch 1970; Ransford 1968; Sears and McConahay 1973; Muller 1972). These studies provide a wealth of attitudinal data on actual and potential participants in ghetto uprisings. Some argue quite forcefully for deprivation-based explanations of the riots. But many of these works have serious theoretical and empirical problems. As methods and ways of defining deprivation have become more precise and theoretically persuasive, deprivation-based models have lost much of their explanatory power.

The first casualty of individual-level analyses was undoubtedly the notion that absolute deprivation would correlate strongly with riot participation. In virtually every study conducted in urban ghettos, riot participants were found to be more highly educated and at least as well off financially as nonparticipants (Sears and McConahay 1970). McPhail (1971), in a review of early riot studies, found little support for any absolute deprivation-based explanations. McPhail also claims to have found no support for *relative* deprivation as a factor in riot participation, but this conclusion appears overstated. The problem is that the measures of deprivation in the studies he analyzed were not based on individual expectations, comparisons, or reference levels but rather on frequently vague indicators of racial inequality. Thus, relative deprivation cannot be so easily dismissed as a potential determinant of individual behavior.

One effort that did advance a reasonable relative deprivation explanation of riot behavior was the thorough analyses by Sears and McConahay (1970; 1973) of participation in the Los Angeles/Watts riot of 1965. These are among very few studies in the literature that explicitly gauge aspiration and comparison levels of urban blacks. They base their explanation on the effects of demographic changes in this century, which first brought blacks northward from the South and then westward in the post–World War II period. By 1960, Northern natives dominated in the Los Angeles ghetto. They allegedly instilled in their children values and expectations vastly different from those of their Southern-native counterparts. The offspring of these Northern blacks became the "new urban black," highly urbanized, relatively well educated, and possessing much higher expectations of life attainment and overall aspirations. These youth were developing strong feelings of black identity (and antiwhite hostility) and expecting more response from the political system to alleviate their grievances. As their expectations went unfulfilled, they experienced significantly more relative deprivation (which Sears and McConahay term "subjective status deprivation"—thus, the frustration that ultimately led the "new urban blacks" to participate disproportionately in the ghetto riots.

This study is unique in its efforts to articulate a social comparison or relative deprivation explanation of civil violence. But several ambiguities in the empirical analysis prevent wholehearted endorsement of the analysis. First, examination of actual comparison levels of the new versus old urban blacks showed no statistically significant differences. Second, the measure of deprivation was constructed solely from the differences between the status of the respondent's present occupation, as determined by the National Opinion Research Center socioeconomic status rating, and the status of his "most aspired to" occupation. But occupational status is obviously but one of many possible bases for relative deprivation; it does not tap overall life satisfactions, expectations, or achievements.

Finally, although there were differences between the new and old urban blacks on the subjective deprivation scale, and between deprived and nondeprived on measures of riot participation, none of these findings was overly powerful. A simple bivariate table showed only a fifteen percentage point difference in riot participation among the highly deprived and self-reported "satisfied" respondents; these findings rose only to a twenty-two point difference when the sample was limited to those between fifteen and twenty-nine years of age. These findings cast considerable doubt on the status of relative deprivation as the key explanatory variable in riot participation; these doubts are magnified by the lack of detailed multivariate analyses and statistical controls in the studies by Sears and McConahay.

A more general method for tapping feelings of relative deprivation was obtained in a series of other riot studies, and their results point to even more problem explanations of this type. Bowen et al. (1968), Crawford and Naditch (1970), and Grofman and Muller (1973) all administered the Cantril-Kilpatrick Self Anchoring Scale to samples of urban respondents in their studies. This scale presents a ladder with ten rungs, with the top rung representing the respondent's "best possible life" and the bottom rung the "worst possible life." Respondents are asked to place themselves on the ladder with respect to their perception of their present situation and, in several of the studies, where they expect to be five years hence and where they were five years ago. In this fashion, the Cantril scale identifies more directly the gap or discrepancy between life aspirations and life achievement, and is able to simulate temporal changes in individual life situations to test more accurately some variants of deprivation theories.

In none of the cases cited above did the Cantril scale produce strong associations with measures of riot participation or even riot approval. The results of the Crawford and Naditch study were in the expected direction, yet were small in magnitude. Other studies using the Cantril measure found little relationship between one's present or future standing on the scale and riot orientation. Grofman and Muller (1973), in fact, found an unexpected relationship between trends in one's perceived situation and protest potential. Respondents who experienced sharp declines in their perceived fortunes, or a greater discrepancy between life aspirations and attainments, scored higher on the protest scale than those experiencing no change. But also scoring higher were those who experienced positive change, those whose aspiration-achievement ratios were becoming smaller. Thus the shape of the graph of protest potential against relative gratifications resembled a V-curve, not a J-curve, as traditional deprivation theories would suggest. In other words, *any* perceived change, whether for better or worse, in life situation was associated with higher levels of violence potential. One explanation for such a finding is a "fluctuation-uncertainty" hypothesis: Any change in life satisfaction leads to uncertainties about the future, serving to activate the individual behavior intended likely to defend gains or rectify negative outcomes. Such a hypothesis was proposed by Miller, Bolce, and Halligan (1977), after analysis of individual-level data of perceptions of blacks' present and future financial situations in the 1960s. Such an explanation obviously differs greatly from a pure deprivation-type explanation.

Although these patterns emerging from the Cantril measures are certainly suggestive, two fundamental problems remain from these analyses. First, the Cantril scale measures, in whatever form, are generally only weakly correlated with measures of riot orientation; moreover, these associations virtually disappear when other factors are entered into more complex statistical models. Second, the Cantril scale itself entails serious conceptual deficiencies as a measure of relative deprivation. Most relative deprivation explanations turn on the discrepancy between an individual's circumstances and his or her *expectations*, whereas the Cantril scale taps the discrepancy between attainments and *aspirations*. The distinction is crucial, for as Gurr argues, "value expectations are defined with reference to *justifiable* value positions, meaning what men believe they are entitled to get or maintain, not merely what they faintly hope to attain" (1970, p. 27). What is needed are measures of deprivation that tap an individual's legitimate expectations and whether he is getting his "just deserts." No study examining ghetto riots used such a measure. Evidence gathered with measures discussed above, however, has been less than overwhelming.

3. *More recent relative deprivation research.*    Many of the uncertainties in measurement and estimation of the effects of relative deprivation have been resolved in the works of Edward N. Muller and his collaborators over the past fifteen years (Muller 1972; 1977; 1979; Muller and Jukam 1973; 1983; Grofman and Muller 1973). More than any others, these studies have pursued relative deprivation and related psychological explanations in various settings, from the racial disturbances considered in the early work (Muller 1972; Grofman and Muller 1973) to samples of urban, rural, and university populations in New York City, West Germany, and Costa Rica in the mid- to late 1970s (Muller, Jukam, and Seligson 1982). Vast improvements in measurement of key variables have been made, actual participation in violent events has been recorded (as distinct from attitudes toward such participation), and sophisticated statistical models have been developed to test the influence of deprivation and other social-psychological factors on violent behavior. Even after these improvements, though, the weight of evidence does not sustain the theory of relative deprivation as it relates to civil violence. Instead, Muller offers an alternative "Expectancy-Value-Norms" approach. This relegates relative deprivation to at most an indirect role in determining aggressive behavior, and elevates attitudes such as regime legitimacy and utilitarian considerations to center stage.

    The first major improvement in research strategy by Muller and his collaborators is their more precise measurement of participation in violent activity. Whereas much earlier work measured approval or sympathy toward violent protest, their later work recorded actual participation in aggressive political behavior. Acts such as fighting with police or demonstrators, taking part in wildcat or unofficial strikes, participating in groups dedicated to violent overthrow of government, and refusal to pay rent or taxes make up the overall index, called "Aggressive Political Participation" (Muller 1979, pp. 36–68). After all, people may approve many things that they would never do themselves. Instead of analyzing support for violence, the Muller studies specify more exactly those factors that determine individual participation in those violent acts.

The measurement of deprivation in these studies is also much improved. Several measures used in previous works, such as the Cantril scale, were included, in addition to new measures designed to gauge what Muller terms "just deserts" frustration. Respondents were asked specifically whether they were "getting what they were entitled to" with regard to material values such as housing, income, medical care, and employment and with regard to life in general. Thus, a comparison pegged to some sense of entitlement or expectation, and not simply to something aspired to in the best of possible worlds. Muller then reasons that even this type of frustration may not have political consequences unless accompanied by some sense that the political system, or state, is responsible for the discrepancy between present outcomes and just deserts. If the individual blames himself, rather than an outside agency for his situation, there should be little motivation to participate in violent antisystem behavior. Thus, Muller framed questions on perceived state responsibility for outcomes in the various deprivation outcomes, and the simple just deserts frustration scores were weighted by these responses to produce a scale of "structural just deserts frustration" (Muller 1979, p. 133).

All the various frustration measures were then correlated with scores on the aggressive participation index in the United States and West German studies, and a consistent pattern emerged. The Cantril scale exhibits its familiar V-curve pattern with aggressive behavior, yet these relationships were of trivial magnitude. The just deserts and structural just deserts frustration variables, though, exhibit relatively strong associations with the same measures of aggressive action. The simple correlation between each of the variables and the behavior index hovers around .4 in the West German and .3 in the New York City sample (Muller 1980, pp. 81–82).

The most important addition that Muller makes to our understanding of aggressive political behavior is the explicit incorporation of social-psychological factors other than relative deprivation into a statistical model. Once this model is estimated, the bivariate relationship found between deprivation and aggressive action largely disappears. Muller concludes that aggressive behavior is more likely among persons who have a strong belief in the efficacy of collective violence, and who believe they can get what they want through violence; are exposed to "facilitative" social norms for aggressive action and are motivated to comply with these norms; and regard aggressive behavior as normatively justifiable, based on either ideological beliefs, or on generalized alienation from the political system (Muller 1979, p. 29).

This last attitude is arguably the centerpiece of his model. Muller contends that no aggressive behavior will occur unless people doubt the moral worth of the political regime as a whole—in other words, unless they come to view the entire system, as opposed to specific policies, leaders, or outputs, as illegitimate. In virtually all of Muller's multivariate models, indicators of political alienation are the single strongest predictor of participation in violent political action. Together with the utilitarian and ideological considerations mentioned previously, they explain a substantial portion of the variance in the aggressive behavior index (Muller 1979). What counts in predicting political violence are low feelings of political support, leftist ideological sentiment, and a strong belief that political violence will "pay off." In addition, "facilitative social norms" also contribute to the explanation; these norms are present mainly in university settings in the samples under investigation. After controlling for these attitudes, the impact of either just deserts or structural just deserts frustration drops to trivial levels; deprivation, in Muller's terms, becomes a "superfluous" factor in predicting civil violence.

But do these findings entirely eliminate the role of deprivation, even within the "Expectancy-Value-Norms" approach? Not entirely, for although direct influence by these factors is ruled out, the possibility does exist that deprivation plays a minor indirect role. In this formulation, deprivation acts on political alienation—in other words, the experience of deprivation leads to a loss of political support, which then leads to violent actions (cf. Pinard 1983a). Muller finds some support for this "facilitative-indirect" role of deprivation. Several other variables appear to have indirect influence as well, for example, satisfaction with specific policy outputs of government, and "post-materialistic value orientations," or concern with environmental and quality-of-life issues. At most, deprivation can be said to play a small role among other factors that cause loss of support for the political system; loss of such support then causes individual participation in violent actions. But even these findings cannot be regarded as conclusive, as the possibility still exists that causality runs in the opposite direction, that is, that feelings about the moral bankruptcy of a particular regime will accentuate or create subjective feelings of deprivation (Muller 1980, p. 98).

The works of Muller and his colleagues give the strongest evidence to date against relative deprivation explanations of civil violence. In their studies, violent political activism appears to stem more from such utilitarian considerations as the consequences of the action, as well as from ideological commitment and lack of moral support for the political system.

Deprivation is neither necessary nor sufficient for aggression to occur; it influences violence only to the extent that it influences more general political attitudes. As Muller and Jukam (1983, p. 23) conclude, "People take part in civil disturbances and political violence because of a multitude of grievances—apparently, alienation from the political system is the only common denominator among them."

## Conclusions

The achievements of Muller and his collaborators are impressive. No other series of studies has pursued the specification of psychological variables in civil violence with such rigor and relentlessness. But what *theoretical* conclusions should be drawn from these studies? Do these researches in fact provide insight into the origins of militant collective action wherever it occurs? Will, as Muller suggests (1979, chaps. 7 and 8), much the same combination of low diffuse support for regimes and high expectations of the efficacy of civil violence yield violent participation wherever these factors co-occur? Will only these factors be responsible?

Clearly this matter is not to be settled a priori. But we are skeptical that the models accounting for violent political action in the settings studied by Muller and his collaborators would necessarily hold across a gamut of historical settings—for example, the American Revolution, the Warsaw Ghetto uprising, or violence among religious communities in modern India. Remember the context in which Muller gathered his key data. Germany at the time of the study had just passed through a period of particular political turmoil, especially in university life. All but a small handful of those scoring high on acts of aggressive political participation were in fact from university communities, which presumably both nurtured and provided the setting for political militancy. Earlier studies by Muller and his collaborators examined the predispositions to militancy among urban black Americans during a time of historical conflict between the races in the United States; here, too, there are questions of the boundedness of the findings to their historical context.

If any psychological explanation for participation in civil violence were the *unique* explanation for civil violence in general, some distinctive implications would follow: We would then expect to find militant action whenever these psychic states manifested themselves, and never in the absence of such states. Variations in culture, the ease of coercion, the facility of organization among potential participants, the accessibility of targets for violent acts—all these and many other variations in the settings and personnel of collective violence would be without significance in predicting and explaining such events. The absence of civil violence, by the same token, could only mean that the psychic states in question had subsided. We confess to doubts that such a categorical theory of civil violence, either in psychological or other terms, can ever be defended. We suspect, rather, that successful social-psychological explanations of participation will hold only within specific historical, cultural, and political contexts. This criticism applies to the works just discussed, as well as for other works that seek to establish the applicability of relative deprivation to other collective protests in other times and places—for example, Useem's (1980) analysis of the Boston antibusing movement. We believe that explanations like these will in the end prove to account for participation in violence during specific places and periods only.

All of this should spur reflection on relative deprivation theory, our original and central concern in this chapter. In their earliest formulations, relative deprivation theories enshrined this variable as virtually the ultimate cause of civil violence. Remember Dollard's sweeping assertion "aggression is always a consequence of frustration" (1939, p. 1) and Gurr's much later but no less sweeping remark (1970, p. 36) that frustration appears to be "the primary source of the human capacity for violence." In these heroic early views, relative deprivation enjoyed a theoretical centrality comparable with that of class relations in Marxist thinking, crowd mentality in the theories of the irrationalists, or moral solidarity in the writings of value integration theorists. Other determinants, though increasingly acknowledged as the relative deprivation literature grew, were depicted as facilitative or contingent influences.

More than other candidates for causal primacy, however, relative deprivation thinking has been subjected to a variety of confrontations with potentially falsifying evidence. Almost from the beginning, both supporters and skeptics have sought to refine methods and close loopholes in the arguments. The result has been a steady dilution of the sweeping theoretical claims for relative deprivation. In the process, other variables have shown equal or greater importance among statistical determinates of occurrence of and participation in violent events. Some studies, as we have seen, gave no support to the relative deprivation position; the minority of empirical studies we have examined that do provide some measure of support usually entail a mixture of causal influences. Gurr's own studies, even if one is to accept at face value his own interpretation of the variables he constructs, have shown greater weights to structural influences than to the variables identified as relative deprivation. His more recent studies have focused more heavily on such structural and historical factors. All things considered, at the time of this writing, forthright defenses of the role of relative deprivation in generating civil violence appear scarce.

In conclusion, perhaps we should review what needs to be established if any episode or series of violent events are to be regarded as accounted for by a relative deprivation explanation:

First, that the participants shared a single standard of justice, appropriateness, equity, minimal acceptability, or the like.

Second, that the timing of the action ensued from the *experience* of the violation of this standard, as registered in evidence from the individual participants.

Third, that actual participants in the violent action were distinguished from nonparticipants in the same population by their sense of violation of the key standard.

A few studies of collective action do take significant steps toward meeting this exacting requirement. An example is Bert Useem's study of neighborhood opposition to school busing in Boston (1980). Using questionnaires of neighborhood residents, Useem shows that protest activism was highest among those reporting themselves most indignant at the perceived violation of various equity standards that seemed salient to them. The protest actions undertaken by these residents were not violent, but one can easily imagine similar cases where violation of deeply held standards leads to violence.

But difficulties with most studies of relative deprivation arise even when they are held to standards less demanding than those cited here. Rarely have relative deprivation researchers been able to specify in advance *what specific standards* of equity, justice, or the like will govern individuals' decisions on participation in violent action. Many studies intended to show relative deprivation have missed even relatively elementary hurdles—for example, they have failed to show levels of dissatisfaction among the rebellious higher than among the quiescent. Only a small handful of studies have reported evidence that proved suggestive or, as in Useem's 1980 article, even stronger. Thus, we conclude that relative deprivation thinking has made a significant contribution to understanding some forms of civil violence. But it falls distinctly short of the status of a viable general theory.

*Chapter Eight*

# Conclusions on Civil Violence

What forces ensure compliance with peaceful, co-operative social arrangements? What conditions, conversely, sharpen latent conflicts into
riot, rebellion, or civil war? What qualities of social organization, objectives, and personnel characterize such outbreaks? Many have regarded
the "problem of social order," embodied in these questions, as *the* fundamental question of all social science. Certainly it abounds in implications
for other long-standing intellectual concerns. Any answer to Hobbes's
problem, after all, is bound to tell us much about the nature of power and
authority; about the origins of social movements and nonviolent forms of
social mobilization; about tensions between claims of governments and
those of other social interests; and about a variety of other enduring thematic questions on the agenda of the social sciences. For this reason, and
because of the sheer urgency of violence as a human concern, the search
for the causes of civil violence has an exceptionally long pedigree in the
history of social thought.

What, then, have the efforts depicted in preceding chapters yielded?
Of intriguing insights and suggestive possibilities we have many. But firm
and dramatic conclusions do not exactly leap to the eye. Often it has been
far clearer where theories of civil violence fail than where they succeed.

This chapter summarizes and assesses the theoretical conclusions on
the origins and character of civil violence that emerge from the preceding
chapters. Much of the evident inconclusiveness of these inquiries, I will
argue, arises from social scientists' ambiguous and unsettled expectations
of theory itself.

## The Theoretical Yearning

All theories afford some form of explanation. But not all explanations are
theoretical. One might explain an urban riot by noting that it began in

warm weather, when routine police brutality attracted especially wide notice in a riot-prone community. One might account for the violence in Prague in August of 1968 as a manifestation of the Czechoslovak people's hatred for Communist domination. One might account for the rise in guerrilla warfare in Cuba in the late 1950s as the result of Fidel Castro's personal pursuit of political power. Such explanations might be entirely correct, in that the violent events in question would not have occurred in the absence of the causal influence cited. But explanations of this kind are not *theoretical*, for they do not tell us how forces and connections in the origin of one case can be expected to play a similar role elsewhere.

The desire to make such links, the yearning for theoretical understanding, is pervasive. Few students of social contention, whether they think of themselves as social scientists or not, can resist seeking essential similarities between the ingredients of one episode and those underlying similar events elsewhere. And this means identifying forces, influences, or conditions conducing to the same results in new and different settings. Whatever else theory may entail, it certainly requires this much.

For this reason theory has been called a "guide to the unknown." Theoretical knowledge is that which warrants some degree of confidence that certain newly encountered situations will be governed by the same sorts of associations and connections found elsewhere. The connections involved may be formulated in the widest variety of ways—qualitatively, mathematically, in terms of binary permutations and combinations of properties, and so forth. But we might think of them all as involving some version of an "If $x$, then $y$" logic. If this community is well organized and mobilized, then it will be more likely to engage in militant action in response to threats to its interests. Or, if a polity experiences an outbreak of private or political violence, then the government must have shown itself weak in its ability to protect the law-abiding pursuit of private well-being. Again, the yearning to extend such theoretical linkages as far as possible is a basic fact of intellectual life.

I offer these thoughts as a minimalist, bare-bones account of empirically relevant theory and explanation; obviously different analysts build on and specify these ideas in many different ways. Yet for some, even this simple model may appear too constraining, too scientistic. They hold that theories in the social sciences may strive only to *interpret* reality, not to predict or explain in the empirical sense suggested here. Theory may lay bare the *essence* of various empirical phenomena, but theoretical statements should never be evaluated in terms of their *fit* with empirical observations.

Advocates of these views desire a variety of insights from theory. They may seek to identify the possibilities for human betterment hidden in the flawed, empirical here-and-now. Or they may seek theories that identify the true moral or political significance of facts or events, as in Marxian analyses aimed at determining whether particular political or social events or trends represent "progressive" or "reactionary" tendencies. The rightness or wrongness of such interpretations, their proponents would insist, is not to be judged by their congruence with any particular facts or evidence.

Proponents of such positions are rarely precise about the alternative they favor to theories contingent on evidence. One must content one's self with statements like the following from Theodor Adorno.

Theoretical speculations on society cannot be confirmed by precisely corresponding sets of empirical data; they elude the latter as persistently as spirits elude the experimental apparatus of parapsychology. . . . If, however, theory does not wish to succumb to dogmatism, . . . [it] must dissolve the rigidity of an object frozen in the here-and-now into a field of tensions between the possible and the actual. . . . In other words, theory is unalienably critical. But for this reason, hypotheses deduced from it, predictions of what may be expected according to the rules, are not fully adequate to it. (1976, p. 238)

I have struggled elsewhere with the interpretation of statements like this (1978, chap. 5). For now, let me simply assert that the implications of these views would be unacceptable even to many of their proponents, if they were clearly understood. Theories are either contingent in some degree on empirical reports, or they are not. To hold they are not contingent at all is to assert they are equally consistent with any and all states of the empirical world. No conceivable findings, evidence, or observations would then warrant theoretical revision. The outlook of a paranoid schizophrenic has this quality of total resilience in the face of what most would consider discordant observations. But this model of theory is hardly appealing to most of us. Indeed, totally nonempirical theories must by definition tell us more about the state of mind of the thinker than about the world he or she inhabits. Whatever the virtues of such theories, they do not provide bases for a community of intellectual inquiry. Somewhere, somehow, there must be empirical statements of the "If $x$, then $y$" variety, statements subject to dispute and revision in terms of some appeal to commonly held standards of evidence.

The classic alternative to these "soft," nondeterministic views of social science theory is a model taken from natural science—the "covering law" view, perhaps the most influential doctrine on theory and explanation in the middle decades of this century. Carl Hempel (1965) and Ernest Nagel (1961) are among its most illustrious proponents among philosophers of science; George Homans (1964; 1967) and others have sought to extend it to social science. In this view, the regularity of the natural universe— social life very much included—is reflected in the lawlike or invariant character of processes governing it. All effects—everything that happens—result from the workings of these universal forces. Scientific progress comes with our increasing ability to specify such invariant forces and the parameters of their action.

Explanation, in the covering law model, occurs when the working of universal principles is applied to specific conditions. To take Hempel's well-known example, the breaking of a car's radiator is explained by citing the fact that the compound $H_2O$ always expands when it reaches zero degrees centigrade, and by specifying that that temperature was indeed reached by the water in the radiator on the occasion in question. The business of explanation, then, is always a matter of linking empirical particularities to the invariant forces that rule an orderly universe. Proponents of this view typically stress that the same logic and structure must govern theorizing and explanation in social science, if the social sciences are ever to achieve "adequate scientific explanations" (Hempel 1965, p. 424).

Thus, a rigorously deterministic view of theory and explanation indeed. Note that the empirical relationships that Hempel and others term "lawlike" are not simply associations registered in large numbers of cases, but *necessary* associations—ones that warrant confidence of being repeated wherever the empirical properties in question co-occur in the future. Although it may be true to assert, "Every coin that has ever been in my pocket is a dime," such statements are nevertheless not lawlike. They do not support further statements of the form, "If $x$ is a coin and $x$ is in my pocket tomorrow, then $x$ must be a dime." Lawlike statements, in other words, require *universal form* and *nonlimited* scope (see Hempel 1965, pp. 266–67).

Statements of this kind must apply to all members of categories of phenomena that could ever occur, where the category involved is open to new instances. Not just *industrial societies that have existed up to the year 1986*, for example, but all societies that might ever meet or have met some criterion defining them as industrial. The category so defined may promise to have only rare instances—for example, hermaphrodites in line of succession to the English throne. But unless the categories covered in statements about empirical relationships refer to things of which new examples can in principle be found, the statements cannot be lawlike (see MacIntyre 1973b, p. 175).

Few if any relationships known to social scientists, I hold, can meet this austere criterion. Indeed, the difficulty in citing convincing examples of universal laws of a social character is one of the most serious difficulties confronting the covering law position in social science. Proponents of the model may point to associations that appear highly durable, such as the propensity of populations in drought-stricken regimes to migrate, or the association of individual support for civil liberties with years of formal education. Yet however frequent such associations have proved in instances studied in the past, they hardly warrant the degree of certainty required in universal form and nonlimited scope. We do not really have grounds for confidence that such relationships must always hold wherever they may be noted, throughout a specified universe of settings.

Social scientists occasionally contend that the lawlike relations most characteristic of their disciplines are statistical, rather than strictly determinate. Indeed, Hempel (1968, p. 61) posits a class of laws that relate one empirical property to another not with absolute certainty but with statistical probabilities. Thus, Mendel's formulations do not entail determinate statements on the colors of specific generations of peas; but they do specify distributions of colors among infinitely large populations from which samples might be drawn. Or atomic physicists may cite lawlike certainties about the decay of radioactive elements—certainties that do not specify the behavior of any particular atom of the element, but the *proportion* of all such atoms that will have decayed after a given period.

The idea of probabilistic laws may appeal to social scientists who feel that their inquiries entitle them to be "fairly certain" about the generalizability of empirical relations that they have established, but not totally so. Thus, a student of industrial societies might hold that the positive association in such societies between social status and voluntary association membership represented a lawlike connection of a probabilistic sort. The argument would be that such associations had been noted in most industrial societies (or at least most non-Communist industrial societies) studied thus far, if not in every such society.

But this knowledge does not really meet the stringent requirements of probabilistic laws. For it is impossible for an investigator to make any definite statement about the entire *universe* of non-Communist industrial societies. For that universe includes not only societies of this description that have existed to date, but any that might ever exist in the future. We have no warrant to believe that the sample of such societies available to investigators today represents a representative sample of that universe; indeed, we have a good deal of reason to believe the opposite. The analyst in this example may have established an *empirical regularity* of real importance. But our knowledge of industrial societies as a class of empirical phenomena will never be so exhaustive as our knowledge of radon atoms or the genetic inheritance of peas. And hence, things that we may establish about those specific industrial societies accessible to us for study are always apt to be peculiar to the historical settings from which our examples are drawn. The associations uncovered by social scientists rarely give grounds for certainty about associations throughout infinitely large populations of settings—that is, about any settings in which the variables in question may occur, whether past, present, or future.

Social scientists have made great strides in quantitative analyses of their materials. But the relationships disclosed through these analyses are not especially likely to hold in new settings simply because they are quantitative. True, many social scientists believe that more exact statistical specification of variables, improvements in multivariate methodology, or other refinements will ultimately yield relations of deterministic or probabilistic lawlike certainty. But such beliefs remain a matter of faith. Social scientists have to date identified few if any empirical relations characterized by universal form and nonlimited scope.

Thus a chronic dilemma. On the one hand, we notice empirical regularities all about us in social life, and most of us take it for granted that the empirical world is governed by forces that are in principle universal. Yet if we are candid, we must admit that we cannot specify with confidence how widely particular regularities that come to our attention may extend. We would like to attain unqualified certainties of the "If $x$, then $y$" sort—to know, for example, that civil violence *must always* be attended or preceded by other empirically specifiable social conditions. But the associations our research establishes typically appear to some degree peculiar to the contexts in which we encounter them; we never know for sure what changes in context may alter such relations.

One response to this dilemma comes from Lewis Coser: "The typical if-then propositions of science can only come into play when, through prior reflection, the researcher has been able to identify which 'if's' are likely to be important and which are not." Thus,

When a plumber is called to the house because a drainpipe needs fixing, he is likely to bring his tool kit along. He is aware that the causes of the malfunction may be many and that he cannot rely on just one tool to put matters right. Analogies are somewhat misleading, but I believe, nevertheless, that one may think of the investigation of specific problems in social analysis as yielding best results when not just one tool, but a set of tools, is employed. (1981, pp. 172–73)

An understated but distinctive position. Social theories do bear falsifiable implications, Coser seems to suggest, but the fact of their falsification should not lead us to discard them. Theories should remain permanently in the conceptual armory of the investigator, awaiting those critical moments when they provide the very insight necessary to unravel the problem at hand. This is an eclectic view of theory indeed.

Coser is certainly right as far as he goes. Any social scientist who failed to invoke Marxian principles in accounting for the formation of social consciousness along class lines, or who ignored Durkheimian formulations in interpreting the moral indignation of a community at a notorious crime, would certainly be unworthy of his or her credentials. But most working sociologists, I suspect, also expect more from sociological theory than the toolbox model might promise.

What we seek is a reliable guide to the unknown. We want to know *in advance* what empirical relations should be expected to hold in what ranges of cases. In Coser's toolbox, all tools are equally important. Yet for both tools and theories, we prefer not to have to try an infinite number before we find the one we need. Surely much of the hold that seemingly profound theories exercise over our imaginations lies in the conviction, warranted or not, that we can count on principles they enunciate to apply to certain sorts of cases wherever we may encounter them. What I call the theoretical yearning is the desire to apprehend relatively enduring connections among empirical properties—connections likely to hold in new settings of specific kinds.

## Another View of Theory and Explanation

Interpretive models of theory and explanation are unsatisfactory when they go to the extreme of offering no formula for revision in the face of discordant empirical findings. In effect, they demand too little of empirical reality. Yet the covering law model, at least in its classic form, demands too much. It demands lawlike principles specifying universal linkages to one another, principles of universal form and nonlimited scope. Absent such principles, authentic scientific explanation is impossible, according to Hempel. Few if any programs of inquiry in the social sciences can meet this stringent standard.

Yet social scientists do establish empirical regularities or generalizations in their subject matter all the time, and on the strength of such regularities propound explanations of individual findings and patterns of findings. What we need is a model of theory and explanation suited to the peculiar logical and empirical constraints of social reality. Such a model should at a minimum:

(1) Identify connections—causal sequences or other durable associations—linking empirically falsifiable properties of social data, connections that can be shown to prevail throughout some range of instances;

(2) Enable us to cite these empirical connections as bases for explanations of particular instances or groups of instances.

In other words, we need a way of identifying significant empirical regularities and mobilizing these patterns as bases for explanations without committing ourselves to the *universality* of such patterns. In fact, one strain of thinking on theory and explanation does afford such a view. Although altogether less influential than the views already considered, this model also has a long pedigree in our intellectual history. For twentieth-century social science, it has had persuasive exponents in the sociologist Robert MacIver (1942) and the philosopher of science Alan Garfinkel (1981).

Let me give my own version of this position, without implicating MacIver, Garfinkel, or anyone else but myself as responsible for its details.*

To explain any event or fact, in social science or in everyday life, one cites a condition or circumstance without which it would not have occurred or would not be the case. Thus, I went to my office *because* I was looking for the keys I had mislaid (if I had not wanted to look for the keys, I would not have gone there). Or, Iakovos is Primate of the Greek Orthodox Church *because* he was elected to this role by the College of Bishops (if he had not been so elected, he would not be Primate).

Now every bit of social behavior, every potential social *explanandum* is contingent on an enormous variety of such necessary conditions, perhaps an infinite list of them. Hence, a potentially infinite list of possible explanations. My going to my office to look for my keys also depended on my believing that the keys were in fact there; on my knowing that the office building was open at the time I went; on the availability of transport to get me to the office, and so on. Any explanation entails singling out a particular one of these dependencies in its significance for the occurrence or fact of interest; other necessary conditions, one might say, are held constant.

Thus *all* explanations are accounts of *differences*—differences between the total situation that produced the *explanandum,* and another situation, similar in other respects, where the *explanandum* is absent. As Robert MacIver put it, in his penetrating but now neglected *Social Causation,*

we identify the situation or type of situations in which the phenomenon occurs, as against a comparable situation from which it is absent, and engage ourselves to discover how the phenomenon is related to the differential organization of the situation containing it. (1942, p. 251)

Identification of the "comparable situation from which . . . [the *explanandum*] is absent" may be made in various ways. In laboratory research, the "otherwise similar situation" may be a control group. In historical studies, it may be a society as similar as possible to the one in which the effect is observed, yet which never manifested the institutions or events to be explained. In medicine, psychology, and sociology, the "comparable situa-

---

*The following exposition is given more fully in "Law and Strategy in Sociological Explanation," *European Journal of Sociology* 25 (1984), pp. 167–82.

tion" may be the same individual, population, or social system at an earlier time, before the intrusion of the causal influence. As Alan Garfinkel puts it,

an explanation always takes place relative to a background space of alternatives. Then different spaces of alternatives may therefore require different explanations. And sometimes we can compare two explanations to see how their contrast spaces differ. (1981, p. 25)

He adds a few pages later:

The contrast space determines, in part, what counts as a successful explanation. (1981, p. 28)

Note that the choice of the "comparable situation" or "contrast set" for analytic comparison to the situation where the *explanandum* occurs can only be the task of the analyst. It does not inhere in the nature of the thing to be explained or the logic of its situation. The philosopher of science Fred Dretske (1972, p. 411) has captured the issue neatly with the following example:

I have three friends who are variously misinformed about one of my recent transactions. The first wants to know why I gave the typewriter to Clyde. I set him straight by telling him that I did not *give* my typewriter to Clyde.

(1) I *sold* my typewriter to Clyde.

Somewhat later my second friend gives it to be understood that he thinks I sold my typewriter to Alex. In correcting him I say,

(2) I sold my typewriter *to Clyde*.

Still later the third asks me why I sold my adding machine to Clyde and, once again, I find myself saying,

(3) I sold *my typewriter* to Clyde.

Dretske's example does two things. First, it reminds us that apparently simple statements of things-to-be-explained may not fully specify the explanatory work required. Explaining the sale of the typewriter to *Clyde* is obviously a different matter from explaining the *sale* of the typewriter to Clyde. Or, to explain why the Paris student rebellion in May 1968 occurred among students (rather than among some other group) is not precisely the same as explaining why these events occurred in May 1968 (instead of some other month or year). Thus a variety of explanations of what may appear to be the same thing may in fact be explanations of rather different things. If all explanations are indeed explanations of differences, specification of *the precise difference* (or contrast) to be explained is an essential part of explanatory work.

Second, Dretske's observations point us to one of the profoundly rich and difficult questions for all social science analysis: How to choose the particular "comparable situations" or "contrast sets" that should serve as bases for explanatory efforts. Which contrasts are apposite and to the point, in other words, and which are distracting, trivial, or misleading?

I could not begin to offer an answer here in the detail that this crucial question demands. But it should be obvious that the interests and values of the analyst and of the larger community are major considerations. Consider an example adapted from Collingwood: I drive my car at sixty miles per hour down a residential street where the legal limit is thirty, and in so doing strike a child who has run into the street. How are we to assess the cause of this event? The child's darting into the street was no less necessary a condition than my fast driving for the occurrence; yet most legal, ethical, and other judgments would place responsibility on the driver. The reasons for this obviously have to do with certain shared interests that guide analyses of such events.

---

Theories are single explanations *writ large*. The quest for a theory of auto accidents involving children—or civil violence, or anything else— requires that we identify dependency between the thing to be explained and another empirical influence or circumstance that holds not just in one case, but in an array of them. In fact, theories of this sort abound, as much in everyday life as in social science. If we note that every time Uncle Ben takes part in a family get-together he sets everyone arguing with one another, and that no arguments occur in his absence from such occasions, we have a rudimentary theory of one set of family arguments in the Mac-Iver—Garfinkel mode. That the explanation applies only to a relatively small number of situations hardly disqualifies it from theoretical status; the logic is not fundamentally different from that underlying much more elaborate and more widely applicable theories of suicide, voluntary association membership, or civil violence.

Note something important about this view of theory and explanation: It entails no assumption that explanatory connections observed in one set of instances must necessarily prevail universally, in all instances of what appears to be "the same" *explanandum*. Such guarded commitments are nothing if not appropriate to our subject matter. The normal state of affairs in social science is to know that a particular causal relation holds in a group of roughly similar settings, without knowing precisely how widely the connection will obtain. For decades economists expected inflation and unemployment in industrial economies to vary inversely with one another; that connection was widely attested. But something changed in many such economies in the 1970s, upsetting the relationship; what that something was is still a matter of debate. Similarly, demographers for decades could demonstrate that fertility was inversely related to socio-economic status in industrial societies; yet this relationship, too, has broken down in some contemporary settings. I see no point in denying the term "theoretical" to our knowledge of these relationships simply be-cause the limits of their applicability were eventually reached—or even because we may not know why or how contextual changes altered the re-lationship. The fact that these empirical dependencies did not extend be-yond a certain range of settings should hardly distract us from the fact that a pattern of such connections did and does exist.

Limited empirical regularities, then, may form bases for informative explanations. We note that tightening of work rules in firms previously marked by much discretion on the job brings resentment among staff and wildcat strikes; or we note that rising levels of formal education bring rising support for civil liberties; or we find that violent protest by peasants is a common result of capitalist encroachment on their traditional means of livelihood. With proper contextual justification, specific strikes, mani-festations of support, or peasant revolts may be explained as instances of such regularities. But social scientists must admit that the relationships thus cited do not entail universal form and nonlimited scope. Indeed, we ought to acknowledge that somewhere, at some time, tightening of work rules will no doubt produce no friction from workers, rises in formal edu-cation will yield reduced support for civil liberties, and expropriation of peasants may spark no protest. We know, in other words, that empirical connections in social systems may hold quite widely, yet remain con-tingent on a great host of contextual conditions, only some of which we can specify.

Thus, it is typically futile for social scientists to seek the invariant, law-like relations heralded by Nagel and Hempel, although the possibility of such relations need not be rejected categorically. For the units of analysis studied by social scientists are rarely so uniform as those studied by natu-ral scientists; their properties can seldom be so exhaustively known. One may specify the characteristics of a cube of lead or a colony of bacteria or a carbon molecule in such a way that they differ in no significant respect from other units of the same description that the scientist might deal with. But we know that industrial societies, families, firms, or revolutions will always have certain idiosyncratic characteristics that cannot be specified in advance, yet may have everything to do with whether causal connec-tions observed in one unit are apt to be repeated in the next.

This guarded view of the regularities uncovered by social scientists hardly implies skepticism about the ultimately orderly or law-governed workings of nature, including the social world. It is entirely compatible, for example, with the classic statement on this subject in Mill's *A System of Logic*.

What happens once, will, under a sufficient degree of similarity of circumstances, happen again, and not only again, but as often as the same circumstances recur. . . . The universe, so far as is known to us, is so constituted, that whatever is true in any one case, is true in all cases of a certain description; the only difficulty is, to find what description. (1893, p. 223)

What we social scientists must acknowledge is that we rarely if ever know exhaustively what constitutes "a sufficient degree of similarity of circumstances." We may sense intuitively that, if poor harvests in rural England in 1622 brought food riots, similar conditions might bring the same results in 1630, as indeed was the case (Beloff 1938, p. 58)—whereas similar conditions in the present century may have quite different results. But it is difficult to give a rigorous defense of our differing degrees of confidence in such connections. We must admit that even under conditions that appear identical in every respect of which we are aware, "the same" cause occasionally does not lead to "the same" effect. Such acknowledgments should hardly deter us from seeking to extend empirical connections as far as we can, nor a fortiori from seeking to specify what conditions must prevail for the connections to hold.

We will do best in these efforts if we conceive of them as an attempt to specify and delimit *causal systems*, rather than simply as attempts to discover relations among variables. By causal systems I mean both empirical connections between properties of interest and the entire set of contextual influences under which these relations prevail. To propound a theory of rural food riots in preindustrial Europe, in other words, one should concern one's self not just with the connections between food prices and violent action, but with all the historical and social conditions that must prevail for these connections to hold. Often the web of such linkages is intricate indeed.

Consider a whimsical example of a causal system where the contingencies were particularly nonintuitive. A woman in California (these stories always seem to come from California) reportedly took her car to a mechanic with a singular complaint. The car stalled when she stopped en route home from work to buy ice cream, but only under peculiar circumstances. When she ordered chocolate, vanilla, or strawberry, the car started as usual on her return from the store. If she purchased pistachio, however, it balked. After much investigation, the following explanation emerged: The car had a defect in the cooling system that caused heat to accumulate excessively when the engine was turned off after running for some time. The build-up of heat was not immediate, so that the car could be restarted for a minute or two, but after three or four minutes it became too hot to start. When the driver stopped for ice cream, the duration of the stop depended on the flavor she chose. Chocolate, vanilla, and strawberry ice cream were sold in prepackaged containers, and the transaction went quickly. Pistachio had to be scooped by hand, and this took several extra minutes—just enough to make the difference between a car that would start and one that would not.

One can imagine attacking an explanatory problem like this with standard multivariate techniques. One might perform a multiple regression analysis aimed at predicting a dummy variable expressing whether the car would start. Independent variables chosen might include—in the absence of foreknowledge of the role of pistachio in this case—the number of stop lights en route to the ice cream store, the length of time since the car was last serviced, the time of day of the trip, and so on. Such investigations might conceivably provide effective insight into the origins of the problem, especially if the investigator thought to include in the equation the duration of the stop at the ice cream shop. But I do not believe that any such investigation could improve on my analysis. Nor would these correlational methods seem to offer the most promising means for investigating the problem before its origins were known.

Was the choice of pistachio really "the cause" of the car's stalling? Or was it the length of time during which the heated engine was left off? Or the malfunction of the car's cooling system? I do not believe that such questions admit of absolute, once-for-all answers. What counts as *the* cause depends on the interests, values, and perspective of the analyst and, by the same token, on the nature of the contrast invoked in the analysis. If the driver normally drove only in very cold climates, where engine heat dissipated so quickly that quick stops never led to subsequent stalling, the cause of the problem might be driving in a warmer locale. Alan Garfinkel gives the following example from an article by Gorovitz.

A match, having been pulled from the assembly line in a match factory, is struck in a supposedly evacuated chamber, the purpose being to test the hardness of the match head. But the chamber has not been properly sealed, and the match lights. . . . The cause can reasonably be said to be the presence of oxygen, and not the striking. (Gorovitz 1965, p. 695)

Again, different kinds of theories, based on different contrast sets or the like, correspond to different values, interests, or perspectives. But this is hardly to say that such differences are arbitrary, that one theory of "the same" thing is as good as any other. Some theories address themselves to differences of wide and lasting analytic interest, whereas others correspond to more limited or parochial interests.

Consider a controversy over the explanation of rioting by black city dwellers in the United States during the 1960s. In a widely publicized analysis, the authors of the *Report* of the National Advisory Commission on Civil Disorders offered the following interpretation of these events: "White racism is essentially responsible for the explosive mixture which has been accumulating in our cities since the end of World War II" (1968, p. 5).

Some years later, James Q. Wilson attacked this conclusion as a defective explanation.

One would suppose that there would be evidence that, not only have these social forces been at work, but that they have led to disorders. There is no such evidence, at least on the latter and fundamental point. Indeed, evidence later gathered by social scientists casts serious doubt on this causal explanation. . . . blacks who believed violence was an appropriate response to ghetto conditions were found as frequently in cities without violence as in cities with it. . . . Later research analyzing the conditions in cities with and without riots suggests that the more violent cities differed chiefly from the others in that they had more blacks. Income inequalities, on the other hand, were not systematically related to violence. (1978, p. 83)

Wilson's theory makes sense only in terms of a "contrast set" counterposing cities that experienced riots *during these specific years* to cities that went without riots during the same period. Such a contrast might be appropriate from a standpoint of the concerns, say, of officials charged with suppressing riots. But it is less satisfactory as a response to what might more properly be termed *theoretical* concerns about why blacks in many or most American cities during these particular years were close to rioting, whereas black residents in the same cities in other periods, or other nations, were not.

Good theories may serve accurately to predict or retrodict the things they explain. But the *interests* underlying the desire to predict are often not the same as those underlying the yearning for theory. The question is, what is the range of cases, and the implicit contrast, for which theory or prediction is sought? A shrewd journalist or other well-informed observer close to the scene of the action might well predict the immediate outbreak of violent events better than any social scientist. Yet even the most impressive predictions of the hour at which a tense situation will erupt into violence, or which of several tense neighborhoods will explode, may not be theoretically satisfying. Like Wilson's critique of racism as a key factor in generating American urban riots of the 1960s and 1970s, such predictions do not address what I have called the theoretical yearning. That yearning is directed at identifying explanatory forces that make the difference between occurrence and absence of the subject under study in a range of cases of evident import. Predictions or explanations lacking this broader reference may have all sorts of important virtues, but theoretical power is not among them.

---

This view of theory and explanation, I hold, fits better the actual constraints and possibilities of social science subject matter than other theoretical strategies. Taking this view seriously obliges us to credit some important caveats otherwise easily overlooked: first, that the task of explaining or theorizing entails important assumptions, often unacknowledged, about which conditions are to remain constant and which are to vary in the setting or settings involved; second, that in light of such subtle assumptions, a variety of equally logically tenable theories or explanations may be offered for what appears to be "the same" *explanandum;* and third, that choice among such alternative accounts often can only be made in terms of the values, interests, or other existential considerations held relevant in the situation at hand.

Such caveats should inform any approach to theories of civil violence. They counsel skepticism about claims for all *general theories*—that is, theories accounting for all manifestations of the *explanandum*, without regard to explanatory context. They encourage us to seek the *specific settings* in which a proposed explanatory factor may make the crucial difference between occurrence and absence of the thing to be explained, even when less imaginative investigations have failed to produce results supporting the theory in question.

With these cautions in mind, let us return to a review and assessment of theories considered in the preceding chapters.

## Theories of Individual Assessment and Calculation

These are the theories considered in Chapter One. They interpret participation in violent events as reflecting individuals' calculating assessments of others' past or future actions. Most versions of these theories posit as bases for individual action what I have called divisible self-interest— "selfish" motives of some sort. But this need not be the case: Granovetter's threshold model, for example, simply pictures the individual as predicating his own action on rates of participation by others, regardless of motives.

All theories of this kind face a conundrum. The individual interests or predispositions from which violent action springs are usually assumed to be relatively enduring. Yet any theory of civil violence must account for *changes* in action, from nonviolent to violent or vice-versa. Obviously such change must arise from changes in individual assessment: The world must look different to people, in other words, for their behavior to change. Where do these perturbations come from?

In Mancur Olson's model of self-interested individual mobilization, only incentives that appeal to divisible self-interest will result in action. Although Olson has little directly to say about participation in violent episodes, selective incentives should clearly be no less necessary for participation in violence than for any other form of mobilization. One should expect riot, revolution, or rebellion only where individual participants expect some form of divisible gratification from their acts—as distinct from the rewards of shared identification with larger causes or collective interests.

Similar assumptions underlie Banfield's analysis of urban rioting in America as a pursuit of "fun and profit." Many conservative thinkers have offered such analyses, seeking to deflate the claims of rebels and revolutionaries to act on behalf of ideal or collective interest. But is there empirical support for any of these positions?

True, satisfaction of individual, divisible interests plays an evident role in many violent actions—for example, the looting accompanying urban rioting in American cities during the 1960s and 1970s. As for the other side of participation, we know that the opponents of rebellion must normally offer pay or other selective incentives to police, strike-breakers, or other specialists in repression. Gary Marx (1974) has noted how provocateurs, presumably acting on selective incentives, may provide the proximate cause of certain riotous episodes. I know of few other studies that conclusively show divisible self-interest as the *trigger* to insurgency. The closest one comes is where changes in repressive capacity suddenly make it in the calculated self-interest of would-be insurgents to rebel.

Note the limits reached by rational choice analysis in Samuel Popkin's distinguished study of peasant activism (1979). Popkin argues that rebellion remains rationally unattractive for individual poor peasants acting on narrowly divisible, selfish interests, despite the evident reality of their exploitation. Potential movements were stymied by the likelihood of "free riding." But arrival of new figures on the scene, in the form of committed activist representatives of outside political or religious movements, injected a qualitatively different element into these calculations. If a *few* actors could be counted on *not* to pursue strict individual rationality, it became rational for others to follow them. I suspect that in-depth examination of many transitions from quiescence to militancy would show processes of this kind.

Now think back to Hobbes. For him, the strength of civil sovereignty

determined whether individuals best served their own interests by acceptance of civil authority, or by rebellion. A shrewd judge of his or her own
self-interest would always support sovereignty—and hence renounce recourse to violence—when doing so would yield a higher probability of
safety and well-being than taking one's chances in a lawless and violent
world.

The difficulty with Hobbes's arguments as bases for empirical inquiry
lies in specifying how much government coercive strength ought to be
"enough." Certainly the potency of governments in ensuring domestic
peace is not simply a linear effect of official coercive might, or of the balance between such forces and popular forces potentially available for
rebellion. Any penetrating empirical investigation of Hobbes's theories
would have to address a strictly perceptual issue: What do people *believe*
about the relations between their own compliance with government-
backed social strictures, the ability of governments to guarantee public
peace, and the importance of that ability for their own private pursuit of
self-interest? These are intriguing but highly subtle matters; the determination and sophistication necessary to pursue them in research is not
yet in sight.

Similar difficulties surround Granovetter's provocative threshold
model. Regarding violent events, thresholds are difficult to assess independently of the behavior they are supposed to explain. This difficulty is
not a matter of logical circularity, but a strictly practical problem. Perhaps
even more than in the Hobbesian case, it would be hard to obtain reliable
reports of people's own thresholds directly from them. Participants or participant observers in crowds where action "builds on itself" are apt to
have gathered one kind of empirical evidence of such processes. Ques-
tioned immediately afterwards, they might give believable reports as to
how others' actions shaped their own or each other's willingness to participate. More painstaking empirical fitting of the details of violent events to
the implications of the model is likely to be difficult.

For those interested in Hobbes's theories, there are some inviting ave-
nues for empirical research. Ability of governments to inspire what Hobbes
called "Awe" on the part of their citizenries sometimes fluctuates sharply
over brief periods. Abrupt declines in ability of governments to guarantee
safety for private citizens' pursuit of private interests (as during police
strikes) and abrupt tightening of coercive power (as in the Turkish military
government's crackdown in 1980) occasionally, though by no means always, lead to Hobbesian results: either sharp breakdowns in compliance,
or restoration of such compliance. Anyone seriously interested in the fit
between Hobbes's theories and empirical reality ought to pay close attention to these cases. We need theoretically sophisticated comparative

analyses of where the power shifts bring results of the sort that might be expected in light of Hobbes's theories, and where no such results occur.

Evidence against individual assessment theories of civil violence as *general theories* is ample. Empirical inquiry attests to many cases where collective rather than individual interest appears to motivate participation in violent events, or where gross fluctuation in government coercive capacity has no effect on popular compliance. But I see no reason why such findings should dampen further inquiry into the empirical possibilities of these theories. For there are various events and periods where individual incentives and calculations may well govern participation. Further attention from shrewd researchers might well disclose how specific calculations of safety, individual opportunity, or other forms of self-interest change in the flux of contentious situations, thus triggering individual participation. The most persuasive thing that proponents of these theories could do would be to document more such instances, and tell us as much as possible about how they differ from cases where individual incentives and calculations seem irrelevant to accounting for civil violence.

## Interaction Theories

Interaction theories are collective behavior theories in line of descent from the irrationalists and Park; one might also characterize them as theories of "crowd mentality" or "collective innovation." In these views, special forms of interaction give rise to distinctive collective dynamics without which violence would not occur. One strain of this view, mass society theory, interprets the lack of connection of participants in "normal" social networks as a key contributor to their tendencies to violent action.

Since the 1960s, this view of civil violence has come under vociferous attack from exponents of competing theories. The attacks have been partly empirical, partly conceptual. Empirically, researchers have demonstrated the continuity of much violent action with participants' "normal" interests, values, and purposes. This rootedness of violent events in the stuff of everyday life, critics claim, discredits theories picturing crowd action as directed by processes sharply different from those guiding "normal" social behavior.

Conceptually, the critique of interaction theories has focused on much the same point—the distinctiveness of the innovative, excited, interactions supposedly necessary for violent collective action. How are these special qualities of crowd interactions to be distinguished? Social theorists increasingly find it difficult to draw rigorous distinctions between innovative and "normal" social process; important elements of creativity and improvisation seem to figure even in the most routine and highly institu-

tionalized social processes. These criticisms, coupled with empirical reports of the highly normative or standardized qualities of much violent
contention, have left proponents of collective behavior theories on the
defensive.

The occurrence and timing of violent action—key targets of these cri-
tiques—are but one kind of falsifiable implication. Collective behavior
theories also yield important implications on the social identities of *participants*. These are what I have termed "scum of the earth" accounts,
both in the more blatant statements by the turn-of-the-century irrationalists and in the more sociologically sophisticated mass society versions of sociometric and political isolation. These theories are eminently
falsifiable and, to judge from various studies to date, eminently false. Participants in a wide variety of violent and other militant collective action
have been shown to be at least as well embedded in social networks and
enduring loyalties as the average for their groups or communities.

Concerning the *content* and *purposes* of violent action, the critics' attack has also been telling. A new generation of social and historical analysts, often inspired by Charles Tilly, William Gamson, or recent Marxist
social historians, have recorded in detail the purposefulness of much violent collective action. The burden of proof now rests on proponents of
collective behavior theory to demonstrate the discontinuities and irrationalities long attributed to civil violence. For most followers of these debates, I suspect, the issue is settled at the expense of collective behavior
theory.

But categorical conclusions on this point are premature. The credibility of the many studies showing purposefulness and continuity is not in
doubt. But such studies may not illuminate all the empirical material relevant to this aspect of the theory. True, the extravagant suggestions by the
irrationalists of total malleability in the directions of crowd action have
properly been discarded. In the entire literature of the empirical studies,
we have virtually no accounts of crowds acting in ways unambiguously
contrary to their "normal" interests, though we often find people pursuing interests in violent situations that are not safe to pursue at other times.
But there is much to suggest that crowd action is not always strictly purposeful, if by this we mean oriented *only* to instrumental ends. Some
militant crowd action is clearly consummatory rather than instrumental,
and such action often includes the sorts of hair-raising sadistic and destructive acts that inspired the anxiety-ridden visions of the irrationalists.
Such actions appear to be ends in themselves, rather than means to some
longer-term end.

Judging these matters is not simple. Again, participation in crowds
may relieve people of entirely realistic concerns about retribution for

their actions. Thus, upper-class observers may be shocked to find that "their" subordinate groups, normally so compliant, have been transformed in the course of violence to raging mobs. No doubt much of what impressed the irrationalists was simply this shock of seeing normally subordinate folk interpret their own interests for themselves, once they had the chance to do so without immediate fear of reprisal. But the irrationalists were also responding to another dimension of crowd action—the gratuitous cruelty, even sadism of revolutionary crowds.

Consider the following account from the diaries of Restif de la Bretonne, a seasoned journalistic observer of the revolutionary events in Paris of 1792; here he recounts the bouts of barely discriminate killing by the mobs that took over many Parisian streets during the revolution.

Outside the Chatelet the corpses were stacked like firewood. And yet the Chatelet takes only common criminals, not political suspects. The curious come up, sniff, and perhaps spit in the gutter; delicate souls pass on the other side of the street—that is the distinction. . . .

It was that morning the Princesse de Lamballe was murdered in the rue St. Antoine outside the prison called La Force. She had been detained there since August 10. The princess was known and detested for being an intimate friend of Marie-Antoinette. She had been in safety in England but had returned earlier this year to be with the Queen. Was her fate merited? Perhaps, but surely not the indignities visited on her body. It is hard to believe but the fact is incontestable that after her death her body was stripped, exposed to all, her head cut off and carried at the point of one pike, her genitals carved out of her corpse and stuck at the end of another, these two obscene trophies carried first to the Palais-Royal, then to the Temple, to frighten the Queen in case she should glance out the window of her prison. (1970, pp. 243–44)

Restif began the revolutionary period as a kind of urban populist; his enthusiasm for the cause became more muted in response to events like these. The authenticity of this account and others like it are not in doubt. To be sure, the violence described here was part of larger actions against entrenched political forces. But it would be hard to argue that all such mayhem contributed to attainment of strategic political goals. Gary Marx, in personal communication, has noted the same mixture of purposeful action with hair-raising instances of maiming, castrating, and killing for their own sake in modern prison riots.

We do not read much about crowd action of this sort in the works of authors like Gamson, Tilly, Rude, or E. P. Thompson. Their theoretical lens focuses better on forms of militancy that serve long-term collective purposes. How frequent vengeance and cruelty for their own sake are, and how they fit into any overall pattern of collective violence, are not questions to be answered a priori. They will have to await empirical investigation by analysts theoretically prepared to look for them. All we know for certain is that much civil violence mixes highly instrumental action with deeds that only make sense as ends in themselves. And these self-gratifying crowd actions range from boisterous but nondestructive street theater to blood-curdling acts of sadism.

Similarly, collective behavior accounts of violent events as results of "shared excitement" have been unduly dismissed. Theories emphasizing the long-term rationality of such action have typically viewed shared emotional states as epiphenomenal, without explanatory significance of their own. Yet many violent sequences appear to depend directly on dissemination of some highly emotional news of no inherent strategic significance. The Indian events following the assassination of Prime Minister Gandhi in 1984 are a conspicuous example. The rioting in the United States following the assassination of Martin Luther King, Jr., simply moves the case closer to home.

Or consider the sweeping popular response throughout the United States in July 1910 to the victory of Jack Johnson, the first black heavyweight boxing champion, over his white challenger. Fights broke out in every corner of the country between blacks and whites, normally in response to racial taunts inspired by the event. At least ten persons died as a result of these attacks, with victims and aggressors in both racial groups; in Texas, a black man held in jail in connection with the altercations was nearly lynched. Violence was especially widespread following the showing of newsreels of the match, to the extent that local officials rushed to ban the screenings in towns and cities throughout the country (*New York Times*, 6–11 July 1910).

Again, such outbreaks of violence would certainly not have occurred in the absence of enduring contention between two racial groups. But it would be hard to argue that the riots following the Johnson victory would have occurred without the special emotional stimulus provided by the event. And note that the goals pursued by rioters in violent status contests like these appear far more consummatory than instrumental.

Finally, do violent collective actions spring from forms of *interaction* different from those underlying nonviolent action? We have no theoretical or empirical reason to believe so. But then, no one has amassed much of the evidence that would be necessary to decide. It appears that few if any violent events take place over issues that participants are indifferent about in "normal" moments. But we know little about whether crowds that turn violent in pursuit of normal interests proceed through interactional phases different from those of crowds that show no violent outcomes. Here, as elsewhere, collective behavior theory needs investigators who can pursue data to support this theory with the same vigor and intelligence shown by exponents of alternative views.

At a minimum, then, some aspects of violent collective events do indeed appear better described by collective behavior theory than by other models. How widespread or typical these are we shall never know unless someone goes systematically looking for them. We need studies geared, in other words, to the *extraordinary* aspects of civil violence and to the differences between the internal dynamics of such actions and similar but nonviolent actions. It is too soon to conclude that such differences must necessarily be nil.

## Theories of Aggregated Individual Support

Two kinds of theories explain the ebb and flow of civil violence in terms of aggregate levels of individual support, approval, or satisfaction. These are the value integration theories considered in Chapter Five and the psychological theories considered in Chapter Seven. For many, differences between the two are no doubt more salient than the similarities. Psychological theories, after all, turn on how well particular social arrangements meet individuals' standards of satisfaction or gratification. In value integration theories, by contrast, likelihood of civil violence is linked to standards of legitimacy held by individuals yet transcending their personal well-being or satisfaction.

But the two views share a crucial logical characteristic—the assumption that overall support for or opposition to established social arrangements is determined by an aggregate of individual levels of some psychic state. For both theories, each individual contributes an equal "vote" to the stability or instability of the larger system; the logic is atomistic and incremental. Both are thus antipathetic to theories that explain civil violence in terms of *differences* in action characteristics of various groups within populations.

Both psychological and value integration theories posit some crucial standard or principle that governs individual support, approval, dissatisfaction, or the like. For value integration theories, this standard is ordinary citizens' evaluation of the moral legitimacy of key institutions and their incumbents. For psychological theories, the standard has most commonly been envisaged as some form of relative deprivation.

For both theories, this crucial standard of evaluation or comparison raises problems that are not generally acknowledged. Researchers seeking to explain particular fluctuations in levels of civil violence have usually found it convenient to assume that the standards are reliably known and relatively enduring over time. Value integration theorists, for example, generally assume that dominant political figures and institutions are held to a single moral standard; thus, decline in support for a particular regime is interpreted as evidence that the regime in question lost legitimacy in the eyes of its people. Proponents of psychological theories similarly identify internal standards said to govern relative satisfaction versus dissatisfaction; they, too, interpret variations in support or compliance as reflecting differences in fulfillment of such standards.

But there is no logical reason why the crucial standards governing propensity to accept or rebel against prevailing social arrangements need be considered unitary and enduring. A particular rebellion or revolution, for example, might be attributable to sensibilities that remained in force no longer than the events themselves. Perhaps the standards of judgment responsible for propelling a particular regime into power will have little to do with those that may eventually result in its ouster. Perhaps, in other words, populations respond to different standards at different moments; such a formulation would fit well enough with what we know of the inconsistencies of individual action, including our own. Or perhaps different standards govern the action or inaction of different segments of populations.

Some relative deprivation thinkers acknowledge that standards governing indignation or perceived just deserts may, in principle, have this transient quality. But in empirical work, both relative deprivation and value integration thinkers typically posit a single standard or set of standards as governing the action to be explained over the time period under study, presumably because entertaining a multiplicity of standards leads to excessive complications in fitting data to the theory.

Such practical difficulties point to problems of a more strictly conceptual kind. *Any* rebellious or coercive action can be considered ipso facto evidence of some kind of dissatisfaction with the world as it is. Theories of these two types do not become interesting until they assert something more than that dissatisfaction is present among the ingredients of rebellion. They need to specify the *content* of the standards governing collective action, the population groups embracing these standards, and the duration of time over which the standards remain in force. Without careful attention to such requirements, researchers are liable to identify rebellious acts or periods, then work backwards in time until they can identify an explanatory standard to fit. When implemented by such research strategies, theories of aggregated individual support are obviously all but unfalsifiable.

Attention to these issues has played an important part in criticism and clarification of relative deprivation studies. Those based on aggregate data have had to confront an entirely legitimate challenge: What justification have we for associating any particular pattern of rebellion or compliance with the standard of satisfaction or deprivation posited by the analyst? What evidence, in other words, warrants the linkage of particular collective actions with particular standards? This nagging question ultimately led investigators to mount individual-level studies of the effects of psychological states on militant action.

These more rigorous studies have hardly shown consistent support for the role of relative deprivation, strictly defined, in individual participation. With a few notable exceptions—for example, Useem (1980)—multivariate analyses of individual-level data have pointed to other determinates as more influential.

But here, as with collective behavior theory, it is too soon for categorical judgments. We can document some forms of action that strongly imply violation of a customary standard as part of their cause. Studies by E. P. Thompson, Tilly, and their allies have often called attention to the importance of traditional standards of entitlement in triggering protest by occupational and community groups threatened by economic change, as in the rural protests by landless laborers described in *Captain Swing* (Hobsbawn and Rude 1969). Also, events such as the rioting that followed price rises for basic foodstuffs in Egypt in 1977 seem to point directly to violation of some crucial standard as a triggering mechanism. If relative deprivation theories have not found support in the more easily researchable forms entertained thus far, perhaps more imaginative framings of "contrast sets"—to use Garfinkel's term—will lead to more positive findings.

In the absence of clear support for relative deprivation theories of individual participation, the work of Edward Muller and his collaborators gives the most convincing account of individual participation for any extensive body of data. In several large surveys of North American and West German respondents in the 1970s, Muller demonstrated a different set of psychological determinants of militant action. Here participants were characterized by a combination of disapproval of government institutions and personnel on principle—withdrawal of legitimacy, one might say— and belief in the effectiveness of violence as a means for improving things.

But if Muller's argument is better attested than relative deprivation theory, it is also less theoretically satisfying. For there is no obvious association between Muller's determinants and any broader states of the social system, such as those alleged to produce relative deprivation. In short, we do not know what conditions lead to the crucial psychic states described by Muller. What Muller proposes, then, is psychological determinism of civil violence par excellence.

It is difficult to believe that Muller's psychological determinants will prove to be general characteristics of participants in militant action. The rebellious individuals in his studies were largely student radicals, and all were responding to broad trends of popular protest characteristic of West-

ern democracies in the 1970s. Thus, they formed a highly distinctive
setting for political action. The costs of participation in violent affrays,
though hardly trivial, were certainly lower than in many other periods.
Moreover, the issues at stake were themselves peculiar to the time. Not
all periods of high levels of civil violence, after all, involve attacks on the
state and its representatives—something neglected by many theorists of
civil violence, including some relative deprivation theorists. In other
times, civil violence may consist of attacks *by* governments against citizens. Or it may entail conflicts among rival political, ethnic, racial, or linguistic groups. Or in still other settings, high rates of violence may be the
results of economic conflicts—peasants occupying land for cultivation,
or local consumers seeking to prevent food produced locally from being
shipped abroad. Although the matter can hardly be settled a priori, I see
no reason why the same psychological profile would characterize participants across such different forms of action.

---

Value integration theories, like relative deprivation theories, offer a
ready plausibility. Hardly anyone would deny that regimes are more
likely to avoid violent challenge to the extent that their citizens regard
them as embodiments of sacred principle. But value consensus theories
strictly speaking must claim much more than this, if they are to occupy a
distinctive position among theories of civil violence. They must establish
that the commitments individuals feel to principles underlying regimes
are strong enough to override the other loyalties, interests, antagonisms,
and uncertainties that are known to motivate participation in civil strife.
They must show that fluctuations in levels of militant popular opposition
versus popular compliance are direct results of fluctuations in moral support. And they must show that widespread commitment to the abstract
principles underlying prevailing social arrangements are the sine qua non
for the maintenance of relatively peaceful, orderly social patterns. These
are large intellectual orders. As with psychological theories, they require
matching of independent evidence on individuals' psychic states to collective levels of militant opposition.

Unfortunately, proponents have rarely given much attention to the requirements facing the theory as an empirical doctrine. Following Parsons
himself, Smelser, Johnson, and other writers in this tradition have simply
taken it as axiomatic that this connection between moral solidarity and
stable sovereignty represents "the fundamental dynamic theorem of sociology" (Parsons 1951, p. 42). Thus while value integration theories need
not be unfalsifiable, the need to establish their falsifiability has hardly
been taken seriously—let alone the need to confront falsifiable implications with potentially falsifying evidence.

One kind of social organization does demonstrate the role of value commitments as a guarantor of compliance. These are charsimatic movements, greedy institutions, and other social units requiring total commitment from their participants. These participants evidently sacrifice competing interests to the central requirements of the group, including sometimes even life itself.

Such forms of value integration mobilize enormous amounts of energy within smaller social units. But they do not appear to sustain entire social systems for long. Value commitments of this intensity are liable either to decay over time, with commensurate declines in loyalty, or to engender internal splits, when competing interpretations of the "true" values of the community emerge. The resulting factional struggles, incidentally, generate much civil violence, as do the collisions between charismatic followings and other social structures. In any case, it is hard to believe that this sort of total commitment characterizes the loyalties of grass-roots citizens of liberal democracies, say, to parliamentary institutions.

No doubt such adherence stems from a variety of influences. But among the most effective are no doubt apathy and resignation. The compliance of most people with most prevailing institutions most of the time, one suspects, results much more from lack of interest or lack of faith that things could be different than from active willingness to undergo significant costs in their support. As resource mobilization theorists are wont to point out, opposition to entrenched regimes almost always carries *costs*. The absence of civil violence is much more likely to indicate unwillingness or inability to sustain such costs than profound moral support.

One subspecies of value integration theories of civil violence deserves special note here. These are the arguments that attribute militant action to "breakdowns" in moral control by single militant groups only—as though quiescent citizens could ipso facto be assumed to be in the best of moral health. Typically these accounts mix value integration assumptions with mass society theory in seeking to account for the allegedly disruptive effects of modernization, as in Mancur Olson's "Rapid Economic Growth as a Destabilizing Force" (1963). But as in those versions of value integration theory where moral breakdown is supposed to affect entire populations, independent evidence of moral breakdown is hard to find. The very fact of rebellion by "uprooted" groups is apt to be taken for evidence of their poor moral health. But I know of no study that has documented a strictly moral explanation for an upsurge of violence by any particular group.

It is extraordinary how persistently social scientists insist in embracing the notion that *any* enduring political regime must enjoy some modicum of legitimacy among those subjected to it. Evidence for such a position has never been more than superficial. True, virtually all regimes put forward claims for such support, and discourage displays of its absence. They sponsor the flourishing of key symbols supposed to affirm legitimacy; encourage manifestations of "civil religion"; sponsor solemn public occasions stressing unity of ideal interests between the powerful and all other sectors of the population; or stage elections, no matter how little real contest is involved. Often it is widely acknowledged that the regime would not last a day without coercion, apathy, or other conditions far removed from moral support. But I suspect that encouraging conspicuous public affirmations of moral support for regimes, and discouraging affirmation of the opposite, at least has the effect of keeping potential opposition off guard, of leaving some part of the population in doubt as to what keeps authority in place. In any case, such gestures certainly should never obscure the forces underlying compliance from the inquiries of social scientists.

Why, then, is the indispensability of legitimacy as an ingredient of any established regime so widely taken as axiomatic by social scientists? Because, I suspect, if this notion is not true, it is at least highly convenient. It would indeed be enlightening if we could assume that every social system not assailed by violent internal conflicts must rest on a coherent system of moral support from its citizens, and that these moral solidarities are effectively mirrored in the official principles claimed sacred by the regime. Thus, key forces underlying social cohesion would be transparent to the analyst, even on relatively superficial acquaintance. But unfortunately we simply have no empirical warrant for this formulation, at least not as a general characterization of regimes. If enthusiasts of moral explanations for civil violence wish to advance the credibility of their position, they should seek evidence for at least one case where empirically demonstrable changes in moral support *throughout an entire population* directly and demonstrably lead to the general rise or decline of violent contention.

## Theories of Group Contention

Theories of group contention include both the classic formulations of Marx and Pareto and those of Charles Tilly and modern resource mobilization thinkers. Collective violence occurs, in this view, where representatives of interest groups within populations struggle for advantage—with one another, or with representatives of the state. Such action may reflect efforts to do better in the ongoing fight for collective advantage, or to avoid doing worse. But whether defensive or offensive, violent action is not for the weak or helpless; like all collective action, it requires both organization and other resources.

The logic of these theories is diametrically opposite to that of value integration and psychological theories. The latter typically explain levels of violence throughout entire polities as aggregated effects of individual states. Theories of group contention, on the other hand, attach little importance to individual states apart from the organization and strategic position of the individuals involved. Moreover, they account for violent affrays in terms of *differences* in the interests and strategic options of groups, rather than in terms of states supposedly shared throughout populations. For these theorists, civil violence is the work of embattled activists, not entire populations. Thus, a distinctly antiholistic position.

What do these theories have to tell us about the *occurrence* and *timing* of civil violence?

Opposition of collective interest here is assumed virtually a constant in political life. But when does the juxtaposition of groups in pursuit of such interest lead to violence? For Marx and his followers, the answer has to do with the fit between underlying material realities and prevailing institutions, hierarchies, and other political and social arrangements. For Pareto, collective violence flares when talented and energetic political elites find themselves excluded from a share in government power. For modern resource mobilization thinkers, violence comes as mobilized groups react to *threats* to their political position or to *opportunities* to improve these positions.

All of these formulations pose at least some problems for derivation of falsifiable implications. For Marxists, the difficulties of specifying precisely how sharp the contradictions between material and "superstructural" realities must be in order to yield violent conflict are acute. Perhaps even more troublesome are Marxian assertions that systems of domination remain unchallenged as long as the underlying mode of production is "on the ascent," but that violent opposition is likely when the material position of the dominant groups has passed its peak. Demonstrating the presence of Marxian "contradictions" in the background of virtually any violent contest is easy enough. But one must wonder whether similar inquiries into quiescent periods would show much the same thing. Perhaps "contradictions" are endemic in all complex social systems.

Analogous problems dog Pareto's theory. Violence is said to occur when elite figures are excluded from official power. But because violence not sanctioned by governments appears ipso facto to give evidence of elite exclusion, how can any violent outbreak fail to conform to the rule? Every exercise of violence other than by government representatives must surely count as a challenge, and so all challengers must appear as nongovernment elites. Without major conceptual revision, this part of Pareto's argument is circular.

Tilly and his allies offer some gain in logical clarity over the positions of Marx and Pareto. But notions like threat and opportunity, or resources and mobilization, are by no means unambiguous in their implications for

the timing and occurrence of civil violence. True, these analysts have established one point of much theoretical interest: the fact that gross variations in levels of civil violence throughout polities are often associated
with variations in other forms of political contention. But when one gets
closer to data on actual episodes, the explanatory concepts become harder
to interpret. At worst, *any* militant action might be held to reflect some
perception of risk or opportunity on the part of the actors. How are proponents of this position to avoid circularity? The solution would be to judge
the degree of risk or opportunity presented by various situations independently of the action or inaction that ultimately resulted. Such a rigorous
method would indeed make the doctrine falsifiable. But no proponent of
the theory has as yet gone this far; instead, writers in this tradition have
generally contented themselves with pointing out notable threats or opportunities underlying specific militant actions, a technique that necessarily leaves one wondering about threats and opportunities that might
have led to no collective action.

Similar problems arise concerning the use of *resources* and *mobilization* as explanatory principles. Here, too, the very existence of militant
action can be taken as evidence for the presence of these influences, a
logically disastrous situation. Needed are criteria for assessing levels of resources and mobilization independent of their supposed results, so that
the actions of groups highly endowed with these features can be systematically compared with those groups rated low. The fact that some authors
(Useem 1980) have found relatively straightforward methods for comparing levels of such states across different groups reminds us that the problem is soluble. But absent such comparisons, the concepts are subject to
logical slippage.

In terms of their implications for personnel involved in violent action,
theories of collective struggle are more direct. The antinomy between
Marx and Pareto, for example, is dramatic: Participants in violent activity
as typical members of the groups whose interests are represented in the
action, versus activists as ambitious, professional power seekers, concerned more with the quest for power than with the resolution of the
immediate issue at hand. This contrast can readily form the basis for
empirical inquiry. No study I have encountered has provided much empirical support for Pareto's position; but then, none of these studies has
been done by a follower of Pareto. Marxian studies have frequently shown
insurgent actors as solid citizens of their embattled constituencies, with
typical social ties and loyalties to the groups whose interests their actions
represent. But did the Bolsheviks of 1917 more closely resemble Marx's
class-conscious representatives of downtrodden grass-roots interests, or
Pareto's power-hungry, insurgent elites? It would be fascinating to have a
response to this question from a sophisticated Paretian.

Charles Tilly and his followers hold simply that participants in militant popular activity will be well integrated in the groups they represent, not social isolates or deviates. For the latter part of this assertion, empirical support seems substantial. If collective violence is ever the work of the deviant, the inept, or the isolated, their sociological chronicler has yet to appear to record it. But neither Tilly's studies nor others in his tradition systematically weigh the possible role of professional power seekers of the Paretian sort in violent activism. Again, we will not know what contribution such activists make until someone focuses theoretically informed attention on the matter.

Finally, consider the *content* and *purposes* of violent action. Here, too, empirical implications of theories of collective struggle are relatively clear. All versions view violent action as contention over authentic interests of the groups represented in it, as against views of violence as discontinuous and "irrational." There is more than a shade of difference here between Marx and Pareto. The former's theories would lead us to expect violence in pursuit of shared material interests, whereas Pareto pictures violence more as directed to the conquest of power for its own sake. These distinctions are empirical in principle, though hardly easy to apply.

Tilly and his followers are agnostic as to whether the ends of militant action are ultimately economic, political, or something else. They assert simply that collective action is purposeful, oriented to furthering the interests of the groups represented in the action. Attesting to these purposeful qualities are a wide array of accounts gleaned by investigators in this tradition.

Yet, acknowledging this purposeful quality of much militant collective action does not exclude what is often seen as the alternative possibility— that fluctuations in violent activity may result from fluctuations in shared excitement, tension, or other extraordinary emotional states. Civil violence, like most other forms of social action, may be consummatory as well as instrumental. Emotional events, exhortations, or gestures may create impulses for violent action as an end in itself, as in the attacks on Iranian students in American universities at the time of the hostage crisis of 1979–1980. Such fluctuations are often closely associated with fluctuations in power relations, strategic opportunities, and other considerations of an instrumental sort. But there are no grounds for asserting that the latter must always create the former. On the contrary, shifting emotional states throughout large populations may reshape opportunities, threats, and power relations, as well as the other way around.

In the mid-1960s, the theories of Charles Tilly and his followers abruptly displaced earlier theories of mass mobilization, notably those derived from Park and mass society theory. The victorious theoretical insurgents provided accounts depicting militant activism as resulting from rational pursuit of objectively reckoned group interest. This approach, in the more than twenty ensuing years, has become virtually a new orthodoxy. Perhaps inevitably, some analysts are beginning, at the time of this writing, to identify determinants neglected in this view—including some emphasized in earlier views. Thus Snow and his collaborators (1986) point out that objective interests may remain latent until activated by changing "frame alignments"—which sound very much like special forms of interaction, definitions of situations, and other processual contingencies considered by Park and his followers. Perhaps another shift of theoretical focus is in the making.

———

Along with psychological theories, theories of group contention have generated the largest amount of empirical inquiry in the literature of civil violence. We now have a wealth of accounts of the personnel, the content, the goals, the rhetoric, the political context, and a wide variety of other aspects of violent contention. These rich accounts, both from Marxian and resource mobilization thinkers, quite overwhelm the discontinuous view of civil violence inherited from the irrationalists. Not surprisingly, the findings of these empirical investigations tend to bear out the empirical expectations of the theories that inspired them.

Therein lies a rub. Studies carried out in this tradition leave little doubt that the theories have wide application. But they make one hungry for research that would give more opportunity for recording results inconsistent with the theory. Marxian investigators have often dug deeply into the history of a district, town, or region and reported class consciousness as a key factor in orienting social contention, for example; one wonders whether alternative sites for investigation that might have yielded different conclusions were considered and rejected. And one wonders whether investigators with different theoretical sensitivities would have come to the same conclusions about the sites actually studied. Such concerns are no special reflection on Marxian thinking; the same problems arise whenever support for a theory comes from case studies carried out by proponents of the theory.

They also arise in the work of Tilly and his followers. One of Tilly's noteworthy contributions has been to introduce sampling and quantification into the study of individual incidents of political upheaval. Yet presentation of results of Tilly's work in formats that would allow for the most direct confrontations between the falsifiable implications of his own versus alternative theories has been relatively rare. There have been a few exceptions—for example, Snyder and Tilly (1972)—but Tilly's main practice has been to use the rich data he and his associates have amassed for *illustration* of the theory, rather than for direct confrontation with other theories. Thus, we have had many demonstrations of the purposefulness of crowd action, of the role of notable opportunities and threats in occasioning such action, and of the importance of resources and mobilization in whether collective action will take place at all.

All of this is satisfactory as far as it goes. But now that the broad applicability of the theory is well established, one yearns to know the limits of that applicability. And this task can only be done through rigorous and demanding steps—by choosing a wide array of instances for study that promise to yield evidence reflecting clearly on the falsifiable implications of the theory and, preferably, of alternative theories as well. Such choices need to be made without advance knowledge of what story the data are apt to tell. And the cases selected require analysis through procedures that can be carried out by proponents of any theoretical view—or of none in particular. Such steps would promise a clear advance in theoretical understanding of civil violence.

## General Theories

"There was once a man," writes Alasdair MacIntyre, "who aspired to be the author of the general theory of holes."

When asked, "What kind of hole—holes dug by children for amusement, holes dug by gardeners to plant lettuce seedlings, tank traps, holes made by road-makers?" he would reply indignantly that he wished for a *general* theory that would explain all of these. He rejected *ab initio* the—as he saw it—pathetically commonsense view that of the digging of different kinds of holes there are quite different kinds of explanations to be given; why then he would ask do we have the concept of a hole? . . . Had he . . . concerned himself not with holes, but with modernization, urbanization, or violence, I find it difficult to believe that he might not have achieved high office in the APSA. (1971, p. 260)

The history of thinking on civil violence gives much evidence of the propensity to claim generality for treasured theories. Virtually all the theories considered here have at one point or another been touted as capturing the ultimate origins and nature of civil violence—wherever and whenever it occurs. In the earliest of these categorical statements, Hobbes assures us that "Feare of Death" (1968, p. 188) is what drives humankind to accept the constraints of sovereignty. No less sweeping are Engels's claims that established regimes are subject to rebellion only "when the mode of production in question has outlived its day" (1962, p. 207). Or consider Parsons's oft-reiterated contention that "the stability of any social system except the most evanescent interaction is dependent on a degree of such [ultimate value] integration may be said to be the fundamental dynamic theorem of sociology" (1951, p. 42). Or Ted Gurr's assertion: "the primary source of the human capacity for violence appears to be the frustration-aggression mechanism. . . . Men who are frustrated have an innate disposition to do violence to its source in proportion to the intensity of their frustration" (1970, pp. 36–37). Or the just slightly more circumspect words of Charles Tilly: "The chief source of variation in collective violence is the operation of the polity" (1978, pp. 181–82).

One could extend the recitation of such claims at length. No doubt such deep theoretical conviction has its uses; a single, incandescent view of the origins of any phenomenon may spark the energy necessary to press that theory as far as it can go. But the more heroic claims of virtually all theories considered here have been significantly blunted by confrontation with empirical evidence and critical reflection. Where not logically flawed to the extent of unfalsifiability, most of the theories appear to fit at least some sets of evidence. But all fall distinctly short of the rigorous requirement of accounting for variation in civil violence whenever and wherever it occurs.

MacIntyre's wry words remind us of something too readily forgotten in contemporary social science: The quest for "the" theory of anything itself reflects a theoretical affirmation, and a highly tendentious one at that. The idea that there must exist underlying causes of civil violence *in general*— or invariant characteristics of its participants, organization, or settings— deserves much skepticism. To be sure, we have no proof of the opposite position, for these are not matters that can be proved in advance. But it would be wiser to proceed from the more prudent assumptions that, for civil violence as for other things, what appears as "the same" effect may proceed from a variety of causes, and that "the same" causal influences may yield a variety of different effects in various settings.

The attractions of seeking a single theory for all instances of what appears to be "the same" phenomenon are clear enough. We nearly all share certain similar *reactions* to civil violence, regardless of its origins: fear, hope, fascination, and other emotionally loaded attitudes. Perhaps the salience of such charged reactions makes it difficult to accept that different manifestations of violence may really be part of quite different social processes, with correspondingly different causes. But other forms of scientific understanding have had to grow by distinguishing which characteristics of phenomena under study were essential, and which were irrelevant, to their explanation. Pioneering physicians had to establish, for example, that not all stomach aches were really the same, that apparently identical *symptoms* could stem from quite different causes. We should approach the study of civil violence with the same assumptions.

The view of explanation derived from MacIver and Garfinkel offers support for such assumptions. For it suggests that empirical connections may be established theoretically over a significant range of cases without being *universal*. Connections between timing, personnel, and content of civil violence and other characteristics and variables may well be valid for certain sets of cases, yet inapplicable elsewhere—without the analyst's being able to specify the reason for the difference. Perhaps even more important, the MacIver–Garfinkel view reminds us that any sociological *explanandum* may admit of a variety of explanations or theories. No phenomenon, indeed no pattern of phenomena is ever explained *tout court*, once and for all. Explaining a violent episode by reference to the states of mind of the participants, for example, need not exclude equally valid explanations of the same behavior in terms of the political organization or power relations among contending groups. In the view entertained here, only the analyst can determine what kinds of comparisons or contrasts, what kinds of *differences* ought to form the basis for a particular explanation or theory. This view obviously leaves room for various alternative theories or explanations of what appears to be "the same" thing.

Even well-attested theories from the natural sciences involve complex assumptions on variable and fixed conditions implicit in the *explanandum* —assumptions that require much unpacking. Consider Alan Garfinkel's discussion of a serious "genetic" disease:

There is a disease called phenylketonuria (PKU), which is an inability to metabolize the protein phenylalanine. This in turn causes overt symptoms. The disease PKU is caused by a genetic defect. That is, the presence of a certain gene causes an inability to metabolize phenylalanine (in the standard womb environment; if genetic surgery were possible, even this causal link could be broken). But the inability to metabolize phenylalanine causes the gross symptoms of PKU only in a certain range of postnatal environments, namely, those containing normal diets, which contain phenylalanine. If the baby is placed on a diet free of phenylalanine, no gross symptoms occur, and the baby is fine. It still cannot metabolize phenylalanine but then it does not have to.

So it would be a mistake to say

genetics ⟶ PKU

The more correct explanatory frame would include the double dependence on two different environments thus:

genetics × womb environment ⟶ trait T

*and*

trait T × normal diet ⟶ PKU

where T stands for "inability to metabolize phenylalanine." (1981, pp. 116–17).

Here as elsewhere, the "cause" of the disease is not given in the nature of things. What factor will appear as cause will depend on the nature of the analyst's *interest* in the disease, in the broadest sense of this term.

Social *explananda* present multiple contingencies at least as complex as those involved in phenylketonuria.

Imagine attempting to build a general theory of traffic accidents. One study might demonstrate that propensity to be involved in traffic accidents varies vastly among individual drivers; in a certain array of cases, indeed, almost all variation in accident rates might correspond to driver differences. Other investigators might attribute great significance to highway design: poorly engineered curves, blind intersections, and absence of stop signals might be shown to result in elevated accident rates. Another set of explanations might show the importance of the sheer numbers of motorists on the road; accident rates are highest, it might be shown, when roads are most crowded. Still another analysis might demonstrate the causal role of interactions among motorists; brandishing of fists and angry attempts to cut other drivers off are more often followed by accidents than other kinds of interactions.

The point is, none of these connections need logically be incompatible with any other. Each invokes a different "contrast set," to use Garfinkel's term, and hence offers a different explanation or theory; none need exhaust the possibilities of the subject matter. Yet we have no reason to think that all theories would be equally salient or germane for any particular set of data—for any time period, driver population, region, set of highways, and so forth. What will appear as a key element of causation, as a basis for satisfying theory, will depend both on the particular data under study and the interests of the analyst.

The logical complexities facing theories of civil violence are at least as challenging as in these hypothetical theories of motor accidents. Here, too, every theory entails some assumptions about what conditions vary and which are in effect "held constant" in accounting for the *explanandum*. And here, as elsewhere, different assumptions result in theories of somewhat different things. Explaining why rioting broke out between *Sikhs and Hindus* in India in 1984 is not the same as explaining why rioting broke out between Sikhs and Hindus in *1984*. Different theories address themselves to different contrasts; some of the apparent incommensurability among theories stems from precisely such differences.

This position is far removed from the unappealing, relativistic doctrine that all theoretical views are correct "in their own terms," or from the thinker's unique viewpoint. Theories can be *wrong*—and some of those considered in this book are, from all available evidence, exactly that. Theories of civil violence are wrong when they specify conditions as necessary for the occurrence of violent episodes that in fact are not, or when they identify characteristics of purposes, participation, or forms of violent actions that are not in fact to be found. But among conditions necessary for an episode or a series of militant events to occur, analysts may pinpoint any one or any combination as crucial, depending on the contrast set they employ.

Understanding these logical contraints should at least alert us to potential multiple explanations that might otherwise go unnoticed. Tilly's theories of timing and content of violent events could, for example, be quite compatible with Muller's psychological determinism. Violent events could well occur at times of political opportunity or threat, and insurgent actions could indeed be directed at authentic political targets; yet the participants in such actions might still be characterized by the psychological profile given by Muller. Much as I doubt that such is often the case, there is no logical reason why it could never be so. Keeping such possibilities in mind is essential for any effort to develop a truly comprehensive theoretical view of civil violence.

Consider the analysis of food riots in preindustrial Europe. These were prominent forms of popular militancy in the late eighteenth and early nineteenth centuries. They often involved capture by local activists of foodstuffs stored by bakers, grain merchants, or speculators and their distribution at a traditional "just" price to consumers who could not afford the market price. Many respected analysts of diverse ideological backgrounds have attributed fluctuations in the occurrence of such events to variation in the price of foodstuffs—for example, Beloff (1938, p. 32); Rude (1972, pp. 200–202); Labrousse (1932, pp. 640–42). In their view, the riots were direct responses to high prices, or to the anticipation of such.

Such an analysis appears to run counter to the position of Charles Tilly, who has also written a great deal about precisely these sorts of events (see Tilly 1970). Tilly typically contends that variation in ability and opportunity for action account for variations in levels of violent action. Although some of his statements on the subject have been quite sweeping, at one point he puts his position more guardedly.

Grievances are fundamental to rebellion as oxygen is fundamental to combustion. But just as fluctuations in the oxygen content of the air account for little of the distribution of fire in the workaday world, fluctuations in grievances are not a major cause of the presence or absence of rebellion. For that, the political means of acting on grievances which people have at their disposal matter a good deal more. (1974b, p. 302; see also his discussion of related issues in *The Contentious French* 1986, pp. 21–24)

In one way, this statement is a reaffirmation of Tilly's usual argument. Yet his words hardly seem inconsistent with a model showing fluctuation in rebellion varying directly with fluctuation in food prices—in settings where resources and opportunities for militant action remained available over a given period. Thus whether grievances or the wherewithal to act on them will appear as the *cause* of militant action depends on the analyst's choice of what "contrast sets" to invoke. Tilly's theories seem oriented to capturing the differences in action among rural communities given high levels of grievances; Beloff, Labrousse, and Rude are accounting for differences in the behavior among the same communities in similar states of political organization, according to whether food is cheap or dear.

Cases like this emphasize one of the key insights of the view of theory and explanation adopted here—that a great variety of explanations of "the same" thing are often possible, depending on the nature of the "contrast set" or crucial difference implied in the explanatory quest. Explanatory factors that account for the difference between quiescence and rebellion in a well-organized rural community across years that include both famine and plenty will not necessarily account for differences in levels of rebellion among communities endowed with varying degrees of internal organization in a single famine year. To profit from such insights, we need more contextual information in theoretical statements—more careful specification of the *causal system* implied by the theory, of the exact nature of the differences the theory aims at accounting for, and of the range of cases to which the theory should be expected to apply.

Any effective effort at building theories of civil violence must cope with logical issues like these; yet they have not received much attention. One of the rare penetrating discussions has come from the noted Canadian political sociologist Maurice Pinard (1983a; 1983b). Reviewing various studies of grass-roots mobilization, violent and nonviolent, Pinard notes what appear to be inconsistent results. In some cases outbreaks of militant action seem to result directly from peaks of deprivation (not necessarily *relative* deprivation) or grievances, as documented in his own study of third-party movements in Canada (1975). Elsewhere, the presence or absence of activism seems to derive directly from variations in mobilization or resources on the part of the populations involved. Can any single theory account for such apparently different findings?

Pinard's answer makes eminent sense in terms of the view of theory and explanation entertained here. If various conditions are necessary for successful activism, he notes, then fluctuations either in mobilization or grievance levels may account for fluctuations in militant action, according to whether other necessary conditions are fulfilled. Unfortunately, many models entertained by analysts of such phenomena fail to allow for such possibilities.

The models used are designed to measure the impact of *fluctuations* through time in the independent variables, not the impact of the stable states of these variables. But given an interaction model, it is possible for the yearly fluctuations in a dependent variable to be triggered by fluctuations in only *one* independent variable, with the other being simply present and constant; for instance, you could have a period during which deprivation and organization would both be present and constant, but during which increases in mobilization efforts would trigger collective violence. With the statistical models employed and given the period studied, the only effect which could be detected would be the *triggering* effect of mobilization; but this would obviously not mean that the other factors did not need to be also present. (1983a, pp. 44–45)

Pinard emphasizes the interactions of deprivation and mobilization variables in the origin of militant action, perhaps the two most salient theoretical possibilities for analysts in the 1980s. But he could as well have cited any number of other conditions the presence or absence of which might, under specific circumstances, have made the crucial difference between occurrence and absence of militant action. These might be anything from the frequency of face-to-face interactions among the population "at risk" to the presence or absence of a "culture of violence." If we assume that all civil violence, like all other social behavior, requires a broad range of necessary conditions for its occurrence—the only reasonable assumption, I hold—then we must admit, at least in principle, that variation in any one of these, with others held constant, *may* account for fluctuations in violent activity. Any one necessary condition might function as the "switch," in other words, depending on the state of other conditions throughout the entire causal system.

Note that these observations hold implications that go well beyond a recommendation for multivariate analyses of complex social processes. It goes without saying that statistical assessments profit from taking into account the largest possible number of variables that might prove to be associated with the outcome of interest. But we need to distinguish between conditions whose variation is associated with the outcome of interest in a particular range of instances and conditions whose fixed states form the unique context in which the action of other variables has its effect. Recall that what Alan Garfinkel calls a "contrast set" involves holding constant a certain array of conditions so that the special weight of the variable of interest comes clear. Thus, in explaining preindustrial subsistence riots, we rely on contextual assumptions about the development of markets, or the power of government repression, or prevailing notions of justice among affected populations. Such assumptions are as integral to the theory as what may be billed as the "theoretical" variable—for example, levels of resources and mobilization within the community, or severity of absolute or perceived deprivation. But such assumptions do often receive less attention, both from creators of such theories and from their "consumers," than do what appear as "theoretical" variables. Such inattention often leads to confusion as explanatory contexts vary, so that what had appeared as "context" in one case becomes the source of variation that triggers the critical outcome elsewhere.

Perhaps the best summary of this position might be in answer to the question, how can theories go wrong? They go wrong, obviously, when they point to conditions as necessary for the *explanandum* that in fact are not. Such was the case with the man who carried out the following investigation into the causes of his own drunkenness: he compared the effects of gin and water, bourbon and water, and scotch and water, finding that all produced the same effect; hence, he pinpointed the causal agent in the one common condition: water.

But in other instances, explanations may go wrong not by identifying as essential what is in fact epiphenomenal, but by invoking inappropriate contrast sets. For certain sets of cases, *opportunity* to act may be crucial in distinguishing between situations leading to drunkenness and those that do not—just as with civil violence. For other contrasts, opportunity may play little role in distinguishing between the presence and absence of the thing to be explained—as in cases where opportunity is rife, but inclination to act is lacking. No "variable," in short, has effect independent of a specified set of comparisons.

What are the implications of these observations for a program of theoretical inquiry? Perhaps some would conclude that the task of the theorist must be to cite every variable that could conceivably affect the outcome in question, or that has ever been observed to do so. But such a strategy would be deadly for theoretical work, if only because the list of such variables is in principle infinite. Again, people must breathe to be able to participate in civil violence, but one would not normally propose a *respirational* theory of the subject. We need a way of doing justice to the variety of possible contingencies without creating theories that turn out to be so all-encompassing as to be uninformative.

MacIntyre, in ridiculing the quest for a general theory of holes, takes an easy shot. He slyly reminds us that we have reason to believe in advance that different sorts of holes have different origins; we would profit from applying the same assumption to civil violence, he suggests. But in fact, we start with much less understanding of the origins of riot, rebellion, and civil war than we do of holes. Carried to its extreme, MacIntyre's position would lead us to assume that the origins and characteristics of any one instance of such a thing have nothing in common with any others. Yet this assumption is no more satisfactory than the a priori conviction that the origins of all members of this category must have something crucial in common.

Theoretical efforts properly take place in a constant intellectual tension between the peculiarities of events and the generality of forces that may constrain them. Some categories of events—some forms of civil violence very much included—show such overt similarities in their origins and characteristics that it hardly takes a social theorist to note them. The rise of vigilantism in communities of the American frontier in response to the weakness of state authority is an example. Another is the marked association of intercommunal violence in India with conspicuous insults by members of one community to another. Similarly, even a casual observer may note parallels in the targets, personnel, and forms of certain historically bounded categories of violent events, such as ghetto riots, land occupations by peasants, intertribal contention among peoples under colonial rule, and battles to organize certain industries by labor unions.

In instances like these, it may be easy to make a case for generalizations. But theorists of civil violence are not liable to rest content with such relatively easy victories. What I have called the theoretical yearning moves us to seek connections binding the largest variety of different kinds of instances in single statements. Such statements offer more informative "guides to the unknown" to the extent that they encompass more and more diverse cases. Many episodes of militant action among American black urban dwellers in the 1960s and 1970s, for example, apparently began with the conspicuous application of police power against ghetto residents, especially brutal arrests in public places. Yet an account of ghetto violence, or even of these events alone, as caused by brutal policing is not wholly satisfying. Nor should it be. The deeper theoretical question has to do with why communities of the sort that yielded violent events during this period were prone to do so at this particular historical juncture, and not at others.

But it will not do to assume, simply because *explananda* appear to share some important quality, that they must necessarily respond to similar causes. The presence of *causal systems* that can be expected to yield similar results over extended ranges of cases has to be demonstrated, not assumed. Where "the same" results stem from quite different causal systems, all the results may really have in common is their name, or perhaps their legal status or moral significance. Such commonalities, of course, do not suffice to support empirically relevant theory.

Theories of civil violence should properly command our attention, then, where they cite explanatory factors accounting for specific differences in outcomes over a specifiable range of cases. The most persuasive thing about the contributions of writers like Tilly or Muller is not any claim of *generality* for their theories. It is that their theories do seem to describe certain key differences between situations that produce violence and those that do not within certain circumscribed settings. If the jury is

still out on relative deprivation theory, the reason must be that its proponents have still not demonstrated an important range of cases where this
factor makes a crucial difference. I strongly suspect that something like
relative deprivation must trigger civil violence in some settings. But proponents of the theory have yet to specify where.

By contrast, much of the unsatisfying character of Smelser's value-
added theory has to do with its lack of commitment as to context. He
posits what amounts to an array of necessary conditions for the occurrence
of collective behavior, such as strain, generalized beliefs, and social control. He assures us that the form taken by these influences will shape the
episode or occurrence in question, as it undoubtedly will. But without
some commitment as to which particular necessary conditions make
which particular differences in outcomes in specific settings, these statements are simply not very informative. We need theories of civil violence
that specify particular connections that should apply in particular settings,
drawing from the infinite range of logical possibilities those particular
linkages that will matter empirically.

Again, all theories of civil violence that are empirically falsifiable probably account for at least some outcomes in some settings. But our interest
is bound to focus on theories that promise reliable "guides to the unknown" for delimited ranges of phenomena. Such is the case for at least
some of the formulations of Hobbes, Marx, Tilly, Muller, and some of the
other authors studied here. Elsewhere, theories of civil violence or anything else may fail to satisfy either because no one has clearly delineated
the range of cases where they apply, or because they apply so obviously to
all instances of the *explanandum* as to offer little that is new, beyond what
its definition already implies.

## Some Substantive Conclusions

The search for *general theories* of civil violence, then, may simply be the
wrong search. Indeed, this quest for quasi-Newtonian formulations on the
origins of civil violence whenever and wherever it occurs has undoubtedly distracted good minds from seeking more informative regularities of
other kinds. As Barrington Moore, Jr., reminded us decades ago, the
most *general* features of social life may simply not be the most informative
or the most important to study (1958, p. 129).

Yet the search for general theories of this subject has not been bootless.
The frustrating attempts to fit actual instances onto the procrustean bed of
theory has dramatized the considerable variability in the heterogenous
category designated as civil violence. Appreciation of this heterogeneity is
one form of general knowledge; it should not be neglected.

We know, for example, that episodes of collective violence within polities vary widely in terms of the *role of governments*. In some violent episodes, government coercive agents are the main, if not the only violent actors. Elsewhere, governments are represented as targets of destructive efforts by nongovernment activists. In still other cases, the only parties are nongovernment actors, and governments are either unwilling or unable to involve themselves.

We know, further, that collective violence varies in terms of the *internal social organization of participants*. Some violent action is governed by role prescriptions and internal division of labor nearly as marked as that in formal organizations. Elsewhere, participation appears highly improvised and unpredictable in these respects. Such variation is probably closely associated with the degree of *advance planning* involved in violent action—another important continuum among instances of civil violence.

Similarly, we know that violent action, like other collective action, varies from the *instrumental* to the *consummatory*. Some is highly purposeful, aimed at closely calculated strategic goals, whereas other instances are expressive actions aimed at venting hatred for opponents or vaunting the virtues of one's own side. Most episodes, I suspect, mix the two ingredients. Calculation may play a big role in consummatory violence, as well, if only as participants seek to avoid suffering repressive consequences from their actions. But the nature of the payoffs obviously differs fundamentally.

Finally, *individual motives* for participating in collective violence appear to vary almost as widely as those underlying other forms of social action. Solidarity with fellow activists obviously plays a large role, but so do other motives, ranging from the lust for rape and plunder to determination to establish the Kingdom of God on earth.

Analysts would be rash to assume that episodes differing along these lines should necessarily be accounted for by the same theories. This may be a negative insight, but it is one that has eluded many acute thinkers to date.

Do we have any more *positive* theoretical conclusions to show for the centuries of analysis of civil violence? Indeed we do. Most of the theoretical strains considered in this book identify distinctive processes in the origins and unfolding of civil violence that do occur. Empirical inquiry, unsystematic though it has often been, has established that much. But only rarely can we specify with certainty where these processes will prevail, as distinct from other possibilities. To oversimplify only slightly, we know a lot of things that are true about civil violence, but we do not know when they are going to be true.

We know, for example, that purposes reflected in violent action are rarely if ever antipathetic to or sharply discontinuous with participants' enduring, everyday interests. Contra the irrationalists, we know that the great bulk of violent collective action within polities follows lines of conflict amply evident in other enduring, nonviolent conflicts. Perhaps more important, research thus far suggests that fluctuations in extent and intensity of violent conflicts are most often directly linked with other changes in relations among the groups whose interests are manifest in the violence, especially power relations. Thus we can assume that changes in social structure will bring changes in the prevailing form and frequency of collective violence.

But such insight does not yield certainty as to which nonviolent conflicts will breed violent ones. We are safe in expecting little violent collective action outside the context of nonviolent conflict, but not in expecting that every nonviolent conflict will yield violence. No one has sought to rate the seriousness of conflicts within populations for independent comparison with the levels of domestic violence with which they may be associated. Short of such a study, our knowledge remains qualified.

Similarly, we know that participants in collective violence are rarely disproportionately drawn from the deviant or the isolated. Contra both the irrationalists and their mass society heirs, participants appear most often typical of the groups whose interests are represented in the fray. But studies to date give little ground for predicting which particular individuals among those whose interests are affected will most likely participate.

From all evidence, civil violence is more likely, the greater the *solidarity* among would-be participants. The strongest forms of solidarity stem from a history of concerted action. But I also mean by solidarity all those forms of mutual acquaintance among would-be participants that might yield bases for predicting how others will act. Thus participants in race riots share a minimal solidarity in being able to recognize potential allies and antagonists in terms of their race, even if the particular individuals involved are unknown to one another. The key falsifiable expectation here would be that little violent action should be carried out by actors not well known to one another, either directly or in terms of their social identities. The exception to this observation is the classical panic, involving no *concerted* action at all.

But we can say little that is categorical about the *kinds* of solidarities required for militant collective action. Contra the most simplistic Marxist expectations, we have no reason to believe that economic issues in general or social class identifications in particular are more prolific of such action than other solidarities. Indeed, I would hypothesize that solidarities form bases for violent collective action roughly in the proportion that they do for nonviolent action. Solidarities based on race, neighborhood, ethnic identification, the workplace, or religion form a high proportion of all bases for militant action, just as they do for other collective action.

*Calculation* of both individual and collective interest clearly plays a major role in the mounting of much civil violence. Few violent actions appear to be initiated in the face of certain disaster, whereas conspicuous hopes for gain often trigger militant action. But we can say nothing categorical about what kinds of calculations will matter for which particular actions. If opportunities for gain plainly incite some violent forays, other such opportunities plainly go unheeded. If repression often works (and the evidence is overwhelming that it does), it is equally clear that some instances of repression, however bloody, sharpen the will to resist. If some individuals are clearly moved to participate in pillage or other violent acts by opportunities for personal gain, such opportunities clearly go unheeded elsewhere. In the current state of knowledge, what *kinds* of calculations will occur, and what outcomes appear to participants to require calculation, can only be discovered contextually, through evidence internal to specific violent episodes or sequences.

Confounding the issue of calculation is the role of *interaction* in shaping interests that fuel participation in civil violence. Tracing calculations of interest involved in any form of action is most informative when the interests can be considered relatively enduring. Yet sometimes, we suspect, the interpersonal dynamics of contentious action may reshape interests felt by participants from day to day or even moment to moment. The attractions of successful activism are not necessarily fixed, for example, but may be constantly revised by the experience of participation. To the extent that people's emotional involvement in issues at stake in violent contention shows sharp fluctuations, assessing the action that should be expected to ensue from participants' rational calculations of their interests becomes problematic. To make matters still more complicated, we cannot specify what kinds of social contention are apt to be fueled by relatively stable interests and where participants' interests are likely to be revised through interaction. As elsewhere, these things can only be known contextually, through study of particular instances.

Similarly, there can be no doubt that standards of justice, equity, and traditional rights enter into the formulation of many violent actions. But here, too, we can specify no invariant rule to tell us what comparisons will matter in what settings. Relative deprivation theorists and their allies rightly alert us to the possible role of such considerations. But this awareness remains among the analytical tools we bring to the study of civil violence, without our knowing in advance when and where it will apply.

Ideal interests such as the ascription or denial of legitimacy may play a role in dampening or sharpening potential violent challenges to regimes.

Any set of social relations is more likely to enjoy peaceful adherence to the extent that people regard it as an embodiment of sacred principle. But we have no reason to imagine that support of this kind is a sine qua non for peaceful or "orderly" social process. Studies that portray revolution or other violent challenges to authorities as resulting from loss of moral solidarity throughout entire populations have never produced the exacting evidence that would be necessary to substantiate such claims.

Finally, shared emotional states have force of their own in explaining the outbreak and subsidence of violent action, independent of the strategic calculations also shaping such action. News of atrocities to a particular group, for example, may move members of the group to violent actions that would never otherwise have occurred. Such sequences are highly unlikely, however, in the absence of enduring tensions or clashes of interest that establish targets of such action. But here, as elsewhere, it is hard to identify in the abstract where such transmission of emotion will play a role, and where such forces will prove relatively unimportant.

Again, the inquiries considered in this book have identified a great variety of processes that clearly play key roles in the origins and unfolding of violent episodes; the trouble is that we often cannot specify in advance where particular processes are apt to come into play. This is a much more reserved conclusion than one might wish, but it is hardly totally equivocal. Recalling Coser's analogy, we have many analytical tools at our disposal, and to this extent our position is a great improvement over theoretical naivete. But a more dramatic form of progress comes with the *exclusion* of once-salient theoretical possibilities—or their certain linkage to specific empirical settings. We can point to a few instances of this kind, as in the rejection of certain doctrines of extreme discontinuity between militant and "normal" collective action. But theoretical conclusions of such apparent robustness are far from plentiful.

## Prospects for Theories of Civil Violence

The preceding statements may strike the reader as spare and guarded. Indeed they are, but this fact should hardly give grounds for despair. For there is no reason to equate the extent of *theoretical knowledge* of civil violence or anything else with the state of *general theory* on the subject.

Better to proceed from the opposite assumption: That the richest, most informative theoretical connections we are likely to make will apply to clearly delineated subsets of the overall category of civil violence. They will illuminate matters like the recruitment to vigilante actions or the timing of such actions in situations of weak central power; or the geographical distributions of violent protests against the enclosure of common lands for market production in a particular country; or the timing of racial violence between specific groups in light of changing ecological and political balances between the two. The connections established in such efforts may prove peculiar to particular historical and social settings. But the circumscribed theories to emerge from such studies will be hardly less valuable for all that.

We have a few exemplary studies of this kind. In Paige's *Agrarian Revolution* (1975), his concern lies neither with civil violence or agrarian conflict in general, nor with analysis of a single case. Instead, he seeks to account for variation in forms and intensities of violence within an important but historically delimited category of settings—developing countries of the mid-twentieth century. Within this category, Paige directs his attention to relations between large landowners and their work forces in plantationlike settings where crops are produced for export. Paige persuasively shows that the forms taken by the many conflicts in such situations are closely linked to the political economy of domination by the landowners—for example, that conflicts follow a less zero-sum pattern where owners are more highly capitalized. Perhaps even more impressive, Paige's analysis is rich in contextual detail that suggests *why* these various empirical relationships hold as they do—and, implicitly, why they may be limited to agrarian conflicts of the kind he is concerned with.

Similar theoretical virtues are apparent in Tilly's writings on the rural, preindustrial subsistence riots mentioned previously. These studies—for example, Tilly (1970)—are most impressive not as defenses of resource mobilization or any other general theory of civil violence, but as analyses of broad juxtapositions of forces and conditions jointly accounting for this historically distinct category of rebellions. Tilly demonstrates that the co-occurrence of popular indignation at high prices and forceful community organization produced these highly standardized riots, but only in a very specific set of historical and social conditions. The classic food riot, he argues, occurred just as areas traditionally self-sufficient in basic foodstuffs began to be absorbed into regional and national markets. Under these circumstances—with the state of communications, coercive organization, local culture, and various other conditions composing the causal system—hard times brought grass-roots local assertions of traditional control over food supplies. When the national economy, and the political forces sponsoring its growth, finally prevailed, these local claims were silenced. The complex set of conditions that produced these distinctive forms of violence had been definitively dissolved.

Both Paige and Tilly, then, offer satisfying and convincing expositions of *causal systems*—arrays of variables and permissive contextual conditions that, in the proper combinations, account for variation in specific forms of violence. In any case of this kind, one can imagine efforts to extend the explanation in question to cover a wider array of cases—popular protest in all preindustrial Europe, for example, or agrarian revolt in all historical periods. Obviously promising leads in such directions always deserve to be followed. But the history of theories of civil violence suggests an enduring hazard for such attempts—the danger that causal forces that can be shown to underlie wider and wider arrays of effects may be specified in such broad terms as to be uninformative. Vague general explanatory schemes based on notions like "strain" or "tension" are the cautionary example here.

Some readers may find this view unexceptionable. Yet the dominant approaches in present-day social science seem to proceed from quite different assumptions—namely, that elaboration of theoretical understanding must come through the "testing" of "variables" in the largest numbers of cases. Embedded in this approach is the conviction that "variables" exist with causal weight transcending wide differences in context. Among investigations considered in this book, this logic has seen its most extravagant development in aggregate studies of relative deprivation "variables." If the results of these studies have not always been inspiring, the fault may lie not with the inherent possibilities of relative deprivation theory, but with the methods adopted to assess it.

An alternative approach would be to begin with a handful of settings showing strong prima facie evidence of the role of relative deprivation in triggering collective violence. Thus one might assemble a list of violent episodes apparently set off by rises in prices or abrogation of long-standing privileges, particularly where, from contextual evidence, one had reason to believe that rioters and their supporters attached special importance to the standard involved. One would want to document such events in the greatest possible depth, seeking to specify what these positive cases had in common, then compare these with other cases, as similar as possible, where violation of what appeared to be important standards resulted in no rioting.

By starting with instances in which a theoretical connection clearly holds, and by extending knowledge of such instances as widely as possible, one gives any theory its best chance to persuade. And comparison between positive and negative cases gives the best chance of delineating the *causal system* that gives the linkage its validity. Obviously it would be rash to assert that the alternative strategy—testing the "variable" in question in the largest possible data set—could never bring informative results. But what we know about explanation in social science hardly suggests that as the most promising strategy. In the case in point, I believe that we would by now have more satisfying understanding of the possibilities of relative deprivation explanations of civil violence, had the strategy I propose been followed.

---

As I look back over the theoretical ideas in this book, one topic seems to offer particular promise for further inquiry. This is the rapid "change of state" from peaceful to violent forms of interaction that Granovetter analogizes to ones studied by physicists, as in that from ice to water. Granovetter has explored the theoretical possibilities of such processes most explicitly in his models of threshold processes. These studies show how social systems that appear quite stable may, by very slight changes in the susceptibility of one or a few members to participation in violent action, switch into intensely violent modes. The same implication, though hardly so explicitly drawn, is to be found in Hobbes's theory of civil violence. Small changes in popular perceptions of government ability to ensure the safety of private contracts would logically lead to less compliance with government-backed strictures, which would lead to still less compliance. The result would plausibly be a quick chain-reaction of devolving social control, leading in the direction of Hobbes's war of all against all.

The possibility of such abrupt breakdowns of restraint against civil violence has been acknowledged from various theoretical standpoints. Parsons's account of "power deflation" as a political analogue to runs on banks is one case in point. Mann's observations on "explosions of consciousness" among workers and students is another, in this case with empirical force (1973, chap. 6). Mann shows how certain militant worker and student movements of the 1960s and 1970s blew up unexpectedly, apparently as much from the standpoint of their participants as from that of outside observers. In such cases, the growth of militancy seemed to "feed on itself," each rise in the level of protest creating conditions for further increase. Stinchcombe (1978, pp. 35–41) seems to point to the same sorts of processes in his discussion of regime authority as sustained or undermined by popular perceptions of its effectiveness or ineffectiveness.

Reflection on such processes suggests a possible rapprochement between theoretical views normally considered antagonistic. Collective behavior theory, in the intellectual line from Robert Park, has typically stressed *shared excitement* or *collective emotional tension* as a cause for outbreaks of violent action. Causes of the shared emotional states have been variously identified as "circular reactions" within crowds or the transmission of emotional stimuli by leaders, either in person or through mass media. Against such accounts, theorists of group contention have posed a more "rational" account, invoking the ability of mobilized groups to respond to threats and opportunities as key explanatory factors.

But consider both positions in light of a scarcely unreasonable assumption: that such "objective" considerations as power relations among embattled interests might be affected by shared emotional states; or similarly, that threats or opportunities for group interests in political struggle are shaped by aggregated individual states of excitement, tension, or readiness for action. Under such assumptions, psychic states and political realities might represent virtually two manifestations of the same thing. American public life went through such a period in 1968, when the assassination of Martin Luther King, Jr., aroused strong emotions throughout the population and thereby briefly created new political opportunities for representatives of blacks. A main concomitant of this changeful period, of course, was considerable civil violence.

The important theoretical point here is that these processes can readily spiral, thus accounting for chain reactions of rising violence. In Granovetter's terms, rising states of shared excitement—or "milling" or "circular" interactions—may simply be manifestations of perceptions by would-be participants that their thresholds for participation are likely soon to be met. The more signs that others may be willing to act, the greater one's own potential readiness, and vice-versa. The higher the levels reached by both these states, the more the political power equation between the forces of stability and the forces of revolt is apt to be altered—thus providing "objective" threats and opportunities where there were none before. Rigid juxtapositions of "rational" versus "irrational" theories of violent action may thus be highly misleading.

There can be no doubt that such abrupt "changes of state" or "explosions of consciousness" do occasionally occur, though they appear relatively rare among all instances of civil violence. Indeed, there seem to be some "implosions," where widespread violence gives way relatively quickly to relative peace, as in the response of the Turkish public to the military coup of 1980. In any case, the theoretical significance of such events far outweighs their statistical frequency. For the fact that such abrupt changes of state do occur reminds us that behavioristic studies of the long-term determinants of "rebellion" or "stability" are apt to miss an important point. Systems that remain behaviorally stable even over very long periods may nevertheless contain the potential for intense outbreaks of violent conflict.

Yet many systems—probably most systems—that appear stable really are. What sort of empirical inquiry would afford the best chance of shedding light on these spirals of rebellion, and of distinguishing where they are and are not likely to occur? My own inclination would be as previously declared—to begin by identifying a handful of cases where these quick shifts in compliance clearly occurred and where rich contextual information about the events and their settings is readily available. Then one would want to compare these positive cases with a number of negative cases, as similar as possible in other respects, where no such chain reactions took place. These steps might well disclose many elements of the *causal system* that obviously does produce such distinctive outbreaks from time to time.

Such inquiries might well lead to questioning of one of the dearest axioms of today's social scientists—the linkage between reported attitudes or opinions and action. Hardly any research strategy is more standard in our disciplines than asking people what they think or feel, then interpreting their reports as bases for explanations of what they will do, or have already done. Clearly such strategies are often eminently reasonable. But quick transitions between routine acceptance of "duly constituted authority" and militant opposition remind us that people may not always be able to give full and accurate reports of how they might act under changed conditions. Moreover, they remind us of the importance of settings where social action shapes attitudes and perceptions, rather than the other way around. If bold activists bring off a dramatic public challenge to an oppressive and feared regime, they may succeed in getting people to think what was previously unthinkable about possibilities for social change. Such dramatic rearrangements of grass-roots cognition are of course what all agitators hope for, and what their regime adversaries exert themselves to prevent.

Anyone who lived through the chaotic times in Western universities in the late 1960s and early 1970s will recall the sweeping processes of student radicalization that often shaped events. Political positions, goals, and doctrines that seemed beyond the pale of consideration at one point became, within days or weeks, taken for granted if not outmoded. Participants in other revolutionary or quasi-revolutionary sequences offer similar reports, as in Poland during the abrupt upsurge of Solidarity after August 1980. In such settings, action taken on the basis of certain beliefs or sentiments—either by one's self or by others—may raise them from the category of fantasy and hypothesis to plausible bases for concrete action and expectations.

Even in rapidly evolving situations like these, of course, participants' actions correspond to *some* sorts of beliefs or attitudes. But the relative unpredictability of these quick shifts in action and belief compel reflection about the nature of the linkage between the two.

What models best describe the relation between political perceptions and attitudes and the participatory actions associated with them? Are cog-

nitive and attitudinal elements within any personality organized in a coherent plan, so that any given situation will result in responses based on a
single set of values, perceptions, or assumptions? Or does any one personality consist of heterogeneous and disparate elements potentially leading
to quite different directions for action, depending on adventitious circumstances and chance events? In short, are the inner bases of human action
more like a computer program or an organization's operating manual, in-
ternally coherent and predictable in their directions—or are they more
like the contents of a kaleidoscope, heterogeneous and unpredictable in
relation to one another and apt to be rearranged in radically different
forms in response to shocks from the outside?

Obviously such questions do not admit of any single answer when
posed in such sweeping form. But for some situations, including some involving civil violence, the kaleidoscope model clearly applies. In certain
turbulent times, people select perceptions, attitudes, and beliefs as bases
for their actions that are quite different from those that might be chosen in
more stable moments. The innovative directions need hardly be antipathetic to long-standing interests or identifications; but they may well represent radically different ways of acting on them. We know virtually
nothing in a systematic way about how such transitions occur. A contribution to their understanding would greatly enrich theoretical grasp of both
civil violence and a variety of other issues.

*Chapter Nine*

# Conclusions on Social Theory

In the study of ideas, as at the movies, the best seats are not always closest to the action. In considering the big questions raised in the introduction to this book on the nature and possibilities of social theory, a measure of distance and comprehensiveness are essential. Individual doctrines on the origins and character of civil violence can of course be assessed largely in their own terms, as to conceptual clarity, internal consistency, plausibility in relation to empirical findings, and the like. But answering larger questions on the overall enterprise requires a view of the whole.

These questions have to do with such matters as the nature and extent of continuity between modern, empirically oriented social science inquiry and its antecedents in the nineteenth century and before. They have to do with the interactions between theory and research—with the constraints imposed on theory by empirical findings, for example, or the role of theory in guiding empirical inquiry. They have to do with the importance of social, cultural and political contexts versus strictly intellectual influences in the elaboration of theory. And they have to do, above all, with that most elusive question of whether the social sciences are capable of anything worthy of the name of *progress*.

Any approach to these weighty questions triggers confrontation with that notorious intellectual red herring—the standing of the social sciences as *scientific*, or the lack of it. Debates on this subject have sputtered on at excruciating length since the earliest days of social inquiry. Their recapitulation in undergraduate courses alone has undoubtedly moved many impressionable students to specialize in computer science or English literature. Yet the question is undoubtedly authentic and full of implications for our expectations of our disciplines.

Notwithstanding endless dispute over the applicability of the term *scientific* to the study of social life, nearly all participants in these debates assume that social inquiry is capable of *some form* of orderly development. Whether the underlying model is seen as deriving from the natural sciences or elsewhere, the idea remains that various contributions to the study of social life may bear fruitful relations to one another, such that one inquiry may complement or add to the next. But those who address these questions typically also complain that the actual practice of social science fails to exploit these opportunities.

Two broad sets of diagnoses are normally offered for this unsatisfactory state of affairs. The first has to do with the epistemologies, conceptual frameworks, paradigms, or meta-theories guiding inquiry; the second, with research methodology, especially quantitative methods. If only one or the other of these aspects of social science practice could be cleaned up, the argument goes, these fields would yield the full measure of enlightening results of which they are capable.

I want to take a slightly different tack. In reviewing the broad historical development of theories of civil violence, I want to consider the role of what one might call *intellectual ecology* in abetting or blocking cumulative growth of understanding. Without ruling out the possible role of strictly conceptual or methodological difficulties, I want to trace the relations between *individual contributions* to these debates and *the larger intellectual wholes* these contributions help constitute. Has inquiry into the origins of civil violence, in other words, been so organized that various single contributions really do build on one another? Or has the organization of intellectual work simply not afforded such orderly cumulation? For this purpose, the overview developed in preceding chapters offers an ideal tool.

In fact, this overview affords fairly direct and uncomplicated answers to some thematic questions raised in the introduction. It is clear, for example, that all the key theories considered in this book bear at least some empirical, falsifiable implications. To be sure, these implications have often been elusive; even the most direct of theoretical statements has required some unpacking and left some room for ambiguity. But none appears absolutely invulnerable to confrontation with evidence. All stand to gain or lose in credibility in light of empirical reports.

Another relatively straightforward conclusion involves the continuity of theoretical concerns. There can be no doubt that modern social science continues to draw on the inspiration of its classical ancestors. Indeed, virtually all the influential theoretical ideas now current draw directly from intellectual sources prior to World War I. The more nettlesome question, of course, is whether any of these long-standing debates has in any sense been resolved. Here matters are much less transparent.

Third, the preceding chapters give ample evidence of *technical prog-*

*ress* in the years since Hobbes, and particularly in the past twenty-five years. From any point of view, modern analysts have a vastly more varied and powerful means for amassing and analyzing information on civil violence than did their predecessors. Computerized means for data storage and analysis and modern statistical techniques are simply the most conspicuous examples. No less important is the compilation of modern information resources bearing on civil violence. The richness and detail of comparisons available to a Tilly or a Gurr by the 1960s would simply have been impossible to a researcher twenty years earlier. Even the painstaking compilations of Sorokin's *Social and Cultural Dynamics* (1937) would have been unthinkable without the resources of an excellent modern library.

Finally, growth in sheer *scale* of scholarly activity since the first studies of civil violence is unmistakable. The American Sociological Society had only 923 members in 1921, the year that Park and Burgess's famous *Introduction* appeared. By 1962, year of publication of Smelser's *Theory of Collective Behavior*, the figure had grown to 7,368. In 1986, membership had reached 11,635, and a special section had formed devoted to the study of "collective behavior and social movements"; membership in the smaller body had by that year grown to 345. No doubt similar profiles would characterize other disciplines participating in the study of civil violence.

But none of these observations affords direct conclusions in matters of greatest interest here—that is, whether knowledge of the subject has really *advanced*. A merry-go-round may add more passengers and pick up speed; yet it still deposits riders more or less where they got on. Again, the crux of the matter lies in the *organization* of ideas. More participants and more powerful methods in a basically inconclusive activity can hardly bring qualitatively new results. What we urgently need to know is whether and how more recent efforts at understanding civil violence *build on* older ones. And this requires a hard look at the relations between individual inquiries and the broad development of theory.

## Elements of Theory

What should count as theoretical cumulation or advancement? How do we reckon *progress* in theoretical development—without committing ourselves to arbitrary tastes or value judgments themselves peculiar to particular theoretical orientations?

The matter is more difficult than it might seem. How, for example, are we to interpret a sequence like this: A single view of a subject dominates scholarly discourse for years or decades. But then, more or less abruptly, it is confronted with a sharp theoretical alternative. The old way of looking at things fails to do justice to the most important characteristics of the subject matter, it is said. Key events, processes, or facts are badly accounted for in the old view—or, worse, that view simply has nothing to say about them. The new, alternative view, by contrast, makes great sense of these crucial matters and hence paves the way for a deeper, fresher, more enlightening program of empirical inquiry. Proponents of the old view find themselves on the defensive; their special viewpoint may no longer excite even themselves. Soon all, or nearly all supporters of the old view drop from the scene, and the new view comes to prevail.

Is such a change to be counted as progress? From the standpoint of the intellectual "consumers" of the innovative, insurgent view, perhaps. But is there any *overarching* standard that warrants such a conclusion? After all, perhaps this schematic account is simply a story of a change of intellectual *taste*, a more or less predictable shift in the aspects of the subject matter that analysts find most interesting or most worth accounting for. Fashions in clothing, cooking, and leisure activities also show shifts from period to period and from one group of consumers to another, often dramatic ones. Here, too, new ways of doing things or looking at things may quickly win general acclaim for satisfying what have suddenly been defined as unmet requirements in the old scheme of things. But few would contend that the long-term pattern of change in these things amounts to *progress*.

Any judgment of progress in the development of theories of civil violence must involve recourse to some standard that might plausibly be held relevant to each and every successive theoretical view. Intellectual tastes are always changing, and each new theoretical approach will to some extent imply a new set of criteria by which it will seek to be judged against other theories. But without *some* overarching criterion of adequacy, by which all theories might be judged, the shifting standards associated with theoretical innovation offer no solid analytical ground to stand on.

The need for some such criterion is one reason why *falsifiability* of theories holds special importance in this book. If theories yield statements in the empirical world that stand to be confirmed or undermined by actual empirical reports, we have the basis for one overarching standard. Suppose one theory of civil violence yields expectations concerning *participants* in violent events that are consistently at variance with empirical reports; an alternative theory, by contrast, withstands repeated attempts to falsify its implications on this subject. Here we might tentatively conclude that the latter theory is the stronger. Suppose that a variety of falsifiable implications of various theories are subjected to such confrontations, and some are rejected while some are retained; then we might reasonably regard the "surviving" implications as an advance over earlier ideas. Falsifiability, then, forms one possible basis for overarching standards of the strength of theories, and hence for registering progress or cumulation.

Note that I say a *possible* basis. The fact that theories of civil violence bear falsifiable implications hardly guarantees that theoretical change describes a progressive sequence. For theories also consist of various other intellectual elements, all of which play some role in their acceptance and currency.

Besides being sources of falsifiable expectations, theories of civil violence, like other social science theories, are broad ways of perceiving the subject. In their most elemental form, such theories consist of a kind of *cartoon* of the phenomenon—that is, a highly schematic account of the origins and characteristics of civil violence, or of deviance, social stratification, labor markets, patrilineal kinship, or whatever. Thus Pareto's theory of civil violence calls to mind an image of ambitious activists, excluded from official power, mobilizing grass-roots followers for a violent assault on the state. To be sure, this thumbnail sketch is highly simplified, indeed oversimplified. But there can be no doubt that such simplified schemes are the intellectual handles by which "consumers" of the theories initially grasp their theoretical wares, with greater or less sophistication as to the distance between such images and the full detail of the theory.

Part of what such intellectual cartoons imperfectly evoke is the *category system* associated with every theory. All theories offer some distinctive way of slicing up reality for analytic attention. Some of these categorical designations may be easily conveyed, as when Pareto enjoins us to consider differences between leaders and followers in insurgent groups. Other distinctive categories may require much exegesis, such as Pareto's notion of residues and derivations. But every theory is a system of selective attention, and its category system is the principle of selection.

Typically theoretical category systems help steer attention to what Alan Garfinkel would term the *contrast set* underlying the explanations afforded by the theories. Pareto's categories highlight the differences between polities where elite political talents are concentrated inside the central "establishment" versus those where talented activists are excluded. Or they call attention to the differences in action potentials of political groups endowed with militant residues versus those characterized by residues of accommodation and compromise. The reason why we are directed to attend to such contrasts is clear enough; both are part of Pareto's account of when and where to expect violence.

As I noted in Chapter Eight, the specification of contrast sets also gives

precise delineation to *explanandum* itself. Not all theories of civil violence, it should now be clear, aim at accounting for precisely the same
thing. Explaining why a crowd of rural consumers in West Oxfordshire
attacked grain merchants and bakers at 2:38 P.M. on 12 July 1830 (instead
of 3:00 P.M. sharp on the same date) is not the same as explaining why the
attack occurred in 1830 instead of 1835, or in the country rather than in
the metropolis. Thus, we need to pay close attention to the dominant contrast sets prevailing in any theory.

All of these attention-focusing elements of theories—and more, for this
description is hardly complete—have the effect of mobilizing attribution
of *meaning* to empirical material. They convey both cognitive and emotional emphases. It is clear enough, for example, that the contrast the irrationalists evoked between crowd action and normal social action was
hardly dispassionate, for all its analytic content. For the irrationalists,
crowd mentality was the enemy of civilization, the destroyer of intelligent
public discourse, the underminer of reason. Similarly, when Tilly and his
followers point to violent action as the voice of groups denied a more formal role in political decision making, the distinction carries more than just
an analytical message. Many consumers of these ideas are no doubt attracted by their highlighting empirical points of compelling evaluative
significance.

Even where a particular theory conveys no clear-cut positive or negative evaluative tone to its subject, it endows the empirical world with
meaning it would not otherwise have. One of the great appeals, one suspects, of highly elaborated category systems such as those of Parsons and
Smelser is their ability to ascribe significance to countless facts and observations that would otherwise remain dubious in their claims on the analyst's attention. The fact that such "determinants" as structural strain and
precipitating factors can always be identified ipso facto creates a program
of intellectual work in charting these states in any particular setting.
Much the same observation might be made for any number of other comprehensive intellectual systems, including those based on the works of
Marx, Habermas, and a variety of others.

———

Now note something important about the cartoonlike "images" conveyed in theory, the category system, the implied contrast sets, their
emotional valence, and their attribution of meaning. None is susceptible
to judgment in empirical terms as "right" or "wrong." Unlike the falsifiable implications that theories may yield, these other elements are to some
degree matters of intellectual taste or inclination. Analysts may ultimately
judge them more or less satisfying or apposite. Yet the standards that

make them appear apposite, suggestive, or fruitful may themselves be peculiar to a particular category of intellectual consumers; it would be hard to cite an overarching criterion to govern such judgments. These elements of theory are empirically *relevant,* in that they relate to properties of the empirical world. But they hardly stand or fall by appeal to any delimited empirical evidence.

I call these the *rhetorical* elements of theory, as distinct from *falsifiable* elements. As in discourse on public issues, the rhetorical elements of theoretical discussion highlight, emphasize, dramatize, and more or less explicitly convey evaluative stances toward the subject—yet they do not themselves stand or fall by appeal to any delimited evidence. They are simply "ways of looking" at the subject. No doubt the rhetorical elements of any theory make the strongest initial impact on anyone encountering it for the first time. For they convey the perceptual texture, the emotional charge, and the political or other cultural valence of the theory. The falsifiable elements are by contrast more elusive, more demanding; as this book has shown, it is often no easy matter to specify just what the key falsifiable characteristics of any theory are.

Now many analysts might view the rhetorical elements of theory as at most a distraction or a source of misperception. What counts, they would hold, is whether the theory is *true*—whether it can withstand the test of encounter with evidence. The emotional, political, or perceptual associations of the theory will at most get in the way of such determinations, it might be said.

Yet for present purposes, such objections will not do. The task here is to account for the *currency* of theories in the study of civil violence. Why and how do they come and go as they do? What wins for some of them the insistent attention of many, and what consigns others to oblivion? For all we know, the answers to such questions may have everything to do with the rhetorical elements of the theories, and rather little to do with their falsifiable implications.

Indeed, some radical relativists attack the very notion of falsifiable implications, at least in the sense of its implying standards of judgment held in common by proponents of contending theories. Contending theories, they might argue, proceed from different and incommensurable paradigms, presuppositions, or epistemologies. The "falsifiable implications" of one theory, it might be held, can only be evaluated from within the domain of assumptions and viewpoints reflected in that theory. Thus, facts that seem to undermine Marxian theories of civil violence, for example, might be held to have such implications only from the standpoint of those outside the Marxian realm of discourse.

The implication is of course solipsistic. If theories can only be evaluated "from the inside," so to speak, then we are bound always to remain imprisoned within our theories. Differences between theories would never stand to be adjudicated by appeal to empirical reports; at most we might hope for something equivalent to religious conversion to bring proponents of discordant theories together.

But another case against the importance of the falsifiable elements of theory is potentially much more telling. One might argue that the falsifiable aspects of theory, whatever their *potential* role in the evaluation of knowledge, in fact have little to do with the forces that govern the ever-changing ecology of ideas. If this were the case, then the implication for progress in our field would be problematic indeed. The rhetorical appeal of theories, after all, is bound to change with changes in political and cultural context. The times are always changing, and with them the forces that tend to raise some theoretical views to prominence, and cause others to drop from sight. What appear as theoretical *advances,* in other words, may simply prove to be *shifts of attention,* or *redefinitions of what aspects of empirical reality are worthy of attention.* If these strictly rhetorical considerations are what predominates in shaping the historical succession of theories of civil violence, then that succession indeed begins to resemble fashion: always changing, but never improving.

Throughout this book, I have devoted much attention to the empirical relevance of abstract theoretical ideas, to their internal coherence, and above all to their falsifiability. Any summary verdict on such matters is bound to be quite mixed. On the one hand, nearly all the most provocative and engaging theoretical ideas considered here have been afflicted with serious vagueness on one conceptual point or another. And the quest for falsifiable implications of these influential theories has often run up against much ambiguity in the original formulations.

Yet I do not believe that these frequent logical lacunae represent the main cause of the considerable inconclusiveness in the history of theories of civil violence. Even the vaguest of these theories, with a bit of pushing and shoving, yields falsifiable empirical expectations at least clear enough to form the basis for meaningful research. Research oriented to such expectations, if carried out systematically by a community of conscientiously engaged analysts, could eventually coax answers to such questions.

What has most decisively stymied such desirable results is neither the logic of the theories nor the possibilities of research, but lack of concertedness in social scientists' intellectual attention. The community of scholars has simply not shown the will, over the length of time required, to wring more conclusive answers from these fundamental theoretical questions. The sheer *trendiness* of both theories and research methods has often blocked the concerted efforts that such answers would require.

For the origins of this episodic quality of intellectual attention, we must look to larger social, political, and cultural contexts of scholarly work.

## Theory as Fashion; Theory as Politics

For many forms of ideas, the expectation of cumulation or progress is quite inappropriate. Art historians hardly judge American abstract expressionism of the 1940s and 1950s as an attempt to improve on German expressionism of the 1920s and 1930s. Nor do we view Shakespeare's tragedies as an effort at progress over the work of Sophocles and Aeschylus. True, we note *technical* progress in works of art and literature—improvements in the ability of painters to render perspective, for example, or in the range of notes and the ease of reproducing them available to musicians. Certainly individual works of art vary in their attainment of the aesthetic ideals that they seek to realize. Sonnets are brilliant or mediocre; symphonies are grand or merely grandiose. But these are judgments of execution, not of aesthetic ideals. The ideals of different artistic forms are independent ends in themselves, rather than approximations of some more distant, ultimate standard.

But what about the study of human affairs? Here, it might appear, all students of the same subject seek a single truth, however difficult such pursuits may be in practice. Surely the steady accumulation of knowledge should lead to what all could agree was overall improvement in understanding, as less reliable insights give way to "hard facts." Or should it? Unfortunately, matters are not clear-cut; again, the answers depend on the kind of progress one has in mind.

The study of history, for example, affords a *form* of progress. Scholars now arguably know more about, say, the French Revolution of 1789 than has ever previously been known, in terms of the sources available, the chronology of events, and the range of facts accessible to study. Yet perhaps these advantages are most comparable to strictly technical progress in the artistic realm. For in matters of *interpretation*, revolutionary scholarship is hardly so conclusive. Judgments of the overall importance, in the ultimate revolutionary outcome, of such forces as the intransigence of the Old Regime, the motives of street crowds, and the importance of the rising commercial bourgeoisie seem perennially in dispute. A clear line of improvement in our understanding of these more interpretive issues is much harder to trace.

The same holds true for other highly charged historical subjects. In his absorbing work *Americans Interpret Their Civil War* (1962 [1954]), Thomas Pressly traces the evolution of scholarly interpretation of this great conflict from generation to generation since the end of last century.

A handful of thematic questions have exercised virtually a hypnotic claim on historians at every stage. How much latitude did various key actors have in the period leading up to the war to take actions that might have averted it? Were the conflicts that ultimately brought about the war primarily economic, political, or moral? What was the precise importance of slavery and abolitionism among these conflicts? And, above all, what *caused* the war? Answers to these questions, buttressed by much scholarship, have come and gone from school to school and from generation to generation, often losing their appeal only to be resurrected in a later inning of the long-running debate.

How are we to account for such turbulence in the supposedly deep waters of scholarship? One might think that these shifts result from discovery of new materials, or refinements of analytic techniques—in short, that they reflect *technical* advances of some sort. But Pressly's conclusion is quite different; the shifting views, he writes,

seem, by and large, to have been due not as much to new evidence about the past as to new experiences in the present. The experiences of historians in the twentieth century, and their reactions to their experiences, disposed many of them to find some new facts, both among those previously known and among those newly discovered, more significant than others. (1962, p. 335)

Among the experiences that move new generations of scholars to embrace new interpretations of the great conflict, Pressly finds none more influential than the state of race relations in the United States as history is being written. Thus the present shapes the past.

Yet how much more complex, one might imagine, is the situation confronting theorists of civil violence. The Civil War, after all, is at least a fait accompli—except perhaps for those who study it. Theorizing about civil violence, by contrast, demands not only interpretations of events and evidence from the past, but also statements about open categories of empirical phenomena—that is, commitments about matters still to be studied, or still to occur. Here, one might expect, the constraint of evidence is even more ambiguous.

Let us agree that students of social life respond to what some sociologists of science call *intellectual interests*—that is, enduring attractions to particular ideas or theoretical views on rhetorical grounds, in terms of their emotional associations or social identifications. Perhaps the most obvious of these intellectual interests are those associated with political identifications—the special appeal to conservative analysts of theories highlighting the unwisdom of rapid change, or the desire of left-wing thinkers for accounts that emphasize the sufferings and resourcefulness of those at the bottom of the social heap.

Such intellectual interests assert themselves even in settings one might have thought well insulated from any political associations. In the early 1980s, debates raged among paleontologists as to the fate of the dinosaurs. An innovative theory held that these creatures had perished because of a collision between the earth and a comet or meteor. The impact was so great, the theory held, that clouds of dust obscured the earth's atmosphere for years; this caused a kind of extended, planetwide winter and thus deprived dinosaurs and certain other life-forms of their livelihood. Discussion of this view became particularly charged when some of its proponents put it forward as a warning of the probable effects of nuclear war. Spokesmen for the Pentagon attacked this interpretation, arguing that a nuclear exchange should not be expected to bring such dire consequences as those that had supposedly ended the reign of the dinosaurs. In the ensuing controversies, scholars who took exception to the comet theory on various scientific grounds found themselves assailed as "militarists" by some of their colleagues, whether they had taken any explicit position on the effects of nuclear war or not (*New York Times*, 2 November 1985, p. 24).

But not all intellectual interests take their charge so directly from politics in the usual sense of the term. Ideas, and a fortiori theories, often bear intense *status implications*—much as do consumption habits in clothing, food, or recreational activities. Any working scholar knows that, at any given moment for any population of thinkers, some ways of looking at things are "in," while others are "out." Moreover, profession of certain key ideas will serve often to define boundaries of groups highly conscious of their identities. One can no more expect to be accepted in Kleinian psychoanalytic circles without correct views on penis envy than one could expect to play a public role in Calvin's Geneva without professing the right position on predestination.

Theories and other ideas, then, unquestionably gain much of their appeal from a vast array of social and political associations that may have nothing to do with their strictly intellectual strengths. But to acknowledge this much tells us little about the precise weight of such considerations versus others, and nothing at all about the development of theories of civil violence.

## The Force of Rhetoric

Have the rhetorical aspects of theories of civil violence shaped their reception and their influence? The indications that this is so are simply overwhelming. True, evidence to this effect is not so direct as one might prefer. We have no in-depth interviews of individual scholars, for example, that might reveal the true, hidden reasons for espousing one theory rather than another. But we do have a great deal of what one might call circumstantial evidence as to the bases for the rise and fall of contending theoretical views, especially where we can compare the reception of two or more theories seeking support from the same intellectual constituencies.

Consider Marx and Pareto. The contrasting rhetorical appeals of their two theories could hardly be more marked. Marx in effect asks his readers to take sides in a struggle of historic dimensions, a struggle between movements on behalf of rationality in human affairs and their antagonists. Pareto by contrast casts doubt on the pretentions of all social movements, and on the prospects for social rationality more generally.

Marx's doctrines obviously threatened the intellectual interests of many conservative and middle-of-the-road intellectuals, especially as his theories became official ideologies of a series of militant movements. Yet there could be no denying their impressive scope and apparent power. What was needed as an alternative view, equally "deep," equally scientific in its claims, equally sweeping in its historical view. Pareto filled precisely this intellectual need, as at least one sophisticated exponent of his ideas has noted in his own intellectual autobiography (Homans 1962, p. 4).

The two theories of civil violence contrast as sharply in their falsifiable implications as in the rhetorical. On the one hand, a view of violent action as direct pursuit of authentic collective interest; on the other, violence as an opportunistic tool of activists ultimately more attracted to the conquest of power than to the interests of their grass-roots constituents. These contrasts, I have argued, imply a research program that should be highly informative; the issues involved are in principle quite accessible to empirical investigation. Yet this program mostly remains to be carried out. The research we have consists largely of case studies of the origins and development of grass-root mobilizations, most often from a Marxian perspective. These studies tend to yield findings, not surprisingly, that fit Marxian expectations. Although they are often persuasive, we have no comparable studies from a Paretian perspective to weigh against them.

Given the state of empirical research on these matters, it is hard to believe that choices between Paretian and Marxian views of civil violence have often been made in terms of their ability to withstand confrontation with potentially falsifying evidence. It is not that the appeal of either theory is unfounded; there is evidence to support both. But in the absence of empirical inquiry that might afford rigorous comparison of the abilities of the two theories to withstand confrontation with the same data, rhetorical appeal seems decisive. Perhaps a few hard-headed analysts have reassigned their loyalty from Pareto's to Marx's theory of civil violence, or vice-versa, in light of rigorous study of evidence, though I have not encountered any such dedicated thinkers. But one suspects that most intellectual consumers simply embrace the account of civil violence associated with the theory that suits their rhetorical predilections.

Next, consider the remarkable career of the theoretical line beginning with the irrationalists: Sighele, Tarde, and LeBon. Their position had much in common with that of their contemporary Pareto, such as the view of crowd action as the result of unconscious impulses beyond the understanding of participants. The doctrines of the irrationalists, particularly those regarding civil violence, commanded attention from an intellectual public much wider than that of professional social scientists. Again, their view of crowd action as manifesting a breakdown of virtually all the forces sustaining civilization seems to have satisfied some particularly compelling intellectual interests. Did the comparative ability of the theory to deal with evidence play any role in this attraction? There is no reason to think that many of the early supporters of the irrationalists' doctrines could have had the chance to weigh such evidence against that for any competing theory. The irrationalists' theories just "fit" the rhetorical needs of a wide swath of early twentieth-century thinkers.

Transformed and relieved of their anticrowd connotation by Robert Park, these ideas became collective behavior theory. For four decades from the publication of Park and Burgess's famous *Introduction* (1921), this was virtually the only perspective available to North American sociologists for the study of militant action. During these years, the doctrine did undergo some theoretical development, though in fact the number of studies published was very small. But with the exception of the historian Crane Brinton's famous *Anatomy of Revolution* (1938), empirical research seems to have played virtually no role in theses changes. Collective behavior theory seemed to persist in an intellectual vacuum, insulated from challenges from other theories and from confrontation with potentially disturbing data.

This theoretical dominance came to an abrupt end in the 1960s. The eclipse of collective behavior and mass society views is the closest we are apt to come in social science to an authentic "paradigm shift." The successful challengers were of course relative deprivation theories such as those of Gurr and group contention theories as advanced by Tilly, Gamson, and various Marxist scholars. Some of the latter developed a critique of the older views that proved extremely persuasive. Far from being a symptom of moral or organizational breakdown, these theoretical insurgents held, violent collective action is a sign of solidarity, a manifestation of the most normal of all facts of social life, the pursuit of collective interest.

Perhaps more than any other element of the attack on collective behavior theory, this alternative *image* of civil violence reshaped scholarly perceptions of the subject. Proponents of group contention theories buttressed this view with impressive research programs, yielding countless examples attesting to the purposefulness and the normative content of violent action. Collective behavior theorists mounted no program of empirical inquiry comparable with the historical researches of group contention theorists, or to the statistical inquiries of relative deprivation thinkers. From the mid-1960s to the time of this writing in 1986, there seem to have been no new converts to collective behavior theory. Its proponents have remained few in number and defensive in stance.

It is ironic that collective behavior thinking should have taken such a beating at the hands of political theories. The natural opponents of the latter are not collective behavior doctrines strictly speaking but theories of moral breakdown and social disorganization, those derived from mass society or value integration theory. Park and his followers, notwithstanding certain statements on the ahistorical or acultural aspects of crowds, generally treated crowd action as a creative process that might well bring innovations for the better. Indeed, the replacement of collective behavior thinking with theories accounting for violent episodes in terms of group contention or relative deprivation represents more of a *shift of attention* or *redefinition of theoretical importance* than a clash of falsifiable implications. For collective behavior theorists typically focused their attention on the details of interaction within crowds, or on the short-term transmission of emotional stimuli—as against their competitors' focus on long-term psychological or structural determinants of militant action. To a significant extent, collective behavior theorists of the Park tradition were simply seeking to explain different things from what Tilly and Gurr were addressing. But in the 1960s students of civil violence found the latter a more compelling target for attention.

---

The significance of these observations deserves emphasis, for they have everything to do with our search for *progress* in theories of civil violence. If collective behavior thinking, dominant among North American social scientists for some four decades, had failed *in its own terms*—if, for example, its falsifiable implications on the origins of civil violence had met with massive falsification—then the meaning of the doctrine's decline might be more clear-cut. Under these circumstances, new doctrines might well have been expected to succeed where collective behavior had failed. But such was hardly the case. As far as the record shows, students of civil violence and other supposedly "unstructured" social processes simply *lost interest* in interactional contingencies. Whereas the "scum of the earth" theories of participation in violent events lost credibility through repeated subjection to falsifying evidence, collective behavior thinking as a broad theoretical view simply seems to have passed out of style. True, students of face-to-face interaction in crowd situations never succeeded in producing the sorts of dramatic, falsifiable formulations yielded by political or psychological theories. But we can hardly say that such formulations could never have been produced, had interest in the collective behavior thinking not waned. Under these circumstances, it is difficult to interpret the shift from collective behavior thinking to political and psychological theories as unambiguously progressive.

In the course of the shift, the exact nature of the differences between collective behavior thinking strictly speaking and the doctrines that displaced it seem to have been blurred in our collective memory. A number of critics have given the impression that the doctrines of Park and his direct followers shared the pathological view of crowd action characteristic of the irrationalists and mass society theorists (Currie and Skolnick 1972; Couch 1968). Perhaps these distortions of historical recall are as inevitable in intellectual revolutions as in the other kind. In the world of social theory, control of the present grants a measure of control over the intellectual past. And crucial to the appeal of any doctrines that are presently "in" is their ability to claim superiority to those that are, at least momentarily, "out."

How, finally, are we to account for this dramatic rewriting of the theoretical map of civil violence in the mid-1960s? One might hold that the force of evidence played a preponderant role. After all, the attention-grabbing empirical researches of Tilly, Gamson, Gurr, Muller, and others surely showed a new image of violent collective action. Yet both the theoretical and empirical ingredients of the intellectual revolt had been available for decades, if not longer. Investigators could have, and certainly should have, noted the purposeful aspects of crowd action even without the elaborate historical sampling of Tilly and his students, for example. Marxism and other doctrines had long provided theoretical bases for purposeful views of violence, just as de Tocqueville had laid down the bases for relative deprivation studies. The intellectual syntheses of the innovators deserve the credit they have received, but one must also ask why the revolution came precisely when it did.

The answer has to lie in the social and cultural context of intellectual work, and in the rhetorical appeal of the new theories. Tilly, Gamson, Gurr, and others were not former collective behavior theorists troubled by the failure of that theory to account for some crucial finding. Rather, they were newcomers to the study of civil violence, responding to new intellectual interests in themselves and their audiences. For an older generation of scholars, militant collective action had had different associations: Naziism and Stalinism abroad, McCarthyism and lynchings at home. For the newer generation, the associations were more likely to be movements for national liberation abroad and peace and civil rights demonstrations at home. Theories with new rhetorical associations were essential. Again, some few conscientious theorists may have sought to weigh the available evidence for one or more of the newer theories versus that favoring alternative positions, although, as I have noted, rather few published studies offer such direct confrontations. But most of the younger social scientists who gave their adherence to these theories must surely have acted on simpler motives: The new views simply accorded with their perceptions of the world of social contention.

In this light, the striking success of Lewis Coser's *Functions of Social Conflict* (1956) appears as a precursor of the massive shift of the 1960s. As I noted in Chapter Four, this book apparently won a great following largely by serving as a badge of "progressive" attitudes on social contention. Though rich in falsifiable implications, it did not inspire research that might confront such implications with potentially falsifying evidence. Indeed, it seems to have shaped rather little empirical research in a direct way. Instead, like so many well-known theoretical ideas, it stood on its own—at first little noticed, but then increasingly prominent as the pace of contentious social change in America quickened. Had it not been for changes in the rhetorical appeal of its ideas, it would presumably have remained as it began, an admirable but rather obscure work.

Did the theoretical shift that began with Coser's book, then continued with a vengeance in the mid-1960s, represent an overall *advance* in understanding of civil violence? In one sense, certainly. For it afforded deepened understanding of aspects of civil violence now considered highly important. And the technical contributions of the new approaches, in terms of new *methods* for study, are manifest.

But at the same time, something appears to have been lost in this shift of theoretical attention—the concern of collective behavior theorists with the details of face-to-face interaction and other forms of communication of emotional stimuli. The new theories do not really deny the importance of such elements in the formulation of civil violence so much as they simply turn away from them. For group contention and relative deprivation theories, the contingencies that shape violent episodes lie much farther back in time. The search for such contingencies requires methods and strategies unsuited for the search for interactional contingencies. We will never know whether or how the latter enter into civil violence until those theoretically prepared to find them go looking.

-----------

The 1960s also brought another important new theoretical force to bear on the study of civil violence, in Smelser's *Theory of Collective Behavior* (1962). The appeal of Smelser's scheme does not seem to have been associated with any political connotations; his view of collective behavior is neither laudatory nor necessarily critical. As far as one can judge—again, the best evidence is indirect—the work gained much attention as an extension of the expanding influence of Talcott Parsons. During the 1950s, Parsons and his followers were successfully persuading many North American social scientists of the generality of their doctrine—not just as an exercise in "pure theory," but as an analytic system that had to be reckoned with in the study of any substantive subfield. Smelser himself, as one of Parson's most eminent apostles, took the lead in extending Parsonian thinking to the study of social change (1959) and to economics (Parsons and Smelser 1956). *Theory of Collective Behavior* was obviously intended to direct this same missionary function toward what had been the theoretical preserve of Robert Park.

The opening pages of the work make this intent explicit. While expressing thanks to his colleague Herbert Blumer, a key exponent of Park's views, Smelser emphasizes his own theoretical distinctness (1962, p. x). He then goes on to *define* collective behavior in such a way as to eschew concepts derived from Park (pp. 8–22). The new conceptual map comes straight from Parsons.

> Collective behavior is analyzable by the same categories as conventional behavior. . . .
>
> Given this position, it is important to assemble a number of categories to describe the components of action at the social level. . . . The result will be a kind of "map" or "flow chart" of paths along which social action moves. In the chapters which follow we shall investigate what happens to these components of action when established ways of acting fall in the face of unstructured situations. . . .
>
> In discussing the principal components of action, we shall rely on the accumulated sociological thought in Europe and America during the last century or so. In a more direct sense, we shall refer most to the work of Talcott Parsons, Edward Shils, B. F. Bales and their associates. (p. 23)

Thus, Smelser launches a massive effort of reclassification, aimed at stamping each major form of collective behavior—from shifts in fashion to earth-shaking social movements—in terms of one Parsonian component of social action or another. Nowhere does he attempt to present evidence linking any particular form of collective behavior with the disturbed "action element" to which it supposedly corresponds. It is simply taken as axiomatic that "value-oriented movements," for example, arise from disturbances in participants' value commitments.

To this classification, Smelser adds his well known "value-added" scheme of stages in the formulation of instances of collective behavior. These categories bear no obvious debt to Parsons. Together, however, the two classifications offer a conceptual agenda for those seeking guidance in understanding particular cases. They evoke a feeling of *comprehensive-ness*—a sense that, when one has filled in the categorical blanks for any particular instance, one has indeed boxed the theoretical compass or completed the "analysis" of the case. In short, Smelser's classifications impart *meaning* to facts that might otherwise appear to lack it.

I have argued that neither scheme is falsifiable—at least, not without considerable further specification as to such things as *how much* or *what form* of structural strain is required for collective behavior to occur. Without such specification, the key concepts are so broad and all-encompassing that a determined observer is bound to find some evidence of them in the background of any situation fitting the definition of collective behavior. Such difficulties should certainly call into question Smelser's claims to offer *explanation* of the phenomenon (1962, p. 1). Yet the vagueness of the schemes and their seeming imperviousness to contrary evidence appears to have been more an asset than a liability in assuring their currency in the literature.

The observation of unfalsifiability is hardly original in these pages. Marx and Wood, in an influential review of the literature, note the "persisting criticism of Smelser's theory: that it is not predictive or falsifiable" (1975, p. 411). Yet this observation does not deter them from citing a long list of studies in which the scheme "has clearly been useful in ordering and helping to understand collective behavior phenomena"; in at least several cases, one reads, these studies "tended to verify" Smelser's approach (1975, p. 407).

This latter claim surely warrants skepticism. One of the studies cited is an account of events at and around Kent State University at the time of the National Guard shootings of students in 1970 (Rudwick and Meier 1972). The key observation here is that the community's perception of student agitation as a "value-oriented movement"—that is, a movement with sweeping and fundamental goals—accounted for its willingness to condone the repression. Another of the studies reportedly "tending to verify" Smelser's scheme was an investigation by Zurcher et al. (1971) of two anti-pornography movements; they reported the presence of such value-added elements in the background of the action as structural conduciveness and structural strain. It is difficult to see how such findings "tend to verify" Smelser's theory. They do demonstrate once again that Smelser's categories are so broad as to apply to virtually any instance of contentious or innovative behavior. But that is surely another matter.

I believe that Marx and Wood's observation of the role of Smelser's scheme as a device for "ordering and helping to understand" the disparate subject matter of collective behavior should be taken seriously. Whatever the logical looseness of these categories, they have provided a way of looking at social reality that many researchers have found attractive. Specifically, Smelser's scheme ascribes meaning to data that would apparently otherwise appear meaningless, disparate, or uninteresting—that is, unclear in their relations to the origins and characteristics of any other instance of collective behavior. The ability of a theoretical scheme to offer such a potent source of meaning is rare and noteworthy. We need to recognize its force in the currency of theories.

———

The varying ability of conceptual systems to impart a commanding sense of importance or meaningfulness to otherwise humdrum material raises a complex question that rarely gets the critical attention it deserves: What marks a subject as an authentic and worthy target of social science concern?

The most superficial acquaintance with social science literature reveals some pervasive rituals relating to this question. Rare is the book or article that does not begin with an invocation of intellectual ancestors, more or less hoary, whose works allegedly form the context for what is about to follow. In sociology, Marx, Weber, and Durkheim are of course the preferred choices for this role, but more recent figures are acceptable if their standing as guarantors of theoretical consequentiality is secure. Ostensibly, the purpose of these incantations is to establish the line of intellectual cumulation whose direction the new work is to follow. More to the point, however, such remarks represent an appeal for the new offering to be considered sociologically *meaningful*.

The truism has it that no facts, observations, or findings are meaningful or scientifically useful without context in a conceptual system. To establish the standing of their work as legitimate contributions to social science, participants in these disciplines must always invoke orienting ideas shared with other participants. In this respect the growth of social science is like that of coral reefs. The reefs grow by accretion, each new organism creating its abode on the accumulated homes abandoned by others, so that finally massive structures result, in which the living constitute but a layer on the countless tombs of the dead.

The difference is that each coral organism contributes approximately equally to the eventual creation of the reef; in scholarship, the contributions of individual participants to consensual definitions of meaningfulness are vastly disproportionate. For the most part, we dwell in intellectual structures created mainly by small handfuls of thinkers whose attributions of meaning especially endure.

At the extreme of potency in ability to confer meaningfulness are works one might call *mythic*. For these, there can be no debate of the importance of the key themes and problems. Establishing one's own contribution as a plausible response to or logical extension of a mythic source assures its standing as a legitimate exercise. In extreme cases, mythic status may even foreclose critical comment on the original work. In studies of civil violence, Smelser's *Theory of Collective Behavior* at least for a time approached mythic status, though this seems by the 1980s to have subsided. At the peak of the work's influence, application of Smelser's categories in itself established an investigation as a meaningful theoretical "analysis."

Perhaps the theoretical work of the middle twentieth century that most fully achieved mythic status is Parsons's *Structure of Social Action.* Obviously the special potency of this work extends far beyond the study of civil violence. So thoroughly has it been apotheosized that questioning of its central claims was for a long time simply suspended. Generations of social scientists have taken it for granted, for example, that no social system may persist without widespread grass-roots moral support for the principles underlying its key social arrangements. Or that utilitarianism went sociologically bankrupt because of its insistence that human beings were incapable of pursuing goals other than narrow self-interest. The fact that both claims are gravely misleading and that neither received reasoned, systematic support in *The Structure of Social Action* or elsewhere in Parsons's work seems to have counted for little.

What qualities are required to confer mythic status on a work or a body of work? A thorough answer is far beyond my powers here. But clearly those who succeed in this direction, whatever else they may have or lack in common, at least share special powers of *imagination*. Their works identify intellectual connections, indeed, rich interweavings of meaning, that most thinkers are incapable of creating for themselves.

But does this ability of a theory to convey an experience of *meaning* have anything to do with the ability of its theoretical implications to withstand confrontation with potentially falsifying evidence? Alas, not necessarily. The rhetorical aspects of a theory may be aesthetically evocative, intellectually labyrinthine, politically congenial, and gratifying to status claims and other intellectual interests, quite regardless of its ability to admit of or withstand subjection to potentially discordant evidence. For many intellectual consumers, the rhetorical appeal of imaginative conceptual schemes—those evocatively "useful in ordering and helping to understand" a subject matter—far outweighs considerations of falsifiability.

## The Constraint of Falsifiability

The rhetorical elements of theories obviously exercise an enormous influence over their currency. The theoretical "map" of civil violence is subject to frequent reshaping by the ever-changing intellectual interests of theorists. As in art and literature, social theory often seems to respond to new ideals or agenda for every new age and school. These observations lend credence to Gouldner's claim that "questions of fact . . . seem to enter surprisingly little into much social theory"—at least as a description of the actual development of theoretical ideas.

But perhaps this is only a partial view. Perhaps certain aspects of our understanding of civil violence are shaped by the constraints of evidence in an enduring way. But how would one establish such a point? The matter is more complicated than it might appear. For the question I am asking has to do not just with the intellectual *possibilities* of theories of civil violence, but also with the empirical realities of how theoretical ideas come and go.

There can be no doubt, I have argued, that theories of civil violence bear important falsifiable implications. These empirically vulnerable aspects of theories might well form the basis for a pattern of enduring progress, if only the attentions of the intellectual community worked in such a way as to exploit them.

Imagine, for example, that the community of students of civil violence did indeed pay unerring attention to the falsifiable implications of theories on the subject; imagine, further, that empirical inquiry were so organized as to subject such implications systematically to potentially falsifying data. Under such conditions, one might imagine, more thoroughly falsified ideas might well gradually give way to those that had better withstood such attempts.

But the intellectual ecology of our disciplines does not necessarily work so coherently. Many rich and relatively clear empirical implications of important theoretical ideas have been admired from afar, yet never subjected to the systematic confrontations with data that might yield closure on them. The ideas of Hobbes, or of Simmel and Coser are cases in point. Other plausible theoretical possibilities, such as the notion that crowds that become violent pass through distinctive phases of interaction, seem simply to have been lost in the shuttle.

Demonstrating that the confrontation of theoretical ideas with empirical evidence has *any* systematic effect on their currency requires some demanding steps. One needs to establish something both about the currency of a particular theoretical idea and the reasons for that currency. It does not suffice to show that a particular empirical expectation is likely to be *justified,* for example, by pointing to a record of unsuccessful attempts at falsification. One must also show that the idea owes some of its salience among all other theoretical ideas to such confrontations with evidence. We can take it for granted that empirical expectations of theories will remain current in the absence of unfavorable evidence, if the rhetorical associations of the theory are agreeable in a particular intellectual community. But will empirical expectations that have fared well in confrontation with empirical reports remain *salient* once the contextual conditions accounting for the original rhetorical interest in the theories have altered?

Perhaps the most conclusive case would be where a given issue had been theoretically salient during periods dominated by a variety of contrasting theories—and where a particular empirical expectation had withstood empirical attention from both those disposed to disbelieve it and from supporters. But I can think of virtually no empirical expectations this well established in our theoretical heritage. Let me then set the standard a little less rigorously: Have any theoretically relevant empirical expectations been salient to proponents of more than one theoretical view, and also withstood confrontation with potentially falsifying evidence, or been decisively falsified, to the consensual satisfaction of those espousing a variety of theoretical convictions? Have any such expectations, in other words, yielded conclusions that have persuasive power extending beyond a particular theoretical community?

Perhaps the strongest candidate is what I have called the "scum of the earth" theory of participation in civil violence. This theme was not only present in the ideas of the irrationalists, but indeed quite central in theoretical importance there. Slightly altered, it continued for decades to have a place in the thinking of mass society theorists, right down to Kornhauser (1959). Yet the notion was antipathetic to the theories that came to the fore in the 1960s, when its rhetorical appeal dropped dramatically. More to the point, a variety of convincing empirical studies appeared with falsifying findings, while virtually no empirical work specifically sustained it.

Today the expectation that participants in violent action will be disproportionately deviant, outcast, or otherwise disconnected from social networks appears without serious support. To be sure, we cannot claim absolute certainty as to what a future revolution of thinking on civil violence might bring. One cannot reject the possibility that some resourceful analyst will produce evidence of violent action dominated by outcasts. Nor indeed can we be sure that future generations of theorists of civil violence will continue to ascribe theoretical importance to the social identities of participants in civil violence. Perhaps it simply will not matter. But I doubt this. The question of who participates is just so thoroughly intertwined with other aspects of thinking on civil violence that it seems to me unlikely to slip from scholarly attention.

Perhaps theories of the *purposefulness* of violent action offer nearly as strong a case as the scum of the earth theories. Here, too, the irrationalists had taken a strong stand, claiming in their more extreme statements almost a randomness of objectives pursued by violent crowds. This idea has been virtually overwhelmed by research since the 1960s showing continuity of crowd action with long-standing interests of crowd participants.

I suspect that this perception of purposefulness will continue to withstand confrontation with evidence, at least as far as it goes. But I also believe that certain other aspects of crowd action will have to be recognized as widespread, notably the actions that serve consummatory rather than strategic purposes. These purposes may be less predictable in light of the structural position of participants—framed, as they may be, by the exigencies of the moment. But the assertion that enduring interests are not dissipated in the solvent of crowd action, I would bet, will continue to be persuasive and to hold the attention of students of civil violence in future theoretical generations. Yet here again, one can offer no grounds for *certainty* that students of civil violence will continue to find this issue theoretically important.

Are there other theoretical statements on which research and reflection have offered clear conclusions, and where such conclusions promise to endure longer than the lifetime of a particular theoretical view? Cases quickly become harder to cite. Perhaps we could point to the rejection of the simplistic coercion theories sometimes ascribed to Hobbes. It is clear that sheer command of coercive strength does not reliably distinguish regimes that preside over highly compliant populations from those beset by disobedience and rebellion. This conclusion emerges both from quantitative studies of large samples of polities and from various case studies. Certainly this insight is worth having. Again, my guess would be that its appreciation is apt not to be lost, even as new theoretical views emerge. But we should also note that Hobbes himself never intended such a crude theory of compliance, and that the subtleties of Hobbes's real doctrine have thus far eluded serious empirical inquiry.

Perhaps we should add to our list the rejection of certain absolute deprivation theories and the crudest version of relative deprivation theories considered in Chapter Seven. We are reasonably certain, in other words, that no objective level of deprivation can be specified that will inevitably result in violent response from the deprived. Similarly, even proponents of some reformed version of relative deprivation thinking would probably join in rejecting the assumption that the causes of relative deprivation can be automatically specified in terms of some objective features of participants' situations, for example, wage levels or political rights. If there is hope for relative deprivation arguments, most would now agree, it lies in exploring people's own specification of their degree of satisfaction as the baseline for reckoning satisfaction or deprivation.

No doubt this list could be extended, particularly with negative conclusions, if we are willing to relax further the criteria for inclusion. As we do so, it would come to resemble the list given toward the end of the preceding chapter—a list of conclusions that I myself find highly persuasive in light of the literature. But for present purposes, a tougher standard is needed. I want to identify empirical statements about civil violence that have both withstood attempts at falsification and promise to retain theoretical interest. The second point is important, for we know that many important theoretical themes simply lose appeal with shifting rhetorical emphases. And again, any judgments on the likely durability of these ideas are bound to be speculative.

Perhaps it is too soon in the history of ideas on civil violence to make such judgments with confidence. Perhaps the durability of empirically sanctioned theoretical ideas will become more clear-cut once a larger community of researchers have the opportunity to address this literature in continuity and depth over a longer period. For the present, however, conclusions have to be guarded. The most important theoretical ideas have not necessarily been pursued in empirical inquiry, and ideas that once seemed important are apt to lose their interest with changes in the social and political context of intellectual work. The fact that some key points have been established and seem likely to retain their claim on theoretical attention suggests that the barriers to cumulation are not insuperable. But how much these insights of 1986 will have in common with their eventual counterparts in the year, say, 2050 has to remain a matter for conjecture.

## The Predominance of Rhetoric

The pretensions of the language used by social scientists are persistently, if unavowedly, scientific. We describe the conceptual or methodological approaches we favor as more or less *enlightening* or *accurate* than their alternatives, implying the existence of overarching standards that all might share. Or we refer to individual writings as *contributions*, suggesting joint efforts at some larger intellectual task addressed by all. Or we implicitly excuse the inconclusiveness of our work by avowing that "further research is needed" to pursue implications raised but left dangling. Implied in such conceits is a view of social science as a joint search for some larger truth whose validity should be compelling.

Yet closure on the big theoretical questions remain scarce. Further research is always needed, it would seem, and indeed further research of some kind is always under way. But the results of this research, in relation to theory, often remain inconclusive. This is not to say, in the instance of civil violence, that we have no accomplishments worthy of pride or nothing likely to endure. But the role of what I have called rhetorical forces in theoretical change is obvious and far-reaching, whereas the constraint of evidence is limited and often ambiguous.

I have tried to identify some obstacles to more clear-cut patterns of cumulation in theories of civil violence. One is the sheer multiplicity of explanatory tasks implicit in theory on this subject: Theories that explain the occurrence of violent episodes within historical time, for example, may tell us relatively little about their timing within the day or hour of a particular crowd's existence. Then there are considerations of the sheer multifariousness of our subject matter: Causal sequences or other empirical connections rigorously established in one setting may well not hold universally. We may find that theories legitimately propounded for certain cases, in other words, have to be abandoned even in what appear to us highly similar conditions.

But although these considerations pose formidable complications, I see no reason to view them as *absolute* blocks to progress. Indeed, the weight of the evidence considered in this book points to a different interpretation: Relatively trustworthy conclusions on theoretically important empirical issues are possible, if only the point in question receives the kind of concerted attention necessary. Where relatively clear-cut empirical expectations of theories have been pursued widely and systematically, conclusive results have often followed, as in the rejection of early interpretations of relative deprivation as a general theory of participation in violent actions, or the discredit suffered by "scum of the earth" theories.

What has blocked more frequent closure of this kind is the shifting nature of social scientists' theoretical attention. Rare are the theoretical questions that have been pursued at the length, and with the attention to the demands of falsification necessary, to yield even moderately conclusive results. It is appealing to use theoretical ideas as exposition devices for particular findings; it is far less appealing to attempt to mobilize evidence that might actually move us to shift our theoretical allegiances. The most fundamental problem, then, is not with the nature of the subject matter so much as with the organization of theoretical work.

The richness of alternative *contrast sets* as bases for explaining what may appear as "the same" thing greatly complicates the organization of such theoretical work. Without conscious and concerted attention to the variety of logically legitimate ways of accounting for civil violence, incommensurable results are virtually inevitable. To weigh properly the strengths of various theories in relation to specific empirical material requires elaborate specification of precisely which conditions are presumed to remain constant, and which to vary. And for the results of such inquiries to acquire maximum persuasiveness among the intellectual community, the same sorts of rigorous assumptions have to be followed by a variety of investigators. Needless to say, such demanding attention to the organization of theoretical inquiry is more the exception than the rule in most of social science. Indeed, theoretical ideas most often serve in quite a different way.

Consider the important book by Doug McAdam, *Political Process and the Development of Black Insurgency 1930–1970* (1982), a study of the vicissitudes of movements of and on behalf of blacks in the United States, analyzed in terms of the political models of activism considered in Chapter Six of this book. An important goal is to demonstrate the superiority of this view over various theoretical alternatives, at least as far as the struggles of black Americans are concerned.

McAdam takes particular exception to the implications of what he calls "the classical theory" of social movements (p. 6); this inclusive category comprises "mass society, collective behavior, status inconsistency, rising expectations, relative deprivation, and Davies' J-curve theory of revolution" (p. 6). Although these positions are not held identical,

the idiosyncratic components of each are relatively insignificant when compared to the consistency with which a general causal sequence . . . is relied on in all versions of the model to account for the emergence of social movements. This sequence moves from the specification of some underlying structural weakness in society to a discussion of the disruptive psychological effect that this structural "strain" has on society. The sequence is held complete when the attendant psychological disturbance reaches the aggregate threshold required to produce a movement. (p. 7)

McAdam gives his own position as follows:

Social movements are not, as the classical theorists contend, only the product of factors endemic to the aggrieved population (alienation, dissonance, etc.). The characteristics and actions of opponents and allies, as well as those of movement groups, must be taken into consideration in accounting for any specific social movement. (p. 12)

Some pages later, he notes:

In contrast to the various classical formulations, a social movement is held to be above all else a *political* rather than a psychological phenomenon. That is, the factors shaping institutionalized political processes are argued to be of equal analytic utility in accounting for social insurgency. (p. 36)

True to his theoretical convictions, McAdam proceeds with a detailed and informative analysis of movements on behalf of black Americans as manifestations of an extended struggle for political power. He takes particular pains to account for rises and declines in the political fortunes of black activism in terms of strategic considerations—resources, organization, opportunities, and threats—rather than predicating his explanations on psychological states of black activists and their allies. The result is a new look at the broad historical sweep of racial activism in America and, not incidentally, a view that implicitly grants activists themselves credit for their hard-won accomplishments.

If anyone had reason to be unhappy with McAdam's words, it would be proponents of the "classical" theories he disparages. One of these was Lewis Killian, veteran analyst of militant phenomena in the collective behavior tradition of Robert Park. Killian compares McAdam's characterization of his theoretical opponents to a political challenger's attack on the incumbent.

Quote the opponent selectively and out of context, carefully deleting any statements of his which do not sustain the caricature. In particular, studiously ignore refutations of charges which have been levelled before by you or others—just repeat the charges. Quote from the opponent's political speeches regardless of the date they were made—never concede that minds do change. At the same time, do not hesitate to borrow freely from the opponent's ideas without acknowledging that despite party differences there is indeed a great deal of overlap in the platforms. Give the ideas you borrow new labels so that the voters won't recognize them. Finally, use guilt by association by putting the opponent in the same bag with others of whom you're sure your constituents will disapprove and then quote what they said as if he agrees with it. (1983, p. 4)

I hardly intend to pass judgment on all the characterizations Killian makes of McAdam's book; they are detailed and critical, yet not without appreciation for certain of the work's substantive accomplishments. But Killian's words do properly alert us to distortions and exaggerations that often accompany collisions of competing theoretical views. There is always a tendency to paint one's theoretical antagonists with a broad brush—for example, to attribute to all of them all of the time shortcomings more correctly ascribed to a few some of the time.

Thus McAdam implies, in the quoted passage, that all "classical" theorists share the mass society view of participants in social movements as somehow dislocated from "normal" social roles. This seems to be his intent, in any case, in ascribing to "classical" theorists a view of participation as resulting from the "disruptive psychological effect" of "underlying structural weakness" in society. I do not see that this claim is true, say, of collective behavior theory in the Park tradition or of relative deprivation thinking as advanced by Gurr, unless it is true by definition of all militant participation. These doctrines certainly do picture participants as responding to something they perceive as amiss in their social environments. But the same could be said for virtually any theory of the same subject.

McAdam's charges would be more precisely accurate had he specified that most empirical studies in the "classical" category simply have little to say about issues on which his study is highly informative, such as the

effects of repression and outside alliances on movement participants in
the formulation of their activism. The other analysts have invoked different *contrast sets*, holding "environmental" considerations constant, while
positing variation in relative deprivation, shared excitement, or whatever.
I suspect that passages could be found in a number of the works McAdam
criticizes that acknowledge in passing the possibility of what they might
consider exogenous influences in social movements; Park and Burgess, for
example, do note at one point that coercion may dampen collective behavior (1921, p. 786). But such remarks *en passant* hardly carry the persuasiveness of McAdam's detailed exposition.

What McAdam calls "classical" theories, then, do have little that is distinctive to say on matters about which McAdam's work tells us a great
deal—the counting of costs and benefits by participants and potential participants in militant action. Like many other proposed "theoretical revi-
sions," his is an effort to dramatize a series of issues, to activate a set of
categories that he feels deserve more importance or centrality than they
have received in other analyses—in short, an appeal for a new set of rhetorical references in the study of this highly politically charged arena of
contention.

Now some might defend the rhetorical style of works like McAdam's on
the grounds that each new "perspective" or "approach" adds some increment to our overall store of theoretical knowledge. As I noted in Chapter
Eight, there is something to be said for such a position. In some sense,
every study may alert us to some new contingency in the origins of militant action. Thus, each item in the total literature might represent one
new addition to the theoretical toolbox.

But without some form of condensation and organization, the usefulness of an ever-expanding list of theoretical possibilities is vitiated. And it
is a sobering fact of theoretical life that, as new "departures," "syntheses,"
and "perspectives" emerge, old ones may be displaced from our collective
memory, as shown by the marked decline in salience of some quite reasonable theoretical possibilities suggested by Park and his followers, in
the wake of the shift to political and relative deprivation theories since the
1960s. A constant succession of one new rhetorical thrust after another,
then, may not bring meaningful cumulation of knowledge. More useful
would be creation of a list of crisp, closely ordered, falsifiable statements
specifying what empirical characteristics are to be expected of militant action in specific settings. If sufficiently condensed, such a list might well
command attention enduring beyond a shift in the rhetorical demands of
particular social and temporal contexts. But the creation of such a body of
theoretical knowledge is a far more demanding task than what most works
in this tradition attempt.

Killian is particularly pointed in his comments on McAdam's concept of "cognitive liberation," essentially the willingness of aggrieved populations to believe that their situation can be changed. Such willingness figures as another *resource* for struggle in McAdam's analysis of the strategic equation of political forces shaping the destinies of black insurgency. Killian does not dispute the importance of such forces, but only the distinctiveness of McAdam's position.

> Do "hope" and "optimism" reflect pure cognition, a "rational" assessment of cues in a changing stimulus field, or do they include an emotional component? McAdam condemns classical theorists for the significance some of them attach to such states of mind as status inconsistency, alienation or relative deprivation . . . but there is no warrant for calling other theorists' attitudinal variables "psychological" and "irrational" but our own "political" and "rational." (1983, p. 2)

What McAdam has done is to attend to different manifestations of phenomena that, as Killian insists, do indeed have an important place in certain other theories. Consistently with his program of viewing these movements as political phenomena, he has designated in political terms facts labeled by others in different language. The essential difference lies not in the facts under consideration, but in their rhetorical presentation.

I note these controversies over *Political Process and Black Insurgency* not because this work is especially vulnerable to such criticism, but because it is an outstanding book that embodies some highly characteristic uses of theory. McAdam uses theory to highlight aspects of reality that he finds insufficiently appreciated, attended to, or understood. And he succeeds in his aims of showing the political power contingencies that shaped the experience of black Americans through decades of political struggles. Where his work contributes less is in clarification of the exact differences among alternative theoretical positions and in evaluation of the falsifiable strengths and weaknesses of theories in their own terms. Such observations could well be made about the bulk of theoretical writing on civil violence.

One might think of theoretical work in social science as resembling civil violence itself—as oriented both to purposeful and expressive ends. The purposeful goals of theorizing, one could say, are the elaboration of clear, empirically falsifiable statements that might serve other thinkers as a "guide to the unknown" in confronting new situations. Yet as we have seen, theoretical language also plays an enormous role in dramatizing, evoking, highlighting, legitimizing, and otherwise repackaging reality in relation to changing intellectual interests. These expressive uses of theory, from all indications, often overwhelm the others.

There seems to be nothing unusual about studies of civil violence in this respect among topics addressed by social scientists. The sociologist of science, Stephen Cole, in an impressive quantitative study of citation patterns, has come to similar conclusions regarding the deviance literature (1975). Cole reviews the intellectual reception accorded over a period of decades to Robert K. Merton's famous "Social Structure and Anomie" (1949 [1938]). His quantitative indices demonstrate what informal impressions also suggest—that Merton's article enjoyed a extraordinarily long hold over the theoretical imaginations of students of deviance. But Cole also shows that, of all the scores of citations to this work, only a small minority came in contexts involving anything resembling an empirical test of its ideas. When the article finally dropped from a central place in the attentions of writers on deviance, it did so not, apparently, because of the success or failure of its key ideas in their own terms, but through the redirection of analysts' attention to a different and basically incommensurable set of concerns, namely those of labeling theory. In short, a shift of attention, a redefinition of importance, a rhetorical revision in theoretical perception.

Again, the history of theories of civil violence gives no reason to believe that more conclusive uses of theory are in principle impossible. As the examination of relative deprivation and a small handful of relatively enduring other issues has shown, truly concerted attention to theoretically relevant empirical points may well yield eventual closure. Yet the scarcity of such concerted research programs is conspicuous.

How are we to account for this persistent shortness in the collective attention span of those addressing theoretical questions? The answer has to lie in the nature of the rewards they seek. Social scientists, compared with natural scientists, do very little *replication* of one another's research. The chance to offer a dramatic new view of a subject, the opportunity to ally one's self publicly with positions with which one seeks identification—the appeals of such expressive opportunites often far outweigh those of helping to bring the issues addressed by many other researchers one step nearer to closure. Under these circumstances, the various literatures of social science tend to give pride of place to stellar solo performances, rather than to relentless working of well-worn but important theoretical issues.

And it is no secret that the skew of scholars' efforts toward dramatic solo departures reflects prevailing systems of reward within the scholarly communities. When we think of notably successful careers in the social sciences, we almost always think of those credited with "new departures," "theoretical breakthroughs," or "pathbreaking investigations." In short, we think of those who generate new sources of meaning for academic work, rather than those who seek closure on intellectual puzzles already before the scholarly community. Such extraordinary emphasis on novelty and innovation within the academy, along with the shifting rhetorical demands of the larger social and political contexts of research and theorizing, make it easy to understand why we have so many more new theoretical departures than we do conclusions.

One manifestation of our exaggerated enthusiasm for virtuosity of individual performances, as against concerted joint efforts at theoretical closure, is our obsession with methodological innovation, especially that in quantitative methods. It should go without saying that such technical advances have afforded all sorts of gains in the study of civil violence. But the disparities between the intellectual energy devoted to quantitative innovation versus systematic effort at clarification and revolution of long-standing theoretical issues is conspicuous. The precious handful of relatively well-attested conclusions on important theoretical issues in the study of civil violence owe much more to breadth and persistence of conscientious attention among communities of researchers than to application of special methodological virtuosity. Theoretical accomplishments are ipso facto the work of *communities* of investigators. And enduring attention from such communities to delimited issues of agreed importance is much more urgently needed for the elaboration of theory than even the most spectacular feats of quantitative innovation.

Could the work of social scientists, then, be organized so as to produce more conclusive theoretical results? I am sure that it could. Consider the vast amounts of time, talent, and other resources that go into generating the long bibliographies of generally inconclusive studies that are comprised in most of our scholarly literatures. These assets could, if we wished, be redirected into a concerted attack on theoretical issues of agreed importance among the intellectual community, along lines carefully planned to yield the best possibilities for unambiguous results. With effective central coordination, I believe that such conclusive results would be very likely. But such an ambitious restructuring of theoretical work could only be accomplished by instituting considerable central coordination over the work of what is now a community of independent scholars. Such centralization, not incidentally, would curtail the expressive possibilities available to analysts in singling out and highlighting the aspects of social reality that they feel deserve most attention. And restrictions of this kind would quite likely undercut the appeals that bring most participants into the world of scholarship in the first place.

But such drastic steps as these would hardly be necessary for us to profit from the insights offered here. Even without imposing some binding form of coordination among researchers, we might profitably attend more to the potential of individual works in our disciplines to contribute to points of enduring and widely shared interest. For each "contribution" to the study of civil violence or anything else, we ought to ask not only whether it is dramatic, innovative, and impressive in itself, but also whether it shows promise of forming part of an eventually persuasive answer to issues of long-standing and widely shared interest. Herein lies the most important role that the study of the *history* of our own disciplines can play for us. We need to study the historical origins and development of our disciplines in order to hone our instincts for what issues are likely to *endure*—to endure at least long enough, in other words, so that our contributions have some hope of mattering to others. This reward, more than the need to mine some long-neglected insights of Marx, Weber, and Durkheim, is the most compelling reason for staying in touch with the works of our immediate and distant intellectual ancestors.

## In Praise of Falsifiable Theory

One can imagine the future of theories of civil violence as an endless succession of shifting emphases, as different intellectual needs and interests give rise to one "new interpretation" or "theoretical revision" after another. Views held to be of incandescent theoretical significance at one point—such as the 1960s' "discovery" of the continuity of violent action with participants' "normal" interests and objectives—might, in this view, lose all interest for future theorists. Perhaps some future theoretical "breakthrough" would entail ignoring the purposeful aspects of violent action in favor of the culture of the participants, or the physical settings of violent action, or the age distributions of various parties to the action. These new interests, for all we know, might well give way in turn to theoretical revivals of the ideas that they eclipsed in the first place.

Each of these succeeding "theoretical breakthroughs" or "paradigm shifts" would, of course, involve a new or revived set of analytical categories, along with a variety of other novel rhetorical elements. Proponents of each new category system would inevitably proclaim its special usefulness in "ordering and helping to understand" previously neglected aspects of the subject. In some sense, all such claims may be correct. Any subject matter, after all, admits of characterization by an infinity of different category systems—any one of them logically coherent, all of them illuminating especially some particular aspect of reality.

Yet evaluating such theoretical views only in terms of the dramaturgical satisfaction they afford the thinker hardly yields a compelling picture of social theory. If an account of social theory as completely impervious to influences from thinkers' personal needs and social context is unappealing, a view of such understanding as governed only by such existential influences is no less so. Nor does the historical development of theories of civil violence suggest any reason why overarching criteria—above all, the falsifiable aspects of theories—ought not to play a crucial role in their reception.

Relativistic observers might well point out that the various falsifiable elements of theories themselves vary enormously in their claims on theorists' attention from period to period and from theoretical school to school. And this claim is certainly true as far as it goes. Students of civil violence might, for example, simply cease to *care* about the fact that implications of a given theory, say, for participation in violent action had been thoroughly falsified; the theory might continue to hold interest for quite different reasons. But there are, I suspect, a core of empirical issues in the study of civil violence that is unlikely ever to be of total theoretical indifference. The social identities of the participants, the relations between deprivation and action, the continuity or discontinuity of violent action with the rest of social life—issues like these, I hope and believe, are likely to command significant attention from theorists at any point. I readily admit that there is no logical reason why this *must* be so; I simply think it likely, in light of the interconnectedness of these issues with others in the study of civil violence, and because of their enduring importance in the subject thus far. Insofar as the issues remain important, the contributions of the last twenty years are apt to represent a significant step in addressing them.

Of course, one may argue that, even if certain *questions* remain important, answers antipathetic to prevailing intellectual needs or interests will simply be ignored. To this extent, Gouldner's dictum will be correct: Facts will really matter rather little for the elaboration of social theory. Indeed, some might even defend such a view of social theory as normatively, as well as descriptively accurate. If the *only* purpose of theory is to meet the intellectual needs of a generation or a school, it might be said, facts inconsistent with such needs ought to play no part.

Such a view amounts to rejection of the best possibilities of social analysis. The social theory of the paranoid, impervious to revision in the face of discordant evidence, is not really attractive to most of us, nor should it be. A key difference between social science, on the one hand, and art and literature is the orientation of social science to an *exterior* reality versus the aesthetic orientation to subjective *experience*. Social scientists seek, or should seek, a form of knowledge that can alert us to features of the world that we would not have expected, that are not intuitively part of our experiences, yet which will constrain our future experiences in dealing with that world. This approach means seeking a form of theoretical knowledge capable of forcing revision of understanding in light of unexpected or indeed unwelcome evidence.

Knowledge of this kind, at best, holds out the hope of less destructive, more realistic bases for human action. Consider the irrationalists' theories. Their idea of crowd activity as a mindless access of unaccountable impulses, especially likely to afflict the least "civilized" individuals, is an elegant evocation of a certain social mood. Its extraordinary popularity in the early decades of this century attests to its correspondence to a certain set of intellectual needs and interests. The key difficulty of these ideas is not that they were peculiar to a particular social viewpiont, or even that that viewpoint was in some sense selfish and retrograde. What matters is that this view of civil violence was *wrong*.

The ability of theoretical understanding to change in the face of discordant empirical findings is invaluable, from the standpoint of human affairs as much as in strictly intellectual terms. For it holds out the hope of bringing human action more in line with durable social realities, or reducing the role of fantasy and wish-fulfillment in public discourse and political action. We have much need for such hope in matters connected with civil violence. Who knows what irrational, insensitive, or blood-thirsty actions might be avoided if the lesson could be well learned that what crowds do is no unaccountable aberration, but most likely a direct expression of abiding tensions and interests in the lives of participants? Perhaps appreciation of these facts has already, in some small ways, reshaped social practice for the better.

We might make similar statements for a precious handful of other areas where theoretical inquiry has overcome evocative theories that accorded all too elegantly with the intellectual needs of those who believed them. Nineteenth-century theories of intelligence differences among races certainly suited the intellectual needs of opponents of racial equality at the time—and might again do so today, had those theories not given way almost totally to the constraints of evidence. One might say much the same for early theories that only members of certain ethnic stock were suited to participation in democratic institutions. Here and there, evidence and theory wear away at potentially destructive ideas, ideas favored by the intellectual interests of groups to whom they promise special advantage. We should do everything in our power to build the kind of theorizing that maximizes these potentials. And that means pursuing those aspects of social ideas with the power to *constrain* the evocative rhetorical appeal of theory—no matter how demanding that task may be. Empirically grounded theories that oblige us to change our minds about one highly charged aspect of social reality or another are the greatest achievement that social science has to offer.

In the climactic chapter of his great and terrible novel *Germinal*, Emile Zola creates an indelible image of a violent strike in the Northern French coal fields of the late nineteenth century. In this scene, several *bourgeois* watch petrified as an enraged throng of working men and women pass.

"Take out your scent-bottles, the sweat of the people is passing by!" murmured Negrel, who, in spite of his republican convictions, liked to make fun of the populace when he was with ladies.

But his witticism was carried away in the hurricane of gestures and cries. The women had appeared, nearly a thousand of them, with outspread hair dishevelled by running, the naked skin appearing through their rags, the nakedness of females weary with giving birth to starvelings. A few of them held their little ones in their arms, raising them like banners of mourning and vengeance. Others, who were younger, with the swollen breasts of amazons, brandished sticks; while frightful old women were yelling so loudly that the cords of their fleshless necks seemed to be breaking. And then the men came up, two thousand madmen—trammers, pikemen, menders—a compact mass which rolled along like a single block in confused serried rank so that it was impossible to distinguish their faded trousers or ragged woolen jackets, all effaced in the same earthy uniformity. Their eyes were burning, and one only distinguished the holes of black mouths singing the *Marseillaise*; the stanzas were lost in a confused roar, accompanied by the clang of sabots over the hard earth. Above their heads, amid the bristling iron bars, an axe passed by, carried erect; and this single axe, which seemed to be the standard of the band, showed in the clear air the sharp profile of a guillotine-blade.

"What atrocious faces!" stammered Madame Hennebeau.

Negrel said between his teeth: "Devil if I can recognize one of them! Where do the bandits spring from?"

And in fact anger, hunger, these two months of suffering and this enraged helter-skelter through the pits had lengthened the placid faces of the Montsou colliers into the muzzles of wild beasts. At this moment the sun was setting; its last rays of sombre purple cast a gleam of blood over the plain. The road seemed to be full of blood; men and women continued to rush by, bloody as butchers in the midst of slaughter.

"Oh! superb!" whispered Lucie and Jeanne, stirred in their artistic tastes by the beautiful horror of it. . . .

It was the red vision of the revolution, which would one day inevitably carry them all away, on some bloody evening at the end of the century. Yes, some evening the people, unbridled at last, would thus gallop along the roads, making the blood of the middle class flow. They would hang up heads and sprinkle about gold from disembowelled coffers. The women would yell, the men would have these wolf-like jaws open to bite. Yes, there would be the same rags, the same thunder of great sabots, the same terrible troop, with dirty skins and tainted breath, sweeping away the old world beneath an overflowing flood of barbarians. Fire would flame; they would not leave standing one stone of the towns; they would return to the savage life of the woods, after the great rut, the great feast-day, when the poor in one night would reduce women to leanness and rich men's cellars to emptiness. There would be nothing left, not a sou of the great fortunes, not a title-deed of properties acquired; until the day dawned when a new earth would perhaps spring up once more. Yes, it was these things which were passing along the road; it was the force of Nature herself, and they were receiving the terrible wind of it in their faces. A great cry rose, dominating the *Marseillaise:* "Bread! bread! bread!"

No work of social science will ever approach a passage like this in its evocation of civil violence. It would be unreasonable to expect as much. True, this passage, like Zola's novel more generally, does convey a particular view of the origins of the miners' violent and desperate revolt. Indeed, we find both here and in other works of the imagination themes strikingly resonant of the theories of civil violence considered in this book: class consciousness, moral indignation, crowd mentality.

But the goals of fiction are different from those of sociology, anthropology, or political science. The evocations in *Germinal* stand or fall in terms of the justice they do to the inner world of human experience. One asks, Do Zola's words really capture the feelings and perceptions triggered by crowd action in the sensibilities of figures like Negrel and his companions? No one, I hope, would seek to judge Zola's book by launching an empirical investigation, say, into whether striking miners' faces "really" come to look like those of animals at moments like these. A passage like this makes it incontrovertible that the experience was real for someone. That alone establishes the success of the literary enterprise.

All the theories of civil violence considered in this book have been true to *someone's* experience. But this fact hardly justifies these accounts as social science. Here we must instead ask, Does this account point to evidence not suggested by other accounts; and do actual investigations yield the sorts of evidence suggested by this account, rather than those suggested by alternative views? Pursuing questions like these is normally a humdrum business, compared to an evocation like Zola's. But success in the social scientist's enterprise promises payoffs that literature cannot offer—above all, the possibility of grasping realities that exercise constraint over social life, whether they form part of anyone's direct experience or not.

Surely these special goals justify the rigor required in their pursuit.

## Coda

If the case for cumulative progress in theories of civil violence is problematic, the same holds a fortiori for the realm of what I call Social Theory with capital "S" and "T." By Social Theory, I mean those literatures addressing the big, context-forming issues of social thought in the widest sense. These include discussions of the fundamental epistemological and strategic issues facing the social science disciplines—studies of the most appropriate logical form of social knowledge and the most fitting methods for its development, for example. And they include speculations on the shape that a "successful" study of society might take, if only the quest for such understanding could be set in the right directions.

Consideration of Social Theory obviously is supposed to take into account substantive areas of inquiry, such as civil violence. But as Social Theory is bound to be less constrained by any particular set of empirical issues or evidence, it appears even more volatile and transient than theories of civil violence per se.

Indeed, the world of Social Theory would shame Detroit with its continuing flow of "theoretical reorientations," "new departures," and innovative syntheses. Especially in sociology, these appeals to put intellectual life on radically new bases appear regularly, like charismatic religions. And like those riveting faiths, they typically subside abruptly after generating intense but short-lived interest—sometimes leaving permanent innovations woven into the fabric of conventional belief, more often not.

Usually these appeals for fundamental revision entail a message relating to intellectual progress, explicit or not. If only we liberate ourselves from our old, unsatisfactory ways of thinking, the message goes, if only we embrace this innovative set of assumptions or new program of inquiry, *then* our efforts will begin to show the dramatic, conclusive developments so long expected of them.

The frequent inconclusiveness of inquiry in our disciplines is no myth, as this book has demonstrated. No doubt the perception of such inconclusiveness has much to do with the appeal of doctrines promising a radical solution to it. Yet these appeals for drastic reorientations of intellectual efforts as solutions to the perceived unevenness in achievements in social science are bound by now to appear suspect, as well. If social inquiry really does hold out possibilities of such great accomplishments, why do Social Theorists so regularly find it necessary to pull the plant up by the roots in order to give it a new start?

In this book, I have argued that the considerable—but by no means total—inconclusiveness of inquiry into civil violence does not mainly stem from conceptual or methodological weaknesses in the usual sense. Instead, it reflects a largely unacknowledged diversity of intellectual interests guiding efforts to create a "general theory" of the subject. The literature on the subject in fact involves pursuit of a variety of more or less distinct questions. The heterogeneity of such questions, their continual reformulation, and their charged political and social contexts must lead to ambiguity in our overall grasp of this subject. Understanding the sources of such ambiguity, I hope, may help us make our expectations of the study of civil violence more realistic. Perhaps it will even afford us the best chance of exploiting the considerable theoretical opportunities that are open to us.

So I hope for the study of civil violence. But what about Social Theory—that is, our expectations for growth and development in all forms of social inquiry? I turn to this question in the sequel to this volume.

# Selected Bibliography

Abel, T. 1937. "The Pattern of a Successful Political Movement." *American Socio-logical Review* 2:347–52.

Aberbach, J. D., and J. L. Walker. 1970. "Political Trust and Racial Ideology." *American Sociological Review* 64:1199–219.

Abercrombie, Nicholas, Stephen Hill, and Bryan S. Turner. 1980. *The Dominant Ideology Thesis.* London: George Allen and Unwin.

Aberle, David F. 1970. "A Note on Relative Deprivation Theory as Applied to Millenarian and Other Cult Movements." In *Millennial Dreams in Action,* ed. Sylvia Thrupp. New York: Schocken Books.

Adorno, Theodor W. 1976 (1957). "Sociology and Empirical Research." In *Critical Sociology,* ed. Paul Connerton. New York: Penguin Books.

Aguirre, Benigno E. 1984. "The Conventionalization of Collective Behavior in Cuba." *American Journal of Sociology* 90:541–66.

Aguirre, Benigno E., and E. L. Quarantelli. n.d. "Methodological, Ideological and Conceptual-Theoretical Criticisms of the Field of Collective Behavior . . ." Texas A&M Sociology Department. Mimeographed copy.

Aminzade, Ronald. 1977. "Breaking the Chains of Dependency: From Patronage to Class Politics in Toulouse." *Journal of Urban History* 3:485–506.

———. 1981. *Class, Politics and Early Industrial Capitalism.* Albany: State University of New York Press.

Amiot, Michel, ed. 1968. *La violence dans le monde actuel.* Paris: Desclee de Brouwer.

Anderson, William A., and Russell Dynes. 1975. *Social Movements, Violence and Change: The May Movement in Curacao.* Columbus: Ohio State University Press.

Apter, David E., ed. 1964. *Ideology and Discontent.* New York: The Free Press.

Archer, Dane, and Rosemary Gartner. 1984. *Violence and Crime in Cross National Perspective.* New Haven: Yale University Press.

Aristotle. 1958. *The Politics.* Edited by Ernest Barker. New York: Oxford University Press.

Aya, Rod. 1979. "Theories of Revolution Reconsidered: Contrasting Models of Collective Violence." *Theory and Society* 8:39–98.

Bagehot, Walter. 1984 (1869). *Physics and Politics.* New York: Knopf.

Bain, Read. 1939. "Cultural Integration and Social Conflict." *American Journal of Sociology* 44:499–509.

Baker, Wayne. 1983. "Floor Trading and Crowd Dynamics." In *Social Dynamics of Financial Markets*, ed. Patricia Adler and Peter Adler. Greenwich, Conn.: JAI Press.

Baldwin, J. Mark. 1910. "The Basis of Social Solidarity." *American Journal of Sociology* 15:817–31.

Bandura, Albert. 1973. *Aggression: A Social Learning Analysis*. Englewood Cliffs, N.J.: Prentice-Hall.

Banfield, Edward C. 1968. *The Unheavenly City*. Boston: Little, Brown.

Barnes, Samuel M., M. Kaase, et al. 1979. *Political Action: Mass Participation in Five Western Democracies*. Beverly Hills, Calif.: Sage.

Barry, Brian. 1968. "Warrander and His Critics." *Philosophy* 48:117–37.

————. 1978. *Sociologists, Economists and Democracy*. 2d ed. Chicago: University of Chicago Press.

Barry, Brian, and Russell Hardin, eds. 1982. *Rational Man and Irrational Society*. Beverly Hills, Calif.: Sage.

Batstone, Eric, Ian Boraston, and Stephen Frenkel. 1978. *The Social Organization of Strikes*. Oxford: Blackwell.

Beetham, David. 1974. *Max Weber and the Theory of Modern Politics*. London: Allen and Unwin.

Belin-Milleron, Jean. 1951. "Les expression symboliques dans la psychologie collective des crises politiques." *Cahiers internationaux de sociologie* 10:158–67.

Beloff, Max. 1938. *Public Order and Popular Disturbances, 1660–1714*. Oxford: Oxford University Press.

Bendix, Reinhard. 1976. "The Mandate to Rule: An Introduction." *Social Forces* 55:242–56.

————. 1978. *Kings or People*. Berkeley and Los Angeles: University of California Press.

Benewick, R. 1969. *Political Violence and Public Order*. London: Penguin.

Bentham, J. 1948. *An Introduction to the Principles of Morals and Legislation*. New York: Hafner.

Berger, Peter, and Thomas Luckmann. 1967. *The Social Construction of Reality*. London: Allen Lane.

Berk, Richard A. 1972a. "The Emergence of Muted Violence in Crowd Behavior: A Case Study of an Almost Race Riot." In *Collective Violence*, ed. James Short and Marvin Wolfgang. New York: Aldine Atherton.

————. 1972b. "The Controversy Surrounding Analyses of Collective Violence: Some Methodological Notes." In *Collective Violence*, ed. James Short and Marvin Wolfgang. New York: Aldine Atherton.

————. 1974a. "A Gaming Approach to Crowd Behavior." *American Sociological Review* 39:355–73.

————. 1974b. *Collective Behavior*. Dubuque, Iowa: William C. Brown.

Berkowitz, Leonard. 1962. *Social Psychological Analysis*. New York: McGraw-Hill.

————. 1968. "Urban Violence: Some Implications of Laboratory Studies of Frustration and Aggression." *American Behavioral Scientist* 11:14–17.

Berkowitz, Leonard. 1975. "Comparisons and Other Studies of Emotional Arousals as Contributors to Social Unrest." *Journal of Social Issues* 28:77–92.

Bienen, Henry. 1968. *Violence and Social Change: A Review of Current Literature*. Chicago: University of Chicago Press.

Bloustein, Edward J. 1978. *Individual and Group Privacy*. New Brunswick, N.J.: Transaction Books.

Blumenthal, Monica D., Robert L. Kahn, Frank M. Andrews, and Kendra B. Head. 1972. *Justifying Violence: Attitudes of American Men.* Ann Arbor, Mich.: Institute for Social Research, The University of Michigan.

Blumenthal, Monica D., Letha B. Chadiha, Gerald A. Cole, and Toby Epstein Jayaratne. 1975. *More About Justifying Violence: Methodological Studies of Attitudes and Behavior.* Ann Arbor, Mich.: Institute for Social Research, The University of Michigan.

Blumer, Herbert. 1937. "Social Disorganization and Individual Disorganization." *American Journal of Sociology* 42:871–77.

———. 1957a. "The Field of Collective Behavior." In *Principles of Sociology*, ed. Alfred McClung Lee. New York: Barnes and Noble.

———. 1957b. "Collective Behavior." In *Review of Sociology: Analysis of a Decade*, ed. Joseph B. Gittler. New York: Wiley.

———. 1965a. *Symbolic Interactionism: Perspective and Method.* Englewood Cliffs, N.J.: Prentice-Hall.

———. 1965b. "The Justice of the Crowd." Review of *The Crowd in History* by George Rude. *Transaction* 2:43–44.

———. 1968. "Fashion." In *International Encyclopedia of Social Science.* New York: The Free Press.

———. 1969. "Fashion: From Class Differentiation to Collective Selection." *Sociological Quarterly* 10:275.

———. 1978. "Social Unrest and Collective Behavior." *Studies in Symbolic Interaction* 1:1–54.

Bohstedt, John. 1983. *Riots and Community Politics in England and Wales, 1790–1810.* Cambridge, Mass.: Harvard University Press.

Boskin, Joseph. 1969. *Urban Racial Violence in the Twentieth Century.* Beverly Hills, Calif.: Glencoe Press.

Boudon, Raymond. 1980. *The Crisis in Sociology: Problems of Sociological Epistemology.* New York: Columbia University Press.

Bourricaud, François. 1981 (1977). *The Sociology of Talcott Parsons.* Translated from the French by Arthur Goldhammer. Chicago: University of Chicago Press.

Bowen, Don R., Elinor R. Bowen, Sheldon Gawiser, and Louis H. Masotti. 1968. "Deprivation, Mobility and Orientation Toward Protest of the Urban Poor." *American Behavioral Scientist* 2:20–24.

Braun, Ernst. 1984. *Wayward Technology.* Westport, Conn.: Greenwood Press.

Breton, A., and R. Breton. 1983. "An Economic Theory of Social Movements." *American Economic Review: Papers and Proceedings* 59:198–205.

Brinton, Crane. 1938. *The Anatomy of Revolution.* New York: Random House.

Brown, Roger. 1954. "Mass Phenomena." In *Handbook of Social Psychology*, ed. Gardner Lindzey. Reading, Mass.: Addison-Wesley.

———. 1965. *Social Psychology.* New York: The Free Press.

Bwy, Douglas. 1968. "Dimensions of Social Conflict in Latin America." *American Behavioral Scientist* 2:27–31.

Calhoun, Daniel. 1970. "Studying American Violence." *Journal of Interdisciplinary History* 1:163–85.

Calvert, Peter. 1970. *A Study of Revolution.* Oxford: Clarendon Press.

Camic, Charles. 1979. "The Utilitarians Revisted." *American Journal of Sociology* 85:516–50.

Canetti, Elias. 1962. *Crowds and Power.* New York: Viking Press.

Cantril, Hadley. 1940. *The Invasion from Mars: A Study in the Psychology of Panic.* Princeton: Princeton University Press.

————. 1941. *The Psychology of Social Movements*. New York: John Wiley and Sons.

Caplan, N. 1970. "The New Ghetto Man? A Review of Recent Empirical Studies." *Journal of Social Issues* 26:59–73.

Caplan, Nathan, and J. M. Paige. 1968. "A study of ghetto rioters." *Scientific American* 219 (no. 2):15–21.

Chagnon, Napoleon. 1977 (1968). *Yanomamo: The Fierce People*. New York: Holt, Rinehart and Winston.

Chamberlin, John. 1974. "Provision of Collective Goods as a Function of Group Size." *American Political Science Review* 68:707–16.

Chapman, Dwight W., ed. 1954. "Human Behavior in Disaster: A New Field of Social Research." *Journal of Social Issues* 10 (no. 3):1–72.

Chevalier, Louis. 1958. *Classes laborieuses et classes dangereuses*. Paris: Plon.

Chorley, Katherine. 1943. *Armies and the Art of Revolution*. London: Faber and Faber.

Clark, Kenneth B. 1944. "Group Violence: A Preliminary Study of the Attitudinal Pattern of Its Acceptance and Rejection: A Study of the 1943 Harlem Race Riot." *Journal of Abnormal and Social Psychology* 19:319–37.

Clark, Kenneth B., and J. Barker. 1945. "The Zoot Effect in Personality: A Race Riot Participant." *Journal of Abnormal and Social Psychology.* 2:143–48.

Cohan, A. S. 1975. *Theories of Revolution: An Introduction*. New York: John Wiley.

Cohn, Norman. 1961. *The Pursuit of the Millennium*. New York: Harper.

Cohn, Samuel Kline, Jr. 1981. *The Laboring Class in Renaissance Florence*. New York: Academic Press.

Cole, Stephen. 1975. "The Growth of Scientific Knowledge." In *The Idea of Social Structure: Papers in Honor of Robert K. Merton*, ed. Lewis A. Coser. New York: Harcourt, Brace, Jovanovich.

Coleman, James. 1973. *Mathematics of Collective Action*. Chicago: Aldine.

Collins, Randall. 1974 (1981). "Three Faces of Cruelty: Towards a Comparative Sociology of Violence." *Theory and Society* 1:415–40. Reprinted in Randall Collins, *Sociology Since Midcentury*. New York: Academic Press.

Connolly, William, ed. 1964. *The Bias of Pluralism*. New York: Atherton.

Conot, Robert. 1967. *Rivers of Blood, Years of Darkness*. New York: William Morrow and Co.

Coser, Lewis. 1956. *The Functions of Social Conflict*. Glencoe, Ill.: The Free Press.

————. 1960. "Durkheim's Conservatism and its Implications for his Sociological Theory." In *Emile Durkheim, 1858–1917*, ed. Kurt H. Wolff. Columbus: Ohio State University Press.

————. 1974. *Greedy Institutions*. New York: The Free Press.

————. 1977. *Masters of Sociological Thought*. New York: Harcourt, Brace, Jovanovich.

————. 1981. "The Uses of Classical Sociological Theory." In *The Future of Sociological Classics*, ed. Buford Rhea. Boston: George Allen and Unwin.

Couch, Carl J. 1968. "Collective Behavior: An Examination of Some Stereotypes." *Social Problems* 15:310–22.

————. 1970. "Dimensions of Association in Collective Behavior Episodes." *Sociometry* 33:457–71.

Crawford, Thomas, and Murray Naditch. 1970. "Relative deprivation, powerlessness, and militancy: the psychology of social protest." *Psychiatry* 33:208–23.

Crosby, Faye. 1979. "Relative deprivation revisited: a response to Miller, Bolce and Halligan." *American Political Science Review* 73:85–113.

Cross, Whitney R. 1965. *The Burned-over District: The Social and Intellectual History of Enthusiastic Religion in Western New York, 1800–1850.* New York: Harper and Row.

Currie, Elliott, and Jerome H. Skolnick. 1972. "A Critical Note on Conceptions of Collective Behavior." In *Collective Violence,* ed. James Short and Marvin Wolfgang. Chicago: Aldine Atherton.

Davies. James Chowning. 1962. "Toward a theory of revolution." *American Sociological Review* 27:5–19.

———. 1963. "Internal War: The Problem of Anticipation." In *Social Science Research and National Security,* ed. Ithiel de Sola Pool et al. Washington, D.C.: Smithsonian Institution.

———. 1969. "The J-Curve of rising and declining satisfaction as a cause of some great revolutions and a contained rebellion." In *Violence in America: Historical and Comparative Perspectives,* ed. Hugh Davis Graham and Ted Robert Gurr. New York: Praeger.

———. 1973. "Aggression, Violence, Revolution and War." In *Handbook of Political Psychology,* ed. J. N. Knutson. San Francisco: Jossey-Bass.

———. 1974. "The J-Curve and Power Struggle Theories of Collective Violence." ✓ *American Sociological Review* 39:607–10.

———. 1979. "The J-Curve of Rising and Declining Satisfactions as a Cause of Revolution and Rebellion." In *Violence in America: Historical and Comparative Perspectives,* ed. Hugh Davis Graham and Ted R. Gurr. Beverly Hills, Calif.: Sage.

De Nardo, James. 1985. *Power in Numbers.* Princeton: Princeton University Press.

Desroches, Frederick J. 1983. "Two Theories of Prison Riots." *Canadian Journal of Criminology* 25:173–90.

de Tocqueville, Alexis. 1955 (1856). *The Old Regime and the French Revolution.* Garden City, N.Y.: Doubleday.

Dollard, John, L. W. Doob, N. E. Miller, O. H. Mowrer, and R. R. Sears. 1939. *Frustration and Aggression.* New Haven: Yale University Press.

Downes, Bryan T. 1968. "Social and political characteristics of riot cities: a comparative study." *Social Science Quarterly* 49:504–20.

———. 1970. "A Critical Reexamination of the Social and Political Characteristics of Riot Cities." *Social Science Quarterly* 51:349–60.

Dretske, Fred I. 1972. "Contrastive Statements." *Philosophical Review* 81:411–37.

Dunn, John. 1972. *Modern Revolutions.* Cambridge: Cambridge University Press.

Durkheim, Emile. 1897. *Le suicide.* Paris: Felix Alcan.

———. 1938. *L'education morale.* Paris: Felix Alcan.

———. 1960 (1893). *The Division of Labor in Society.* Glencoe, Illinois: The Free Press.

———. 1962. *Socialism.* New York: Collier Books.

Easton, David. 1975. "A Re-Assessment of the Concept of Political Support." *British Journal of Political Science* 5:435–57.

Eckstein, Harry, ed. 1964. *Internal War: Problems and Approaches.* New York: The Free Press.

318 *Bibliography*

Edelman, Murray. 1964. *The Symbolic Uses of Politics*. Urbana: University of Illinois Press.
Edwards, Lyford Paterson. 1965 (1927). *The Natural History of Revolution*. New York: Russell and Russell.
Eissler, Ruth. 1949. "Riots." *Psychoanalytic Study of the Child* 3–4:449–60. New York: International Universities Press.
Ellis, Desmond. 1971. "The Hobbesian Problem of Order: A Critical Appraisal of the Normative Solution." *American Sociological Review* 36:692–703.
Ellis, Desmond, Harold G. Grasmuck, and Bernard Gilman. 1974. "Violence in Prisons: A Sociological Analysis." *American Journal of Sociology* 80:16–43.
Ellis, John. 1974. *Armies in Revolution*. New York: Oxford University Press.
Ellul, Jacques. 1970. *Violence*. London: S.C.M. Press.
Ellwood, Charles. 1906. "A Psychological Theory of Revolutions." *American Journal of Sociology* 11:49–59.
Elster, Jon. 1985. *Making Sense of Marx*. Cambridge: Cambridge University Press.
Engels, Frederick. 1959 (1884). "On the History of Early Christianity." In *Marx and Engels: Basic Writings on Politics and Philosophy*, ed. Lewis Feuer. New York: Doubleday.
——— . 1962. *Anti-Duhring: Herr Eugen Duhring's Revolution in Science*, 3d ed. Moscow: Foreign Languages Publishing House.
——— . 1970. "The Role of Force in History." In *Marx and Engels, Selected Works*, 3 vols. Moscow: Progress Publishers.
Evans, E. S. 1968. "Ghetto Revolts and City Politics." In *Riots and Rebellion*, ed. Louis Masotti and Don R. Bowen. Beverly Hills, Calif.: Sage.
Evans, Robert R., ed. 1969. *Readings in Collected Behavior*. Chicago: Rand-McNally.
Fanon, Frantz. 1963. *The Wretched of the Earth*. New York: Grove Press.
Feagin, Joe R., and Harlan Hahn. 1973. *Ghetto Revolts*. New York: MacMillan Publishing Co.
Feierabend, Ivo, and Rosalind Feierabend. 1966. "Aggressive Behavior Within Polities, 1948–1962: A Cross-National Study." *Journal of Conflict Resolution* 10:249–71.
——— . 1972. "Systemic Conditions of Political Aggression: An Application of Frustration-Aggression Theory." In *Anger, Violence and Politics*, ed. Ivo Feierabend, et al. Englewood Cliffs, N.Y.: Prentice-Hall.
Feierabend, Ivo K., R. L. Feierabend, and Betty A. Nesvold. 1969. "Social Change and Political Violence: Cross-National Patterns." In *Violence in America*, Hugh Davis Graham and Ted R. Gurr. Washington, D.C.: U.S. Government Printing Office.
——— . 1973. "The Comparative Study of Violence." *Comparative Politics* 5:393–424.
Feree, Myra Marx, and Frederick D. Miller. 1985. *Sociological Inquiry* 55:38–61.
Feuer, Lewis S. 1969. *The Conflict of Generations*. New York: Basic Books.
Finkel, Steven E., and James B. Rule. 1986. "Relative Deprivation and Related Psychological Theories of Civil Violence: A Critical Review." In *Research in Social Movements, Conflicts and Change*, vol. 9, ed. Kurt Lang and Gladys Engel Lang. Greenwich, Conn.: JAI Press.
Fireman, Bruce, and William A. Gamson. 1979. "Utilitarian Logic in the Re-

source Mobilization Perspective." In *The Dynamics of Social Movements*, ed. Mayer N. Zald and John D. McCarthy. Cambridge, Mass.: Winthrop.

Fishbein, Martin. 1967. "Attitude and the Prediction of Behavior." In *Readings in Attitude Theory and Measurement*, ed. Martin Fishbein. New York: Wiley.

Fogelson, R., and R. Hill. 1968. "Who Riots? A Study of Participation in the 1967 Riots." In *Supplemental Studies* for the National Commission on Civil Disorders. Washington, D.C.: U.S. Government Printing Office.

Ford, William Freithalter, and John H. Moore. 1970. "Additional Evidence on the Social Characteristics of Riot Cities." *Social Science Quarterly* 51:339–48.

Foreman, Paul B. 1953. "Panic Theory." *Sociology and Social Research* 37: 295–304.

Forward, J., and J. Williams. 1970. "Internal-External Control and Black Militancy." *Journal of Social Issues* 26:75–92.

Foster, John. 1974. *Class Struggle and the Industrial Revolution: Early Industrial Capitalism in Three English Towns*. London: Weidenfeld and Nicholson.

Frank, J. A., and Michael Kelly. 1977. "Etude preliminaire sur la violence collective en Ontario et au Quebec, 1963–1973." *Revue Canadienne de Science Politique* 10:145–57.

———. 1979. "Street Politics in Canada: An Examination of Mediating Factors." *American Journal of Political Science* 23:593–614.

Freeman, Jo. 1973. "The Origins of the Women's Liberation Movement." *American Journal of Sociology* 78:792–811.

Freeman, Michael. 1972. "Review Article: Theories of Revolution." *British Journal of Political Science* 2:339–59.

Freese, Lee. 1972. "Cumulative Sociological Knowledge." *American Sociological Review* 37:472–82.

Freud, Sigmund. 1967 (1921). *Group Psychology and Analysis of the Ego*. New York: Livewright Publishing.

Frohlich, Norman, and Joe Oppenheimer. 1970. "I Get by with a Little Help from My Friends." *World Politics* 23:104–20.

Frohlich, Norman, Joe A. Oppenheimer, and Oran R. Young. 1971. *Political Leadership and Collective Goods*. Princeton: Princeton University Press.

Gamson, William. 1975. *The Strategy of Social Protest*. Homewood, Ill.: The Dorsey Press.

Gamson, William A., and James McEvoy. 1972. "Police Violence and Its Public Support." In *Collective Violence*, ed. James F. Short and Marvin Wolfgang. Chicago: Aldine Atherton.

Garfinkel, Alan. 1981. *Forms of Explanation*. New Haven: Yale University Press.

Garve, Mark. 1974. "Hobbes and His Audience: The Dynamics of Theorizing." *American Political Science Review* 68:1542–56.

Gauthier, David P. 1969. *The Logic of Leviathan*. Oxford: The Clarendon Press.

———, ed. 1970. *Morality and Rational Self-Interest*. Englewood Cliffs, N.J.: Prentice-Hall.

Geschwender, James. 1964. "Social Structure and the Negro Revolt: An Examination of Some Hypotheses." *Social Forces* 43:248–56.

Gibbs, Jack. 1972. *Sociological Theory Construction*. Hinsdale, Ill.: The Dryden Press.

Giddens, Anthony. 1965. "The Suicide Problem in French Sociology." *British Journal of Sociology* 16:1–18.

———. 1966. "A Typology of Suicide." *European Journal of Sociology* 7:276–95.

————. 1979. *Central Problems in Social Theory.* Berkeley. University of California Press.

Glick, C. E. 1948. "Collective Behavior and Race Relations." *American Sociological Review* 13:287–94.

Goode, William J. 1960. "Norm Commitment and Conformity to Role-Status Obligations." *American Journal of Sociology* 66:246–58.

————. 1972. "Presidential Address: The Place of Force in Human Society," *American Sociological Review* 37:507–19.

————. 1973. "Violence Between Intimates." In *Explorations in Social Theory,* ed. William J. Goode. New York: Oxford University Press.

————. 1973. "A Theory of Role Strain." In *Explorations in Social Theory,* ed. William J. Goode. New York: Oxford University Press.

Gordon, Robert A., James E. Short, Jr., Desmond S. Cartwright, and Fred L. Strodtbeck. 1963. "Values and Gang Delinquency: A Study of Street Corner Groups." *American Journal of Sociology* 69:109–28.

Gorovitz, Samuel. 1965. "Causal Judgment and Causal Explanation." *Journal of Philosophy* 42:695–711.

Gottschalk, Louis. 1944. "Causes of Revolution." *American Journal of Sociology* 50:1–8.

Gouldner, Alvin. 1970. *The Coming Crisis of Western Sociology.* New York: Basic Books.

Granovetter, Mark. 1978. "Threshold Models of Collective Behavior." *American Journal of Sociology* 83:1420–43.

Granovetter, Mark, and Roland Soong. 1983. "Threshold Models of Diffusion and Collective Behavior." *Journal of Mathematical Sociology* 9:165–79.

Grimshaw, Allen. 1961. "Urban Racial Violence in the U.S.: Changing Ecological Considerations." *American Journal of Sociology* 66:109–19.

————. 1968. "Three Views of Urban Violence: Civil Disturbance, Racial Revolt, Class Assault." *American Behavioral Scientist* 11:2–7.

Grofman, Bernard, and Edward N. Muller. 1973. "The Strange Case of Relative Gratification and Potential for Political Violence: The V-Curve Hypothesis." *American Political Science Review* 67:514–39.

Gunning, Patrick. 1972. "An Economic Approach to Riot Analysis." *Public Choice* 13:31–46.

Gurr, Ted Robert. 1968a. "A Causal Model of Civil Strife: A Comparative Analysis Using New Indices." *American Political Science Review* 62:1104–24.

————. 1968b. "Urban Disorder: Perspectives from the Comparative Study of Civil Strife." *American Behavioral Scientist* 11:50–55.

————. 1970. *Why Men Rebel.* Princeton: Princeton University Press.

————. 1972a. "Psychological Factors in Civil Violence." In *Anger, Violence and Politics,* ed. Ivo K. Feierabend and Rosalind L. Feierabend. Englewood Cliffs, N.J.: Prentice-Hall.

————. 1972b. "Sources of Rebellion in Western Societies: Some Quantitative Evidence." In *Collective Violence,* ed. James Short and Marvin Wolfgang. New York: Aldine Atherton.

————. 1973. "The Revolution Social Change Nexus: Some Old Theories and New Hypotheses." *Comparative Politics* 5:359–92.

Gurr, Ted Robert, and Raymond Duvall. 1973. "Civil Conflict in the 1960s: A Reciprocal Theoretical System with Parameter Estimates." *Comparative Political Studies* 6:135–71.

Gurr, Ted Robert, and Charles Ruttenberg. 1967. *The Conditions of Civil Violence: First Tests of a Causal Model.* Center for International Studies, Princeton University, Research Monograph no. 28. Princeton, N.J.: Center for International Studies.

Gusfield, Joseph. 1963. *Symbolic Crusade.* Urbana: University of Illinois Press.

———. 1970. *Protest, Reform and Revolt: A Reader in Social Movements.* New York: Wiley.

Guthrie, Chester L. 1937. "Riots in Seventeenth Century Mexico City." Ph.D. dissertation. Berkeley: University of California.

Halaby, Charles N. 1973. "Hardship and Collective Violence in France: A Comment." *American Sociological Review* 38:495–501.

Hamblin, Robert L., et al. 1963. "The Interference-Aggression Law?" *Sociometry* 26:190–216.

Hardin, Russell. 1982. *Collective Action.* Baltimore: Johns Hopkins University Press.

Hauser, Philip. 1963. "The Social, Economic and Technological Problems of Rapid Urbanization." In *Industrialization and Society,* ed. Bert Hoselitz and Wilbert Moore. The Hague: Mouton for UNESCO.

Hawkes, Roland K. 1975. "Norms, Deviance and Social Control: A Mathematical Elaboration of Concepts." *American Journal of Sociology* 80:886–908.

Heberle, R. 1949. "Observation on the Sociology of Social Movements." *American Sociological Review* 14:346–57.

Heberle, Rudolf. 1951. *Social Movements.* New York: Appleton-Century-Crofts.

Heirich, M. 1971. *The Spiral of Conflict.* New York: Columbia University Press.

Hempel, Carl. 1965. *Aspects of Scientific Explanation.* New York: The Free Press.

———. 1968. "Explanation in Science and History." In *The Philosophy of Science,* ed. P. H. Nidditch. Oxford: Oxford University Press.

Hibbs, Douglas A., Jr. 1973. *Mass Political Violence: A Cross-National Causal Analysis.* New York: Wiley.

Hill, Robert B., and Robert Fogelson. n.d. *A Study of Arrest Patterns in the 1960s Riots.* Final Progress Report, Public Health Service Research Grant No. 1R12 MH 15826-01, National Institute of Mental Health.

Hilton, Rodney. 1973. *Bond Men Made Free: Medieval Peasant Movements and the English Rising of 1381.* New York: The Viking Press.

Himes, Joseph. 1980. *Conflict and Conflict Management.* Athens: University of Georgia Press.

Hirsch, Herbert, and David C. Perry, eds. 1973. *Violence as Politics: A Series of Original Essays.* New York: Harper and Row.

Hobbes, Thomas. 1949. *De Cive.* Edited with an introduction by Sterling P. Lamprecht. New York: Appleton-Century-Crofts.

———. 1968. *Leviathan.* Edited by C. B. McPherson. New York: Penguin Books.

Hobsbawn, Eric J. 1963. *Primitive Rebels: Studies in Archaic Forms of Social Movements in the 19th and 20th Centuries,* 2d ed. New York: Praeger.

———. 1965. *Primitive Rebels: Studies in Archaic Forms of Social Movements in the 19th and 20th Centuries,* 3d ed. New York: W. W. Norton.

———. 1974. "Peasant Land Occupations." *Past and Present* 62:120–52.

———. 1984. *Workers: Worlds of Labor.* New York: Pantheon.

Hobsbawn, Eric J., and George Rude. 1969. *Captain Swing.* London: Lawrence and Wishart.

Hoerder, Dirk. 1977. *Crowd Action in Revolutionary Massachusetts: 1765–1780*. New York: Academic Press.

Hoffer, Eric. 1951. *The True Believer*. New York: Harper and Row.

Hofstadter, Richard, and Wallace Michael, eds. 1970. *American Violence: A Documentary History*. New York: Knopf.

Hollon, W. Eugene. 1974. *Frontier Violence*. New York: Oxford University Press.

Homans, George C. 1962. *Sentiments and Activities*. New York: The Free Press.

———. 1964. "Contemporary Theory in Sociology." In *Handbook of Modern Sociology*, ed. Robert E. L. Faris. Chicago: Rand McNally.

———. 1967. *The Nature of Social Science*. New York: Harcourt, Brace and World.

Honderich, Ted. 1976. *Political Violence*. Ithaca, N.Y.: Cornell University Press.

Hopper, Rex. 1950. "The Revolutionary Process: A Frame of Reference for the Study of Revolutionary Movements." *Social Forces* 28:270–79.

Hovland, Carl, and Robert Sears. 1940. "Minor Studies in Aggression, VI: Correlation of Lynchings with Economic Indices." *Journal of Psychology* 9:301–10.

Hughes, H. 1972. *Crowds and Mass Behavior*. Boston: Allyn and Bacon.

Hume, David. 1957 (1751). *An Enquiry Concerning the Principles of Morals*. Edited by Charles W. Hendel. New York: Bobbs-Merrill.

Huntington, Samuel P. 1968. *Political Order in Changing Societies*. New Haven: Yale University Press.

Ikle, Fred Charles. 1971. *Every War Must End*. New York: Columbia University Press.

Isaac, Larry, Elizabeth Mutran, and Sheldon Stryker. 1980. "Political Protest Orientations Among Black and White Adults." *American Sociological Review* 45:191–213.

Janowitz, Morris. 1964. "Converging Theoretical Perspectives." *Sociological Quarterly* 5:113–22.

———. 1968. *Social Control of Escalated Riots*. Chicago: University of Chicago Center for Policy Studies.

———. 1975. "Sociological Theory and Social Control." *American Journal of Sociology* 81:82–108.

Jenkins, Craig, and Charles Perrow. 1977. "Insurgency and the Powerless: Farm Workers Movements." *American Sociological Review* 42:249–68.

Jiobu, Robert. 1971. "City Characteristics: Differential Stratification and the Occurrence of Interracial Violence." *Social Science Quarterly* 52:508–20.

———. 1974. "City Characteristics and Racial Violence." *Social Science Quarterly* 55:52–64.

Johnson, Chalmers. 1982 (1966). *Revolutionary Change*. Boston: Little, Brown and Co.

Johnson, D. M. 1945. "The 'Phantom Anesthetist' of Mattoon: A Field Study of Mass Hysteria." *Journal of Abnormal and Social Psychology* 40:175–86.

Keith, Thomas. 1965. "The Social Origin of Hobbes' Political Thought." In *Hobbes Studies*, ed. K. C. Brown. Oxford: Basil Blackwell.

Kelley, H. H., J. C. Condry, Jr., A. E. Dahlke, and A. H. Hill. 1965. "Collective Behavior in a Simulated Panic Situation." *Journal of Experimental Social Psychology* 1:20–54.

Kerckhoff, Alan C., and Kurt W. Back. 1968. *The June Bug*. New York: Appleton-Century Crofts.

Kerr, Clark. 1954. "Industrial Conflict and Its Mediation." *American Journal of Sociology* 60:230–45.

Killian, Lewis M. 1952. "The Significance of Multiple Group Membership in Disaster." *American Journal of Sociology* 57:309–14.

———. 1964. "Social Movements." In *Handbook of Modern Sociology*, ed. R. E. L. Faris. Chicago: Rand McNally.

———. 1980. "Theory of Collective Behavior: The Mainstream Revisited." In *Sociological Theory and Research: A Critical Appraisal*, ed. Hubert M. Blalock, Jr. New York: The Free Press.

———. 1983. Review of *Political Process and the Development of Black Insurgency 1930–1970*, by Doug McAdam. *Critical Mass Bulletin* 8:1–6.

Kim, Quel-Young. 1983. *The Fall of Syngman Rhee*. Korea Research Monograph, no. 7. Berkeley: University of California Institute of East Asian Studies.

King, C. Wendell. 1956. *Social Movements in the United States*. New York: Random House.

Klandermans, Bert. 1984. "Social-Psychological Expansions of Resource Mobilization Theory." *American Sociological Review* 49.

Klapp, Orrin E. 1969. *Collective Search for Identity*. New York: Holt, Rinehart and Winston.

———. 1972. *Currents of Unrest: An Introduction to Collective Behavior*. New York: Holt, Rinehart and Winston.

———. 1978. *Openings and Closings: Strategies of Information Adaptation in Society*. New York: Cambridge University Press.

Kornhauser, William. 1959. *The Politics of Mass Society*. Glencoe, Ill.: The Free Press.

Korpi, Walter, and Michael Shalev. 1980. "Strikes, Power and Politics in the Western Nations, 1900–1976." In *Political Power and Social Theory*, ed. Maurice Zeitlin. Greenwich, Conn.: JAI Press.

Kriesberg, Louis. 1973. *The Sociology of Social Conflicts*. Englewood Cliffs, N.J.: Prentice-Hall.

Labrousse, C.-E. 1932. *Esquisse du mouvement des prix et des revenues en France au XVII siècle*. Paris: Librarie Dalloz.

Ladner, R. A., B. V. Schwartz, S. J. Rokiv, and L. S. Titterud. 1981. "The Miami Riots of 1980: Antecedent Conditions, Community Responses and Participant Characteristics." In *Research in Social Movements, Conflicts and Change: A Research Annual* 4, ed. L. Kriesberg. Greenwich, Conn.: JAI Press.

Lamprecht, Sterling P. 1940 "Hobbes and Hobbism." *The American Political Science Review* 34:31–53.

Lang, Kurt, and Gladys Engel Lang. 1961. *Collective Dynamics*. New York: Thomas Y. Crowell Company.

———. 1968. "Racial Disturbance as Collective Protest." In *Riots and Rebellion*, ed. Louis Masotti and Don R. Bowen. Beverly Hills, Calif.: Sage.

———. 1968. "Collective Behavior." In *International Encyclopedia of the Social Sciences*. New York: The Free Press.

———. 1970. "Collective Behavior Theory and the Escalated Riots of the Sixties." In *Human Nature and Collective Behavior: Papers in Honor of Herbert Blumer*, ed. Tamotsu Shibutani. Englewood Cliffs, N.J.: Prentice-Hall.

Langness, L. L. 1972. "Violence in the New Guinea Highlands." In *Collective Violence*, ed. James Short and Marvin Wolfgang. New York: Aldine Atherton.

LaPiere, Richard. 1938. *Collective Behavior*. New York: McGraw-Hill.

LeBon, Gustave. 1899. *The Psychology of Peoples*. London: T. Fisher Unwin.

————. 1912. *La revolution française et la psychologie des revolutions*. Paris: Flammarion.

————. 1917. *Les opinions et les croyances*. Paris: Flammarion.

————. 1921. *The World in Revolt: A Psychological Study of Our Times*. London: T. Fisher Unwin.

————. 1960. *The Crowd: A Study of the Popular Mind*. New York: The Viking Press.

Lederer, Emil. 1940. *State of the Masses*. New York: W. W. Norton.

Lee, Alfred McClung, and Norman D. Humphrey. 1943. *Race Riot*. New York: The Dryden Press.

Lees, Lynn, and Charles Tilly. 1975. "Le peuple de juin 1848." *Annales: Economies, Sociétés, Civilisations* 29 (no. 5):1061–91.

Leggett, John C. 1963. "Uprootedness and Working-Class Consciousness." *American Journal of Sociology* 68:682–92.

Lammers, C. J. 1969. "Strikes and Mutinies." *Administrative Science Quarterly* 14:558–72.

Lenin, V. I. 1970 (1918). *The State and Revolution*. Peking: Foreign Languages Press.

Lerner, Daniel. 1959. *The Passing of Traditional Society*. Glencoe, Ill.: The Free Press.

Lewis, Jerry M. 1972. "A Study of the Kent State Incident Using Smelser's Theory of Collective Behavior." *Sociological Inquiry* 42:87–96.

Lieberson, Stanley, and A. R. Silverman. 1965. "The Precipitants and Underlying Conditions of Race Riots." *American Sociological Review* 30:887–98.

Lieske, Joel A. 1978. "The Conditions of Racial Violence in American Cities: A Developmental Synthesis." *American Political Science Review* 72:1324–40.

Lintott, Andrew. 1968. *Violence in Republican Rome*. Oxford: The Clarendon Press.

————. 1982. *Violence, Civil Strife and Revolution in the Classical City*. Baltimore: Johns Hopkins University Press.

Lipset, S. M. 1964 (1955). "The Sources of the 'Radical Right.'" In *The Radical Right*, ed. Daniel Bell. New York: Doubleday.

————. 1985. *Consensus and Conflict: Essays in Political Sociology*. New Brunswick, N.J.: Transaction Books.

Lockwood, David. 1964. "Social Integration and System Integration." In *Explorations in Social Change*, ed. George K. Zollschan and Walter Hirsch. New York: Houghton Mifflin Company.

Lofland, John. 1981. "Collective Behavior: Its Elementary Forms." In *Social Psychology: Sociological Perspectives*, ed. Morris Rosenberg and Ralph Turner. New York: Basic Books.

Logan, John. 1978. "Rural-Urban Migration and Working-Class Consciousness: The Spanish Case." *Social Forces* 56:1159–78.

Lohdi, Abdul Q., and Charles Tilly. 1973. "Urbanization, Crime and Collective Violence in 19th Century France." *American Journal of Sociology* 79:296–318.

Lukacs, Georg. 1971. *History and Class Consciousness: Studies in Marxist Dialectics*, trans. Rodney Livingstone. Cambridge, Mass.: The MIT Press.

Lukes, Steven. 1973. *Emile Durkheim, His Life and Work*. London: Allen Lane-The Penguin Press.

Lupsha, Peter A. 1971. "Explanation of Political Violence: Some Psychological Theories *versus* Indignation." *Politics and Society* 2:89–104.

MacIntyre, Alasdair. 1971. *Against the Self-Image of the Age.* New York: Schocken Books.

———. 1973a. "Ideology, Social Science and Revolution." *Comparative Politics* 5:321–42.

———. 1973b. "Is a Science of Comparative Politics Possible?" In *The Philosophy of Social Explanation*, ed. Alan Ryan. Oxford: Oxford University Press.

MacIver, Robert. 1942. *Social Causation.* New York: Ginn and Company.

Mack, Raymond. 1965. "The Components of Social Conflict." *Social Problems* 12:388–97.

Mackay, Charles. 1980 (1841). *Extraordinary Popular Delusions and the Madness of Crowds.* New York: Harmony Books.

Maier, Norman R. F. 1949. *Frustration: The Study of Behavior Without a Goal.* Ann Arbor: University of Michigan Press.

Mann, Michael. 1970. "The Social Cohesion of Liberal Democracy." *American Sociological Review* 35:423–39.

———. 1973. *Consciousness and Action Among the Western Working Class.* London: Macmillan.

Manning, Roy. 1973. "Fifteen Years of Collective Behavior." *Sociological Quarterly* 14:279–86.

Marsh, A. 1974. "Explorations in Unorthodox Political Behavior: A Scale to Measure Protest Potential." *European Journal of Political Research* 2:107–29.

———. 1977. *Protest and Political Consciousness.* Beverly Hills, Calif.: Sage.

Martin, Everett Dean. 1920. *The Behavior of Crowds.* New York and London: Harper and Brothers.

Martin, Joanne, and Alan Murray. 1984. "Catalysts for collective violence: the importance of a psychological approach." In *The Sense of Injustice: Social Psychological Perspectives*, ed. Robert Folger. New York: Plenum Press.

Marwell, Gerald, and Ruth Ames. 1979. "Experiments on the Provision of Public Goods 1. Resources, Interests, Group Size, and the Free Rider Problem." *American Journal of Sociology* 85:926–37.

———. 1980. "Experiments on the Provision of Public Goods 2. Provision Points, Stakes, Experience and The Free Rider Problem." *American Journal of Sociology* 85:926–37.

Marx, Emmanuel. 1976. *Social Context of Violent Behavior.* London: Routledge and Kegan Paul

Marx, Gary T. 1969. *Protest and Prejudice. A Study of Belief in the Black Community.* New York: Harper and Row.

———. 1972. "Issueless Riots." In *Collective Violence*, ed. James F. Short and Martin Wolfgang. New York: Aldine-Atherton.

———. 1974. "Thoughts on a Neglected Category of Social Movement Participants: The Agent Provocateur and the Informant." *American Journal of Sociology* 80:402–42.

———. 1980. "Conceptual Problems in the Field of Collective Behavior." In *Sociological Theory and Research: A Critical Approach*, ed. Hubert M. Blalock, Jr. New York: The Free Press.

Marx, Gary, and James L. Wood. 1975. "Strands of Theory and Research in Collective Behavior." *Annual Review of Sociology* 1:363–428.

Marx, Karl. 1968. *Karl Marx on Colonialism and Modernization*, ed. and introd. Shlomo Aveneri. Garden City, N.Y.: Doubleday.

———. 1968. *Selected Essays.* Freeport, N.Y.: Books for Libraries Press.

———. 1971. *Karl Marx: Economy, Class and Social Revolution*, ed. and introd. Z. A. Jordan. London: Joseph.

———. 1972. *The Karl Marx Library*, ed. Saul K. Padover. New York: McGraw-Hill.

———. 1973 (1847). *The Poverty of Philosophy*. Moscow: Progress Publishers.

———. 1977. *Selected Writings*, ed. David McLelland. Oxford: Oxford University Press.

———. 1979. *The Essential Marx: The Non-Economic Writings*, ed. and trans. Saul K. Padover. New York: New American Library.

———. 1983. "Revolution in China and in Europe." Reprinted in *The Portable Karl Marx*. New York: The Viking Press.

Marx, Karl, and Frederick Engels. 1937. *Revolution and Counter-Revolution or Germany in 1848*. London: George Allen and Unwin.

———. 1971. *Writings on the Paris Commune*, ed. Hal Draper. New York: Monthly Review Press.

———. 1972. *The Revolution of 1848–49*. Articles from the *Neue Rheinische Zeitung*. New York: International Publishers.

———. 1975. *Collected Works*. New York: International Publishers.

Masotti, Louis H., and Don R. Bowen, eds. 1968. *Riots and Rebellion: Civil Violence in the Urban Community*. Beverly Hills, Calif.: Sage.

Mazrui, Ali A. 1976. "Black Vigilantism in Cultural Transition: Violence and Viability in Tropical Africa." In *Vigilante Politics*, ed. H. Jon Rosenbaum and Peter C. Sederberg. Philadelphia: University of Pennsylvania Press.

Mazur, Allan. 1972. "Comment on 'Causes of Black Riots.'" *American Sociological Review* 37:490–93.

McAdam, Douglas. 1982. *Political Process and the Development of Black Insurgency 1930–1970*. Chicago and London: University of Chicago Press.

———. 1986. "Recruitment to High-Risk Activism: the Case of Freedom Summer." *American Journal of Sociology* 92:64–90.

McCarthy, John D., and Mayer N. Zald. 1977. "Resource Mobilization and Social Movements: A Partial Theory." *American Journal of Sociology* 82:1212–41.

McClelland, David. 1973. *Karl Marx: His Life and Thought*. New York: Harper and Row.

McCloskey, Donald N. 1985. *The Rhetoric of Economics*. Madison: University of Wisconsin Press.

McCord, William, and John Howard. 1968. "Negro Opinions in Three Riot Cities." *American Behavioral Scientist* 11:24–27.

McDougall, William. 1920. *The Group Mind*. Cambridge: Cambridge University Press.

McNeil, Elton B. 1959. "Psychology and Aggression." *Journal of Conflict Resolution* 3:195–293.

McPhail, Clark. 1968. "Student Walkout: A Fortuitous Examination of Elementary Collective Behavior." *Social Problems* 16:441–55.

———. 1971. "Civil Disorder Participation: A Critical Examination of Recent Research." *American Sociological Review* 36:1058–73.

McPhail, Clark, and David Miller. 1973. "The Assembling Process: A Theoretical and Empirical Examination." *American Sociological Review* 38:721–35.

McPhail, Clark, and Ronald T. Wohlstein. 1986. "Collective Locomotion as Collective Behavior." *American Sociological Review* 51:447–63.

Meadows, Paul. 1941. "Sequence in Revolution." *American Sociological Review* 6:702–709.
———. 1946. "Theses on Social Movements." *Social Forces* 24:408–12.
Medalia, Nahum, and Otto Larsen. 1958. "Diffusion and Belief in a Collective Delusion." *American Sociological Review* 33:180–86.
Meerloo, Joseph A. M. 1950. *Patterns of Panic.* New York: International Universities Press.
Merriman, John, ed. 1975. *1830 in France.* New York: New Viewpoints.
Merton, Robert K. 1938. "Social Structure and Anomie." *American Sociological Review* 3:672–82. Revised version published in Robert K. Merton, *Social Theory and Social Structure.* Glencoe, Ill.: The Free Press, 1949.
Michelson, William. 1971. "Some Like it Hot: Social Participation and Environmental Use as Functions of the Season." *American Journal of Sociology* 76:1072–83.
Milgram, Stanley, and Hans Toch. 1969. "Collective Behavior: Crowds and Social Movements." In *Handbook of Social Psychology,* 2d ed., ed. Gardner Lindzey and E. Aronson. Reading, Mass.: Addison-Wesley.
Mill, John Stuart. 1893. *A System of Logic, Ratiocinative and Deductive.* New York: Harper and Brothers.
Miller, Abraham, Louis Bolce, and Mark Halligan. 1977. "The J-Curve Theory and the Black Urban Riots: An Empirical Test of Progressive Relative Deprivation Theory." *American Political Science Review* 71:964–82.
Mills, C. Wright. 1940. "Situated Actions and Vocabularies of Motive." *American Sociological Review* 5:904–13.
Moore, Barrington, Jr. 1955. "Sociological Theory and Contemporary Politics." *American Journal of Sociology* 61:107–15.
———. 1958. *Political Power and Social Theory.* Cambridge, Mass.: Harvard University Press.
———. 1978. *Injustice: the Social Bases of Obedience and Revolt.* New York: M. E. Sharpe.
Morgan, William R., and Terry N. Clark. 1973. "The Causes of Racial Disorders: A Grievance-Level Explanation." *American Sociological Review* 38:611–24.
Morris, Aldon. 1984. *The Origins of the Civil Rights Movement.* New York: The Free Press.
Morrison, Donald G., and Hugh Michael Stevenson. 1972. "Integration and Instability: Patterns of African Political Development." *American Political Science Review* 66:902–27.
Muller, Edward N. 1972. "A Test of a Partial Theory of Political Violence." *American Political Science Review* 66:928–59.
———. 1977. "Behavioral Correlates of Political Support." *American Political Science Review* 71:454–67.
———. 1979. *Aggressive Political Participation.* Princeton: Princeton University Press.
———. 1980. "The Psychology of Political Protest and Violence." In *Handbook of Political Conflict,* ed. Ted Robert Gurr. New York: The Free Press.
———. 1985. "Income Inequality, Regime Repressiveness and Political Violence." *American Journal of Sociology* 50:47–61.
Muller, Edward N., and Thomas O. Jukam. 1977. "On the Meaning of Political Support." *American Political Science Review* 71:1561–95.

————. 1983. "Discontent and Aggressive Political Behavior," *British Journal of Political Science,* 13:159–79.

Muller, Edward N., Thomas O. Jukam, and Mitchell Seligson. 1982. "Diffuse Political Support and Anti-System Political Behavior: A Comparative Analysis." *American Journal of Political Science* 26:240–64.

Muller, Edward N., and Karl-Dieter Opp. 1986. "Rational Choice and Rebellious Collective Action." *American Political Science Review* 80:471–87.

Nagel, Ernest. 1961. *The Structure of Science.* New York: Harcourt, Brace and World.

Nardin, Terry. 1972. *Violence and the State: A Critique of Empirical Political Theory.* Sage Professional Papers, Comparative Politics Series, vol. 2. Beverly Hills, Calif.: Sage.

National Advisory Commission on Civil Disorders. 1968. *Report.* Washington, D.C.: U.S. Government Printing Office.

Nettl, J. P. 1967. *Political Mobilization.* London: Faber and Faber.

Nieburg, H. L. 1962. "The Threat of Violence and Social Change." *American Political Science Review* 56:856–870.

Nye, Robert A. 1975. *The Origins of Crowd Psychology: Gustave LeBon and the Crisis of Mass Democracy in the Third Republic.* Beverly Hills, Calif.: Sage.

Oakshott, Michael. 1962. "The Moral Life in the Writings of Thomas Hobbes." In *Rationalism in Politics and Other Essays.* London: Methuen.

Oberschall, Anthony. 1973. *Social Conflict and Social Movements.* Englewood Cliffs, N.J.: Prentice-Hall.

————. 1978. "Theories of Social Conflict." *Annual Review of Sociology* 4:291–315.

Oliver, Pamela. 1984. "If You Don't Do It, Nobody Else Will: Active and Token Contributors to Local Collective Action." *American Sociological Review* 49:601–10.

Olson, Mancur. 1963. "Rapid Economic Growth as a Destabilizing Force." *Journal of Economic History* 23:529–52.

————. 1971 (1965). *The Logic of Collective Action.* Cambridge, Mass.: Harvard University Press.

Oquist, Paul. 1980. *Violence, Conflict and Politics in Colombia.* New York: Academic Press.

Orbell, John M., and Brent M. Rutherford. 1973. "Can Leviathan Make the Life of Man Less Solitary, Poor, Nasty, Brutish and Short?" *British Journal of Political Science* 3:383–407.

Orum, Anthony. 1972. *Black Students in Protest: A Study of the Origins of the Black Student Movement.* Washington, D.C.: The American Sociological Association.

Paige, Jeffrey M. 1971. "Political Orientation and Riot Participation." *American Sociological Review* 36:810–20.

————. 1975. *Agrarian Revolution.* New York: The Free Press.

Palmer, Monte, and William R. Thompson. 1978. *The Comparative Analysis of Politics.* Itsace, Ill.: F. E. Peacock.

Pareto, Vilfredo. 1902. *Les systèmes socialistes,* 2 vols. Cours professé à l'Université de Lausanne. Paris: V. Giard et E. Brière.

————. 1935 (1916). *The Mind and Society,* 4 vols. New York: Harcourt, Brace and Co.

————. 1971. *Manual of Political Economy.* New York: Augustus M. Kelley. (Translated from French edition of 1927.)

Park, Robert E. 1927. "Human Nature and Collective Behavior." *American Journal of Sociology* 32:733–41.

————. 1930. "Collective Behavior." In *Encyclopedia of the Social Sciences.* New York: The Macmillan Company.

————, ed. 1939. *Outline of the Principles of Sociology.* New York: Barnes and Noble.

————. 1967. *On Social Control and Collective Behavior,* ed. Ralph Turner. Chicago: University of Chicago Press.

————. 1972. *The Crowd and the Public; and Other Essays,* ed. and introd. Henry Elsner, Jr. Chicago: University of Chicago Press.

Park, Robert, and Ernest W. Burgess. 1969 (1921). *Introduction to the Science of Sociology,* 3d ed., rev. and introd. Morris Janowitz. Chicago: University of Chicago Press.

Parsons, Talcott. 1937. *The Structure of Social Action.* New York: McGraw-Hill.

————. 1951. *The Social System.* New York: The Free Press.

————. 1955. "McCarthyism and American Social Tension: A Sociologist's View." *Yale Review,* Winter:226–45.

————. 1958. "Authority, Legitimation and Political Action." In *Authority,* ed. Carl J. Friedrich. Cambridge, Mass.: Harvard University Press.

————. 1959a. *An Approach to the Sociology of Knowledge.* Transactions of the Fourth World Congress of Sociology. Milan.

————. 1959b. "*Voting* and the Equilibrium of the American Political System." In *American Voting Behavior,* ed. Eugene Burdick and Arthur Brodbeck. Glencoe, Ill.: The Free Press.

————. 1960. *Structure and Process in Modern Societies.* Glencoe, Ill.: The Free Press.

————. 1961a. "Some Considerations on the Theory of Social Change." *Rural Sociology* 26:219–39.

————. 1961b. "An Outline of the Social System." In *Theories of Society,* ed. Talcott Parsons, et al. New York: The Free Press.

————. 1963a. "On the Concept of Influence." *Public Opinion Quarterly* 27:37–62.

————, 1963b. "On the Concept of Political Power." *Proceedings of the American Philosophical Society* 107:232–62.

————. 1964. "Some Reflections on the Place of Force in Social Process." In *Internal War,* ed. Harry Eckstein. Glencoe, Ill.: The Free Press.

————. 1966. *Societies: Evolutionary and Comparative Perspectives.* Englewood Cliffs, N.J.: Prentice-Hall.

Parsons, Talcott, Robert F. Bales, and Edward A. Shils. 1953. *Working Papers in the Theory of Action.* Glencoe, Ill.: The Free Press.

Parsons, Talcott, and Neil Smelser. 1956. *Economy and Society: A Study in the Integration of Economic and Social Theory.* Glencoe, Ill.: The Free Press.

Parsons, Talcott, Edward Shils, Kaspar Naegele, and Jesse R. Pitts, ed. 1961. *Theories of Society.* New York: The Free Press.

Pawelczynska, Ann. 1979. *Values and Violence in Auschwitz: A Sociological Analysis.* Berkeley: University of California Press.

Peacock, Alfred James. 1965. *Bread or Blood; A Study of the Agrarian Riots in East Anglia in 1816.* London: Victor Gollancz.

Pettee, G. S. 1971 (1938). *The Process of Revolution.* New York: Harper.

Pettigrew, Thomas F. 1969. "Racially Separate or Together." *Journal of Social Issues* 25:43–69.

Pfautz, Harold W. 1961. "Near Group Theory and Collective Behavior: A Critical Reformulation." *Social Problems* 9:167–74.

———. 1963. Review of *Theory of Collective Behavior*, by Neil J. Smelser. *Social Research* 30:541–46.

Pinard, Maurice. 1975. *The Rise of a Third Party.* Montreal: McGill–Queen's University Press.

———. 1983a. "From Deprivation to Mobilization: I. The Role of Some Internal Motives Reexamined." Paper presented at the Collective Behavior/Social Movements Section Roundtables, American Sociological Association Meetings, Detroit, Mich. McGill University Department of Sociology. Mimeographed copy.

———. 1983b. "From Deprivation to Mobilization: II. Incentives, Ideals and a General Motivation Model." Paper presented at the Collective Behavior/Social Movements Roundtables, American Sociological Association Meetings, Detroit, Mich. McGill University Department of Sociology. Mimeographed copy.

Pinard, Maurice, and Richard Hamilton. 1983. "The Motivational Dimensions in a Nationalist Movement: The Quebec Case." McGill University Department of Sociology. Mimeographed copy.

Pitcher, Brian, Robert Hamblin, and Jerry L. L. Miller. 1978. "The Diffusion of Collective Violence." *American Sociological Review* 43:23–35.

Plamenatz, John. 1963. *Man and Society*, vol. 2. London: Longman.

Popkin, Samuel L. 1979. *The Rational Peasant: The Political Economy of Rural Society in Vietnam.* Berkeley: University of California Press.

Pressly, Thomas J. 1962 (1954). *Americans Interpret Their Civil War.* New York: The Free Press.

Pruden, Durward. 1949. "A Sociological Study of a Texas Lynching." In *Sociological Analysis*, ed. L. Wilson and W. L. Kolb. New York: Harcourt Brace and Co.

Przeworski, Adam. 1985. *Capitalism and Social Democracy.* Cambridge: Cambridge University Press.

Quarantelli, Enrico. 1954. "Nature and Conditions of Panic." *American Journal of Sociology* 60:267–75.

———. 1970. "Emergent Accommodation Groups: Beyond Current Collective Behavior Typologies." In *Human Nature and Collective Behavior*, ed. Tamotsu Shibutani. Englewood Cliffs, N.J.: Prentice-Hall.

———. 1977. "Response to Social Crisis and Disaster." *Annual Review of Sociology* 3:23–49.

———. 1978. *Disasters: Theory and Research.* Beverly Hills, Calif.: Sage.

Quarantelli, Enrico L., and Russell R. Dynes. 1968. "Looting in Civil Disorders: An Index of Social Change." *American Behavioral Scientist* 11 (no. 4):7–10.

———. 1970. "Property Norms and Looting: Their Patterns in Community Crises." *Phylon* 31 (Summer):168–82.

———. 1970. "Editors' Introduction: Organizational and Group Behavior in Disasters." *American Behavioral Scientist* 13:325–30.

Quarantelli, Enrico, and James R. Hundley, Jr. 1969. "A Test of Some Propositions About Crowd Formation and Behavior." In *Readings in Collective Behavior*, ed. Robert R. Evans. Chicago: Rand-McNally.

Quarantelli, Enrico, and J. M. Weller., 1974. "The Structural Problems of a Sociological Specialty: Collective Behavior's Lack of a Critical Mass." *American Sociologist* 9:59–68.

Quinault, Roland, and John Stevenson. 1974. *Popular Protest and Public Order: Six Studies in British History, 1790–1920.* New York: St. Martin's Press.

Ransford, H. Edward. 1968. "Isolation, Powerlessness and Violence: A Study of Attitudes and Participation in the Watts Riot." *American Journal of Sociology* 73:581–91.

Rapoport, Anatol. 1960. *Fights, Games and Debates.* Ann Arbor: University of Michigan Press.

Renshaw, Patrick. 1967. *The Wobblies: The Story of Syndicalism in the U.S.* New York: Doubleday.

Restif de la Bretonne. 1970. *My Revolution: Promenades in Paris: 1789–1794.* New York: McGraw-Hill.

Reynolds, Harry W., Jr. 1968. "Black Power, Community Power and Jobs." In *Riots and Rebellion,* ed. Louis Masotti and Don R. Bowen. Beverly Hills, Calif.: Sage.

Roeder, Phillip G. 1982. "Rational Revolution: Extensions of the 'By-Product' Model of Revolutionary Action." *Western Political Quarterly* 35:5–23.

Rogowski, Ronald. 1974. *Rational Legitimacy.* Princeton: Princeton University Press.

Rose, Jerry D. 1982. *Outbreaks: The Sociology of Collective Behavior.* New York: The Free Press.

Rosenbaum, H. Jon, and Peter C. Sederberg. 1976. *Vigilante Politics.* Philadelphia: University of Pennsylvania Press.

Rosenberg, Morris, and Ralph Turner, eds. 1981. *Social Psychology: Sociological Perspectives.* New York: Basic Books.

Rosenhaft, Eve. 1983. *Beating the Fascists: The German Communists and Political Violence 1929–1933.* Cambridge: Cambridge University Press.

Rosenthal, Naomi, M. Fingrudt, M. Ethier, R. Karant, and D. McDonald. 1985. "Social Movements and Network Analysis: A Case Study of Nineteenth-Century Women's Reform in New York State." *American Journal of Sociology* 90:1022–54.

Ross, Edward Alsworth. 1908. *Social Psychology.* New York: MacMillan.

———. 1969 (1901). *Social Control.* Cleveland: Press of Case Western Reserve University.

Rude, George. 1959. *The Crowd in the French Revolution.* Oxford: Oxford University Press.

———. 1962. *Wilkes and Liberty.* Oxford: Oxford University Press.

———. 1964. *The Crowd in History: A Study of Popular Disturbances in France and England, 1730–1848.* New York: Wiley.

———. 1972. *Europe in the Eighteenth Century: Aristocracy and the Bourgeois Challenge.* New York: Praeger.

Rudwick, Elliott, and August Meier. 1972. "The Kent State Affair: Social Control of a Putative Value-Oriented Movement." *Sociological Inquiry* 2:81–86.

Rule, James B. 1978. *Insight and Social Betterment.* New York: Oxford University Press.

———. 1984. "Law and Strategy in Sociological Explanation." *European Journal of Sociology* 25:167–82.

Rule, James, and Charles Tilly. 1975. "Political Process in Revolutionary France, 1830–1832." In *1830 in France,* ed. John Merriman. New York: Franklin Watts.

Russell, Diana E. H. 1974. *Rebellion, Revolutions and Armed Force: A Comparative Study of Fifteen Countries with Special Emphasis on Cuba and South Africa.* New York: Academic Press.

Salert, Barbara. 1976. *Revolutions and Revolutionaries.* New York: Elsevier.

Schuler, Edgar A., and Vernon Parenton. 1943. "A Recent Epidemic of Hysteria in a Louisiana High School." *Journal of Social Psychology* 17:221–35.

Schwartz, Michael. 1976. *Radical Protest and Social Structure: The Southern Farmer's Alliance and Cotton Tenancy, 1880–1890.* New York: Academic Press.

Scott, James C. 1976. *The Moral Economy of the Peasant: Rebellion and Subsistence in Southeast Asia.* New Haven: Yale University Press.

Searles, R., and J. A. Williams. 1962. "Negro College Students' Participation in Sit-Ins." *Social Forces* 40:215–20.

Sears, David O., and John B. McConahay. 1967. *The Los Angeles Riot Study: The Politics of Discontent.* Los Angeles: Institute of Government and Public Affairs, University of California.

———. 1970. "Racial Socialization, Comparison Levels, and the Watts Riots." *Journal of Social Issues* 27:121–40.

———. 1973. *The Politics of Violence.* Boston: Houghton Mifflin.

Seeman, Melvin. 1972. "The Signals of 1968: Alienation in Pre-Crisis France." *American Sociological Review* 37:385–402.

Seton-Watson, Hugh. 1951. "Twentieth Century Revolutions." *Political Quarterly* 22:251–65.

Shibutani, Tamotsu, ed. 1970. *Human Nature and Collective Behavior: Papers in Honor of Herbert Blumer.* Englewood Cliffs, N.J.: Prentice-Hall.

Short, James F., Jr., and Marvin E. Wolfgang, eds. 1972. *Collective Violence.* Chicago and New York: Aldine Atherton.

Shorter, Edward, and Charles Tilly. 1974. *Strikes in France, 1830–1968.* New York: Cambridge University Press.

Sighele, Scipio. 1892. *La foule criminelle: Essai de psychologie collective.* Translated from the Italian by Paul Vigny. Paris: Felix Alcan.

———. 1898. *Psychologie des sectes.* Translated from the Italian. Paris: V. Giard et E. Brier.

Silver, Allan. 1967. "The Demand for Order in Civil Society." In *The Police: Six Sociological Essays,* ed. David J. Bordua. New York: John Wiley and Sons.

Silver, Morris. 1975. "Political Revolution and Repression: An Economic Approach." *Public Choice* 17:63–71.

Simmel, Georg. 1955. *Conflict,* trans. Kurt H. Wolff. Glencoe, Ill.: The Free Press.

Skocpol, Theda. 1979. *States and Social Revolutions.* Cambridge: Cambridge University Press.

Smelser, Neil. 1959. *Social Change in the Industrial Revolution: An Application of Theory to the British Cotton Industry.* Chicago: University of Chicago Press.

———. 1962. *Theory of Collective Behavior.* London: Routledge and Kegan Paul.

———. 1964. "Theoretical Issues of Scope and Problems." *Sociological Quarterly* 5:116–22.

———. 1972. "Some Additional Thoughts on Collective Behavior." *Sociological Inquiry* 42:97–101.

———. 1972. "Two Critics in Search of a Bias: A Response to Currie and Skolnick." In *Collective Violence,* ed. James Short and Marvin Wolfgang. New York: Aldine Atherton.

Snow, David A., Louis Zurcher, Jr., and Sheldon Ekland-Olson. 1980. "Social Networks and Social Movements: A Microsociological Approach to Differential Recruitment." *American Sociological Review* 45:787–801.
———. 1983. "Further Thoughts on Social Networks and Social Movements." *Sociology* 17:112–20.
Snow, David, E. Burke Rochford, Jr., Steven K. Worden, and Robert D. Benford. 1986. "Frame Alignment Processes, Micromobilization, and Movement Participation." *American Sociological Review* 51:464–81.
Snyder, David. 1976. "Theoretical and Methodological Problems in the Analysis of Governmental Coercion and Collective Violence." *Journal of Political and Military Sociology* 4:277–93.
———. 1977. "Early North American Strikes: A Reinterpretation." *Industrial and Labor Relations Review* 30:325–41.
———. 1978. "Collective Violence: A Research Agenda and Some Strategic Considerations." *Journal of Conflict Revolution* 22:499–534.
———. 1979. "Collective Violence Processes: Implications for Disaggregated Theory and Research." In *Research in Social Movements, Conflict of Change*, vol. 2., ed. L. Kriesberg. Greenwich, Conn.: JAI Press.
Snyder, David, and Charles Tilly. 1972. "Hardship and Collective Violence in France, 1830 to 1960." *American Sociological Review* 37:520–32.
———. 1975. "On Debating and Falsifying Theories of Collective Violence." *American Sociological Review* 39:610–13.
Soares, G. A. D. 1986. "Marxism as a General Sociological Orientation." *British Journal of Sociology* 19:365–74.
Soboul, Albert. 1958. *Les sans-culottes Parisiens en l'an II*. La Rodre-sur-Yon: Potier.
Sorokin, Pitirim A. 1925. *The Sociology of Revolution*. New York: Lippincott.
———. 1962 (1937). *Social and Cultural Dynamics. Vol. 3: Fluctuation of Social Relationships, War, and Revolution*. New York: The Bedminster Press.
Spence, Michael. 1974. *Market Signalling*. Cambridge, Mass.: Harvard University Press.
Spilerman, Seymour. 1970. "The Causes of Racial Disturbances: A Comparison of Alternative Explanations." *American Sociological Review* 35:627–49.
———. 1971. "The Causes of Racial Disturbances: Tests of an Explanation." *American Sociological Review* 36:427–42.
———. 1972. "Strategic Considerations in Analyzing the Distribution of Racial Disturbances." *American Sociological Review* 37:493–99.
———. 1976. "Structural Characteristics of Cities and Severity of Racial Disorders." *American Sociological Review* 41:771–93.
Stalling, Robert. 1973. "Patterns of Belief in Social Movements: Clarifications from an Analysis of Environmental Groups." *The Sociological Quarterly* 14:465–80.
Stewart, Dugald. 1855 (1828). *Philosophy of the Active and Moral Powers of Man*. In *Collected Works*, ed. W. Hamilton. Edinburgh: Constable and Co.
Stinchcombe, Arthur. 1975. "Social Structure and Politics." In *Macropolitical Theory*, ed. Fred Greenstein and Nelson Polsby. *Handbook of Political Science* 3:557–622.
———. 1978. *Theoretical Methods in Social History*. New York: Academic Press.
———. 1982. "Should Sociologists Forget Their Mothers and Fathers?" *The American Sociologist* 17:2–11.

Stohl, Maurice. 1976. *War and Domestic Political Violence: The American Capacity for Repression and Reaction.* Beverly Hills, Calif.: Sage.

Strauss, Anselm. 1947. "Research in Collective Behavior: Neglect and Need." *American Sociological Review* 12:353–54.

Street, David, and John C. Leggett. 1961. "Economic Deprivation and Extremism." *American Journal of Sociology* 67:53–57.

Sullivan, David S., and Martin J. Sattler. 1971. *Revolutionary War: Western Response.* New York: Columbia University Press.

Swanson, G. E. 1953. "A Preliminary Laboratory Study of the Acting Crowd." *American Sociological Review* 18:522–33.

Szatmary, David P. 1980. *Shays' Rebellion: The Making of an Agrarian Revolution.* Amherst: University of Massachusetts Press.

Talmon, Yonina. 1970. "Pursuit of the Millennium: The Relation Between Religious and Social Change." In *Protest, Reform and Revolt,* ed. Joseph Gusfield. New York: John Wiley.

Tarde, Gabriel. 1893. "Foules et sectes; au point de vue criminel." *Revue des Deux Mondes* 120:349–87.

———. 1895. *Essais et mélanges sociologiques.* Lyon: A. Stovck.

———. 1898. *Etudes de psychologie sociale.* Paris. V. Giard and E. Brière.

———. 1901. *L'opinion et la foule.* Paris: Felix Alcan.

———. 1921. *Les lois sociales.* Paris: Felix Alcan.

———. 1969. *On Communication and Social Influence,* ed. and introd. Terry N. Clark. Chicago: University of Chicago Press.

Thompson, E. P. 1968 (1963). *The Making of the English Working Class.* Harmondsworth, U.K.: Penguin Books.

———. 1971. "The Moral Economy of the English Crowd in the Eighteenth Century." *Past and Present* 50:76–136.

Tilly, Charles. 1963. "Queries on Social Change and Political Upheaval in France." Princeton: Center for International Studies. Mimeographed copy.

———. 1964a. "Reflections on the Revolutions of Paris: An Essay on Recent Historical Writing." *Social Problems* 12:99–121.

———. 1964b. *The Vendée.* Cambridge, Mass.: Harvard University Press.

———. 1966. "A Travers le Chaos des Vivantes Cites." Mimeographed copy.

———. 1969. "Quantification in History, as Seen From France." Center for Advanced Study in the Behavioral Sciences: Mimeographed copy.

———. 1970. "The Changing Place of Collective Violence." In *Essays in Theory and History; An Approach to the Social Sciences,* ed. Melvin Richter. Cambridge, Mass.: Harvard University Press.

———. 1972a. "The Modernization of Political Conflict in France." In *Perspectives on Modernization: Essays in Memory of Ian Weinberg,* ed. Edward B. Harvey. Toronto: University of Toronto Press.

———. 1972b. "How Protest Modernized in France." In *The Dimensions of Quantitative Research in History,* ed. William O. Aydelotte, Allan G. Bogue, and Robert William Fogel. Princeton: Princeton University Press.

———. 1973a. "Does Modernization Breed Revolution?" *Comparative Politics* 5 (April):425–47.

———. 1973b. "Les vagues de grèves en France 1830–1960." *Annales* 28 (no. 4):857–87.

———. 1974a. "Do Communities Act?" *Sociological Inquiry* 43:209–40.

———. 1974b. "Town and Country in Revolution." In *Peasant Rebellion and*

*Communist Revolution in Asia,* ed. John Wilson Lewis. Stanford: Stanford University Press.

———. 1975a. "Food Supply and Public Order in Modern Europe." In *The Formation of National States in Western Europe,* ed. Charles Tilly. Princeton: Princeton University Press.

——— 1975b. "Reflections on the History of European State-Making." In *The Formation of National States in Western Europe,* ed. Charles Tilly. Princeton: Princeton University Press.

———. 1978. *From Mobilization to Revolution.* Reading, Mass.: Addison-Wesley.

———. 1979a. "Collective Violence in European Perspective." In *Violence in America,* ed. Hugh Davis Graham and Ted Robert Gurr. Beverly Hills, Calif.: Sage.

———. 1979b. "Repertoires of Contention in America and Britain, 1750–1830." In *The Dynamics of Social Movements,* ed. Mayer Zald and John D. McCarthy. Cambridge, Mass.: Winthrop Publishers.

———. 1981. *As Sociology Meets History.* New York: Academic Press.

———. 1986. *The Contentious French.* Cambridge, Mass.: Harvard University Press.

Tilly, Charles, and Lynn Lees. 1974. "Le Peuple de Juin 1848." *Annales* 29 (no. 5):1061–91.

Tilly, Charles, Louise Tilly, and Richard Tilly. 1975. *The Rebellious Century.* Cambridge, Mass.: Harvard University Press.

Tilly, Charles, and James Rule. 1965. *Measuring Political Upheaval.* Princeton: Center of International Studies.

Tilly, Louise A., and Charles Tilly, eds. 1981. *Class Conflict and Collective Action.* Beverly Hills: Sage.

Toch, Hans. 1965. *The Social Psychology of Social Movements.* New York: Bobbs-Merrill.

Tomlenson, T. M. 1968. "The Development of a Riot Ideology Among Urban Negroes." *American Behavioral Scientist* 11:27–31.

Tomlenson, T. M., and David O. Sears. 1967. *The Los Angeles Riot Study: Negro Attitudes toward the Riot.* Los Angeles: Institute of Government and Public Affairs.

Touraine, Alain. 1981. *The Voice and the Eye: An Analysis of Social Movements.* Cambridge: Cambridge University Press.

Traugott, Mark. 1978. "Reconceiving Social Movements." *Social Problems* 26:38–49.

———. 1980a. "The Mobile Guard and the French Revolution of 1848." *Theory and Society* 9:683–720.

———. 1980b. "Determinants of Political Orientation: Class and Organization in the Paris Insurrection of 1848." *American Journal of Sociology* 86:32–49.

———. 1983. "The Mid-Nineteenth Century Crisis in France and England." *Theory and Society* 12:455–68.

———. 1984. "Durkheim and Social Movements." *Archives Européenes de Sociologie* 25:319–26.

———. 1985. *Armies of the Poor.* Princeton: Princeton University Press.

Trimberger, Ellen Kay. 1978. *Revolution from Above.* New Brunswick, N.J.: Transaction Books.

Trotsky, Leon. 1974 (1932). *History of the Russian Revolution.* Ann Arbor: University of Michigan Press.

Trotter, W. 1964. *Instincts of the Herd*, 2d ed. London: Oxford University Press.

Tullock, Gordon. 1971. "The Paradox of Revolution." *Public Choice* 11:89–99.

Turner, Ralph. 1964a. "Collective Behavior." In *Handbook of Modern Sociology*, ed. Robert E. L. Faris. Chicago: Rand McNally.

———. 1964b. "New Theoretical Frameworks." *Sociological Quarterly* 5:122–32.

———. 1969a. "The Public Perception of Protest." *American Sociological Review* 34:815–31.

———. 1969b. "The Theme of Contemporary Social Movements." *British Journal of Sociology* 20:390–405.

———. 1974. "Collective Behavior." *Encyclopedia Britannica Macropedia* 4:842–53. Chicago: Benton.

———. 1981. "Collective Behavior and Resource Mobilization as Approaches to Social Movements." In *Research in Social Movements*, ed. Louis Kriesberg, 4:1–24.

———. 1957. *Collective Behavior.* Englewood Cliffs, N.J.: Prentice-Hall.

Turner, Ralph, and Lewis Killian. 1972. *Collective Behavior.* Revised Edition. Englewood Cliffs, N.J.: Prentice-Hall.

Turner, Ralph H., and Servace, Samuel J. 1956. "Zoot Suiters and Mexicans: Symbols in Crowd Behavior." *American Journal of Sociology* 62:14–20.

Useem, Bert. 1980. "Solidarity Model, Breakdown Model and Boston Anti-Busing Movement." *American Sociological Review* 45:357–69.

———. 1981. "Models of the Boston Anti-Busing Movement: Polity Mobilization and Relative Deprivation." *The Sociological Quarterly* 22:263–74.

———. 1985. "Disorganization and the New Mexico Prison Riot." *America Sociological Review* 50:677–88.

Useem, Michael. 1973. *Conscription, Protest and Social Conflict: The Life and Death of the Draft Resistance Movement.* New York: Wiley.

———. 1975. *Protest Movements in America.* Indianapolis: Bobbs-Merrill.

Vidich, Arthur, and Stanford Lyman. 1985. *American Sociology.* New Haven: Yale University Press.

Viner, Jacob. 1958. "Bentham and J. S. Mill: The Utilitarian Background." In *The Long View and the Short.* Glencoe, Ill.: The Free Press.

Von der Mehden, Fred R. 1973. *Comparative Political Violence.* Englewood Cliffs, N.J.: Prentice-Hall.

Walter, Eugene V. 1964. "Violence and the Process of Terror." *American Sociological Review* 29:248–57.

———. *Terror and Resistance.* New York: Oxford University Press.

Walton, John. 1984. *Reluctant Rebels.* New York: Columbia University Press.

Wanderer, J. J. 1969. "An Index of Riot Severity and Some Correlates." *American Journal of Sociology* 74:500–505.

Watkins, J. W. N. 1973. *Hobbes' System of Ideas: A Study in the Political Significance of Philosophical Theories.* London: Hutchinson University Library.

Weber, Max. 1946. *From Max Weber: Essays in Sociology.* Trans., ed., and introd. Hans Gerth and C. Wright Mills. New York: Oxford University Press.

———. 1951. *The Religion of China.* Glencoe, Ill.: The Free Press.

———. 1958. *The Religion of India.* Glencoe, Ill.: The Free Press.

———. 1964. *The Theory of Social and Economic Organization,* ed. and introd. Talcott Parsons. Glencoe, Ill.: The Free Press.

———. 1968. *Economy and Society,* 2 vols., ed. Guenther Roth and Claus Wittich. Berkeley: University of California Press.

Welch, Claude E., Jr. 1980. *Anatomy of Rebellion*. Albany: State University of New York Press.

Weller, Jack, and E. L. Quarantelli. 1973. "Neglected Characteristics of Collective Behavior." *American Journal of Sociology* 79:665–85.

Westley, William. 1956. *The Formation, Nature and Control of Crowds*. Ottowa: Department of National Defense, Defense Research Board.

———. 1957. "Nature and Control of the Hostile Crowd." *Canadian Journal of Economics and Political Science* 23:33–41.

———. 1970. *Violence and the Police: A Sociological Study of Law, Custom and Morality*. Cambridge, Mass.: The MIT Press.

Willer, David, and George Zollschan. 1964. "Prolegomenon to a Theory of Revolutions." In *Explorations in Social Change*, ed. George K. Zollschan and Walter Hirsch. Boston: Houghton Mifflin.

Williams, Robin. 1975. "Relative Deprivation." In *The Idea of Social Structure: Essays in Honor of Robert K. Merton*, ed. Lewis Coser. New York: Harcourt, Brace.

———. 1976. "Relative Deprivation Versus Power Struggle? 'Tension' and 'Structural' Explanations of Collective Conflict." *Cornell Journal of Social Relations* 2:31–38.

Wilson, James Q. 1978. "Social Science and Public Policy: A Personal Note." *In Knowledge and Policy*, ed. Laurence E. Lynn. Washington, D.C.: National Academy of Sciences.

Wilson, John. 1973. *Introduction to Social Movements*. New York: Basic Books.

Wittfogel, Karl A. 1957. *Oriental Despotism*. New Haven: Yale University Press.

Wolin, Sheldon. 1973. "The Politics of the Study of Revolution." *Comparative Politics* 5:343–58.

Wolf, Eric R. 1973. *Peasant Wars of the Twentieth Century*. New York: Harper and Row.

Wright, James D. 1976. *The Dissent of the Governed*. New York: Academic Press.

Wright, Sam. 1978. *Crowds and Riots: A Study in Social Organization*. Beverly Hills, Calif.: Sage.

Wrong, Dennis. 1961. "The Oversocialized Conception of Man." *American Sociological Review* 35:184–93.

Yoder, Dale. 1926. "Current Definitions of Revolution." *American Journal of Sociology* 32:433–41.

Zald, Mayer, and John D. McCarthy. 1979. *The Dynamics of Social Movements: Resource Mobilization, Social Control and Tactics*. Cambridge, Mass.: Winthrop Publishers.

Zald, Mayer, and Roberta Ash. 1970. "Social Movement Organizations: Growth, Decay and Change." In *Protest, Reform and Revolt*, ed. Joseph Gusfield. New York: Wiley.

Zanden, James W. Vander. 1963. "The Non-Violent Resistance Movement Against Segregation." *American Journal of Sociology* 68:544–50.

Zimmermann, Ekkart. 1977. *Soziologie der politischen Gewalt*. Stuttgart: Ferdinand Enke Verlag.

———. 1980. "Macro-Comparative Research on Political Protest." In *Handbook of Political Conflict: Theory and Research*, ed. Ted Robert Gurr. New York: The Free Press.

———. 1983. *Political Violence, Crises and Revolutions: Theories and Research*. Cambridge, Mass.: Schenkman.

Zurcher, Louis A., R. George Kirkpatrick, Robert G. Cushing, and Charles K. Bowman. 1971. "The Anti-Pornography Campaign: A Symbolic Crusade." *Social Problems* 19:217–38.

Zurcher, Louis A., and David A. Snow. 1981. "Collective Behavior: Social Movements." In *Social Psychology: Sociological Perspectives*, ed. Morris Rosenberg and Ralph Turner. New York: Basic Books.

# Index

Abercrombie, Nicholas et al., 121, 145
absolute deprivation, 205, 297
Adorno, Theodore, 226
aggregate data: in studies of participation in civil violence, 248; in studies of relative deprivation, 206, 209, 270
aggression. *See* coercion; frustration; mobilization
aggressive political participation, 219
AGIL model, four-function model, in Parsons, 153–54
agitators, 94
alienation, 220
altruism, 39
American Association for the Advancement of Science, 209
American Revolution, 160
American Sociological Society, 277
Aminzade, Ronald, xiv
anomie, 159
antiholism, in Pareto, 138
antiholistic character of political theories of civil violence, 171
apathy, as basis for compliance, 249
Arendt, Hannah, 108
aristocracies, 79
Aristotle, 200
Arjomand, Said, xiv
aspirational deprivation, 210
atomism, 133–35, 245; in relative deprivation theory, 202, 245
awe, 26, 28

Banfield, Edward, 34, 190, 239
Barber, Bernard, xiv
Barry, Brian, 26, 137, 156
Batstone, Eric, 117

Beetham, David, 127
Beloff, Max, 235, 259–60
Bendix, Reinhard, 146, 159
Bentham, Jeremy, 32, 137
Berk, Richard, 105, 111
black Americans, militancy by, 207, 213–18
blackouts, 28, 41
Blumer, Herbert, 47, 98, 101, 105, 111, 291
Bolshevik Party, 83, 252
Bourricaud, Francois, 143
Bowen, Don R., 217
breakdown theories, 173, 186–87, 202, 249, 288
"breakthrough" in theory, 306
Brinton, Crane, 104, 287
bureaucracy, 180–81
Burgess, Ernest, 96

calculation, 22–23, 52, 61, 62, 117–18, 133–35, 179, 190–91, 197, 267, 302–3
Camic, Charles, 90, 107
Canetti, Elias, 116
Cantril, Hadley, 106
Cantril scale, 217
capitalism, "late," 58
Caplan, Nathan, 184, 215
cartoons of social processes, as conveyed in social theories, 279
category systems, as invoked by theories, 279, 306
causal systems, role in theory of, 235–38, 260, 263, 269–70, 273
challengers, in Tilly's polity model, 192
change, rapid social, 173, 209
change of state, 147, 271

339

multivariate analysis, 210, 236
mythic status of influential works, 293–94

Nagel, Ernest, 226, 234
National Advisory Commission on Civil
  Disorders, 237
National Science Foundation, 174
nationalist movements, 69
natural history theories, 104, 161
nature, law of, in Hobbes, 24
Nature, State of, 21, 22, 23
Nazi movement, 195, 207, 289
networks, in collective action, 182
"new urban blacks," 216
Nobel Prize, 116
nonlimited scope, 227, 229, 234
nonnormative character of militant action,
  99–100
nonrationality, 78
normative character of militant action, 175
normative content of civil violence,
  287–88
normative content of collective behavior,
  100–101
normative justification, for militant action, 219–20
normative thinking, in Parsons, 135–36
norms, emergent, 101, 113
novelty, attractions of to theorists, 304

Olson, Mancur, 33, 173, 188, 203, 239,
  249
opportunity, 178, 187, 206, 251–52, 267,
  272, 300
Orbell, John M., 26
organic solidarity, 121
organization, 178, 187, 265, 300
Ortega y Gasset, José, 95, 108
Orwell, George, 108

Paige, Jeffrey M., 72, 88, 172, 260
Palestine Liberation Organization, 111
Palmer, Monte, 212
panic, 97, 100, 162
paradigm shifts, 287, 306
paradigms, 276
paranoid world-view, 6
Paretian models of civil violence, 286–87
Pareto, Vilfredo, 8, 9, 11, 14, 43, 76, 90,
  93, 95, 136, 138–39, 195, 250–55, 279
Paris Commune, 91, 183
Park, Robert, 8, 47, 92, 94, 95, 99, 100,
  111, 116, 160, 197, 241, 253–54, 271,
  277, 287, 291, 301, 302
Parsons, Talcott, 29, 32, 132–69, 248,
  255, 280, 291–93, 294

participation in violence, 183–84
passions, Hobbes's view of, 20
Peacock, Alfred James, 73
Pettigrew, Thomas, 213
philanthropic action, 37
phlogiston, 149
Pinard, Maurice, xiv, 109, 163, 220,
  260–61
PKU disease, 257
Plamenatz, John, 137
pluralism, 172
police strikes, 28
*Political Process and the Development of
  Black Insurgency 1930–1970* (Doug
  McAdam), 300–303
polity, Tilly's model of, 176, 192
Popkin, Samuel, 49–53, 239
Popper, Karl, 7
positivism, 132, 135, 137
positivistic claims of social science, 17
power, 154
power deflation, 29, 156, 158–60, 168,
  271
precipitating factors, 162
Pressley, Thomas, 283–84
primitive forms of collective action, 175,
  196
problem of order, 224. *See also* Hobbesian question
progress in social theory, 275–312
progressive deprivation, 210
Przeworski, Adam, 61
psychoanalysis, 152
psychological theories, 245–50
public good, 33
purposeful character of civil violence,
  287, 296–97
purposeful quality of militant collective
  action, 170, 181, 188, 191, 253
quantitative techniques, 305
Quarantelli, Enrico, 100

racial intelligence, theories of, 308
randomness of human ends, 133–35, 140
Ransford, H. Edward, 215
rational choice theory, 32, 61
rationality, 23, 24, 52, 54, 105, 117–18,
  133–35, 170, 180, 272, 303
reactionary forms of collective action, 175
redefinitions of theoretical importance,
  288
regression, 93
relations of production, 57
relative deprivation, 188, 200–23, 245–
  48, 264, 270, 297, 299, 301, 304
relative deprivation theories, 177, 188

thresholds, 29, 44
threshold processes, 240
Tilly, Charles, xiv, 10, 59, 62, 113, 146,
    159, 170–99, 242, 243, 247, 250, 255,
    256, 259, 263–64, 268, 277, 280,
    287–89
timing of collective violence, 184
"tool box" model of social theory, 229–30
totalitarian movements, 183
totalitarianism, 23–25
traditional society, 108
Traugott, Mark, 11, 122 – 24, 194
Trotsky, Leon, 73–76, 86, 127, 178
Tullock, Gordon, 34
Turkey, 29, 272
Turner, Ralph, 97, 99, 101, 106, 113, 182

unconscious, the, 77, 93
unfalsifiability, 205
universal form, 227, 229, 234
urbanization, 173
Useem, Bert, 220–21, 247, 252
utilitarianism, 18, 30–32, 132–36

value-added scheme, Smelser's, 161, 264
value consensus, 20, 51, 120, 125, 132–
    69, 143, 150, 152–54, 203, 245
value-oriented movements, 291–92
values, common, 152–54, 156
values, ultimate, 79, 138
Van Den Berg, Axel, xiv
V.J. Day, 189, 196

*The Vendée* (Charles Tilly), 173
Vidich, Arthur, 96
Vietnam, 50
vigilantism, 263
voting, 140, 155, 158, 168

want formation, 208–10
want satisfaction, 208–10
war of all against all, 21
Weber, Max, 2, 19, 46, 79, 89, 119, 125,
    136, 138–39, 142, 293, 306
Weller, Jack, 114
Wells, Orson, 106
Westley, William, 111
white racism, as an explanation for riots,
    237
Wiener, Norbert, 153
Wilson, James Q., 237
Windelband, Wilhelm, 96
Wittfogel, Karl A., 66
Wolf, Eric R., 72, 88
Wrong, Dennis, 144

Zald, Mayer, 172
zero-sum situations, 20
zero-sum views of social power, 155–56,
    169
Zimmermann, Ekkart, xiv, 111, 212
Zola, Emile, 309–10
"zoot suit" riots, 106
Zurcher, Louis A., 292

Compositor: G&S Typesetters
Text: 10/11.5 Caledonia
Display: Caledonia
Printer: Maple-Vail Book Mfg. Group
Binder: Maple-Vail Book Mfg. Group